Ireland in the World

This international edited book collection of 10 original contributions from established and emerging scholars explores aspects of Ireland's place in the world since the 1780s. It imaginatively blends comparative, transnational, and personal perspectives to examine migration in a range of diverse geographical locations including Ireland, Scotland, Wales, Australia, New Zealand, the United States, Canada, Argentina, Jamaica, and the British Empire more broadly. Deploying diverse sources including letters, interviews, press reports, convict records, and social media, the contributors canvass important themes such as slavery, convicts, policing, landlordism, print culture, loyalism, nationalism, sectarianism, politics, and electronic media. A range of perspectives including Catholic and Protestant, men and women, convicts and settlers are included, and the volume is accompanied by a range of striking images.

Angela McCarthy is Professor of Scottish and Irish History at the University of Otago, New Zealand.

Routledge Studies in Modern History

1 **Isolation**
   Places and practices of Exclusion
   Edited by Carolyn Strange and Alison Bashford

2 **From Slave Trade to Empire**
   European colonisation of Black Africa 1780s—1880s
   Edited by Olivier Pétré Grenouilleau

3 **Revolution, Counter-Revolution and Revisionism in Postcolonial Africa**
   The case of Mozambique, 1975–1994
   Alice Dinerman

4 **Charity and Mutual Aid in Europe and North America since 1800**
   Edited by Paul Bridgen and Bernard Harris

5 **Churchill, Roosevelt and India**
   Propaganda during World War II
   Auriol Weigold

6 **Genocide and Fascism**
   The eliminationist drive in Fascist Europe
   Aristotle Kallis

7 **Scientific Research in World War II**
   What scientists did in the War
   Edited by Ad Maas and Hans Hooijmaijers

8 **Restoration and History**
   The search for a useable environmental past
   Edited by Marcus Hall

9 **Foundations of Modernity**
   Human agency and the imperial state
   By Isa Blumi

10 **Transpacific Revolutionaries**
   The Chinese Revolution in Latin America
   By Matthew D. Rothwell

11 **First World War Nursing**
   New perspectives
   Edited by Alison S. Fell and Christine E. Hallett

12 **The Ideological Cold War**
   The politics of neutrality in Austria and Finland
   Johanna Rainio-Niemi

13 **War and Displacement in the Twentieth Century**
Global conflicts
Edited by Sandra Barkhof and Angela K. Smith

14 **Longue Durée of the Far-Right**
An international historical sociology
Edited by Richard Saul, Alexander Anievas, Neil Davidson and Adam Fabry

15 **Transnational Perspectives on Modern Irish History**
Edited by Niall Whelehan

16 **Ireland in the World**
Comparative, Transnational, and Personal Perspectives
Edited by Angela McCarthy

Ireland in the World
Comparative, Transnational, and Personal Perspectives

Edited by Angela McCarthy

NEW YORK AND LONDON

First published 2015
by Routledge
711 Third Avenue, New York, NY 10017

and by Routledge
2 Park Square, Milton Park, Abingdon, Oxon OX14 4RN

Routledge is an imprint of the Taylor & Francis Group,
an informa business

© 2015 Taylor & Francis

The right of the editor to be identified as the author of the editorial material, and of the authors for their individual chapters, has been asserted in accordance with sections 77 and 78 of the Copyright, Designs and Patents Act 1988.

All rights reserved. No part of this book may be reprinted or reproduced or utilised in any form or by any electronic, mechanical, or other means, now known or hereafter invented, including photocopying and recording, or in any information storage or retrieval system, without permission in writing from the publishers.

Trademark notice: Product or corporate names may be trademarks or registered trademarks, and are used only for identification and explanation without intent to infringe.

Library of Congress Cataloging-in-Publication Data
Ireland in the world : comparative, transnational, and personal perspectives / edited by Angela McCarthy.
    pages cm. — (Routledge studies in modern history ; 16)
    Includes bibliographical references and index.
  1. Ireland—Emigration and immigration—History. 2. Ireland—Relations. 3. Transnationalism—History. 4. Irish—Migrations—History. 5. Ireland—Biography. 6. Ireland—History—1691–
  I. McCarthy, Angela, 1971–
    JV7711.I75 2015
    305.8916'2—dc23   2015006150

ISBN: 978-1-138-81206-2 (hbk)
ISBN: 978-1-315-74902-0 (ebk)

Typeset in Sabon
by Apex CoVantage, LLC

Contents

List of Figures   ix
List of Tables   xi
Acknowledgements   xiii

Introduction: Ireland in the World: Comparative, Transnational, and Personal Perspectives   1
ANGELA MCCARTHY

1   Ireland, Jamaica, and the Fate of White Protestants in the British Empire in the 1780s   15
TREVOR BURNARD

2   From Cronelea to Emu Bay to Timaru and Back: Uncovering the Convict Story   34
JOAN KAVANAGH AND DIANNE SNOWDEN

3   Policing Ireland, Policing Colonies: The Irish Constabulary 'Model'   61
RICHARD HILL

4   'From beyond the Sea': The Irish Catholic Press in the Southern Hemisphere   81
STEPHANIE JAMES

5   'In Harmony': A Comparative View of Female Orangeism, 1887–2000   110
PATRICK COLEMAN

6   An Irish Landlord and His Daughter: A Story of War and Survival in America and Ireland   137
PHILIP BULL

7 Coming from over the Waves: The Emergence
   of Collaborative Action in Ireland and Wales   161
   ROBERT LINDSEY

8 Ireland and Scotland: From Partition to Peace Process 181
   GRAHAM WALKER

9 Emigration in the Age of Electronic Media: Personal
   Perspectives of Irish Migrants to Australia, 1969–2013 198
   FIDELMA BREEN

   Contributors   235
   Index   239

Figures

2.1	Wicklow Gaol, Ireland, where Eliza Davis was imprisoned before her transportation to Van Diemen's Land	38
2.2	The Female Convict Depot at Grangegorman, Dublin, where Eliza Davis awaited her embarkation in 1845	42
2.3	Eliza Davis and Amos Eastwood	47
4.1	Masthead of Australia's *Catholic Advocate*, 24 June 1911, showing round tower, shamrocks, and Celtic cross	100
4.2	Masthead of Australia's *Freeman's Journal*, 21 January 1915, with shamrocks and wattles intertwined	100
4.3	Masthead of the Adelaide *Southern Cross*, 18 November 1892, showing harp and shamrocks	101
4.4	Masthead of the Sydney *Catholic Press*, 13 January 1900, with Southern Cross constellation, waratah, sun, and dead trees	102
5.1	ALOI membership in Ireland, 1919–67	114
5.2	Orange female lodge numbers in England, 1882–2003	115
5.3	Male and female Orange membership in Scotland, 1911–2001	117
5.4	Orange ladies' lodge numbers in the United States, 1911–2008	119
5.5	Membership figures for LOBA, Canada, 1923–59	120
5.6	Male and female Orange lodge numbers in New Zealand, 1908–2000	122
5.7	Members of the ladies' and junior lodges, Twelfth of July Parade, Christchurch, circa 1950s	125
5.8	Margaret and William R. Norris Memorial LLOL No. 228 marching in the Annual Twelfth of July celebrations, Bath Street, Glasgow, 1976	128

Figures

6.1	Monksgrange, County Wexford	138
6.2	Edward Moore Richards (1826–1911) in December 1849, a year after he went to America	139
6.3	Dorothea Sargent, the mother of 'darling Eddy'	141
6.4	Edward's second wife, Ellen Aird, in clothes Edward designed to conform to the rational dress movement	146
6.5	Edward Moore Richards in the outfit he regularly wore	147
6.6	Edward's daughter Adela, 'the young emigrant', age five-and-a-half years	152
9.1	The Irish population of Australia, 1901–2011	200
9.2	The Irish-born as a percentage of the Australian population, 1921–2010	200
9.3	Skill and family visa categories, 2012–13: Onshore versus offshore	202
9.4	Permanent and long-term arrivals and departures of Irish-born persons, 1993–94 to 2012–13	202
9.5	Temporary skilled (subclass 457) visa holders in Australia: Top five citizenship countries	203
9.6	World map showing destinations of Irish emigrants (2007)	204
9.7	Survey 1 visa categories	212
9.8	Survey 2 visa categories	213
9.9	Advice sought by migrants in online forums	215
9.10	Timeline of arrivals for Survey 1 respondents	220
9.11	Timeline of arrivals for Survey 2 respondents	221

Tables

4.1 Irish Catholic Newspapers: Dates, Locations, Founders, and Significant Editors and Their Backgrounds — 83

9.1 Numbers of Irish-born in the Australian Population, 1921–2011 — 199

Acknowledgements

The chapters in this collection were first presented at the nineteenth Australasian Irish Studies conference held in December 2012 at the University of Otago, Dunedin, New Zealand. Since then, they have been extensively revised as the result of individual anonymous peer refereeing, and I would like to thank all those colleagues who generously offered their expertise to critique the chapters. I am likewise grateful to Dr Enda Delaney for his feedback on my introduction. My thanks also to the contributors who responded swiftly to numerous queries.

Introduction
Ireland in the World
Comparative, Transnational, and Personal Perspectives
Angela McCarthy

Between 1607 and 2007, approximately ten million people left the island of Ireland, seeking new lives in North America, Europe, Asia, and the Pacific, among other destinations.[1] This outflow means that today, around 80 million individuals worldwide claim some connection with Ireland, either as their place of birth or as their ancestral origin. The changing dimensions of this migrant stream are now generally acknowledged, with continental Europe and North America looming large as destinations until 1800, while North America, Britain, and Australasia proved attractive in the nineteenth century, and Britain became the destination of choice for many decades after 1930. Much of the scholarly literature on Irish migration which emanated from the twentieth century onwards has been directed towards individual countries—and places—within these regions with a focus on issues of motivation, adjustment and settlement, experience, and identities.[2] Within this historiography, however, and particularly since the later twentieth century, two key approaches—comparison and transnationalism—together with the use of personal testimonies, have especially advanced our knowledge of Ireland's place in the wider world.

This book seeks to demonstrate the ongoing importance of those three strands for Ireland's 'diaspora'. Conceptualised variously by scholars as a scattering or enforced exile, contributors in this volume tend to view diaspora according to Rogers Brubaker's formulation: dispersal in space, orientation to the homeland, boundary maintenance, and 'a category of practice'.[3] They do so over three centuries ranging from the 1780s to the present day, a period when Ireland went from having its own government (1782), to being ruled by Westminster (from 1801), to partition and independence (1920–22). There are then many 'Irelands' incorporated in this volume, and the experiences of both Catholic and Protestant, male and female, and the Irish-born and descent group are all to the fore. Although presenting a range of fascinating case studies, the authors do not claim representativeness. Rather, they seek to highlight the diversity of comparative, transnational, and personal approaches to Irish migration and, in some cases, the ways that the Irish deviated from 'social norms'.

COMPARISON

Two main comparative approaches dominate approaches to Ireland's diaspora, the first being contrasts between the Irish and other migrant groups, especially the Scots. Comparing the movement of the Catholic Irish with the Scots to the United States in the nineteenth century, T. M. Devine concludes that 'divergence rather than convergence was often the norm'.[4] He identifies several key differences to explain the more positive reception towards the Scots: their Protestantism, dispersed settlement, and skill base. By contrast, the Irish were negatively typecast for their Catholic faith, their poverty, the scale of their migration, and their unskilled occupations.[5] Meanwhile, the key variable contributing to 'differentiation in the immigration experience', derives, Devine reckons, from the 'contrasting paths of development of the countries from which they had come after the 1850s'. Scotland, more industrial than Ireland's rural agricultural economy, supplied a more skilled workforce.[6] My own exploration of the personal testimonies of Irish and Scottish migrants who ventured to a range of destinations in the twentieth century, meanwhile, points to 'subtle differences rather than yawning cultural gaps . . . similarities in attitude and expectation are more common than divergent or unique experiences'.[7] More recently Louise Ryan, drawing on her research into Irish, Polish, and Muslim migration, calls for comparative research of migrants in Britain because findings are often interpreted as being related to Irishness rather than the migration process more broadly.[8] She further and acutely rues the 'historical myopia of much migration research' among social scientists because 'patterns being hailed as new and innovative were being exhibited by the Irish decades ago'.[9]

Part of the rationale for comparing the Irish and Scottish migrant flows lies in the importance of outward migration for both societies. During the era of mass migration between 1815 and 1930, when at least 50 million people (but more likely 60 million) left Europe, the outflow from Britain and Ireland comprised around 18.7 million which was approximately 36 per cent of all European migrants (at a time when Britain and Ireland constituted 10–11 per cent of Europe's total population). Ireland's share was 7 million of the total and that from Scotland around 2 million.[10] Such was the cumulative outflow from Ireland and Scotland that they were among the top three countries per head of population experiencing emigration in the nineteenth and earlier twentieth centuries.[11]

This agenda of examining comparative migration from Ireland and Scotland also emerged out of a history of comparison between the domestic histories of these societies which began from the late 1970s with a series of edited collections. Much of the earlier work focused on the differing domestic economies and social structures of the two societies.[12] Comparisons were made of agricultural productivity, trade, cities, banking, income, landed society, wages, unrest, Poor Law, industries, and policy, among other themes. More recent comparisons incorporate cultural aspects including literature, cinema, and language.[13] Such was the success of these comparative initiatives that centres for Irish and Scottish Studies emerged in the Northern and Southern Hemispheres.[14] Comparison has also been undertaken between Ireland and India, particularly in relation to Irish nationalism and the struggle for freedom in India. Comparative studies of famines and the land question have also been undertaken.[15] More recently, however, this focus on Ireland and India has become more transnational in orientation, as outlined in the following section.

Comparisons also exist with countries in Europe. D.H. Akenson, for instance, has compared Ireland and Sweden in the nineteenth century, both countries being geographically peripheral, largely without resettlement through military conquest, and in possession of good datasets for studies of population and migration. In this work, D.H. Akenson posits a threefold framework of a pioneering stage of out-migration, a period of axial stress (the Great Famine and Great Deprivation), and an era of emigration culture (1870–1914).[16] He considers that 'much of what happened in Ireland occurred elsewhere in Europe' but observes that Ireland was unique in preventing many at home from reproducing thus restricting population increase. The key to this, Akenson concludes, was the Catholic Church.[17] For the twentieth century, Enda Delaney situates an analysis of post-war Irish migration to Britain in a comparative context with southern Europe. He notes that outward movement from the Irish Republic was similar to southern Europe in respect of timing, rate, and the regional incidence of migration but, conversely, observes that the Irish state did not encourage migration, nor did the Irish face language barriers in Britain.[18]

Apart from comparing Ireland with other ethnic groups and nation states, the second key comparative framework to have developed in the wider migration historiography is comparison between the Irish in different destinations.[19] Australia and the United States figure in David Doyle's comparative agenda with a focus on similarities rather than difference. Doyle censures scholars for misreading the Irish American situation, noting that the proportions of all migrants leaving Ireland were similar for the Irish in Australia and the United States. But he plays down the greater percentage—and numbers—of Famine Irish moving to the United States compared with Australia.[20] In his comparison of Australia and the United States, Malcolm Campbell, by contrast, draws attention to environmental differences. Deploying case studies of Minnesota and New South Wales and of California and eastern Australia, Campbell assesses the respective influences of the migrants' cultural heritage versus the local conditions encountered in new lands. He concludes that the economic and political factors that Irish migrants encountered abroad were more influential in shaping their adjustment to new lands than their prior experiences or cultural attributes.[21] In this way, then, he differs from scholars such as Devine and Kerby Miller, who prioritise origins and prior experience to explain migrant adjustment and experience. Historical geographer William Jenkins' comparative research is also instructive. Comparing the Irish and their descendants in Buffalo in the United States with Toronto in Canada between 1867 and 1916, he points to the importance of incorporating religious outlooks and socio-economic backgrounds among the Irish in North America. Migrants from west and southwest Munster, for instance, did not arrive with the capital accompanying Ulster Protestants, and this affected their standing in society.[22]

Indeed, the issue of antecedent factors is a key debate in studies of Irish migration. In his award-winning *Emigrants and Exiles*, Miller portrays the Irish in America 'not as voluntary, ambitious emigrants but as involuntary, nonresponsible "exiles," compelled to leave home by forces beyond individual control, particularly by British and landlord oppression'.[23] This rhetoric, according to Miller, arose from 'a distinctive Irish worldview' which 'led Irish emigrants to interpret experience and adapt to American life in ways which were often alienating and sometimes dysfunctional'.[24] But if their cultural background was so influential we need to ask why historians more positively interpret Irish settlement in Canada, New Zealand, and Australia. As Miller's most vocal critic, Don Akenson, puts it, '[i]f one New World history sees the Irish homeland as producing economically handicapped, lachrymose exiles and another one depicts the same homeland as producing aggressive and at least competent pioneers, something is wildly out of kilter'.[25] Akenson suggests that the answer may lie with each destination within the diaspora receiving a 'markedly different sort of person'.[26] Certainly David Fitzpatrick points to key migrant destinations being linked to particular counties in Ireland.[27] But no research has identified whether such divergent backgrounds influenced adjustment and experience.

TRANSNATIONALISM

While comparative history emerged partly in order to overcome accusations of introspection and parochialism directed towards national histories, the explicit engagement with transnationalism in recent years is seen as a result of disillusionment with the nation state as the unit of comparison and a need to consider the connections between cases being compared.[28] It is, however, a concept imprecisely conceptualised at times as movement across borders, but if defined so simply, its explanatory power is limited. In its original conceptualisation, transnationalism was designed to examine 'the processes by which immigrants build social fields that link together their country of origin and their country of settlement'.[29] These transnational 'social fields' include family, economic, political, and religious ties that transcend borders. Communication exchanges, flows of information and remittances, and the role of social networks are all fundamental.[30] As such, transnationalism is best conceptualised with a focus on the consequences emerging out of transfers, exchanges, and connections.[31] At their most fruitful, transnational links are not just one-way but are reciprocal.[32] Enda Delaney has recently emphasised this aspect in his persuasive call for a transnational history of Ireland to move the country's past from 'an older island-centric history to a more inclusive global one' which charts the connections and entanglements of 'people, ideas and objects over time'.[33] Delaney recommends several avenues for such transnational investigation including popular politics, labour, class, and power dynamics.[34]

This is not to say that transnationalism has been absent within studies of Ireland's diaspora, but its presence has been largely implicit.[35] In his recent edited volume on Ireland and transnationalism, Niall Whelehan charts these antecedents including Atlantic history and migration history.[36] Whelehan notes, however, that such contributions have been spatially limited, whereas 'transnational approaches hold the potential to extend in multiple directions'.[37] In noting the dearth of explicitly transnational perspectives in Irish history writing, Whelehan suggests that geographical separateness, language difficulties, and revisionist debates have all played a part in the resistance of historians of Ireland to take up the transnational baton.[38] Yet the future for a transnational history of Ireland is promising as demonstrated by Whelehan's work on dynamiters and Ciaran O'Neill's study of transnational education.[39] A number of chapters in Whelehan's recent edited collection on transnational Ireland are similarly rewarding. Fearghal McGarry's examination of the 1916 rebellion, Delaney's exploration of the Irish Famine, and Jonathan Jeffrey Wright's consideration of Sir James Emerson Tennent are all model approaches in explicitly conceptualising transnationalism as concerned with the outcomes of interactions and encounters rather than loose definitions (without consideration of their impact) of mobile people, commodities, and ideas.[40]

Further promising advances in the historiography are evidenced from work on Ireland's transnational connections with India. This includes Barry Crosbie's examination of networks and communication between Ireland and India in the nineteenth century. He explores merchants and entrepreneurs, soldiers and missionaries, colonial science, and education to show the exchange of ideas, practices, and goods.[41] Michael Silvestri, meanwhile, seeks the interactions between Irish and Indian revolutionary nationalists in the nineteenth and twentieth centuries, while Kate O'Malley likewise examines relations between Irish and Indian nationalists from 1919 until the 1964.[42]

Despite the potential promise of explicit transnational approaches, some scholars argue for the blending of comparison and transnationalism. According to Heinz-Gerhard Haupt, '[w]ithout explicit comparison, historical studies of transfers and of entanglements are in danger of becoming airy and thin'.[43] And, as Ian Tyrrell, argues, '[c]omparative history must be set within broader themes of transnational history, so as to demonstrate the contingent and ever-changing character of the nation'.[44] Among historians of Ireland calling for its diaspora to be analysed in a comparative transnational framework, Kevin Kenny has led the charge. He argues convincingly that '[n]ation-based comparisons cannot capture the fluid and interactive processes at the heart of migration history . . . But a strictly transnational approach can underestimate the enduring power of nation-states and the emergence within them of nationally specific ethnicities'.[45] And what issues might be analysed? Kenny recommends settlement patterns, labour, race, and nationalism, themes common to migrant groups globally.[46]

PERSONAL TESTIMONIES

Deployed hand in hand with a focus on transnationalism is the role of formal and informal migrant networks, emphasising the knowledge and the assistance migrants received from their connections abroad which helped with the decision to migrate as well as initial and ongoing settlement.[47] A particularly useful source for exploring these issues is migrant letters for they reveal the quality and range of information exchanged between sending and receiving societies and dominated much of the communication across shores throughout the nineteenth and twentieth centuries. And it is the use of personal testimonies, including letters and oral testimonies, which constitutes the third key methodological approach to have shaped the writing of Ireland's migration history.

Arnold Schrier was among the first to use migrant letters to examine the 'lure' of America for the Irish. Indeed, letters, Schrier argues, were 'the greatest single source of knowledge' for those considering life elsewhere.[48] It would be almost 30 years before Kerby Miller produced his monumental *Emigrants and Exiles* which utilised personal testimonies to advance his highly contested exile thesis. More recently, Miller has again turned to letters and memoirs, producing (with Schrier and David Doyle and Bruce Boling) transcripts and analyses of accounts from the Irish in revolutionary America with a focus on patterns and processes of migration and adaptation and on identities.[49]

The other key region from where significant work on personal testimonies has emerged is Australasia. Patrick O'Farrell's examination of letters seeks to identify aspects of Irishness, noting that the Irish kinship mentality declined 'into a residual social atomism marked by separation, isolation, loneliness and eventual alienation'.[50] Yet it was David Fitzpatrick's *Oceans of Consolation* which was the high watermark in the methodology of utilising migrant letters. As Fitzpatrick observes, previous explorations of migrant letters 'paid little heed to the rhetoric and personal functions of correspondence'.[51] Fitzpatrick did so and, importantly, included letters sent from Ireland to Australia, and provided full transcripts of the correspondence. Private letters were also used to investigate the Irish in New Zealand and were among the diverse forms of testimonies deployed to examine Irish and Scottish migration in Australasia and North America in the early to mid-twentieth century.[52]

Despite their benefits in being able to reveal quite vividly the migration experience and provide a two-way perspective on the migration saga (even though scholars usually only have access to correspondence in one direction), such sources are not without problems especially the reliability of information, issues of representativeness, and methodological concerns about authenticity and transcription. Drawbacks also surround the use of oral testimonies especially the validity, reliability, and interpretation of memory. Yet their benefits are likewise profound, enabling exploration of the past that would be lost to researchers and mapping accounts over time. These oral testimonies are also utilised within studies of the Irish diaspora and further illuminate the diversity of the migrant experience. Sociologist Louise Ryan, for instance, examines women who left Ireland for Britain in the 1930s and reveals that they conceptualised migration as 'a journey of improvement', their clothing symbolising that transition.[53] Johanne Devlin Trew, meanwhile, explores outward migration from Northern Ireland between 1921 and 2011, with a focus on issues of identity as well as multigenerational memory or 'narrative inheritance' in migration stories which reveal the presence of 'loss'.[54]

A further form of personal testimony is that of autobiography and memoir which literary scholar Liam Harte examines as 'both social history and cultural product' to explore the 'multiple ways of being Irish in Britain' since the 1700s.[55] Incorporating the life writings of prominent authors together with more 'ordinary' migrants, these writings, formulaic or otherwise, offer 'intimate glimpses of interior worlds'.[56] Home, place, belonging, exhilaration, triumph, exclusion, struggle, and alienation emerge from the pages.

THIS BOOK

This book showcases these key strands to the study of Ireland in the world since the later eighteenth century, especially through migration. It commences with Trevor Burnard's chapter on Ireland and Jamaica in the 1780s, with a specific focus on each country's white Protestant loyal minorities in the eighteenth century through in-migration. A focus on the 1780s is important in light of debates surrounding Maya Jasanoff's claim of the emergence of a second British Empire after 1783. Burnard aligns with those who contest this, arguing that continuity rather than change in the imperial state is discernible when assessing Ireland and Jamaica. But he notes that the 1780s, while not seeing a shift in imperial policies, did see existing policies harden. Viewed positively in prior times, West Indians were from the 1780s perceived as non-British and castigated by abolitionists for their cruelty and immorality among other 'revolting habits'. By contrast, white Protestants in Ireland were not subject to similar denigration, a puzzle Burnard ponders, given the similarities of Jamaica and Ireland including the backing of poor whites in Jamaica and Volunteers in Ireland in supporting the ruling elite.

The answer, he asserts, is that religion was less contestable than race and Catholics were receiving concessions.

A vastly different environment awaited those bound for Australia in the nineteenth century and early Irish settlement there was primarily the result of transportation. In 1845, Eliza Davis, a single Protestant servant from County Wicklow, was among those banished as a result of being found guilty for the infanticide of her infant son. Sentenced to death, her crime was commuted to transportation for life. Joan Kavanagh and Dianne Snowden draw on a wealth of official sources and family history materials to tell Eliza's story. Their use of information from descendants permits consideration of Eliza's legacy and analysis of the 'convict stain' or 'stigma' of shame, not just among migrants but their descendants as well. It is an account that reminds us of the key interchange between historians and genealogists so aptly utilised in Fitzpatrick's *Oceans of Consolation*. Kavanagh and Snowden also illuminate the complexities of individual stories, demonstrating the need to examine convict lives after emancipation. As Kavanagh and Snowden argue, '[t]o ignore the post-sentence life of any convict woman is to ignore a major part of her story.'

Some migrants either continued—or adopted—a life of crime in the colonies. In doing so they were subject to an environment where Irish policing models were the controlling mechanism. Richard Hill's comparative and transnational approach facilitates his striking overview of Irish policing in the British Empire. Hill deftly charts the historiography surrounding both the Irish or Royal Irish Constabulary model and the English or Metropolitan model, noting that whereas the English model was considered minimally violent, the Irish model was renowned for harsh methods of control and was the main policing style applied throughout the colonies. New research, however, suggests that those who trained under the English model also deployed coercive practices in colonial environs. It was, then, not much different from the Irish model. Hill notes the transnational impulse of policing with colonial New Zealand taking its steer from Sydney's Metropolitan policing system, although as the colony developed, RIC-influenced policing was imposed. Colonies, he observes, generally took their lead from the Irish policing rulebooks, in some cases copied verbatim, though adaptation rather than replication is now acknowledged. Hill's survey, part of a larger international comparative project on policing, suggests, however, that the Irish and English models contain elements of each other as well as other policing practices, including indigenous. Nevertheless, Hill concludes that it was the RIC model used for colonial control and it had 'global resonance'.

Policing manuals were not the only form of print culture in the colonies. Stephanie James assesses the circulation of the Irish Catholic press in Australia, New Zealand, and Argentina. With a focus on eight Irish Catholic newspapers, James examines the system of newspaper exchanges, whereby newspapers around the diaspora could reproduce items published elsewhere, and which was crucial in correcting press bias about Ireland in other publications. Such exchanges also ensured wide circulation of appeals for financial assistance for Ireland and facilitated the dissemination of information about Ireland including political detail and discussion of historical events; Home Rule featured significantly as did the centenary of the 1798 rebellion. These topics were designed to appeal to a sense of Irishness, as did business advertisements which used Irish cues of greetings to attract potential customers. The theme of identity is also traced in James's assessment of the relationship between editors and the Catholic Church which not only charts tensions but maps the church takeover of the Catholic press which resulted in less overt Irish identification. The comparative dimension to this identity is also examined through Irish Catholic newspaper mastheads with the Dunedin *Tablet* void of visual references to Ireland or New Zealand, whereas the Australian *Catholic Advocate* featured a round tower, Celtic cross, and shamrocks.

Studies of the Protestant Irish within Ireland's diaspora historiography have been less sustained, despite key works on Irish Protestants and Orangeism. Although again examined in this volume, the focus is on the female element, with Patrick Coleman undertaking a comparative and transnational analysis of Orangewomen's lodges in Ireland, Scotland, England, Canada, the United States, New Zealand, and Australia. He looks at the origins, as well as membership peaks and declines, and notes that the growth of many lodges coincided with the suffragette movement and increasing female participation in voluntary associations, while lodge stability owed much to founding individuals. Coleman also identifies the importance of interaction between lodges, asserting that lodges around the world were more inclined to seek inspiration from other diaspora lodges rather than from Ireland. This transnational focus continues in Coleman's examination of issues of ritual. Again, Ireland was less important than diaspora lodges in this regard. He concludes that 'what separates Ireland from all the other jurisdictions [was that] the Orange diaspora wanted uniformity, but lodges in Ireland wanted to be different'.

Not all Protestants, however, ascribed to an Orange worldview. Edward Moore Richards and his daughter Adela were two such individuals who fly in the face of many assumptions about Irish Protestants. Utilising a rich collection of private letters, Philip Bull traces Edward's story from Monksgrange in County Wexford to Virginia and Kansas in the United States and back to Ireland. Bull's main thrust is to consider how the father's and daughter's experiences in the United States influenced and changed them. In doing so, Bull chooses five key themes to explore: work, nation, religion, women, and slavery. The diversity of the migrant experience is once again revealed and supplemented by striking contemporary images of the Richards family.

As the twentieth century progressed, Ireland's diaspora increasingly moved to destinations closer to home, including Wales. Robert Lindsey examines this collaboration between Ireland and Wales with a focus on nationalist and cultural organisations in the post-1945 period. Conceptualising this collaboration as 'moral, organisational, and material', Lindsey succinctly charts the period before 1945 when Irish and Welsh members of Parliament sought to co-operate on issues of Home Rule and land reform. It was not, however, until the creation of the Anti-Partition League after the end of the Second World War that this collaboration took off. An initiative of Irish migrants, the League received moral support from Welsh branches and speakers at League events. Most cooperation, however, was among cultural organisations and Lindsey explores the Welsh Language Society which sought to assert language rights through direct action. These actions, or 'Welsh methods', included protests and refusals to pay bills, and were adopted by groups in Ireland including the Gaelic League. More violent collaboration also took place with Welsh extremist groups such as the Free Wales Army seeking relationships with organisations, such as the Irish Republican Army, to train in guerrilla warfare and obtain weapons. Lindsey emphasises, however, that media coverage was the main mechanism for the exchange of ideas and information between nationalist and cultural organisations in Ireland and Wales.

Ireland's special relationship with Scotland is again examined in this volume, but with a focus on sectarianism, and political relations, especially devolution and constitutional change. Graham Walker describes politics in early-twentieth-century Scotland as two-party-based and characterised by social and political turbulence but that 'local tensions and squabbles rarely achieved any national political profile or purchase'. Scotland's 'national question', he points out, was 'politically muted between the wars'. This he contrasts with Northern Ireland where the national question dominated politics. Walker also incorporates a transnational approach to his discussion, including Scotland's Home Rule movement's engagement with the devolved Stormont parliament in Northern Ireland, the Scottish National Party's use of Ireland's 'Celtic Tiger' economic success to support the drive for Scottish independence, and connections emanating from Ulster support for Glasgow Celtic and Rangers football teams. Other transnational themes, Walker notes, still require analysis particularly how Northern Ireland's Troubles influenced Scotland, how political developments in Scotland had purchase in Northern Ireland, and how Scotland may learn lessons from Ireland's integrated education system. Hindering past opportunities for interaction and cooperation was, Walker points out, the Troubles in Northern Ireland which prevented attempts to address sectarianism in Scotland. Indeed 'Scotland's shame' only emerged more fully in public discussion after the commencement of the Northern Ireland Peace Process.

The volume concludes with Fidelma Breen's examination of the role of technology among Irish migrants in contemporary Australia. Drawing on her own archive—two sets of questionnaires conducted electronically with Irish migrants who moved to Australia between 1969 and 2013 (and divided between pre-1980 and post-2008 movers)—Breen considers the use of technology as a means to connect with family and friends in Ireland and

Australia, and for concerns about the quality of life abroad. Breen's findings are not only compared with other studies of Irish migrants in contemporary Australia but with an emigration report from Ireland. Comparisons between the two groups reveal not only differences (the pre-1980 group were less inclined to return to Ireland, contact with 'home' was less frequent, the post-1980 migrants had higher skill levels) but also similarities (the prevalence of homesickness). Indeed, Breen notes that despite a greater ease of connectedness for twenty-first-century transnational migrants, with access to electronic technology such as Skype, 'the human aspect—feelings of fear, trepidation, loneliness, excitement, freedom, adventure, despair, and homesickness—has not changed' from earlier migrants.

Through their engagement with the three key frameworks outlined earlier, these chapters contribute to ongoing analysis of Ireland in the world. In particular, three key aspects emerge. First, several chapters move beyond a two-country comparative or a transnational approach to incorporate contrasts and linkages between multiple destinations. Here we can think of Hill's examination of Irish (and other) policing models throughout Empire, James's examination of exchanges within the Irish Catholic press in Australia, New Zealand, and Argentina, and Coleman's exploration of Orangewomen in Britain, North America, Australasia, and Ireland.

Second, the volume contributes to the ongoing inclusion of the Irish Protestant experience as part of Ireland's history. In this volume that experience stretches from Burnard's broad overview of Protestants in Jamaica and Ireland in the 1780s, Kavanagh and Snowden's recovery of the convict Eliza Davis's life in Ireland and Australia, Coleman's examination of Orange women from the later nineteenth century, and Bull's focus on landlords Edward Moore Richards and his daughter Adela in the nineteenth and twentieth centuries.

Third, the volume gives due attention to Ireland's place in the world beyond the often-examined long nineteenth century. Coleman's and Bull's chapters, already noted, engage with this significant period when Ireland's political landscape changed, from independence in 1921 through to 1949 when it left the Commonwealth. Chapters from Lindsey and Walker also show the comparative and transnational aspects of Ireland's past in the twentieth century and importantly engage with political aspects. Breen's engagement with electronic media brings the volume up to date with twenty-first-century diasporic connections.

NOTES

1. P. Fitzgerald and B. Lambkin, *Migration in Irish History, 1607–2007* (Houndmills: Palgrave Macmillan, 2008), pp. 293–34.
2. D.H. Akenson, *Half The World From Home: Perspectives on the Irish in New Zealand, 1860–1950* (Wellington: Victoria University Press, 1990); C.J. Houston and W.J. Smyth, *Irish Emigration and Canadian Settlement:*

Patterns, Links and Letters (Toronto: University of Toronto Press, 1990); K. Kenny, *The American Irish: A History* (Harlow: Longman, 2000); M. J. Mitchell, *The Irish in the West of Scotland, 1798–1848: Trade Unions, Strikes and Political Movements* (Edinburgh: John Donald, 1998); P. O'Farrell, *The Irish in Australia* (Kensington: New South Wales University Press, 1986); P. O'Leary, *Immigration and Integration: The Irish in Wales, 1798–1922* (Cardiff: University of Wales Press, 2000).
3. R. Brubaker, 'The "Diaspora" Diaspora', *Ethnic and Racial Studies*, 28:1 (2005), p. 3.
4. T. M. Devine, *To the Ends of the Earth: Scotland's Global Diaspora, 1750–2010* (London: Allen Lane, 2011), p. 126.
5. Ibid., pp. 142–43.
6. Ibid., pp. 143–44.
7. A. McCarthy, *Personal Narratives of Irish and Scottish Migration, 1921–65: 'For spirit and adventure'* (Manchester: Manchester University Press, 2007), p. 222. See also A. McCarthy, *Scottishness and Irishness in New Zealand since 1840* (Manchester: Manchester University Press, 2011).
8. L. Ryan, 'Compare and Contrast: Understanding Irish Migration to Britain in a Wider Context', *Irish Studies Review*, 21:1 (2013), p. 12.
9. Ibid., p. 9.
10. D. Baines, *Emigration from Europe, 1815–1930* (Houndmills: Macmillan, 1991).
11. Ibid., p. 10.
12. T. M. Devine and D. Dickson (eds), *Ireland and Scotland, 1600–1850: Parallels and Contrasts in Economic and Social Development* (Edinburgh: John Donald, 1983); R. Mitchison and P. Roebuck (eds), *Economy and Society in Scotland and Ireland, 1500–1939* (Edinburgh: John Donald, 1988); R. J. Morris and L. Kennedy (eds), *Ireland and Scotland: Order and Disorder, 1600–2000* (Edinburgh: John Donald, 2005).
13. L. McIlvanney and R. Ryan (eds), *Ireland and Scotland: Culture and Society, 1700–2000* (Dublin: Four Courts Press, 2005).
14. For example, Centres at the University of Aberdeen, Trinity College, Dublin, and University of Otago.
15. For a summary of recent works and the literature to date see M. Conly, 'Ireland, India, and the British Empire: Intraimperial Affinities and Contested Frameworks', *Radical History Review*, 104 (2009), pp. 159–72.
16. D. H. Akenson, *Ireland, Sweden and the Great European Migration, 1815–1914* (Liverpool: Liverpool University Press, 2011), p. 230.
17. Ibid., 7, 178.
18. E. Delaney, 'Placing Postwar Irish Migration to Britain in a Comparative European Perspective, 1945–1981', in A. Bielenberg (ed.), *The Irish Diaspora* (Harlow: Pearson, 2000), p. 350.
19. See, for instance, D. N. Doyle, 'The Irish in Australia and the United States: Some Comparisons, 1800–1939', *Irish Economic and Social History*, 16 (1989), pp. 73–94; L. Ryan, 'Compare and Contrast: Understanding Irish Migration to Britain in a Wider Context', *Irish Studies Review*, 21:1 (2013), pp. 6–19; B. Walter, *Outsiders Inside: Whiteness, Place and Irish Women* (London and New York: Routledge, 2001). Although not strictly comparative, some interesting similarities and differences between destinations are made in D. H. Akenson, *The Irish Diaspora: A Primer* (Toronto and Belfast: P. D. Meany, 1996). See also J. M. Gallman, *Receiving Erin's Children: Philadelphia, Liverpool, and the Irish Famine Migration, 1845–1855* (Chapel Hill and London: University of North Carolina Press, 2000). Gallman's study, primarily one of urban development, considers the key factors in these cities

differing responses to Irish Famine incomers as 'material conditions, dominant ideologies, and the magnitude of the migration in each port' (p. 211).
20. D. N. Doyle, 'The Irish in Australia and the United States: Some Comparisons, 1800–1939', *Irish Economic and Social History*, 16 (1989), pp. 78–80.
21. M. Campbell, *Ireland's New Worlds: Immigrants, Politics, and Society in the United States and Australia, 1815–1922* (Madison: University of Wisconsin Press, 2008), p. 183.
22. W. Jenkins, *Between Raid and Rebellion: The Irish in Buffalo and Toronto, 1867–1916* (Montreal: McGill-Queen's University Press, 2013).
23. K. A. Miller, *Emigrants and Exiles: Ireland and the Irish Exodus to North America* (Oxford: Oxford University Press, 1985), p. 556.
24. Ibid., p. 4.
25. D. H. Akenson, 'Reading the Texts of Rural Immigrants: Letters from the Irish in Australia, New Zealand, and North America', in D. H. Akenson (ed.), *Canadian Papers in Rural History*, 7 (Ontario: Langdale Press, 1990), p. 390.
26. Ibid., p. 389.
27. D. Fitzpatrick, 'Irish Emigration in the Later Nineteenth Century', *Irish Historical Studies*, 22:86 (1980), pp. 126–43.
28. H-G. Haupt and J. Kocka, 'Comparative History: Methods, Aims, Problems', in D. Cohen and M. O'Connor (eds), *Comparison and History* (New York: Routledge, 2004), p. 32.
29. N. G. Schiller, L. Basch, and C. Blanc-Szanton, 'Transnationalism: A New Analytic Framework for Understanding Migration', in N. G. Schiller, L. Basch, and C. Blanc-Szanton (eds), *Towards a Transnational Perspective on Migration: Race, Class, Ethnicity, and Nationalism Reconsidered*, Annals of the New York Academy of Sciences, 645 (New York: New York Academy of Sciences, 1992), p. 1.
30. S. Vertovec, 'Conceiving and Researching Transnationalism', *Ethnic and Racial Studies*, 22:2 (1999), p. 456.
31. J. Kocka and H-G. Haupt, 'Comparison and Beyond: Traditions, Scope, and Perspectives of Comparative History', in Haupt and Kocka (eds), *Comparative and Transnational History*, p. 2.
32. I. Tyrrell, *Transational Nation: United States History in Global Perspective since 1789* (Houndmills: Palgrave Macmillan, 2007), p. 8.
33. E. Delaney, 'Our Island Story? Towards a Transnational History of Late Modern Ireland', *Irish Historical Studies*, 37 (2011), pp. 85, 104.
34. Ibid.
35. Ibid., D. Hoerder, 'Losing National Identity or Gaining Transcultural Competence: Changing Approaches in Migration History', in H-G. Haupt and J. Kocka (eds), *Comparative and Transnational History: Central European Approaches and New Perspectives* (New York and Oxford: Berghahn Books, 2009), p. 253.
36. N. Whelehan, 'Playing with Scales: Transnational History and Modern Ireland', in N. Whelehan (ed.), *Transnational Perspectives on Modern Irish History* (New York: Routledge, 2015), pp. 16–18, 20–22.
37. Ibid., p. 17.
38. Ibid., pp. 7, 13–16.
39. N. Whelehan, *The Dynamiters: Irish Nationalism and Political Violence in the Wider World, 1867–1900* (Cambridge: Cambridge University Press, 2012); C. O'Neill, *Catholics of Consequence: Transnational Education, Social Mobility, and the Irish Catholic Elite, 1850–1900* (Oxford: Oxford University Press, 2014).
40. F. McGarry, ' "A Land Beyond the Wave": Transnational Perspectives on Easter 1916', pp. 165–188; E. Delaney, 'Ireland's Great Famine: A Transnational

History', pp. 106–26; J.J. Wright, '"The Perverted Graduates of Oxford": Priestcraft, "Political Popery" and the Transnational Anti-Catholicism of Sir James Emerson Tennent', pp. 127–48, all in Whelehan (ed), *Transnational Perspectives*.
41. B. Crosbie, *Irish Imperial Networks: Migration, Social Communication and Exchange in Nineteenth-Century India* (Cambridge: Cambridge University Press, 2012).
42. M. Silvestri, *Ireland and India: Nationalism, Empire and Memory* (Basingstoke: Palgrave Macmillan, 2009); K. O'Malley, *Ireland, India and Empire: Indo-Irish Radical Connections, 1919–64* (Manchester: Manchester University Press, 2008). See also T. Foley and M. O'Connor (eds), *Ireland and India: Colonies, Culture and Empire* (Dublin: Irish Academic Press, 2006).
43. Kocka and Haupt, 'Comparison and Beyond', p. 20.
44. I. Tyrrell cited in G. Sluga, 'The Nation and the Comparative Imagination', in Cohen and O'Connor (eds), *Comparison and History*, p. 109.
45. Ibid., p. 135.
46. K. Kenny, 'Diaspora and Comparison: The Global Irish as a Case Study', *Journal of American History*, 90:1 (2003), p. 135.
47. See the chapters in E. Delaney and D.M. MacRaild (eds), *Irish Migration, Networks and Ethnic Identities Since 1750* (Abingdon: Routledge, 2007).
48. A. Schrier, *Ireland and the American Emigration 1850–1900* (Chester Springs: Dufour, 1997; first published 1958), p. 18.
49. K.A. Miller, A. Schrier, B.D. Boling, and D.N. Doyle, *Irish Immigrants in the Land of Canaan: Letters and Memoirs from Colonial and Revolutionary America, 1675–1815* (Oxford: Oxford University Press, 2003).
50. P. O'Farrell, *Letters from Irish Australia, 1825–1929* (Kensington: New South Wales University Press, 1984), p. 6.
51. D. Fitzpatrick, *Oceans of Consolation: Personal Accounts of Irish Migration to Australia* (Cork: Cork University Press, 1995).
52. A. McCarthy, *Irish Migrants in New Zealand, 1840–1937: 'The Desired Haven'* (Woodbridge: Boydell Press, 2005); McCarthy, *Personal Narratives*.
53. See, for instance, L. Ryan, ' "I'm Going to England": Women's Narratives of Leaving Ireland in the 1930s', *Oral History*, 30 (2002), pp. 42–53.
54. J.D. Trew, *Leaving the North: Migration and Memory, Northern Ireland 1921–2011* (Liverpool: Liverpool University Press, 2013), pp. 67, 85.
55. L. Harte, *The Literature of the Irish in Britain: Autobiography and Memoir, 1725–2001* (Basingstoke: Palgrave Macmillan, 2009), pp. xxvii, xx.
56. Ibid., p. xix. See also L. Harte (ed), *Modern Irish Autobiography: Self, Nation and Society* (Basingstoke: Palgrave Macmillan, 2007).

1 Ireland, Jamaica, and the Fate of White Protestants in the British Empire in the 1780s

Trevor Burnard

At the conclusion of the American Revolution, the white Protestant residents of Jamaica in the West Indies and Ireland in the British archipelago faced a different imperial prospect than that which they had anticipated in the 1760s and 1770s. In those halcyon days for 'dominant minorities'[1] in the British Empire, white Protestants were part of an expanding settler population of white colonials. Most of these white Protestant colonials lived in the thirteen colonies of British America that were to break away from Britain in the American Revolution that started in 1776. Before that breakaway, however, white Protestants in the British Empire looked as if they might match in numbers and importance the large and growing population of white people in England, Wales, and Scotland.

Benjamin Franklin predicted in 1760 that in a few generations white settlers in British North America would eventually outnumber the number of people in the metropolis, to the mutual benefit, he thought, of both areas, adding to the great glory of a glorious empire. He crowed in *Observations on the Increase of Mankind* that rapid population increase in North America will mean that there 'will in another Century be more than the People of England, the greatest Number of *Englishmen* will be on this Side of the Water. What an Accession of Power to the *British* Empire by Sea as well as Land! What Increase of Trade and Navigation! What Numbers of Ships and Seamen!' These new Britons would be firm defenders of empire, as 'there is not a single native of our country who is not firmly attached to our King by principle and affection'. Britain had to do nothing to maintain that affection. There was no danger, he thought, of America 'uniting against their own nation, which protects and encourages them, with which they have so many connections and ties of blood, interest and affection and which 'tis well known they all love more than they love one another'. Indeed, Franklin continued: 'I will venture to say, an union amongst them for such a purpose is not merely improbable, it is impossible'.[2]

The American Revolution put paid to Franklin's dream. In the mid-1780s, the white population of empire had declined dramatically from what it had been in the mid-1770s. The loss of 3 million white North Americans from the imperial population ledger meant an irreplaceable diminution of settler numbers. By the mid-1780s, white Protestants were a minority population in their own lands—the Anglo-Irish made up about the same proportion (10 per cent) of the Irish population that whites accounted for in the British West Indian population. In addition, white Protestants in colonial settings were now a minority of the population of the empire as a whole. That empire was now clearly a black and brown empire rather than a white empire. Indeed, the British Empire was probably less white in the mid-1780s than at any other time in imperial history. The last quarter of the eighteenth century signalled a brief period, before the mass emigration of Britons to the white dominions following Waterloo in 1815, in which the empire had few white settlers, especially white Protestant settlers.[3] White colonists were a minority of the population of the empire as a whole, an empire in which inhabitants in Britain's colonies were coloured rather than white, enslaved, or otherwise coerced, rather than free, subjects more than citizens, and much more likely to live in India than in America, the West Indies, or Ireland.[4]

British politicians tried to reassure these minority populations (the attention in this chapter is on Protestant Irishmen and white Jamaicans) that they were still foremost in their attentions, even as they started to think of the empire in more authoritarian terms than previously. In 1785, for example, William Pitt told the House of Commons that Great Britain and Ireland were 'now the only considerable members . . . in what yet remained of our reduced and shattered empire'. He implored that '[t]here ought to be no object more impressive on the feelings of the House' than how to maintain the Anglo-Irish connection.[5] The message to Jamaicans was not quite as positive and was a little different, as might be expected from a politician who was soon to become the most prominent supporter of a burgeoning abolitionist movement. Jamaicans were not conceived of as kin in the same way as Protestant Irish people were often conceived. Indeed, the feelings of kinship between white West Indians and metropolitan Britons noticeably declined during the course of the American Revolution. As Stephen Conway has argued, Americans were perceived in the metropolitan imagination not so much as fellow countrymen as foreigners, and, after the entry of France into the American Revolution in 1780, as traitorous foreigners at that. White West Indians, to their horror and amazement, were caught in the wake of such a tidal wave of change in public opinion. Their decline in public reputation was compounded both by the rise of the abolitionist movement from 1785 and by the fact that many of the most prominent American opponents of the British—George Washington, Thomas Jefferson, James Madison, and Alexander Hamilton, just to name four—were planters whose behaviour and character could easily be compared to West Indians.[6]

THE IMPORTANCE OF JAMAICA

The message that Jamaicans received related to their continual geopolitical importance, rather than to their character or to their frequent claims of Englishness. Jamaica, it was argued, was the indispensable island, the colonial possession that Britain was determined to hold onto, by hell or high water, and at almost any cost.[7] Indeed, by diverting its navy in September 1781 from outside Yorktown to confront an imminent invasion of Jamaica that they thought would happen in the first few months of 1782, the British, as Andrew O'Shaughnessy has argued, gave the Americans the chance to pull off a decisive victory that secured American independence.[8] By 1782, even George III was willing to let the troublesome 13 colonies have their independence.[9] But neither the King, nor anyone else was prepared to have the same fate occur for Jamaica. When Admiral George Rodney won the Battle of the Saints in April 1782, outside Dominica, thus preserving Jamaica from invasion, the British public was beside itself, delirious with joy.[10] The high military importance of Jamaica continued after peace with America had been declared. Troops continued to be sent to Jamaica during the 1780s, including a new unit led by Lord Charles Montagu, ex-governor of South Carolina and the brother of the government minister, the Duke of Manchester.[11]

This chapter compares two colonies—Ireland and Jamaica—that were placed in a different situation than they expected as a result of the tumultuous changes initiated by a war in which they were anxious observers rather than active participants. White Protestants in Ireland and white planters and merchants in Jamaica were both relatively satisfied in the early 1770s with their position within the British Empire and found it difficult to understand the motivations that led Americans to foment revolution in 1776.[12] The focus in this chapter is on the 1780s, a decade that is often overlooked between the tumults of the 1770s, as the 13 colonies slid into rebellion, and the conflagrations of the 1790s, in which the world was turned upside down by the global ramifications of the French Revolution. In this latter decade, both Jamaica and Ireland were swept up in the maelstrom of the French Revolution, even more than had been the case in the years of the American Revolution. In the case of Ireland, the tumults started by the French Revolution led to the failed Irish Rebellion of 1798 and the incorporation in 1801 of Ireland into a new national entity, the United Kingdom. That becoming a formal part of Britain was never an option for Jamaica points to one significant difference between the two colonies. In the case of Jamaica, the 1790s were not as dramatic in their consequences as the 1790s were in Ireland. Nevertheless, the island faced massive pressure from two interrelated outside forces: the Saint Domingue revolt of 1791–1804 and the gathering strength of Britain's first and most humanitarian reform movement, the movement to abolish the Atlantic slave trade.[13]

THE VALUE OF COMPARISON

Despite the differences between the two colonies, there is good reason why a comparison of each place in the 1780s makes sense. As the introduction to this chapter suggests, they both shared a common experience in the 1780s. They were places full of people loyal to the British Empire who found themselves living in a quite different imperial polity than what they had envisaged living in a decade earlier. It is useful to look at these conspicuously loyal (at least loyal as measured by attitudes among colonial governing elites) colonies as loyalist enclaves after what Maya Jasanoff calls the '1783 moment'. By the '1783 moment', she is referring to the year in which a different kind of British Empire emerged out of the rubble of British defeat in British North America. Jasanoff's argument is intriguing but not wholly convincing and is somewhat overstated. Not everything changed after 1783, despite her claims to the contrary. Nevertheless, what is correct about her contentions is that Britain had to decide important matters about those remaining colonies in which there were substantial proportions of white Protestants. It had to decide whether it would learn the sort of lesson that rebellious Americans had intended them to learn through their actions taken after 1776. Essentially, the lesson that American revolutionaries had wanted Britain to learn was that colonials who were loyal to Britain and who had legitimate claims to being thought of as equal to metropolitan Britons should have a considerable degree of local autonomy, especially over areas of local expertise. These areas of expertise included the right to control Catholics in Ireland and the right to determine policy towards slaves in Jamaica.[14]

What became clear, however, was that after 1783 rewards given to individuals and societies for staying loyal during the American Revolution were slight. Ireland did better in the 1780s in getting concessions from the imperial state than did Jamaica. Nevertheless, their relative success came about less because metropolitan Britons recognised and accepted their constitutional pretensions than because Ireland was both able to exert greater political pressure on the metropolis than was the case anywhere else in the empire and also because the Protestant Irish, especially Anglicans in Dublin, were seen as more unequivocally white than were white Jamaicans, whose claims to being British were increasingly disputed.[15]

What needs to be stressed in this comparison is that the experience of whites in Jamaica during the 1780s had poignant relevance for episodes later than the 1780s in Irish history. White West Indians were the first group of loyalist white colonials to experience what Richard Bourke, drawing on the work of J.G.A. Pocock in the mid-1970s, has acutely described as the 'Ulsterisation' of small groups of colonials whose values came to be seen as aberrant to metropolitan opinion and who were abandoned by the people they most looked up to as cultural models.[16] By Ulsterisation, Bourke means the treatment of a loyal population of people of British descent as if they were illegitimate or unreal Britons, people whose claims to Britishness could, for a variety of reasons, be denied or downgraded from the importance given to it by those who proclaimed Britishness as a cardinal virtue. This process of Ulsterisation, or, to use an ugly neologism 'Un-Britishing', occurred, Bourke contends, again and again in the history of the British

Empire. It happened with increasing frequency and ferocity in the twentieth century as Britain tried to shed itself of empire and its imperial trappings. We can trace Ulsterisation in the treatment of Anglo-Indians in India and Pakistan after partition in 1947, in the demonisation of South Africans and Rhodesians in the 1960s and, of course, to the residents of Ulster in the time of troubles in the 1970s and 1980s.[17]

ULSTERISATION IN JAMAICA

The earliest example of Bourke's 'Ulsterisation' process happened in Jamaica, most prominently in the 1780s. Before this decade, white West Indians were generally viewed positively in Britain as people who brought wealth to Britain and who were generally ornaments of empire.[18] The image of the West Indian before the American Revolution was not entirely positive. They were sometimes resented as nouveau riche parvenus with dubious genealogical inheritances who had too much money and too much influence (mostly thought of as malign) within English politics. In short, they were thought of like American soldiers in Britain during the Second World War— overpaid, oversexed, and over here. But if West Indians were resented, they were also respected, as people who made a vital contribution to the British Empire through their islands' massive and growing production of luxury tropical goods such as sugar, rum, indigo, cotton, and mahogany. They tended to get their way in imperial disputes and their massive constitutional pretensions to be a largely self-governing country of free and independent British subjects was generally accepted as correct.[19]

During the 1780s, however, despite their conspicuous loyalty to the British Crown during the tumults of the American Revolution, the image of the West Indian planter went through a sea change. West Indians came to be seen in metropolitan opinion as profoundly disturbing people who were fundamentally non-British. There was a variety of reasons for the sudden denigration of white West Indians in the 1780s, but the main reason why they lost so spectacularly in the public relations battle for representation in the 1780s was because their cultural style came to be increasingly depreciated. Cast against their self-image as proud, loyal, productive sons of the Empire was another image produced by a growing band of abolitionists. The white West Indian was relentlessly portrayed by abolitionists as a degenerate person of revolting habits. Abolitionists especially emphasised their indolence, their cruelty, their avarice, their irreligiosity, and, most of all, their sexual extravagance and fondness for interracial sexual liaisons. In short, they were 'orientalised'. As Mimi Sheller accurately describes the image of the white West Indian in the late eighteenth century, planters were seen through an Orientalist discourse, itself a discourse predicated on a humoralist understanding of the malign effects that changing a temperate climate and lifestyle for a tropical way of life meant for Europeans. Depictions of planters' wealth were undercut by intimations of decadence coded as luxury, effeminacy, gluttony, racial degeneracy, and sexual hybridity.[20]

What especially damaged their reputation was their inability, so it was perceived, of resisting the siren charms of black and especially free coloured women. This devotion to the sins of the flesh was made in a British social context where fears of interracial contamination were increasingly conspicuous. Planters' sexual abandon and racial preferences in their sexual partners made many of the people who might have had positive feelings towards white West Indians feel wary about them.[21] White West Indians' propensity to 'riot in the goatish embraces' of coloured 'Jezebels', as the historian Edward Long colourfully put it, whose sexual tricks and sexual allure apparently put to shame the denizens of London's Drury Lane, was too much for people who may have been their erstwhile supporters to bear. White West Indians should have had a lot of support for their character, activities, and political positions among Regency libertines and rakes. Georgian libertines had little reason to feel a sense of commonality with the evangelical moralists who made up the vanguard of the abolitionist community. Proponents of having fun and people with a relaxed late-eighteenth-century attitude to morals were very well aware of what the advent of William Wilberforce's moralistic humanitarianism meant—it foreshadowed the starchy and repressive Victorian age. But while proslavery had a number of advocates, the defence of white Jamaicans was relatively muted during the fierce early stages of abolitionism. Interracial sexual connections were a step too far for any group to make in societies marked by hardening racial lines and in which embryonic scientific racism was making its appearance.[22]

What we can see from the 1780s is a transformation of the image of the West Indian and usually Jamaican planter. From being seen as a valuable, if admittedly vulgar, friend of the empire, the Jamaican planter became demonised. Unlike North American planters, notably George Washington, who was lionised for his empathetic qualities despite being the most significant enemy of Britain during the revolutionary years, Jamaican planters were characterised as slothful, cruel, diseased, and immoral. The abolitionists were remarkably successful in being able to portray planters as fundamentally un-British. The notorious *Zong* case of 1781–83 in which sailors on a slave ship threw 132 slaves overboard and then made a claim for insurance for their presumed loss of property that was contested by their insurers was such an outrageous violation of ethical practice that it galvanised public opinion against not just the slave trade but also against Jamaican planters.[23] To some extent planters got the press they deserved. Some early abolitionist works, notably the best-selling work of 1784 by the Reverend James Ramsay, previously and unhappily a parson in St Kitts, were directly inspired as much by dislike for the West Indian planter class as by distaste for slavery and sympathy for Africans. What also contributed to the denigration of Jamaican planters were a number of imperial scandals in the mid-1780s, such as the well-publicised pursuit by Edmund Burke of the ex-governor of

Calcutta, Warren Hastings. While the Hastings case was not connected to events in the West Indies per se, this case, and other cases like it, cast doubt in the British public's mind about both the efficacy and the morality of imperial activities.[24]

This change of attitude to imperial matters developed in the 1780s in a Britain brimming with confidence in a period of sustained economic prosperity. What is interesting to consider is why this attack on white Jamaicans and on officials of the East India Company serving in India was not extended to an attack on Irish Protestants in Ireland, especially Church of Ireland Protestants. This group of loyal imperial colonists, like white Jamaicans, was potentially vulnerable to charges both that their self-view of themselves was harmed by their vicious behaviour towards Catholics and that their adherence to ideals of settler rights and settler autonomy was antithetical to assumptions about British parliamentary sovereignty. Why did white Jamaicans face such opposition when the character and behaviour of Irish Protestants were less often impugned?

THE POSITIVE IMAGES OF IRELAND

The obvious retort to such a question is, of course, that Ireland—usually seen as a kingdom rather than a colony per se—was not Jamaica. It could be argued that the differences between the two British possessions were so great as to make comparisons invidious. Such a retort has considerable validity. Ireland was indeed not Jamaica and Catholics were not easily equated with enslaved Africans. What is worth doing, however, is not to concentrate on the ways in which Ireland and Jamaica were different—all of which differences are too obvious to require extensive enumeration—but to suggest ways in which they were similar. These similarities are not usually canvassed in historical works, mainly because Jamaica and Ireland are seldom discussed together. A slave colony with a small population of white people and a kingdom with an ambivalent constitutional position situated in western Europe and full of white people, who although divided by religious affiliation were united in their Christianity and even more so by their shared whiteness at a time when colour bars were beginning to emerge with greater force, do not seem to have much in common. But it is worth discussing the ways in which Jamaica and Ireland shared some similarities. In part this comparison is worth making because what happened to white Jamaicans in the 1780s through to the 1800s prefigured later events in Ireland in surprising ways. In part it is also worth making because a comparison of similarities of the two places helps us understand some of the peculiar dynamics of changes in imperial thinking that occurred in the 1780s.

The first, if not most obvious, similarity between the two colonies was that the ruling elites in both colonies were conspicuously loyalist in a period where the majority of white colonials had shown disloyalty to the empire and to the king. Both colonies expected to be rewarded for their loyalty after the American Revolution was finished. One sign of white Jamaicans' expectation that they would be rewarded for their loyalty to king and country was their delirious delight after Admiral Rodney had saved their country from invasion by winning the Battle of the Saints and their willingness to expend vast sums on building an elaborate memorial in the island's capital, Spanishtown, depicting Rodney in classical garb. The act was intended to be the grateful response of loyal Britons to a fortunate deliverance and a not-too-subtle sign to British imperial officials of their wealth and geopolitical importance.[25] But white Jamaicans were to be disappointed. They were not rewarded in any ways that they recognised. Indeed, they suffered a great deal from British actions after 1783, notably from British refusal to allow the new United States to trade with the islands. This decision prevented the United States from resuming after 1783 an important trade that had sustained Jamaica before the American Revolution. Britain's decision to keep the United States out of its mercantilist system was mostly related to Britain's desire to teach the United States a lesson about the consequences of independence. But its imposition (mostly easily avoided by Jamaicans but symbolically important nevertheless) was seen in Jamaica, rightly, as an economic blow. It was also seen, more worryingly, as an indication that the previous easy access to imperial influence over Caribbean affairs that Jamaican politicians had enjoyed prior to the American Revolution was now much more difficult.

During the American Revolution, when Britain needed all the Loyalists it could get, Jamaica tended to be treated reasonably well in imperial counsels. One noticeable example of the relatively high regard in which Jamaica was held could be seen in 1781–82 when Jamaica and Barbados received large sums of money (£40,000 for Jamaica) as welfare relief for the considerable losses that each had suffered during a catastrophic hurricane that hit western Jamaica in October 1780.[26] It also placed Jamaica at the heart of its geopolitical strategy in the lead-up to the Battle of the Saints. But British officials were unimpressed by Jamaicans' lack of effort during the American Revolution, especially their reluctance to serve in the military and thought them unduly self-interested. As P. J. Marshall comments, the 'planters seemed to be unreliable partners in empire, putting their own interests before the common good'.[27]

Ireland fared better than Jamaica did in the 1780s, as Britain reconfigured its imperial commitments and aspirations. To an extent the favours extended to Ireland in this period were surprising. Britain was not as certain of Ireland's loyalism as it was of Jamaicans' fidelity. Jamaicans may have been self-interested and self-seeking, but they were not disloyal. By contrast, Britain was suspicious about the motives and behaviours of many Irish patriot leaders during the American Revolution. British politicians, both in Britain and in Ireland, knew that many Irish patriot leaders had been sympathetic to American rebels. They knew that many Irish patriots shared similar views about the desired imperial–colonial connection as their

North American cousins. Nevertheless, even though there was little likelihood that Irish Protestants would have gone further than fond thoughts in their sympathy for American rebels and no chance that they would have transformed those fond thoughts into actual rebellion, given the danger that Catholic rebellion posed to Protestant dominance, British officials were always fearful about what might happen in Ireland. They worried about even the slightest sign of discontent in Ireland, conscious that the island was always a tinderbox of potential unrest. Ireland's proximity to Britain always made British leaders much more worried about what might happen there than they were about places like Jamaica that were very distant from the metropolis. Britain was thus more prepared in the case of Ireland than in the case of Jamaica to try to dampen down any sign of local discontent.

IRELAND AND THE AMERICAN REVOLUTION

The entry of France in the American revolutionary war in 1778 heightened the long-term danger of Catholic rebellion. Britain feared that France would take the opportunity of war to foster a Catholic uprising in order to help them attack Britain from the west. Interestingly, British officials were more concerned about this hypothetical possibility than they were about the reality of a planned French invasion of Jamaica in 1782. The latter was important in geopolitical thinking, of course, but it was only a few politicians, and those most connected to military strategy, who became really concerned about what the loss of Jamaica might mean. On the other hand, the loss of Ireland was always inconceivable. It also seemed much more likely. The reactions of the British to the 1798 rebellion indicate just how central Ireland and its connection to Britain were in the British imperial imagination.[28]

Consequently, Ireland was granted a number of concessions during the American Revolution, all of which helped counter some long-standing Irish resentment against Britain. The most important concession was the repeal in 1782 of the 1720 Declaratory Act made by the British parliament that asserted British parliamentary sovereignty over the Irish parliament. Henceforth, Ireland had something akin to dominion status (to use an anachronism from the constitutional arrangements of empire in the early twentieth century). It had attained by 1782 the status within the empire that the Americans had revolted about in order to obtain. And they had done so without going to war. From 1782, Ireland was to be a distinct kingdom, in which the king of England and Wales, Scotland, and now Ireland, and his Irish lords and commoners in the Irish parliament alone had the right to make laws. The much-hated Poynings' law of the seventeenth century was also amended so that the Privy Council no longer had the power to suppress or alter Irish bills.[29]

More concrete help was given in regard to the parlous state of Irish finances, which had been badly hurt by disruptions to the lucrative Atlantic trade during the American Revolution, especially after 1778. The British, however, in contrast to their actions with regard to Jamaica in the mid-1780s, lifted export restrictions on goods going into Britain. In addition, there was support given for Irish Volunteers. These Volunteers had done much to force the British government to concede the legislative independence of the Irish parliament in 1782. Britain also gave some modest relief for Catholics, even though most of their legal and political disadvantages remained—Irish Protestants guarded zealously their rights to keep Catholics in check through various kinds of social and legal discrimination. Both of these latter actions were not entirely well received by the Irish ruling elite. They were especially upset about the limited but constitutionally significant relief given to Irish Catholics.[30]

For some Irish Protestant leaders, the gains they had made during the years of the American Revolution presaged the beginnings of a 'Golden Age'. Henry Grattan, the major Irish Protestant leader, declared that Ireland was now a free country with a free people.[31] But Henry Flood, Grattan's rival patriot leader, was not fooled by British concessions. He warned the Irish House of Commons that 'the repeal of a declaratory law (unless it contains a renunciation of the principle) is only a repeal of the declaration, and not of the legal principle. The principle remains fully in force, unless to be renounced'.[32] For Flood, the fundamental problem with the seemingly new rapprochement of Irish and English Whigs in office on both sides of the Irish Sea was that it could not be a genuine alliance of equals. 'Office in Ireland' was, in his view, 'different from office in England; it was not a situation held for Ireland, but was held for an English government, often in collision with, and frequently hostile to Ireland'.[33]

Ireland may have become a kingdom (now officially) but it was also thought of as a colony. When push came to shove, British ministers, despite their common Whig sympathies with Irish patriots (even after the Tories had taken control of government with the accession to power of William Pitt, the younger, in 1784), were not prepared to alter the old system of management of Irish affairs through inducements and rewards. They found two ideas that circulated in this period as incompatible with regard to Ireland as they had done in the 1760s with respect to British North America. These ideas were the colonial idea of a Whig empire of equality between its members, regardless of which part of the empire they came from, and the parliamentary insistence that the settlement of 1688 between Crown and monarch necessitated an ever-vigilant concern with maintaining parliamentary supremacy. Jamaica found out in the late 1780s, especially with the advent of an abolitionist movement, that Britain was not prepared to loosen its grip over exercising power in the colony. Britain interpreted the result of the American Revolution as meaning that the imperial government had to exert more, rather than less, control over settler colonies. If there was any constitutional lesson that was drummed into British politicians from their reflections on the American Revolution it was that the imperial–colonial relationship was not a negotiated relationship but was instead a relationship with a clear master (Britain) and a clear insubordinate (the colony).[34] Ireland did not find out this fact in the 1780s, but it found it out, with a vengeance, in the nineteenth century.[35]

PARLIAMENTARY REFORM

One problem Ireland faced was that British concessions were not accompanied by real parliamentary reform. Three-quarters of the members of the Irish House of Commons were elected as members of rotten boroughs. Those rotten boroughs were invariably controlled by British landlords. The main outcome of the concessions of 1782, therefore, was to allow such aristocratic patrons, answerable to no one but themselves, to be able to drive even harder bargains with a British administration than they had done previously. What this meant in practice was that it became even more important for the British Parliament than before to maintain control over the Irish parliament. As S.J. Connolly puts it, 'without parliamentary reform all that had been achieved [from the Declaratory Act] was a transference of arbitrary power from despotism abroad to aristocracy at home'.[36] For some Irish politicians, this absence of reform was troubling. Grattan and Flood occasionally spoke as if they wanted actual reform. But when voices were raised in favour of reform, as at the third Dungannon Convention in September 1783, fears about what might happen if Catholics used the prospect of reform to agitate for voting rights soon led Irish Patriots to back down from any extreme position. The Irish zeal for reform, such as it was, quickly dissipated after legislative independence of a sort had been gained in 1782.[37]

In short, both white Jamaicans and Irish Protestants, despite the initial greater favouritism seemingly shown to the latter, were to be ultimately disappointed. Their desire to increase the amount of autonomy they had over their own affairs was stymied by the intransigence of Britain in respect to any loosening of its insistent claims that the British Parliament was sovereign in all things. These are significant historiographical issues. The question of imperial reform or imperial continuity in the 1780s has elicited historical argument. Historians disagree over what happened in the imperial sphere in the 1780s. Maya Jasanoff believes that 1783 and the Peace of Paris in that year marked a rupture and a crisis in imperial thinking. She is inclined to believe that there was a Second British Empire from the '1783 moment' that was conceptually different with regard to imperial willingness to allow colonial elites more latitude than was previously possible before the American Revolution. P.J. Marshall, on the other hand, argues that the fundamental features of the British imperial state that had been manifested before the American Revolution continued essentially unchanged after the loss of the American colonies. He denies that there was any shift from a First British Empire to a Second British Empire after 1783.[38]

Marshall has the better of the argument, rather than Jasanoff. Examining the experience of Jamaica and Ireland in the 1780s supports a contention that continuities were more important than change in the imperial state during the 1780s. If there was a change in imperial decision-making and imperial thinking, it occurred in the 1740s. In that period, previous understandings that involved a general acceptance of settler claims to political equality with Britain and an acceptance at the highest levels that settler colonies should have a certain amount of autonomy were replaced by an increasingly fervent insistence on British parliamentary insistence. This policy was initiated under the Earl of Halifax, one of whose protégés was George Grenville, who became prime minister in the 1760s. Grenville followed in the 1760s Halifax's position—that the colonies needed to be kept under fierce control—with disastrous results. But no major British politician ever resiled from the idea that the duty of colonies was to obey when Britain said they had to do so; this was as true in the early nineteenth century as it had been in the period of the Seven Years' War. Britain refused to accept settler claims that settlers living outsider Britain were the equals of Britons living in Britain. Britain also denied that colonists' homemade parliaments were the functional equivalent in the colonies of the British Parliament in Britain. It also rejected the second tenet of the settler position, which was that local elites were entitled to have control over those issues that most delineated the colonies from Britain and in which colonial elites had special interest and knowledge. Thus, white Jamaican's claims that what they did with their slaves and how they purchased slave property was Jamaica's concern and not Britain's was dismissed in London. So too, even given British indulgence of Irish Protestant desires in the 1780s, the Irish Protestant claim to special knowledge and power over their local Catholic population was not a proposition that British politicians ever accepted.

POORER WHITES IN JAMAICA AND PROTESTANT IRELAND

It was understandable, however, that Irish Protestants did not really believe in the 1780s that Britain would insist on asserting its own authority in Ireland. It was not just that Ireland was thought of as a kingdom as well as a colony and thus, as a kingdom, that it exercised its own sovereign power. Ireland's elite was both more powerful in British affairs (where many sat in the House of Lords) than were Jamaicans and more able to flit successfully and easily between their estates in Britain and in Ireland than was the Jamaican elite. But both elites had much in common. In particular, they were dominant minorities—small if powerful and outnumbered by their domestic enemies. The smallness of the ruling elite in both colonies and their reliance on uncertain support from the poorer people who were attached to them by race (Jamaica) or religion (Ireland) was striking. In Ireland, more than 80 per cent of the population was Roman Catholic and thus was denied any active participation in politics. No Roman Catholic could vote or sit in parliament. Moreover, the number of Protestant dissenters who could vote or participate in politics was very small. The Irish parliament thus represented only the propertied Anglo-Irish adherents of the Church of Ireland—about 10 per cent of the population, a figure about equal to the number of whites in the Jamaican population (the great majority of whom, if they met property qualifications, could vote).

What also united the elites of the two countries and made their situation functionally similar was the role of poor whites in Jamaica and ordinary Church of Ireland Protestants in Ireland. The latter we might think of in shorthand as the men who formed and staffed the Volunteers. Volunteers were Protestants, drawn from the middling and upper ranks of Irish Protestant society, who came together—perhaps as many as 40,000 men by 1780—at their own expense to resist any foreign invasion and, increasingly, to maintain the Protestant ascendancy. What is interesting about the poorer members of the dominant minorities in both colonies is how structurally similar as groups they each were. The groups respected hierarchical relationships, in part because they themselves benefited from being part of a hierarchy in which their connection to the ruling elite placed them above other groups in society. These were deferential societies in which there were great disparities of wealth even within the dominant minorities. Poorer whites and Volunteers knew their place and did not contest that place too often. Yet if they were members of a society in which deference mediated relationships in a way that was satisfactory to all parties, they were not especially characterised by deferential behaviour. They knew that they were important cogs in the machinery of government and even more so in supporting the leaders of dominant minorities against their enemies (slaves and Catholics, respectively). They required something for their political and social acquiescence to the authority of dominant elites. They expected to be consulted, they expected to be deferred to, and they expected their interests to be catered to. Outlining the details of how this works is beyond the compass of this chapter, but what is important to note is that poor Jamaican whites, especially those who worked as plantation employees and thus responsible for the maintenance of order on plantations, and Volunteers, who formed the backbone of social and military organisation that was used to keep Catholics relatively passive, were not incidental but central to the continuation of elite rule.[39] Both groups supported elite rule but a crucial precondition for that support was elite recognition that Jamaica and Ireland were more than just class societies. In Jamaica, the caste privilege was race; in Ireland, it was religion. Thus, being a white man in Jamaica brought privileges, no matter how poor any white man was. Being a Protestant in Ireland brought poor white men similar advantages. Or so poor white men thought.[40]

The 1780s, however, saw a different valence to the respective issues of race and religion. In short, attitudes to racial separation hardened as scientific racism developed. At the same time, and probably as a consequence of a developing sense that whiteness needed to be valorised against blackness, the religious differences dividing whites from each other started for the first time to be not that important. We can see hints of this developing in the differing relationship Britain had to Ireland as compared to Jamaica. It is also true in the willingness of the British government to countenance giving greater freedoms to Catholics brought into the empire, as in the Quebec Act of 1774, even if that act had been thought of by North Americans as one of the 'intolerable acts' that justified armed resistance.[41] Britain kept the basic principles of that Act, despite the part that the Quebec Act had played in inflaming American Patriots in 1774, in their far-reaching Canada Act of 1791.[42] Race was thus becoming more of a dividing issue in imperial relations from the late eighteenth century onwards. The turn to the east in imperial matters, as India became more important, and the reformulation of the British Atlantic as being a place full of black or brown people, made it difficult for imperial officials to think that the whites who remained in empire were terribly important.[43] By contrast, the importance of differences in religion declined in the latter part of the eighteenth century as Enlightenment dicta was increasingly used to dictate that religious differences were small and manageable. At roughly the same time that white Jamaicans began to harden their attitude towards free coloureds and as it became a society divided along caste lines, some small lessening of Catholic disenfranchisement in Ireland showed that Britain was more willing to tolerate religious difference than it had been.[44] Ireland and Jamaica were thus moving in different directions in significant aspects of their social makeup and ideological discourse.

For Ireland, the 1780s seemed to be a period of Protestant political ascendancy. But there were worrying signs that this 'golden age' was temporary rather than permanent. Jamaicans realised with alarm in the late 1780s that metropolitans were beginning to think of enslaved people as humans as much as property and thus were people who had 'rights' that needed to be considered just as white 'rights' were not as sacrosanct as they imagined. So, too, ruling Irish patriots were concerned about what they saw as the British government displaying some worrying leniency towards Catholics. The leniency the British displayed mainly came about for pragmatic reasons: Britain needed Irish Catholic soldiers as cannon fodder in their many wars. Irish Protestants feared that any extension of rights to Catholics would be the thin edge of the wedge. They were very well aware of the demographic realities that existed in an Ireland in which Catholics were far and away the majority of the population. Any diminution of British or Irish anti-Catholicism could lead to disaster for such a small Irish Protestant population. As one Irish politician argued, if Catholics got the right to vote, then no Protestant would ever again be elected. Soon, he insisted, the seventeenth-century land settlement, guaranteeing Protestant landed dominance, would be reversed, with Protestants being thrown off the land.[45]

1780s AND CHANGES IN IMPERIAL THOUGHT

What we see happening in the 1780s, therefore, was the beginning of a division between the British and the Irish governments. The Irish parliament and British imperial officials in Ireland noticeably hardened their attitude in this period towards Catholics—one predictable result of being given more autonomy was the use of such autonomy to devise more restrictive legislation against Catholics. The revival of earlier anti-Catholic Whiteboy movements, usually termed 'Rightboys', from 1785 to 1788 was one sign of how agitation for increased rights was linked to anti-Catholic sentiment.[46] These groups and Irish Protestants in general treated former Catholic allies with suspicion. They insisted that 'the ascendancy of Protestants must be accomplished with 'more firmness and security'.[47] Prime Minister Pitt was sympathetic to such assertions. He decided that 'too much pains cannot be taken to encourage the salutary jealousy of the designs of the Catholics which begins to show itself . . . The Protestant interest must be the bond of union between Ireland and this country'.[48] Nevertheless, the British government's previous actions during the American Revolution belied his strong words. Britain gave numerous concessions to Catholics during that period—a dismantling of the worst penal laws, an end to economic discrimination, an allowance of freedom of worship, and better access to land than had existed in the first half of the eighteenth century.[49]

Irish Protestants saw such actions as naïve metropolitan meddling into matters that the metropolis little understood with results that would be unpredictable. Irish Protestants predicted they would need to cope with whatever mess ignorant imperial meddlers concocted. They used the same sort of language about Catholic emancipation that white Jamaicans used to counter abolitionists. In particular, they mimicked white Jamaicans in believing that metropolitan indulgences to the subordinate majority imperilled the dominant majority and would lead to social unrest and rebellion. They argued, as did white Jamaicans with regard to enslaved people, that Catholics were ungrateful and would not see the concessions given to them with grateful eyes but as signs of weakness that they would exploit for their own gain. Indulgence of Catholics, they argued, would foster and encourage Catholic extremism, not Catholic moderation.[50]

There were other similarities between these two seemingly disparate colonies. One similarity was that the end result of the American Revolution was, in the final resort, unsatisfying for both Irish Protestants and also white Jamaicans. The result of the American revolutionary war was twofold for the imperial state. First, the loss of the war convinced Britain that the imperial centre had to be stronger, more authoritarian, and less willing to bend than it had seemed to be before the start of the Seven Years' War. Britain's defeat in America did not suggest to them that some latitude towards settlers, especially with regard to settler insistence that they had all the rights of native born Englishmen, would be a good idea. Rather, they felt that settlers needed to be kept in check. White Jamaicans' tendency towards tyranny to their enslaved people if left unchecked and Irish Protestants' relentless determination to prevent Irish Catholics from having any stake in society only convinced metropolitan observers that they were not dealing with reasonable people but with bullies and tyrants.[51] Second, neither Ireland nor Jamaica could be, as they were previously, imperial places that were largely out of sight and invisible to metropolitan inspection. One noticeable change that occurred in the 1780s was a considerable and growing interest in imperialism and in empire. Although empire had always been important as part of the British psyche during the eighteenth century, it was inconsequential alongside the much greater importance of Europe in the British geopolitical imagination.[52] But the American War of Revolution and the scandals over India in the mid-1780s made empire a much more pressing concern. Metropolitans started to take notice of imperial matters.[53]

Previously, as in the 1740–41 famine in Ireland and in Tacky's slave rebellion in Jamaica in 1760, provincial elites had been able to deal with colonial crises without much metropolitan attention being placed on what they did. They dealt with crises themselves, without much imperial assistance. Even if sometimes they over reached themselves, as in Tacky's revolt, where what white Jamaicans did to punish slaves evoked some degree of repulsion in polite circles in Britain, colonial elites for the most part were unencumbered in their actions by any metropolitan restraint. By the 1780s, however, Britain was far more aware of empire than before and much more critical of what they saw as objectionable colonial behaviour by colonial elites.[54] What white Jamaicans and Irish Protestants came to realise was that the trend towards firmer imperial control of colonial affairs, begun tentatively in the 1740s and leading to the American Revolution in the mid-1770s, was exercised over settler colonies more frequently in the 1780s. Britain was now an interventionist imperial power. Both possessions were henceforth shaped by that spirit of intervention. That in the end was the ultimate lesson the 1780s and the aftermath of the American Revolution for white Loyalists everywhere in the British Empire.

NOTES

1. The phrase comes from the influential work of Nicholas Canny, comparing white Protestants in seventeenth-century Ireland with white settlers in seventeenth-century Virginia. N. Canny, 'Dominant Minorities: English Settlers in Ireland and Virginia, 1550–1650', in A. C. Hepburn (ed), *Minorities in History* (London: Arnold, 1978), pp. 51–69.
2. B. Franklin, *Observations on the Increase of Mankind*, in L. W. Labaree et al. (eds), *The Papers of Benjamin Franklin*, vol. 4 (New Haven: Yale University Press,1959), pp. 225–34.
3. For mass British and Irish emigration to the British World in the nineteenth century, see J. Belich, *Replenishing the Earth: The Settler Revolution and the Rise of the Anglo-World, 1783–1939* (New York: Oxford University Press, 2009).
4. Among a large literature, see in particular C. A. Bayly, *Imperial Meridian: The British Empire and the World, 1780–1830* (London: Longman, 1989);

P. J. Marshall, *Remaking the British Atlantic: The United States and the British Empire after American Independence* (Oxford: Oxford University Press, 2012); and J. P. Greene, *Peripheries and Center: Constitutional Development in the Extended Polities of the British Empire and the United States, 1607–1788* (New York: W. W. Norton & Co., 1986).
5. William Pitt, Speech, 12 May 1785, House of Commons, *Parliamentary Register*, XVIII: 266.
6. S. Conway, 'From Fellow-Nationals to Foreigners: British Perceptions of the Americans, circa 1739–1783,' *William and Mary Quarterly*, 3rd ser., 59 (2002), pp. 65–100. I have developed this theme in several publications, most notably T. Burnard, 'Harvest Years: Reconfigurations of Empire in Jamaica during and after the Seven Years' War', *Journal of Imperial and Commonwealth History*, 40 (2012), pp. 533–55. The depiction of American planters in Britain was complicated by a grudging admiration for them. See T. Bickham, *Making Headlines: The American Revolution as seen through the British Press* (DeKalb: Northern Illinois University Press, 2009).
7. P. J. Marshall, 'Britain and the World in the Eighteenth Century: II, Britons and Americans', *Transactions of the Royal Historical Society*, 6th ser., 9 (1999), p. 12.
8. A. O'Shaughnessy, *An Empire Divided: The American Revolution and the British Caribbean* (Philadelphia: University of Pennsylvania Press, 2000).
9. A. O'Shaughnessy, *The Men Who Lost America: British Leadership, the American Revolution, and the Fate of Empire* (New Haven, CT: Yale University Press, 2013).
10. S. Conway, '"A Joy Unknown for Year's Past": The American War, Britishness and the Celebration of Rodney's Victory at the Saints', *History*, 86 (2001), pp. 180–99
11. Marshall, *Remaking the British Atlantic*, pp. 249–51.
12. Burnard, 'Harvest Years'.
13. For Jamaica in the 1790s, see D. Geggus, 'The Enigma of Jamaica in the 1790s: New Light on the Causes of Slave Rebellions', *William and Mary Quarterly*, 3rd ser., 44 (1987), pp. 274–99; and D. Ryden, *West Indian Slavery and British Abolition, 1783–1807* (New York: Cambridge University Press, 2009). For Ireland, see, inter alia, R. B. McDowell, *Ireland in the Age of Imperialism and Revolution, 1760–1800* (Oxford: Oxford University Press, 1979); T. W. Moody and W. E. Vaughan (eds), *A New History of Ireland: IV: Eighteenth-Century Ireland, 1691–1800* (Oxford: Clarendon Press, 1986); and J. Smyth (ed.), *Revolution, Counter-Revolution and Union: Ireland in the 1790s* (Cambridge: Cambridge University Press, 2000).
14. M. Jasanoff, *Liberty's Exiles: American Loyalists in the Revolutionary World* (New York: Alfred A. Knopf, 2011).
15. T. Burnard, 'White West Indian Identity in the Eighteenth Century', in J. D. Garrigus and C. Morris (eds), *Assumed Identities: Race and the National Imagination in the Atlantic World* (College Station, TX: Texas A & M Press, 2010), pp. 71–87.
16. R. Bourke, 'Pocock and the Presuppositions of the New British History', *Historical Journal*, 53 (2010), p. 750; J.G.A. Pocock, 'British History: A Plea for a New Subject: A Reply', *Journal of Modern History*, 47 (1975), p. 627. Pocock's lament for a new kind of British history was inspired by his feeling of dismay that Britain had abandoned his native New Zealand to economic disarray in order to join the European Economic Community.
17. Jasanoff, *Liberty's Exiles*. See also D. Kennedy, *Islands of White: Settler Society and Culture in Kenya and Southern Rhodesia, 1890–1939* (Durham, NC: Duke University Press, 1987).

18. W. Sypher, 'The West-Indian as a "Character" in the Eighteenth-Century', *Studies in Philology*, 36 (1939), pp. 503–20.
19. T. Burnard, 'Et Ego In Arcadia: West Indian Planters in Glory, 1674–1784', *Atlantic Studies*, 9 (2012), pp. 65–83; J.P. Greene, 'The Jamaica Privilege Controversy, 1764–1766: An Episode in the Process of Constitutional Definition in the Early Modern British Empire', *Journal of Imperial and Commonwealth History*, 22 (1994), pp. 15–53.
20. M. Sheller, *Consuming the Caribbean: From Arawaks to Zombies* (London: Routledge, 2003), p. 114; C. Petley, 'Gluttony, Excess and the Fall of the Planter Class in the British Caribbean', *Atlantic Studies*, 9 (2012), pp. 85–106.
21. F. Nussbaum, *The Limits of the Human: Fictions of Anomaly, Race, and Gender in the Long Eighteenth-Century* (Cambridge: Cambridge University Press, 2003).
22. The subject of abolitionism has attracted a wide literature. See for important recent works C.L. Brown, *Moral Capital: The Foundations of British Abolitionism* (Chapel Hill: University of North Carolina Press, 2006); S. Drescher, *Capitalism and Antislavery: British Mobilization in Comparative Perspective* (New York: Oxford University Press, 1987); and J.R. Oldfield, *Popular Politics and British Anti-slavery: The Mobilization of Popular Opinion, 1787–1807* (Manchester: Manchester University Press, 1995). Pro-slavery thought has been less studied. But see D.B. Davis, *The Problem of Slavery in the Age of Emancipation* (New York: Alfred Knopf, 2014), and for the practical politics of pro-slavery, see D.B. Ryden, 'Sugar, Spirits, and Fodder: The London West India Interest and the Glut of 1807–15', *Atlantic Studies*, 9 (2012), pp. 41–64.
23. J. Walvin, *The Zong: A Massacre, the Law and the End of Slavery* (New Haven, CT: Yale University Press, 2011).
24. N.B. Dirks, *The Scandal of Empire: India and the Creation of Imperial Britain* (Cambridge, MA: Harvard University Press, 2009).
25. O'Shaughnessy, *Empire Divided*.
26. M. Mulcahy, *Hurricanes and Society in the British Greater Caribbean, 1624–1783* (Baltimore: Johns Hopkins University Press, 2006), pp. 165–74.
27. Marshall, *Remaking the British Atlantic*.
28. J. Kelly, '"Era of Liberty": The Politics of Civil and Political Rights in Eighteenth-Century Ireland', in J.P. Greene (ed.), *Exclusionary Empire: English Liberty Overseas, 1600–1900* (New York: Cambridge University Press, 2010), pp. 104–6.
29. V. Morley, *Irish Opinion and the American Revolution, 1760–1783* (Cambridge: Cambridge University Press, 2002); M. Bric, 'Ireland and the Reassessment of a Special Relationship, 1760–1783', *Eighteenth-Century Ireland*, 11 (1996), pp. 88–119; J. Kelly, *Poynings' Law and the Making of Law in Ireland, 1660–1800* (Dublin: Four Courts Press, 2007).
30. Moody and Vaughan (eds), *A New History of Ireland: IV*, pp. 217–20.
31. *Speeches of the Late Rt. Hon. Henry Grattan, in the Irish Parliament, in 1780 and 1782* (London: James Ridgeway, 1821), pp. 1–19
32. Cited in P. Jupp, 'Earl Temple's Viceroyalty and the Question of Renunciation, 1782–3', *Irish Historical Studies*, 17 (1971), p. 503.
33. H. Grattan, *Memoirs of the Life and Times of Henry Grattan*, 5 vols. (London: Henry Colburn, 1839–46), II: p. 225.
34. J.P. Greene, *The Constitutional Origins of the American Revolution* (New York: Cambridge University Press, 2011).
35. Kelly, 'Era of Liberty,' pp. 91–101.
36. S.J. Connolly, *Divided Kingdom: Ireland 1630–1800* (Oxford: Oxford University Press, 2008).
37. Marshall, *Remaking the British Atlantic*, p. 138.

38. Jasanoff, *Liberty's Exiles*; P.J. Marshall, 'Empire and Authority in the Later Eighteenth Century', *Journal of Imperial and Commonwealth History*, 15 (1987), pp. 105–22.
39. T. Burnard, *Creole Gentlemen: The Maryland Elite, 1691–1776* (New York: Routledge, 2002); T. Burnard, *Planters, Merchants, and Slaves: The Rise and Development of Plantation Societies in British America, 1650–1850* (Chicago: University of Chicago Press, 2015). For an important treatment of the topic for colonial British North America, see M.J. Rozbicki, *Culture and Liberty in the Age of the American Revolution* (Charlottesville: University Press of Virginia, 2011). An earlier treatment for Ireland is N. Canny, *Making Ireland British: 1580–1650* (Oxford: Oxford University Press, 2001). For Ireland in the 1780s see J. Kelly, 'The Parliamentary Reform Movement of the 1780s and the Catholic Question', *Archivium Hibernicum*, 43 (1988), pp. 95–117. For volunteers, see P.D.H. Smyth, 'The Volunteers and Parliament, 1779–84', in T. Bartlett and D.W. Hayton (eds), *Penal Era and Golden Age: Essays in Irish History, 1690–1800* (Belfast: Ulster Historical Foundation, 1979), pp. 113–36.
40. T. Burnard and J. Garrigus, *Tropical Transformations: St Domingue, Jamaica, and the Making of Racial Order, 1748–1791* (forthcoming). For Ireland, see I.R. McBride, *Scripture Politics and Irish Radicalism in the Late Eighteenth Century* (Oxford: Clarendon Press, 1988).
41. H. Neatby, *Quebec: The Revolutionary Age, 1760–1791* (Toronto: University of Toronto Press, 1966).
42. Marshall, *Remaking the British Atlantic*, pp. 172–75.
43. For India, see R. Travers, *Ideology and Empire in Eighteenth-Century India: The British in Bengal* (Cambridge: Cambridge University Press, 2007). For hardening attitudes to race in British America in the late eighteenth century (ironically at the same time as opposition to slavery also hardened) see Brown, *Moral Capital*. For a wider perspective see J.G.A. Pocock, *Barbarism and Religion: Barbarism, Savages and Empires* (Cambridge: Cambridge University Press, 2008).
44. For later developments in Ireland, see F. O'Ferrell, *Catholic Emancipation: Daniel O'Connell and the Birth of Irish Democracy, 1820–30* (Dublin: Gill and Macmillan, 1985).
45. Connolly, *Divided Kingdom*, p. 419. See also T. Bartlett, *The Fall and Rise of the Irish Nation: The Catholic Question, 1690–1830* (Dublin: Gill and Macmillan, 1992).
46. J.S. Donnelly, 'The Rightboy Movement 1785–8', *Studia Hibernica*, 17–18 (1977–78), pp. 120–202.
47. J.B. Kelly, 'Inter-denominational Relations and Religious Toleration in late Eighteenth-Century Ireland: The "Paper War" of 1786–88', *Eighteenth-Century Ireland*, 3 (1988), pp. 39–67.
48. William Pitt, Speech, 12 May 1785, House of Commons, *Parliamentary Register*, XVIII, p. 266
49. A full account of Pitt's commercial relations with Ireland can be found in J. Kelly, *Prelude to Union: Anglo-Irish Politics in the 1780s* (Cork: Cork University Press, 1992), pp. 76–209.
50. M.J. Bric, 'Priests, Parsons, and Politics: The Rightboy Protest in County Cork, 1785–1788', *Past & Present*, 100 (1983), pp. 100–23.
51. For Jamaica, see T. Burnard, 'Powerless Masters: The Curious Decline of Jamaican Sugar Planters in the Foundational Period of British Abolition', *Slavery & Abolition*, 32 (2011), pp. 185–98.
52. B. Simms, *Three Victories and a Defeat: The Rise and Fall of the First British Empire, 1714–1783* (London: Allen Lane, 2007).
53. Dirks, *Scandal of Empire*.
54. J.P. Greene, *Evaluating Empire and Confronting Colonialism in Eighteenth-Century Britain* (New York: Cambridge University Press, 2013).

2 From Cronelea to Emu Bay to Timaru and Back
Uncovering the Convict Story

Joan Kavanagh and Dianne Snowden

Cronelea is a townland in the parish of Mullinacuffe, south County Wicklow, Ireland. Emu Bay is on the north coast of Tasmania, Australia. Timaru is on the east coast of the South Island, New Zealand. These three places are connected by Eliza Davis, a foundling admitted to the Dublin Foundling Hospital as an infant. In January 1841, when she was 22, Eliza was apprenticed by the governor of the Foundling Hospital as a servant to James Twamley, a farmer of Cronelea in County Wicklow. In July 1845 she was charged, tried, and found guilty of the crime of infanticide. The sentence of death was later commuted to transportation for life to the penal colony of Van Diemen's Land.

Eliza was one of approximately 80,000 convicts transported to Van Diemen's Land between 1803 and 1853. Few historians have analysed the colonial experience of individual convict women, particularly in Van Diemen's Land.[1] These women often dropped out of sight once they emerged from the convict system. This chapter adds to the body of knowledge about the individual convict experience and the migration of convict families from the colony. It also considers the 'convict stain' as an important historiographical issue as well as its impact on family history and popular memory.

In 1998, A.G.L. Shaw expressed scepticism about the value of the contribution of many of the books and articles on female convict history.[2] However, Kay Daniels, Deborah Oxley, and Kirsty Reid have all carefully examined the development of convict historiography generally, and female convict historiography specifically.[3] The debate about female convict historiography has been complex and far-reaching.

An important strand of the female convict historiographical discussion has been predicated on the existence of a criminal class and its corollary, the habitual criminal. Daniels and Reid both suggest that much of the early writing on convict women was moulded by this belief; this is especially evident in the work of Shaw, Manning Clark, and Lloyd Robson.[4] Although Shaw later clarified what he meant by 'criminal class'—that is, that it was not a group of professional criminals who hoped to live exclusively by criminal means but a moral grouping of opportunistic poor people, 'perennially petty thieves'[5]—his focus on convict background has persisted. More recently, Oxley argued for a reopening of the debate about female convict origins but on a much broader scale than indicated by a mere qualitative study.[6]

A fundamental concern with the origins of convicts—who they were and where they came from—included consideration of whether the female convicts were whores or prostitutes. This stereotype was adopted uncritically, even by feminist historians such as Anne Summers and Miriam Dixson,[7] until questioned by Michael Sturma in his seminal article 'Eye of the Beholder'.[8] Sturma argued that prostitution was not synonymous with cohabitation and that middle-class values had been imposed on established working-class relationship patterns. In other words, the majority of convict women were not whores or prostitutes: it was a question of semantics.[9] Sturma's views are evident in Robinson's presentation of the convict woman, not as a whore but as a family woman.[10] She argued that the 'damned-whores' stereotype was the product of the behaviour of a minority, the troublesome few. Her argument was picked up by other historians, including Marian Aveling and Monica Perrott.[11]

Deirdre Beddoe's study of Welsh convict women followed on from the work of Irish convict historians, in acknowledging there might be significant differences in convict experience depending on where they were tried. Her study examined the circumstances, motives, demographic and occupational features, and voyage experience of convict women tried in Wales.[12] Increasingly, there have been a number of recent county and regional convict studies, albeit mostly quantitative.[13]

An important point made by Richard Davis is that the examination of individual lives may help untangle some of the intricacies of female convict historiography.[14] Although his article dealt with only three women, it is significant for the detail that it provides about their lives. The provision of such detail clearly indicates the complexity of individual convict lives. Babette Smith's study of her ancestor, Susannah Watson, provides another example of how the detailed examination of individuals can add to a clearer understanding of the convict experience.[15] Daniels and Reid both implied that quantification of the convict experience provides only part of the picture and that many convicts do not fit into sharply defined statistical or descriptive categories.[16] As Reid stated, '[p]eople are much more than the abstract composites of the demographic facts and figures relevant to their history'.[17]

Historiographically, it may be the approach and techniques of the family historian that best allow insight into the complexities of individual lives. By concentrating on the individual, much more is revealed, not only of the life of the individual convict woman but also the discrepancies and anomalies of the convict system, the multilayered constraints of colonial Van Diemen's Land, and the intricacies of the social system. There is growing acknowledgement of the role that family history has to play in providing the necessary detail.[18] In 1998, Shaw acknowledged that family historians had been able to do what academic historians had not: 'What we need generally are personal studies of the type some of our genealogists have been able to carry out—the examination of court records, of local press, of petitions for mitigation of sentence and such similar material'.[19] Shaw's suggestion was not new; as early as 1989, John Spurway, in 'The Growth of Family History in

Australia', commented that family historians had received scant attention from academic historians, despite influencing the direction of contemporary history.[20]

One implication of this historiographical shift to the detailed study of individuals is a focus on convict life after emancipation. For most historians, a convict's life was a life under sentence. Relatively few historians have considered the possibility of studying the convict experience after sentence. In Daniels's *Convict Women*, the chapter 'Freedom' is almost a postscript.[21]

This historiographical overview demonstrates the inadequacy of traditional approaches in explaining the complexity of convict life. To ignore the post-sentence life of any convict woman is to ignore a major part of her story. In the case of the convict women, it is this search for detail which adds richness and enables the women to be seen as individuals. To this end, the following analysis of Eliza Davis's life is in three sections: her conviction, transportation to Australia and her life there, and her legacy (including the migration of some of her family to New Zealand).

Irene Levin, in 'Silence, Memory and Migration', suggests that within memory, 'there are things one wants to remember and other parts that one does not remember or take to the new country'.[22] Failure to acknowledge a convict past has been attributed to shame—the convict stigma or convict stain.[23] Grace Karskens maintains that because early Australian historians portrayed the convict period as shameful, the origins of the colony 'tended to be quarantined', ignored, or forgotten. It was not until the publication in 1958 of Russell Ward's book *The Australian Legend* that convicts were included 'into a national narrative, not just as pioneers but as "founding fathers"'.[24] Williams suggested that many Irish convicts 'probably escaped the stigma of convictism by moving to mainland colonies', while those that remained had 'nothing to fear from their convict heritage'.[25] This was because most were 'basically honest men and women caught in the poverty, famine and conflicts that were part of Irish history during the 1840s and 1850s'.[26] Elsewhere, however, he acknowledged that convict heritage was either concealed or considered shameful until well into the twentieth century: 'most families hid the fact that they had convict ancestors . . . Tasmanians wished to distance themselves from what they believed to be a sordid past and a stain on their society'.[27]

The story of Eliza Davis enables consideration of the 'convict stain' in relation to an individual convict woman and her descendants. Was Eliza being deliberately silent about her past in Ireland and then in Van Diemen's Land? Did her silence have any bearing on the decision of some of her family to leave Tasmania for New Zealand?

ELIZA'S CONVICTION

In early February 1845, when she was 19 and still living in County Wicklow, Eliza Davis gave birth to a son. No information has come to light about the father of her child, except that he was most likely a fellow servant who took advantage of her reduced circumstances.[28] Tragically, Eliza's infant son died and a police constable from Killabeg Barracks about two miles from Cronelea was called to investigate. On 3 March 1845, the constable ordered the draining of a pond at Coolkenna. The baby's body was found in the pond, dressed in a cotton gown and two caps which had been given to Eliza. An inquest was held the next day. The surgeon who attended the inquest and examined the body told the court that 'the child had received injury on the head, but [he] thinks the immediate cause of death was suffocation, it appeared previously to have been taken care of, it was a healthy male child'.[29]

Eliza was indicted for the murder of her male child at Cronelea, at the Wicklow assizes on 8 July 1845. The verdict of the jury was guilty. The sentence passed by the chief justice, John Doherty, was that she was to be executed. Doherty 'appointed a distant day (16 August) for the execution in order to afford his Excellency (Lord Heytesbury, Lord Lieutenant of Ireland) ample time for the consideration of this case'.[30] As will be seen, there was much to consider in this particular case.

On 12 July 1845 Chief Justice Doherty replied to a letter from the chief secretary's office requesting information on Eliza Davis, then under sentence of death in Wicklow Gaol (see Figure 2.1). He regretted to state that he could 'not discern any mitigating circumstances which would in [his] opinion warrant [him] in recommending the prisoner as a proper object of mercy'. Doherty enclosed the notes of the evidence given at the trial for the Lord Lieutenant's 'perusal'. If grounds were discovered for extending mercy to 'this unfortunate woman, it would afford me sincere satisfaction', he concluded.[31]

The trial notes contain the sworn evidence of five local women: Mary Deegan, Catherine Foley, Eliza Gahan, Bess (Eliza) Carr, and Margaret Hopkins. Police Constable Francis Culhane and Henry William Morton, surgeon, also gave sworn evidence. All five women knew the prisoner before the crime was committed. Mary Deegan stated that Eliza had lodged with her before Christmas and 'was confined there sometime in February and delivered of a male child'. Eliza had informed Mary Deegan that she was not a married woman. After the birth she remained in the house for a fortnight. The witness told how she had given clothes to the prisoner for the baby and that she had identified these same clothes, a frock and two caps, at the inquest on 4 March in Killabeg Barracks. Under cross-examination she stated she had never heard Eliza call the baby by any name.[32]

Catherine Foley, meanwhile, claimed to have seen the prisoner with a baby about a fortnight old in her arms. She had come into a house where the witness was and sat by the fire where they talked for about an hour and a half. The child appeared to be in good health.[33] Eliza Gahan had been asked by the prisoner for a night's lodging, which she granted, on a Monday night. This was the day before the inquest, 3 March. Eliza stayed until about 12 o'clock the next day. She had no child with her.[34]

Figure 2.1 Wicklow Gaol, Ireland, where Eliza Davis was imprisoned before her transportation to Van Diemen's Land

Source: Reproduced with the permission of Joan Kavanagh.

The next witness, Bess Carr, was a significant witness, as we shall see later, for what she revealed about Eliza Davis's background. Unfortunately, her important evidence does not appear to have been brought out at the trial. Bess stated she met Eliza coming out of Eliza Gahan's house and they walked together for a while. The prisoner had told her she had had a child about a fortnight old and that she had left him with a Mrs Deegan of Baltinglass and was at that time making her way back for him. Bess asked her to go to her father's house to clean up. It seemed at first that Eliza was inclined to do so, but she then said she was afraid of Mrs Deegan if she did not go to collect the child.[35]

The evidence of Margaret Hopkins is undoubtedly questionable, a fact which the Revd Soloman Donovan, who later petitioned on Eliza's behalf, brought to the attention of the Lord Lieutenant. Margaret Hopkins claimed that on the evening of Monday, 24 February, at about six o'clock, she saw a woman sitting at the edge of Mrs Ashe's Pond, wrapping a cloth around a child. The woman put the child down into the water and it cried at first. She then pushed it down two or three times more. The witness claimed she was seven or eight perches from the woman, standing on the road while the woman was at the far side of the pond. The woman in question came out and passed the witness, saying nothing. The witness saw this woman at the inquest and identified her as the prisoner Eliza Davis. Under cross-examination Margaret Hopkins stated that she was the mother of several children. At the time of the incident she had a burden on her back which she claimed prevented her from running down to the pond. Neither did she call out to the woman. With hindsight she admitted that this would have been a wise thing to do.[36] The scene described by Margaret Hopkins would seem to be improbable. Could she have conceivably seen Eliza putting a cloth around the baby's head and then pushing the baby down into the pond at six o'clock on a winter's evening in February? Evidence from other quarters would later cast considerable doubt on her testimony.

Police Constable Francis Culhane, stationed at Killabeg Barracks, testified that he found the body of a child in Mrs Ashe's Pond, in Coolkenna, on 3 March. The inquest was held the next day. He found the body by draining the pond.[37] It is not clear from the records who alerted him to the death of the baby. There are several similar minor anomalies in the evidence. The surgeon who examined the body, Henry William Morton, stated that the child had several injuries on the head but that the immediate cause of death was suffocation. It appeared to him that the child, a healthy male, had been previously taken good care of.[38]

What prompted the chief secretary's office to request information regarding Eliza Davis from Chief Justice Doherty was a petition, or memorial, on the prisoner's behalf written by the jury at Eliza's trial. Although 'compelled' by the evidence placed before them to find Eliza Davis guilty, they entreated the Lord Lieutenant to commute the sentence to transportation for life. It appeared to them that the child was properly taken care of and that she acted from a sudden impulse. They were also informed by the sub-inspector of the district that she was prone to fits.[39] This is the first indication given that there may have been extenuating circumstances.

Revd Donovan, former incumbent of the parish of Mullinacuff, made a sworn affidavit before W.R. Farmer, magistrate for County Wexford, to the effect that Eliza Davis was 'subject to fits'. These were of a peculiar kind which 'frequently seized her at her work in which she has lain as in a sleep for upwards of twenty-four hours. That she frequently had a bewildering look and remained on these occasions silent when spoken to'.[40] There was no doubt, according to Revd Donovan, but 'that her intellect was impaired'. He claimed that Bess Carr was in the best position to comment on Eliza's condition because she, being a fellow servant with Eliza, had shared a room and a bed in the servant's quarters, until the discovery of Eliza's pregnancy. Bess had sworn to the fact that Eliza was not 'alright in the head'. Revd Donovan had known Eliza himself for four years. While incumbent of Mullinacuff parish he had lodged in the house of James Twamley, Cronelea. He also, then, was in a good position to observe Eliza's affliction and to comment on it.

The minister also cast extreme doubt on the evidence of Margaret Hopkins and asserted that her allegation that she saw Eliza Davis drown her child was 'totally undeserving of the least credit, that if she Margaret Hopkins was cognisant of the fact she could not in my opinion have kept it a secret for so long'. He told of Margaret's background which was one of poverty, her husband and herself having a large family. Sometime previously she had been summoned to Carlow to give evidence in a similar case. She had received a sum of money to cover her expenses. 'A hope of obtaining a similar or greater sum was in my opinion the motive that induced Margaret Hopkins to volunteer evidence against Eliza Davis', wrote Revd Donovan. He also reported that Margaret Hopkins had made several statements to the effect that he, Revd Donovan, had advised her to go forward with this evidence, giving her money to cover the expenses of the journey. Revd Donovan attested that these were 'totally false and without foundation'.

The chairman and commissioners of the Borough of Wicklow also sent a memorial to Lord Heytesbury.[41] Having made enquiries into the case they had come to the belief that the crime had been committed as a 'result of a weakness of the mind and deficiency of the intellect'. It is through this memorial that more details of Eliza's life are revealed. It was alleged that while Eliza was a servant in Twamley's house she was seduced by a person in the house. She became pregnant, and Eliza brought her infant back to her place of employment 14 days after its birth. She offered to support the child if the father would allow her £2 a year. No offer of support was given. This, according to the commissioners, 'drove her into such a state of desperation as to commit the melancholy deed being seized with one of the fits alluded to by the Revd Mr. Donovan'.

The chairman and the commissioners also asserted that affidavits corroborating Revd Donovan's statement were lodged with the deputy clerk of the Crown; one was made by a policeman showing Margaret Hopkins's evidence could not have been true. The other was made by Eliza (Bess) Carr, Eliza's fellow servant. The reason why these facts were not put forward in Eliza's defence, they stated, was because her counsel had not been appointed in time to make a case. The jury had made a strong recommendation for mercy 'but by some fatality it was not given until sentence was passed'. Chief Justice Doherty told the court that the matter was now out of his hands and any pleas for mercy should be placed before the Lord Lieutenant. The Commissioners concluded their memorial by asking for Eliza's sentence of death to be reprieved. They reminded the Lord Lieutenant that 'no execution of a female has occurred in this county for the last ninety eight years'. The chairman of the commissioners was Andrew Nolan, a medical doctor who also acted as the local inspector of Wicklow Gaol.

A memorial signed by Henry Pakenham, on behalf of the governors of the Foundling Hospital in Dublin, was received at Dublin Castle on 18 July.[42]

In this it is stated that Eliza Davis had been placed as a foundling under their care and had been reared from infancy in the institution. On 6 November 1840 she was apprenticed as a servant to a farmer in County Wicklow for four years. It was the norm for inspectors from the Hospital to visit apprentices annually and to report on their state and condition. According to Eliza's reports, 'her character and conduct were irreproachable until seduced by a fellow servant who well knew her destitute circumstances and who depended upon not being obliged to marry her, he being of the Roman Catholic persuasion and she a Protestant'. The appointment of both counsel and attorney, only the night before the trial, was again brought to the attention of Lord Heytesbury. The governors felt that this situation had hampered the preparations for her case and the procurement of witnesses for her defence.

Bess Carr's relevant evidence was omitted. Since the trial she had made a sworn statement that Eliza Davis had suffered from epilepsy; 'she would be during the interval before and after, not right in the head', she stated. Bess had gone to court determined to state this fact, but as she had never been a witness before 'she was so very nervous and frightened that she did not know when to come forward, not having been called for'. The governors believed, therefore, that there was every reason to suppose that the crime was not one of premeditation but was committed while the unfortunate girl was labouring under the effects of one of these fits.

A further memorial was written by concerned gentlemen from Wicklow and its environs.[43] Among them were a number of clergymen of both persuasions from the locality, as well as justices of the peace. The Church of Ireland chaplain of the Gaol, Revd Robert Porter, signed, as did Dr William Hamilton, medical superintendent of the Gaol. Francis Synge of Glanmore Castle was also a signatory.

This memorial again alludes to the statements made by Revd Donovan and Eliza Carr which pointed to the prisoner having 'exhibited strange inclinations to imbecility or aberration of the mind'. They also referred to a report which had been made to the judge that, within one year, nine cases of infanticide had been uncovered in the neighbourhood where Eliza Davis lived. It was also claimed that the prisoner had been charged with a similar offence previously. The falsity of this report had been proved without any doubt because the police returns had shown that only three infanticide cases had occurred in the preceding two years. Of these three cases, those charged with the offences in two of the incidents had been acquitted while the third was Eliza Davis. These gentlemen were convinced that the act was committed due to 'a sudden and momentary phrensy' as the evidence given by Mr Morton, surgeon, that the baby had been well taken care of proved that 'maternal feelings were strong in the heart of the said convict'.

The Society of Friends, or Quakers, petitioned on Eliza's behalf, probably as a matter of course.[44] Their belief 'that man is not under any circumstances authorised to deprive his fellow man of life' more than likely prompted the Quaker families resident in Wicklow to sign the petition, beseeching the

Lord Lieutenant to change 'her sentence to whatever may appear to thee best from that of death'; these Quaker families included Joseph Pym, senior and junior; Samuel and Henry Greer; Josiah Fayle; and Joseph Morton. Could this last name have any connection with Henry William Morton, surgeon, who testified at the trial? At the time Eliza 'committed the melancholy act she was without a friend, refused at the poor house, without a home, without food and afflicted with epilepsy'. This state of affairs, they believed, warranted a favourable review of her case.

Eliza's case is remarkable for the way in which it was handled by the authorities who went to some time and trouble to investigate it, and for the compassion that it aroused in the community. But what happened to Eliza Davis following this tragic set of circumstances? Her sentence was commuted by the Lord Lieutenant from death to transportation for life.[45] Eliza was removed from Wicklow Gaol on 12 August 1845 and committed to the Female Convict Depot at Grangegorman Lane (see Figure 2.2) to await embarkation on a ship bound for the penal colonies of Australia.[46]

Figure 2.2 The Female Convict Depot at Grangegorman, Dublin, where Eliza Davis awaited her embarkation in 1845

Source: Reproduced with the permission of Joan Kavanagh.

TO AUSTRALIA

Transported women waiting to be sent to Van Diemen's Land were housed at Grangegorman Convict Depot in Dublin. From the Grangegorman Prison Register, additional information about Eliza comes to light. The Gaol Register for Wicklow Gaol before 1846 is no longer extant. The only entry for Eliza in Wicklow Gaol is in the Transportation Register which gives the minimum amount of information: name, age, crime, sentence, and occasionally the transporting ship, although not in Eliza's case.[47] It is the Grangegorman Register which provides a physical description of Eliza Davis: she was five feet three inches tall, with dark blue eyes, dark hair, and a fair complexion and with no marks on the body. She was listed as single, Protestant, and a servant girl who could read, although not write.[48]

Nearly 12,500 women were transported to Van Diemen's Land, mostly for petty theft. Transportation to the penal colony of New South Wales ceased in 1840, and Van Diemen's Land became the main penal colony receiving more than 36,000 convicts between 1840 and 1853 when transportation ceased.[49] The Irish made up almost one-third of that figure.[50] The convicts' clothes and food were provided by the settlers in return for cheap labour. Those who behaved could look forward to earning a ticket of leave which allowed them relative freedom and the right to work for wages. The granting of a conditional pardon or absolute pardon normally followed sometime later.

Eliza left from Kingstown (now Dun Laoghaire) on 2 September 1845 on the convict transport *Tasmania* (2).[51] There were 138 female prisoners on board the *Tasmania*; only one woman died during the voyage.[52] A newspaper report confirmed that Eliza embarked on the *Tasmania*:

> As it was expected that the above vessel would sail on Saturday from Kingstown Harbour, a number of persons proceeded to the pier to witness the impressive and melancholy sight. The day was beautiful . . . and everything indicated peacefulness and happiness; but when the eye turned to the gloomy form of a convict ship as it lay upon those calm blue waters, a floating dungeon, the prison-home of the felon, exile, a sadness came o'er the mind from the reflection that however bright and lovely, and joyous all things round it seemed to be, within its dark and tomblike bosom were enclosed many suffering spirits, whose crimes had expatriated them from their native land . . . side by side knelt the miserable creature who poisoned her husband in Kilkenny and she who had drowned her infant in Wicklow when driven from the door of her seducer.[53]

The woman referred to in this newspaper article, transported for 'strangling her infant in Wicklow', could only be Eliza Davis.

The *Tasmania* reached Hobart Town on 3 December 1845 with 137 women and 35 children. En route one woman, Ellen Sullivan, and a six-month-old baby, Patrick Ferguson, died. The journey, according to the ship's surgeon, Jason Lardner, was without any great mishap, although a number of the women suffered great distress through seasickness while the dampness below decks also caused much discomfort. This latter problem was alleviated through additional stoves being brought down to the prison section. Ironically, the women were given extra rations of potatoes in September 1845, just as the blight was making its first appearance in Ireland. While two people died onboard, a baby was also born during the voyage to Sarah McArdle, a 28-year-old Waterford City convict sentenced to transportation for vagrancy.[54]

Although female convicts were transported to Van Diemen's Land from 1803 there was no female factory built in the colony until 1821. A factory was designed as a place of labour, a hiring depot, and place of punishment for those convicts who were pregnant or ill. Initially the number of female convicts in the colony was small, and the demand for these convicts as servants or wives was great. Refractory female convicts were imprisoned. With the increasing number of female convicts arriving into Van Diemen's Land the officials in Hobart decided that it was necessary to build a factory where the women could be put to work and from where they could be hired. It could also act as a reception centre for the new arrivals. The Cascades Female Factory, built in 1828, replaced the Hobart Town Female Factory. The probation system was introduced in 1844 for convicts who arrived after this time. Under this system women underwent a probationary period of six months before they could be hired out. The probationary period was completed on the hulk, the *Anson*, moored on the River Derwent.[55]

HMS *Anson*, a former naval vessel, transported 499 male convicts to Hobart in 1844. It was then fitted out as a female probationary establishment. Over the course of its lifetime, 3,000 women were lodged on board the *Anson* at its berth in the Prince of Wales Bay, Risdon, on the River Derwent until 1850 when it was broken up.[56] Eliza Davis was one of those women. According to her convict conduct record, Eliza spent six months aboard the *Anson*, where she was listed as a class 3 prisoner.[57] She was released on 16 June 1846 and was then eligible for employment to an approved master or mistress. The convict conduct record also recorded some regulatory and personal details, including Eliza's applications for a ticket of leave and a pardon as well as her marriage to fellow convict, Joseph Roebuck. Joseph Roebuck arrived in Van Diemen's Land in October 1841 on the *David Clarke*.[58] A native of Pennington, Yorkshire, he was tried at York in July 1840 and was sentenced to 10 years' transportation for stealing wearing apparel. Because he had already been imprisoned for three months on two previous occasions, once for poaching and once for having skeleton keys in his possession, his sentence of transportation would have come as no surprise. His convict record states that he had an idle, bad character but that on board ship his behaviour was good. In 1841 he was a widower, aged 36.

Joseph Roebuck served a period of probation of 18 months at Brown's River (now Kingston). In April 1843 he was charged with 'misconduct in improperly receiving a half loaf from the bakehouse'. He received three months' imprisonment in return. By September 1843 he was residing at Campbell Town, and in 1847, he was granted a ticket of leave. Joseph was recommended for a conditional pardon in April 1848 which was approved in July 1849. According to his convict record, he was 5 feet 6¾ inches tall, with brown hair and whiskers and brown eyes. He was described as 'pock-pitted', with two rings tattooed on the fingers of his left hand, and a hair mole on his left arm.[59]

It is impossible to say how Eliza and Joseph met, but because Eliza and Joseph were convicts, they were required to apply for permission to marry.[60] This was approved, and the marriage took place on 26 July 1847 in Campbell Town at St Luke's Church 'according to the rites and ceremonies of the United Church of England and Ireland'. Joseph, aged 43, signed his own name, while Eliza signed with an 'X'.[61] Two months before the marriage took place, on 20 May 1847, Eliza had given birth to twin daughters in St John's Hospital, Launceston.[62] They were christened in Campbell Town in St Luke's Church on 27 June under the name of Davis and not Roebuck. The twins were named Amelia Eleanor and Elizabeth.[63] The family then appears to have moved south; by June 1850, a son, Joseph Henry, was born to the couple in Hobart.[64]

In 1856 Joseph Roebuck was charged in the police office in Hobart Town with being of 'unsound mind, unfit to be at large and unable of maintaining himself'.[65] On 24 September, evidence was taken by Duncan McPherson and the chief superintendent of police, J. Burgess, as to the condition of Joseph. A question as to his wife's ability to assist towards his maintenance while in the asylum was posed. It would appear that this option had already been investigated by the examining magistrate, who decided that this would not be possible because she had three children to provide for. On the sworn evidence of Dr Edward Bedford, Joseph was to be 'confined in His Majesty's General Hospital at Hobart Town while awaiting the decision of his Excellency, The Governor'. Dr Bedford stated that he had seen Joseph on a number of occasions, once two years previous and again some months prior to the hearing. He found him to be 'subject to epileptic fits and temporary insanity'. This piece of evidence from Dr Bedford is ironic because Eliza similarly suffered from epilepsy. It was this disability which many believed led Eliza to drown her baby. Its revelation after her trial was considered a circumstance which led to the commutation of her sentence from death to transportation for life.

Eliza's sworn evidence provides an insight into her life with Joseph. According to Eliza, Joseph had been unable to work for almost four years, and it was through her labour that the family survived: 'Sometimes I earn thirty shillings a week and sometimes less by taking in washing and mangling. I have no other means of procuring support for myself and family. And I am not able to pay for my husband's treatment in hospital'.[66] A further statement sheds some light on her life with Joseph as his condition deteriorated:

> My husband threatened me last week. He said he would kill me. He was in a worse state of mind then than he is at present. He was more violent. He threatened me on last Friday and Saturday—I am afraid that he will do me some bodily injury unless he is placed under restraint.[67]

Joseph was committed to the New Norfolk Asylum for the Insane where he remained until his death in September 1873.[68] His cause of death was recorded as 'disease of the brain and natural decay', verified by the superintendent medical officer, G. F. Huston. Joseph was described as a pauper, aged 73.

Life for Eliza at this time must have been extremely hard, because she, most likely, continued to take in washing to keep herself and the three children, now aged nine (the twins) and six. She possibly remained in Hobart Town for some time, but by May 1860 when she gave birth to another daughter, Alice, she was living in northern Van Diemen's Land.[69] Eliza had reverted to her maiden name of Davis, and Alice's father was recorded as Amos Eastwood (see Figure 2.3). The union between Eliza and Amos Eastwood produced six children in all: Sarah sometime in 1859,[70] Harriet in September 1862,[71] Hannah in May 1864,[72] Amos in December 1865,[73] and James in July 1869.[74] During this 10-year period Eliza was still married to Joseph Roebuck, but it is likely that Eliza and Amos lived together quite openly as the children were registered under the name of Eastwood and not Davis.

What of this man Amos Eastwood? He, too, was a convict, sent to Van Diemen's Land via Colaba, near Bombay, India, where he was courtmartialled for striking a superior officer.[75] Like Joseph Roebuck, Amos was a Yorkshire man, from Doncaster. He was in the 78th Regiment stationed in India and struck Sergeant Scott in December 1850. For this, he was transported, arriving aboard the *Royal Saxon*. He was of the Church of England denomination, could read and write a little, and was 26 years of age when he arrived in 1851. His trade was recorded as wheelwright. His probationary period was for three-and-a-half years, and he was stationed first in the prison barracks (presumably in Hobart) and then in 1852 at Impression Bay, near the notorious convict depot at Port Arthur. By October of that year he was a pass holder, having completed his probation period; he was then available for hire.

From 1853 to 1855 Amos Eastwood's convict record sheet contains details of a number of colonial offences. There are five instances listed where

Figure 2.3 Eliza Davis and Amos Eastwood
Source: Reproduced with the permission of Gail Mulhern.

he was sentenced to various periods of confinement for drunk and disorderly conduct. Each offence occurred in Hobart; the first in November 1853 when he was confined to 10 days' solitary confinement in the prison barracks and then returned to service. On the second occasion in April 1854, he received 14 days' solitary confinement. By June of that year, as well as being drunk and disorderly he was also charged with being out after hours and was sentenced to two months' hard labour, after which he was returned to service. September saw him again in the prison barracks, this time for six months' hard labour for being drunk and for misconduct in resisting a constable. A note to the effect that he was not to return to service in Hobart was recorded. This pattern of offending continued with another offence recorded in February 1855 when the charge was 'misconduct in returning late under the influence of liquor and assaulting a constable'. He received six months' hard labour. A few days later, he had absconded. Nothing more is known of this episode.

The last entry relates to his certificate of freedom in 1858, an official acknowledgement that he had served his sentence. It is possible that around this time he came in contact with Eliza Davis Roebuck and they formed a relationship. From the places of birth of their children, Eliza and Amos obviously moved from Hobart in the south to the northern region of Morven (Evandale), Longford, and Launceston, and eventually to the Emu Bay port settlement district, later named Burnie.

Emu Bay was established by the Van Diemen's Land Company as a port and service centre for stock and farm supplies.[76] The Van Diemen's Land Company was set up in 1825 by English investors keen to exploit the great wealth to be found in Australia. An area of 350,000 acres was settled by the Company, 120,000 acres of which were in the Emu Bay (Burnie) district. It was one of the few areas of the north-western coastline with deep water potential. The landscape, however, was heavily forested with almost impenetrable rainforest stretching from the shoreline 30 or 40 miles inland. Only a handful of people lived there and it functioned merely as an outpost. In the 1840s, when the land was cleared, it was discovered that the land had a deep, rich loam of remarkable fertility. Settlers moved into the area but few wished to stay in Emu Bay, which was accessible only by sea. The mining of tin at Mt Bischoff in 1871 changed Emu Bay dramatically.

According to the sesquicentenary publication *Pioneers of Burnie*, Amos Eastwood married 'a Launceston girl' (as Eliza was described, no doubt in an attempt to sanitise her convict background), and moved to Burnie in 1868.[77] There he lived in a house on Marine Terrace at the junction of Brickwell Street. It was a felicitous move for Amos, coinciding as it did with the growth in the Mt Bischoff mine. Working as a wheelwright for Burnie blacksmith John Mylas, Amos 'faced a major challenge in building and repairing wheels for the dozens of bullock wagons carting Mt Bischoff ore and general goods'.[78] Mt Bischoff and the Van Diemen's Land Company were a significant source of employment for the family: Amos Eastwood Junior, born in 1865, 'as a boy spent a half day at school and the remainder working for the Van Diemen's Land Company swimming numerous horses, working the Mt Bischoff tramway, in the sea'. Amos Eastwood Junior later joined the Emu Bay and Mt Bischoff Railway Company and became a train driver. In 1905 he bought a 34-acre dairy farm. He died in 1931, aged 65 years. His son, Cliff, bought a 270-acre property which he worked up to his retirement in 1969. In 1964, Cliff donated eight acres of his land to the Burnie Council; this is now a tennis court centre and park and has been named Eastwood Reserve.

The penultimate document relating to Eliza is her marriage to Amos Eastwood, dated 12 October 1898, almost 40 years after the birth of their first child.[79] Eliza, as 'Elizabeth Roebuck', was recorded as a widow aged 68. The wedding ceremony was conducted in Emu Bay 'according to the usages of the Primitive Methodist Church'. Amos was a bachelor and a wheelwright. He was 72 and was born in Doncaster, Yorkshire. His parents were Amos and Mary Eastwood and his father had also been a wheelwright. Eliza's husband, it states, had died at New Norfolk Asylum. A comment of 'cannot remember the year' was recorded. Her birthplace was Wicklow, Ireland, and her parents were not known. Elizabeth signed the certificate with her mark. On her transportation record in 1845 she had been able to read only. Fifty-three years later it would appear that she could still only read.

Elizabeth stated that she had only three children living (this statement is true in that she had only three children alive bearing the name Roebuck but also by this time she had given birth to six additional children, all of whom were registered under the surname of Eastwood). The marriage was witnessed by Amelia Helen Coldhill from Latrobe, and Harriet Whitton, from Burnie. Both were Eliza's daughters: Amelia from her first marriage[80] and Harriet, born in 1862,[81] who was in fact witnessing her parents' marriage.

One week later, on 19 October, Eliza Davis Roebuck Eastwood died. She was, according to the death certificate, aged 69, and the cause of death was 'Cerebral Apoplexy'.[82] The closeness of these dates—her marriage on 12 October and her death on 19 October—begs the following questions: Were Eliza and Amos aware of her impending death, or was it a mere coincidence? Did Amos wish to make 'an honest woman' of Eliza before her death? Why did they marry? Why had they not married earlier, after Joseph Roebuck's death in 1873? These questions have been put to various people in Tasmania and New Zealand, but no definitive conclusion has been reached.

ELIZA'S LEGACY

In one respect, the story of Eliza Davis ends with her death in 1898. But, of course, Eliza's story does not end there as seven of her nine children married and had numerous children; her legacy endures in them and their descendants. It is intriguing to consider what her large family knew of Eliza's background: what story of her early life was passed down within the family? Certainly, her obituary in the local paper was coy about her past:

> A very old resident of Burnie in the person of Mrs. Amos Eastwood passed away at her late residence on Wednesday morning. Deceased, who had reached the advanced age of 78 years, had been failing in health for some time, and a short while back was attacked with paralysis, from which she never recovered. Her demise is regretted by a large circle of friends, as she was universally liked and respected.[83]

No reference here to a convict past but this was not unusual. Lucy Frost in her book *Abandoned Women* suggested that fear of the convict stain may have induced a descendant of a Scottish convict to create 'a paper trail which would delete his grandmother, the convict Margaret Christie' from his mother's obituary in 1902.[84] Similarly, when Amos died suddenly in August 1903, his obituary described him as 'an old colonist [who] in his early days served in the British army'.[85] Again, no reference is made to a convict past in his obituary. Often, but not always, 'an old colonist' was code for a former convict.

The obituary of their daughter Alice, who died in 1932, provides some interesting information about her parents' life in the early years: 'By the death of Mrs Alice Jones last week another link with early days of Burnie has been severed'. The writer, Richard Hilder, describes how the family endured a perilous sea voyage to convey them from Danbury Park to the Cam River so Amos could take up a position as a wheelwright in a sawmill: 'The weather proved so boisterous in Bass Strait that for the family's safety they were battened below for two or three days'. They survived the ordeal and remained on the Cam Road as Amos worked in the mill before settling on Marine Terrace in Burnie, located on Emu Bay. From this obituary we also learn that 'Mrs. Eastwood was known for her excellent work as a maternity nurse for many years'. Again no reference is made to a convict past for either Eliza or Amos.[86]

One local history, *Pioneers of Burnie*, provides an alternative perspective on Amos's beginnings in Van Diemen's Land: 'The Burnie Eastwoods had their origins in the Indian Mutiny of 1857–58. After the mutiny, grandfather Amos Eastwood, of Yorkshire, chose to come to Tasmania rather than return to England'.[87] Where did this information come from? It is noteworthy that Amos Eastwood chose to come to Tasmania and not Van Diemen's Land. According to this account Amos chose to come; he was not forced to. While this book was published in 1977 the author is correct in using Tasmania as indeed the colony had gained self-government in 1856 and the name change had occurred. The calls to end the system of transportation had begun with the Molesworth Report in 1838. Transportation to New South Wales had ceased in 1843, which meant all convicts were henceforth sent to Van Diemen's Land and to Western Australia from 1850 till 1868. The anti-transportation movement really came to the fore in 1844 with the introduction of the probation system.[88] The catastrophic effects of the blight on the potato in Ireland led to greater numbers of convicts being shipped from Ireland after 1846. Finally, when the transportation system was halted in 1853 and the convict colony became a self-governing colony in 1856 there was much rejoicing. A new name was given and all was changed. Van Diemen's Land was no longer; instead, the prosperous self-governing colony of Tasmania had arisen, like a phoenix from the ashes of a society that had been formed as an open prison with the majority of the population having a convict background.

There has been no examination, however, of another possible explanation: that many hardworking rural and working-class families lived from day to day and that the past generally was not an important consideration. In Eliza's case, there may have been other reasons apart from the stigma of convictism that resulted in quietness about the past, including Joseph's admission to the asylum, children born out of wedlock, and even being a foundling.

Eliza and Amos's marriage record in 1898 states that Eliza's place of birth was Wicklow, Ireland, yet she was raised in a Foundling Hospital in Dublin, and there is no other evidence to suggest she was born in Wicklow.[89] Eliza's death record states her place of birth as England. The informant was Francis C. Wills, police clerk in Burnie.[90] It may never be known whether these examples of misinformation were deliberate or arose from ignorance of the facts.

Intergenerational narratives shed light not only on the experiences of transportation and migration but also on their silences. George Hughes is the great-great-grandson of Eliza Davis and Amos Eastwood. Their daughter, Sarah, born in 1859, married Alfred Hughes in 1877 and had 11 children. Four of these children went to New Zealand and settled there. George's reaction to being contacted about his family history was, in part, delight, but then he admitted 'to being a bit taken back at first. We were led to believe that Elizabeth Davis had been transported for stealing. One can only feel the pain for her, to have been driven to do something like that'.[91] Perhaps George's response exemplifies Robert Hughes's description, in *The Fatal Shore*, of the 'twin pressures to forget and mythologise' in which convicts were stereotyped as 'innocent victims of unjust laws, torn from their families and flung into exile on the world's periphery for offences that would hardly earn a fine today'.[92]

George had already commenced researching his family history and was aware that Eliza had two families. Although it was known that Eliza had a convict past, the crime for which Eliza was transported was assumed to have been a petty one. Once the truth of her past was revealed 'Eliza's convict past was considered with empathy and compassion. We all felt for her and admired the life she made for herself in Australia. To marry twice and mother two families was something to be proud of'.[93]

Beverley Gellatly is also a descendant of Eliza and Amos through their daughter Sarah and her husband, Alfred Hughes. She learned of her convict ancestry from her second cousin George Hughes. Her mother, Melba Wright (née Hughes), told her 'of the names of her uncles and aunties and how much her Father (Alfred Hughes Junior, who came to New Zealand with his three brothers in search of work) loved and missed his sisters, especially Elaine. She was reluctant [to] speak to me of Tasmanian family history at all, said it was too sad'.[94] Once she knew of Eliza's background, Beverley accepted 'that we cannot change the past yet without Eliza and her convict past I would not be here today. To me she is the jewel in the crown of my family history research'.

Another descendant, Gail Mulhern, in Queensland, is Eliza's great-great-granddaughter, through Eliza's daughter Amelia Eleanor Roebuck, who married David Coldhill in 1863.[95] On learning of research into Eliza's life,

Gail wrote, 'I can hardly type this letter because I am crying—I am just so happy and amazed that I have received your letter and enclosures'.[96]

Gail commenced researching her great-great-grandmother's past when a cousin mentioned a connection to an Eastwood family that a friend was researching.[97] No one in Gail's family was aware of a convict past until Gail unearthed Eliza's convict record. Gail's experience is not an uncommon one.[98] In the preface to his book *The Great Shame*, Thomas Keneally referred to his Irish ancestry and the vague knowledge of some 'forebears who were convicts'. He then discovered that his wife's family tree also had convict antecedents. He suggested that 'earlier generations of Australians would have suppressed what they conceived as genealogical stains'. He chose to 'tell the tale of the Irish in the new world and the old through the experiences of those transported to Australia for gestures of social and political dissent'.[99]

It was only through the convict record that so much of Eliza's past was revealed. Unlike her distant cousin George Hughes, neither Gail nor her family was aware that the second family, the Eastwoods, existed. When asked how Eliza's past was viewed by the family, Gail replied, '[W]hen I explained what had happened, I don't think anyone I know judged her as we really couldn't judge people from so long ago. . . . [I] for one admire how strong she must have been. She just "got on with life". How wonderful that she became a midwife, and how she loved her children. I do not know of any descendants who do not wish to acknowledge Eliza's past'.[100]

No one in the family knew of Eliza's past as a convict. How was that? What information had been passed down? How soon was Eliza's past glossed over to reflect a different beginning in Van Diemen's Land? What about Amos? How was his past reflected? How and when did this cloak of respectability fall over the family and, indeed, Tasmania? In Tasmania, it seems that there was a collective amnesia, and hiding the convict stain was carried out on two levels—individual and state (reflected in the name change from Van Diemen's Land to Tasmania).

Did Eliza and Amos's life together in Van Diemen's Land mirror what was happening in the colony? Eliza received her ticket of leave in March 1854 and was recommended for a conditional pardon in May 1855; this was approved in 1856.[101] Amos received his certificate of freedom in 1858.[102] Although Babette Smith wrote of the pervasiveness of the concept of the convict stain throughout the entire convict era and locations, Van Diemen's Land is unique in that its population was made up in the main of convicts or emancipists. How best to hide your past than to have an entire population working with you to hide that past? According to Hamish Maxwell Stewart, hiding the past was about allowing people to live and let live:

> My own feeling on forgetting convict origins is that it was a collective act. It would have only worked if everybody played the game (family, friends and enemies). I think that such a large proportion of Tasmanians had convict links because of the shortage of colonial women that no

one dared accuse anyone else in case a skeleton was found in their cupboard. Even many of the colonial elite had married native born girls in the early decades who were themselves the children of liaisons between officers and convicts.[103]

Sarah Eastwood, born about 1859, married Alfred Hughes in 1877 and had 11 children born between 1877 and the late 1890s.[104] Four sons, Alfred (Alf),[105] Joseph Henry (Joe),[106] Milton (Mick),[107] and Bertram (Terry)[108] went to New Zealand in the early 1900s.[109] Because Tasmania was experiencing a depression at this time, the Hughes boys went to New Zealand seeking work and remained there. They initially worked in the timber industry and then later in the coal mines in the Southland and then in the flax mill industry. George felt that the past was not deliberately hidden. It was just a case that the past had not been spoken of, and therefore, they were not aware of it. The Hughes people, he stated, 'were all straight talkers and very honest and open people'.[110]

While it is understandable that a former convict might want to hide his or her past and not refer to it, surely a descendant, knowing the early history and origins of Tasmania, might have asked questions as to their origins on the island? Was it a case of later generations not wanting to ask the question because they might get an answer? George did concede that his grandfather, Milton (Mick), lived in a different age:

> I was not aware that the marriage had taken place so close to Eliza's death. Likewise with the fact that she had been married before. My grandfather did not even tell the name of his mother. Had I, of course, asked it may have been different. An Australian in New Zealand is always hearing jokes about convicts etc. So by nature they are always a bit coy. My grandfather kept most things to himself. Perhaps now I know why. His age was not so well enlightened as now.[111]

Mick Hughes was born in Burnie, Tasmania, in 1887. At the time of Eliza's death in 1898 Mick would have been 11 years old. He would have known his grandmother and grandfather. Being so close to her in time, is it possible that Mick and his siblings, along with his first cousins, were not aware of the convict past in their family?

As in Eliza's early life in Ireland there are many unanswered questions in relation to the concept of the convict stain and the stigma which clung to the individual, even when emancipated. Was this a deliberate act on the part of Eliza and her children to hide her past in order to bring respectability to their family and a better future for her children? Was it a case of once free, out of sight out of mind—a sort of convict amnesia similar to the Famine amnesia of the Irish who emigrated to North America?[112] Was it a three-pronged approach of individuals, communities, and government to reinvent Van Diemen's Land into a Tasmania whose origins were more about free settlers than about convicts? Was it a case of having done her time Eliza was now free to put this one-off criminal act behind her and live a normal life? Was it a case of different times and people did not talk about the past because they had enough to do to just survive each day? Why talk about yesterday when today and tomorrow were more pressing? Were Eliza, Amos, and many other former convicts deliberately suppressing their past 'in order to avoid reliving psychic trauma or suffering the shame of having experienced it?'[113] Were they '[h]iding the stain?', as Chad Habel has suggested in his paper on Christopher Koch's *Out of Ireland?*[114] In this novel and in Koch's earlier book *Highways to a War*,[115] the convict past of the central character, Robert Devereux, is hidden from his son. According to Habel, 'Koch offers a form of ancestral identification that enables individuals to both reconcile with the past and move with purpose into the future'. Koch was himself a descendant of an Irish female convict, Margaret O'Meara, transported aboard the *Tasmania* (2) alongside Eliza Davis.[116] His convict connection was successfully hidden: 'Like many other Tasmanians, I was innocent of any serious knowledge of the history of my island'.[117] Koch wrote that when he was a young man:

> That past—still so close to us—was full of curious gaps. It was a past which many Tasmanians still did not want to know about, in 1960, for fear of disturbing an ancestor in chains. . . . The Hidden Convict has been until recently the ghost at the feast for many Tasmanians. He (or she) was hidden by our parents and grandparents with great cunning . . .
>
> My mother led us to believe that her family contained no convicts—those ancestors whom Tasmanians most dreaded to discover. I asked her several times if she could be sure of this; after all, convict ancestors were to be found in a great many families that had settled here before 1850. Her eyes would widen, her lips would purse, and she would deny it with the same indignation she would have shown had I suggested she was a criminal herself. *No!* her family were entirely respectable.[118]

Now the past has come full circle: later generations wish to know about a convict past in their family and wish not only to acknowledge it but also to celebrate it. With time the shame and stigma attached to a family with convict antecedents has evaporated. Has the spread of democracy and equality for all assisted in this reappraisal of the past?

Distance in time and space has brought compassion, empathy, and pride for an ancestor whose tragic early life was eclipsed by her colonial experience: a mother, a grandmother, and a highly respected community midwife. Gail, George, and Beverley have returned to Wicklow Gaol to see where Eliza was held and tried; the uncovering of Eliza's story has come full circle.

There is no evidence that her epilepsy impeded Eliza's life in Van Diemen's Land. The statement at the inquest by Dr Morton that the child found dead in Mrs Ashe's Pond was a healthy child, with signs of having been well cared for would suggest that the alleged killing of her two-week-old son by Eliza was a momentary mental aberration. Eliza's colonial life in Van Diemen's Land surely justified those who had written numerous memorials on her behalf. Eliza Davis, it would appear, certainly was 'a proper object of mercy'.[119]

CONCLUSION

Eliza Davis's story is remarkable because of the way it has captured the imagination of researchers and her descendants, even inspiring a poem about her life and proposals for a film and a play. Yet her story has only recently been uncovered as the result of diligent and persistent investigation. In Eliza's case, family stories have surfaced as a result of research, not as the result of family memories; her convict past remained hidden, either by design or by default.

Eliza's narrative forms part of a significant historical revision. No longer is a convict past seen as shameful; rather, it is celebrated. Recently, historians such as Alexander, Smith, and Boyce have explored the cultural amnesia of convictism and the impact it has had on more recent generations.[120] Eliza's descendants exemplify this. Perhaps more important, Eliza's story highlights that there is much more to a convict life than a crime, a trial, and a sentence. Daniels, noting the complexity of individual convict lives, warned against stereotyping and this is borne out by Eliza's story.[121] Little has been written about a post-sentence life and even less about post-sentence migration of emancipated convicts or their families. Eliza's many descendants have embraced the difficult details of her early years, as a foundling, as a woman who committed infanticide, and as an Irish convict sentenced to transportation for life. She is accepted with compassion and understanding. The ramifications of a convict life were not limited to the individual transported but flowed through to the next generation and beyond. The migration experience of convict families illuminates and enriches the narrative. In Eliza's case, this is exemplified by those family members who settled in Timaru and their search for an understanding of their past and their convict ancestor. Her story provides a constructive framework for understanding not only intergenerational narratives and their place in identity formation but also the restitution of a suppressed past.[122]

ACKNOWLEDGEMENTS

The authors are deeply indebted to the following people without whose assistance the initial research into Eliza Davis's life in Tasmania and New Zealand would not have been possible: the late Denise McNeice, Thelma McKay, Ray Thorburn, George Hughes, Gail Mulhearn, and Beverley Gellatly.

NOTES

1. Recent studies include D. Snowden, '"A White Rag Burning": Women who Committed Arson in Order to be Transported to Van Diemen's Land' (unpublished PhD thesis, University of Tasmania, 2005); T. Cowley, *A Drift of Derwent Ducks* (Hobart: Research Tasmania, 2004); L. Frost, *Abandoned Women: Scottish Convicts Exiled Beyond the Seas* (Sydney: Allen & Unwin, 2012); T. Cowley and D. Snowden, *Patchwork Prisoners: The Rajah Quilt and the Women who Made it* (Hobart: Research Tasmania, 2013).
2. A.G.L. Shaw, 'The Convict Question, 1866 and 1998', *Tasmanian Historical Studies: Exiles of Empire*, 6:2 (1999), p. 10.
3. K. Daniels, *Convict Women* (St. Leonard's, NSW: Allen & Unwin, 1998); D. Oxley, *Convict Maids. The Forced Migration of Convict Women to Australia* (Cambridge: Cambridge University Press, 1996); K.M. Reid, 'Work, Sexuality and Resistance: The Convict Women of Van Diemen's Land, 1820–1839' (unpublished PhD thesis, University of Edinburgh, 1995).
4. For the existence of a criminal class, see A.G.L. Shaw, *Convicts and Colonies. A Study of Penal Transportation from Great Britain and Ireland to Australia and other parts of the British Empire* (Carlton, Vic: Melbourne University Press, 1978); L.L. Robson, *The Convict Settlers of Australia: An Enquiry into the Origin and Character of the Convicts Transported to New South Wales and Van Diemen's Land 1787–1852* (Carlton, Vic: Melbourne University Press, 1965); C.M.H. Clark, 'The Origins of the Convicts Transported to Eastern Australia 1787–1852', Parts 1 & 2, *Historical Studies*, 7:26–27 (1956), pp. 121–35, 314–27.
5. Shaw, 'The Convict Question', p. 4.
6. Oxley, *Convict Maids*, p. 3. See also S. Nicholas (ed), *Convict Workers: Reinterpreting Australia's Past* (Cambridge: Cambridge University Press, 1988), especially S. Nicholas and P.R. Shergold, 'Unshackling the Past', pp. 3–13, for arguments against the existence of a criminal class.
7. A. Summers, *Damned Whores and God's Police: The Colonization of Women in Australia* (Ringwood, Vic: Penguin Books, 1976); M. Dixson, *The Real Matilda: Women and Identity in Australia, 1788–1975* (Ringwood, Vic: Penguin Books Australia, 1976).
8. M. Sturma, 'Eye of the Beholder: The Stereotype of Female Convicts 1788–1852', *Labour History*, 34 (1978), pp. 3–10.
9. For a recent study of convicts as prostitutes, see C.J. Leppard, 'The Unfortunates: Prostitutes Transported to Van Diemen's Land' (unpublished PhD thesis, University of Tasmania, 2013). In her detailed study, Leppard questions the labelling of convict women as prostitutes.
10. P. Robinson, *The Hatch and Brood of Time: A Study of the First Generation of Native-born White Australians 1788–1828* (Melbourne: Oxford University Press, 1985); P. Robinson, *The Women of Botany Bay* (Ringwood, Vic: Penguin revised edition 1993; first published 1988).
11. M. Aveling, '"Bending the Bars": Convict Women and the State', in K. Saunders and R. Evans (eds), *Gender Relations in Australia: Domination and Negotiation* (Sydney: Harcourt Brace Jovanovich, 1992), p. 156; M. Perrott, *A Tolerable Good Success: Economic Opportunities for Women in New South Wales, 1788–1830* (Sydney: Hale & Iremonger, 1983). See also Robinson, *Botany Bay*; J. Williams, 'Irish Female Convicts and Tasmania', *Labour History*, 44 (1983), pp. 1–17; S.R. Allan, 'Irish Convicts—Hampdens or Hardened Criminals? A Review of the Work of Lloyd Robson and

John Williams: A Comparative Case Study', *Tasmanian Historical Studies*, 7:2 (2001), pp. 95–118.
12. D. Beddoe, *Welsh Convict Women: A Study of Women Transported from Wales to Australia, 1787–1852* (Carmarthen, Wales: S. Williams, 1979).
13. See, for example, the following chapters in B. Reece (ed), *Irish Convicts: The Origins of Convicts Transported to Australia* (Dublin: University College Dublin, 1989): S. Curley, 'Transportation in Clare Before and After the Famine', pp. 81–113; B. Mooney, 'Women Convicts from Wexford and Waterford 1836–40', pp. 113–27; S. Byrne, '"The Law Must Take its Course": Crime and Transportation in Donegal, 1836–42', pp. 129–59; L. Irwin, 'Women Convicts from Dublin', pp. 161–91.
14. R. Davis, '"Victims or Initiators?" Three Irish Women Convicts from Van Diemen's Land', in Reece (ed), *Irish Convict Lives*, pp. 199–30.
15. B. Smith, *A Cargo of Women. Susannah Watson and the Convicts of the Princess Royal* (Kensington, NSW: New South Wales University Press, 1988).
16. Daniels, *Convict Women*, p. 10; Reid, 'Work, Sexuality and Resistance', pp. 37–39.
17. Reid, 'Work, Sexuality and Resistance', p. 37.
18. See P. McIntyre and J. Dwyer, 'Family History, "Professional" History and Academic History: Who Owes What to Whom?', *Descent*, 29:2 (1999), pp. 78–1. Family historians have been acknowledged by R. Reid in his work on assisted immigration from Ireland; N. Townsend and D. Kent on machine breakers; T. McClaughlin on Irish orphans; and G. Karskens in *The Rocks: Life in Early Sydney* (Carlton, Vic: Melbourne University Press, 1997). More recently, academic historians who have acknowledged the contribution of family historians include L. Frost and H. Maxwell-Stewart (eds), *Chain Letters: Narrating Convict Lives* (Carlton, Vic: Melbourne University Press, 2001), p. 3.
19. Shaw, 'The Convict Question', p. 4.
20. J. Spurway, 'The Growth of Family History in Australia', *The Push from the Bush: A Bulletin of Early Social History*, 27 (1989), pp. 53–112.
21. Daniels, *Convict Women*, pp. 214–40.
22. I. Levin, 'Silence, Memory and Migration', *Journal of Comparative Family Studies*, 44:6 (2013), http://www.questia.com/read/1G1–356454936/silence-memory-and-migration (accessed 5 March 2014).
23. A. Alexander, *Tasmania's Convicts: How Felons Built a Free Society* (Sydney: Allen & Unwin, 2010), and B. Smith, *Australia's Birthstain: The Startling Legacy of the Convict Era* (Sydney: Allen & Unwin, 2008).
24. G. Karskens, 'The Settler Evolution: Space, Place and Memory in Early Colonial Australia', *Journal of the Association for the Study of Australian Literature*, 13:2 (2013), pp. 1–21, at www.nla.gov.au/openpublish/index.php/jasal/issue/view/257/showToc (accessed 5 March 2014).
25. J. Williams, 'Irish Convicts in Tasmania', in *Bulletin for Tasmanian Historical Studies*, 2:3 (1989), p. 29.
26. Ibid., p. 29.
27. Williams, 'Irish Female Convicts', p. 17. See also A. Alexander, 'The Legacy of the Convict System', *Tasmanian Historical Studies*, 6:1 (1998), pp. 48–49.
28. National Archives of Ireland (hereafter NAI), Dublin, Convict Reference File (hereafter CRF) 1845 D18. The details of Eliza's case and her early life have been extracted from this Convict Reference File.
29. NAI, CRF 1845, D18/2.
30. NAI, CRF 1845, D18/9, letter from John Doherty, Wexford, to E. Lucas Esq, 12 July 1845.

31. Ibid.
32. NAI, CRF 1845, D18/1.
33. NAI, CRF 1845, D18/1/2.
34. NAI, CRF 1845, D18/2.
35. Ibid.
36. Ibid.
37. Ibid.
38. Ibid.
39. NAI, CRF 1845, D18/3.
40. NAI, CRF 1845, D18/6/7/8. There are two copies of Revd Donovan's statement in the file.
41. NAI, CRF 1845, D18/14.
42. NAI, CRF 1845, D18/4.
43. NAI, CRF 1845, D18/13.
44. NAI, CRF 1845, D18/12.
45. NAI, CRF 1845, D18/5, letter from E. Lucas, Dublin Castle, to Andrew Nolan, Chairman of the Commissioners of Wicklow, 18 July 1845. NAI, CRF 1845, D18/11, letter from E. Lucas, Dublin Castle, to the Governors of the Foundling Hospital, 19 July 1845.
46. NAI, Registry of Female Convicts Grangegorman Depot, Ref 1/9/07.
47. NAI, Transportation Register 6, p. 361.
48. NAI, Registry of Female Convicts Grangegorman Depot; Ibid.
49. J. Williams, *Ordered to the Island—Irish Convicts and Van Diemen's Land* (Sydney: Crossing Press, 1994), p. 101.
50. D. Snowden, 'Female Convicts', in *The Companion to Tasmanian History* (2008), accessed at www.utas.edu.au/library/companion_to_tasmanian_history. See also Williams, *Ordered to the Island*.
51. Because it was the second voyage of the *Tasmania* as a convict ship, it was styled the *Tasmania* (2).
52. C. Bateson, *The Convict Ships, 1787–1868* (Sydney: Library of Australian History, 2004), p. 393.
53. 'Scene on Board the *Tasmania* Convict Ship', *The Courier* (13 December 1845), p. 4, col. 4–5.
54. The National Archives, London, TNA ADM 101/71/2.
55. Female Convict Research Group, (Assignment System), http://www.femaleconvicts.org.au/index.php/administration/assignment-system.
56. I. Brand, *The Convict Probation System, VDL 1839–54* (Hobart: Blubber Head Press, 1990), p. 271.
57. Tasmanian Heritage and Archives Office, Hobart (hereafter TAHO), CON41/1/8, Image 41.
58. TAHO, CON33/1/13, Image 237.
59. Ibid.
60. TAHO, CON52/1/2, p. 178, RGD37/1/6, 1847/624.
61. TAHO, RGD37/1/6, 1847/624.
62. TAHO, RGD33/1/23, Launceston 1847/1722.
63. TAHO, NS1190/1/1, Register of Baptisms for the Parish or District of Campbell Town (Church of England).
64. TAHO, RGD33/1/3, Hobart 1850/2531.
65. TAHO, HSD285/21.
66. Ibid.
67. Ibid.
68. TAHO, RGD35/1/42 New Norfolk, 1873/374.
69. TAHO, RGD33/1/38 Morven, 1860/1590.
70. No record of Sarah's birth has yet been located.
71. TAHO, RGD33/1/40 Longford, 1862/966.

72. TAHO, RGD33/1/42 Launceston, 1864/216.
73. TAHO, RGD33/1/44 Launceston, 1866/1307.
74. TAHO, RGD33/1/47 Launceston, 1869/2319.
75. Details about Amos Eastwood are extracted from TAHO, CON37/1/7, Image 75.
76. R. Pike, *Pioneers of Burnie—A Sesquicentenary Publication 1827–1977* (Tasmania: R. Pike, 1977), pp. viii-xi.
77. Ibid., pp. 30–1.
78. Ibid., p. 30.
79. TAHO, RGD37/1/59, 1898/109.
80. TAHO, NS686/1/5. Amelia Roebuck married David 'Couldhill', a labourer and former convict per *Pestongee Bomangee*, in St George's Church, New Ground, on 30 September 1863.
81. TAHO, RGD37/1/50, 1891/89.
82. TAHO, RGD35/1/67 Emu Bay, 1898/193.
83. *Launceston Examiner*, 21 October 1898, p. 7, col. 4.
84. Frost, *Abandoned Women*, pp. 118–19.
85. *North Western Advocate and The Emu Times*, 24 August 1903, p. 2 col. 5.
86. *Advocate*, August 1932, p. 2, col. 3.
87. Pike, *Pioneers of Burnie*, p. 30.
88. A. Alexander, 'Reality and Reputation: Convicts and Tasmania in the Nineteenth Century', *Tasmanian Historical Research Association*, 54:1 (2007), pp. 50–65.
89. TAHO, RGD37/1/59, 1898/109.
90. TAHO, RGD 35–1–67/1898.
91. Letter from G. Hughes to J. Kavanagh, 10 June 1995.
92. R. Hughes, *The Fatal Shore* (London: Pan Books Ltd, 1988), pp. 158–59.
93. E-mail from G. Hughes to J. Kavanagh, 9 October 2012.
94. E-mail from B. Gellaty to J. Kavanagh, 4 November 2012.
95. Letter from G. Mulhern to J. Kavanagh, 8 February 1996.
96. Letter from G. Mulhern to J. Kavanagh, 2 April 1996.
97. E-mail from G. Mulhern to J. Kavanagh, 1 October 2012.
98. See, for example, C. Kenneally's interview with Professor Janet McCalman, Chief Investigator, and members of the Founders and Survivors project team published as 'Convict Kin Find History Ain't No Ball and Chain', *The Age*, 23 September 2012, accessed at www.theage.com.au/national/convict-kin-find-history-aint-no-ball-and-chain-20120922–26dzm.html. The Founders and Survivors Project is a partnership between historians, genealogists, demographers, and population health researchers which seeks to record and study the founding population of 73,000 men, women, and children transported to Tasmania; http://foundersandsurvivors.org/project.
99. T. Keneally, *The Great Shame: A Story of the Irish in the Old World and the New* (London: Chatto & Windus, 1998), p. xi.
100. E-mail from G. Mulhern to J. Kavanagh, 1 October 2012.
101. TAHO, CON41/1/8, Image 41.
102. TAHO, CON37/1/7, Image 75.
103. E-mail from H. Maxwell Stewart to J. Kavanagh, 2 November 2012.
104. TAHO, RGD37/1/36, 1877/812.
105. TAHO, RGD33/1/58 Emu Bay, 1880/88.
106. TAHO, RGD 33/1/64 Emu Bay, 1885/1331.
107. TAHO, RGD 33/1/67 Emu Bay, 1888/1234.
108. TAHO, RGD 33/1/72 Emu Bay, 1891/1311.
109. Letter from G. Hughes to J. Kavanagh, 10 June 1995, and email, 9 October 2012.
110. E-mail from G. Hughes to J. Kavanagh, 9 October 2012.
111. Letter from G. Hughes to J. Kavanagh, 10 June 1996.

112. For a discussion of 'famine amnesia', see, for example, C. O'Grada, *Black '47 and Beyond: The Great Irish Famine in History, Economy and Memory* (Princeton, NJ: Princeton University Press, 2000), especially his chapter on 'Famine Memory', pp. 210–12.
113. C. Habel, 'Christopher Koch, *Out of Ireland*: No More "Hiding the Stain"', in P. Mead (ed), *Australian Literary Studies in the 21st Century*, Proceedings of the 2000 ASAL conference, Hobart, pp. 127–34, http://www.nla.gov.au/openpublish/index.php/jasal/article/view/2706/3127 (accessed 25 March 2014).
114. Ibid.; C. Koch, *Out of Ireland* (Milsons Point: Doubleday, 1999).
115. C. Koch, *Highways to a War* (Victoria: Minerva, 1995).
116. For Margaret O'Meara, see A. Alexander, 'A Novelist Pictures his Convict Ancestor: Margaret O'Meara and Christopher Koch', in L. Frost (ed), *Convict Lives at the Ross Female Factory* (Hobart, Female Convicts Research Centre, Tasmania: Convict Women's Press, 2011), pp. 210–14; D. Snowden and J. Kavanagh, 'Irish Shipmates from the *Tasmania*', in Frost (ed), *Convict Lives*, pp. 70–76.
117. Alexander, 'Margaret O'Meara and Christopher Koch', in Frost (ed), *Convict Lives*, p. 210.
118. Ibid.
119. NAI, CRF 1845, D18.
120. Alexander, *Tasmania's Convicts*; Smith, *Australia's Birthstain*; J. Boyce, *Van Diemen's Land* (Melbourne: Black Inc., 2008).
121. K. Daniels, *Convict Women*.
122. For further discussion, see C. Habel, Ancestral Narratives: Irish-Australian Identities in History and Fiction (Saarbrucken, Germany: VDM Verlag, 2008).

3 Policing Ireland, Policing Colonies
The Irish Constabulary 'Model'

Richard Hill

Ireland famously exported people to the ends of the earth in the nineteenth century. Less obviously, but arguably of equal or even greater significance, it exported knowledge on how to *control* people. Within the British sphere of influence, the Irish policing model of the empire was deemed generally more suitable for colonies than that of the British imperial metropole. This chapter will take critical stock of the development and current state of scholarship on the two policing models.[1] It will assess their past applicability within the British Empire and their present usefulness. It will end by suggesting that conceptual rethinking needs to go beyond the revision of the models which has occurred in the last few decades. Rather, the models need to be placed in the context of a more flexible conceptual way of approaching sociopolitical control—namely, a strategic coercive continuum of controls on which models can be located (and relocated).[2] Recontextualising Irish and Irish-influenced policing in terms of its (adjustable) positioning on this continuum, allows us to better appreciate its undoubtedly significant contribution to British imperial history.

POLICING MODELS IN THE METROPOLE

Of the two broad models which have dominated British policing studies, the main focus has been on England and Wales, which reflects the foundational principles and afterlife of the London Metropolitan Police ('the Met', established by Robert Peel in 1829).[3] The Met's guiding precepts aimed to garner popular consent for policing. This would be secured by a number of factors, including the use of the minimal amount of violence necessary in any given situation, the official assertion that policing operated independently of politics, and the improvement of social lifestyles by reducing disruption to person and property.[4] These principles have since been characterised by different labels, including the British, London, Metropolitan, and (now most commonly) English model.[5] Their application is said to have resulted in 'the soundest police system in the world [because of] the confidence which the public repose in it'.[6]

In the colonial context the English model has been seen as applicable mostly to urban areas (usually those of sizeable European population) where the constable could (like his London counterpart, according to the Met's instruction book) 'always find the respectable portion of the public willing to assist him in an emergency, and the uniform which he wears gives him great moral power and weight against any lawless character he may be dealing with.'[7]

The second model is that of the Irish Constabulary (from 1867, the Royal Irish Constabulary, or RIC) and its predecessor police forces. This was essentially a rural-based mode of policing control renowned for the harshness of its methods. Its overtly repressive approach to the population reflected Britain's response to endemic resistance to its occupation of Ireland, and (relatedly) to the high degree of 'disorder' in the Irish countryside. As Home Secretary Robert Peel put it, the force in its various iterations was created to effect 'the reduction of Ireland to peaceful habits', and that meant a significant and unapologetic use of coercion.[8] Its principles, and its operational methods, have generally been seen to constitute *the* model for policing the vast spaces and often resistant peoples of the nineteenth- and twentieth-century British Empire.[9]

RE-VISIONING THE MODELS

The academic study of police history is a relatively new pursuit, dating back some half-century or so. Before then, historians presented a Whiggish 'onwards and upwards' story of police involvement in the emergence of a civilised Britain following the establishment of Peel's 'new police' in 1829.[10] English 'bobbies' were depicted as a new and improved version of the holders of the ancient office of constable. They were supposedly no more than 'citizens in uniform' who impartially enforced an increasingly impartial law with minimal violence and maximal respect for citizens' rights. Despite some initial resistance to police intrusion into lives, so the argument went, good sense won out, and the great majority of the population gave their 'willing cooperation' to policing. They gave their *consent* to constables deterring and detaining, in civilised fashion, those who continued to threaten the peace.[11]

This Metropolitan model was contrasted, during and after the Whig phase of historiography, with that prevalent in Ireland. The constables policing the 'internal colony' across the Irish Sea were men whose basic mode of social intervention was *conflictual*. Given the resistance of large portions of the Irish population to British rule and requirements, minimum force had been quite out of the question. A heavily armed paramilitary police had been needed to suppress popular behaviour deemed by the authorities to threaten 'peace and good order'. The state-decreed definition of 'good order' centred on the security of property and profit, and those sections of the population who threatened this were subject to severe discipline being visited on them.[12]

This seemed all so different from the mainland policing depicted by Whig historians who had taken the new police precepts at face value. They stressed the foundational instructions to London's beat police: 'the principal object to be attained is the Prevention of Crime', with the aim of 'security of person and property, the preservation of the public tranquillity, and all the other objects of a Police Establishment'.[13] The public supported strong state surveillance (visible patrolling, and less visible detecting) as a quid pro quo for feeing safe, making policing easier and cheaper as time went by, with miscreants to be deterred by a high risk of arrest from a patrol-based police system. This approach evolved into nine English 'police principles' based, in Charles Reith's 1956 formulation, on the precept that 'the power of the police to fulfil their functions and duties is dependent on public approval of their existence, actions and behaviour and on their ability to secure and maintain public respect [and] willing co-operation'.[14]

Within a couple of decades after this was written, however, revisionist scholars were beginning to challenge the quintessential benignity of the *origins* (at very least) of the English new police and to emphasise that, despite their many imperfections, bobbies were organised in an efficiently disciplined hierarchy whose aim was highly interventionist. They noted that new police aims were no less socially transformational than those of the RIC's 'peelers'—not just suppressing activities deemed to be harmful but also instead turning popular energies towards productive pursuits and peaceful pastimes. The London bobbies and their provincial counterparts acted as 'domestic missionaries' of the political and other decision-makers within the state.

They were a new coercive bureaucracy to meet new circumstances of social disruption prompted by the industrial revolution. Scholars noted that the official version of police aims and methods downplayed the very element which set constables aside from other servants of the Crown: the legitimated right, on behalf of the state, to deter and detain citizens at any time of the day and night, with force if necessary. Their job was to impose a *harsh* social discipline that reflected the agenda of the political economy. They were engaged in an internal 'civilising mission' that would subject the population to required ways of doing and being, at work, at home, and in the public spaces between.[15] This picture became generally accepted, *pace* some continued efforts to depict police as social workers acting as 'guide, philosopher and friend',[16] and it was built upon by scholars working on contemporary policing. Robert Reiner's 1985 *The Politics of the Police*, in particular, stressed that maintenance of order depended on fundamental factors over and above those relating to the efficiency or otherwise of police personnel and methods—policing has always been an inherently political function of state, a powerful agency within the political economy whose roles and responsibilities require demystification.[17]

Despite soothing foundational statements of method and intent, then, Peel had created his new police for the same reason he had inaugurated a system of armed constables in Ireland some 15 years previously. If his bobbies were not (at least at first) benign men in blue who impartially applied an impartial law, then, it was no longer feasible to posit a tight demarcation between Irish and English models. Revisionist works in the last quarter of the twentieth century, in fact, increasingly depicted the boundary between police models as porous.

By the later 1980s, in turn, scholars were both beginning to take a more critical stance with regard to the violence which had long been acknowledged as saturating the Irish system and tracing Irish influences on the English model—most notably in Stanley Palmer's magisterial survey of the policing of protest in England and Ireland over the crucial seven decades before 1850.[18] By 1990, scholarship could no longer downplay the coercion and violence inherent in the policing role, and stressed its instrumental purposes in Ireland, although some corelativity between consensual principles and English policing practice continued to be accepted.[19] More broadly, comparativist scholarship had begun the task of investigating similarities (and differences) between British and other systems—Clive Emsley's focus on French gendarmes, 'men of arms', for example, as part of his broad studies of criminal justice and police history. Emsley was in fact for decades at the forefront of groundbreaking research on both forces within territories and the links between them, leading to what might be called an 'Open University School'. His pioneering typologies were tempered by his appreciation of the complexities of policing and his cautioning of over reliance on models and their portable utility.[20] Scholars of this school, especially Georgina Sinclair and Chris A. Williams, together with others, worked on (among other things) the mutual influencing of the empire and the metropole.[21]

COLONIAL POLICING

Academic study of *colonial* policing (outside of Ireland) is even newer than that of revisionist scholarship on new police, and so its pioneers were able to take this into account. Because there had been little interrogation of the generally accepted outlines of the Irish model, however, the Irish export model was initially seen principally through a traditional lens, as overtly coercive. They differed in one sense, however. The RIC–colonial nexus had most prominently been outlined in a seminal 1952 treatise on colonial police by Sir Charles Jeffries, deputy undersecretary of state for the colonies; essentially, he followed Whig historians of the RIC, seeing it in approving terms as using minimal force within its own necessary operational parameters.[22] When revisionist studies of the RIC eschewed uncritical approval of its methods, such critical stances began to be transferred to colonial policing.[23] This added a theoretical overlay to and reaffirmed what case-study histories in colonies were already finding—that colonial policing was suffused with violence and conflict.

But the entrenchment of the Irish model meant that a number of scholars, remaining at least residually influenced by traditional historiography on the RIC, underestimated the degree of violence associated with it and especially with empire. Conversely, some who accepted a very high degree of endemic violence resiled, as a consequence, from applying the RIC model to settler colonies, where 'humanitarian' attitudes were believed to have had influence. All the same, whether they were critical or underestimated the violence of police interactions with the indigenes of the empire, scholars generally accepted that RIC-style policing had been applied.

By 1988, however, when the first conference on policing the British Empire was held, the export of an Irish model to the colonies was coming under scrutiny, something that resonated with the revisionist dismissal of *tight* dichotomising into two models—*civilian* police in the metropole and *paramilitary* police elsewhere.[24] It had long been acknowledged that the Met had been a sub-model for colonies. Reith, an avid reader of police files, noted an 'unceasing demand for full details of organization, and of orders, uniforms and equipment, and request for the transference of [Metropolitan policemen], which came to the Commissioners in the eighteen-thirties from every part of the Empire.'[25] But integrated scholarship on the new police, at home and abroad, now showed increasing appreciation that it was the coercive practice (as opposed to the public precepts) of London's bobbies which made them readily adaptive to colonial urban streets.

Australasian colonies were among those providing evidence on this matter. New South Wales had quickly applied the Metropolitan beat surveillance system in Sydney and other urban areas.[26] Although these towns and cities retained much of the character of the raw frontier of a convict colony, some degree of order had been imposed.[27] Thus, the urban authorities needed a combination of both the coercive practice and the aspirational precepts embodied in Metropolitan-style policing. Sydney's policing system was in turn transferred for control of the beachhead settlements of New Zealand in early 1840, when officials arrived to establish a Dependency of New South Wales.[28] At first (and from time to time later, as in turbulent urban areas associated with goldfields) antipodean Peelism focused on the coercive element to beat surveillance (while also paying obeisance to the attributes implicit in the benign precepts of 1829).[29]

As the urban frontier of the empire was gradually 'tamed' by, among other things, the police, their coercion lessened, and public assistance to and trust in them grew. At the founding of some colonies, and during their development, then, the influence of the Met in empire was greater than believed in the days when scholars were contrasting benign bobbies with pugnacious peelers. But for many decades, paramilitary control characterised policing in most spaces of the empire. In New Zealand, when expansion into the indigenous hinterlands began and (relatedly) significant Maori resistance formed, RIC-influenced policing was imposed on the whole colony, including the urban areas.

Revisionist scholarship which stressed the coercion inherent in *both* policing the metropole and controlling Ireland helped better explain the relative ease of rapid switching from one type of policing system to the other—and the gradual emergence of a more consensual form when the threats to public order had subsided. Thus in New Zealand, the militarised forces of the 1840s developed into consensual style forces in areas where, especially, Maori had either not rebelled or had been subdued—until that is, they became a threat again. Policing was policing, be it situated within a conflictual or a consensual model, a device to impose 'correct' ways of behaviour on the great majority of people. Even when operating within the most compliant of communities, consent needed to be seen as forged in the context of willingness to use main force—on a daily basis against individuals, and against collectivities of people from time to time. With the new police precepts more aspirational than actual at the time of their drafting, the English model was not at root much different from the Irish. The first of the English 'Nine Principles' had in effect recognised this: 'To prevent crime and disorder, as an alternative to their repression by military force and severity of legal punishment.'[30]

EXAMINING THE IMPACT OF IRISH PRINCIPLES

All forces were, in the final analysis, institutions of singular ilk, given that the key characteristic separating police from other public-sector agencies was their legitimated capacity, at all times, to use force against members of the public. This now seems to be generally accepted in the world of police historical studies. That being said, there is little demur from the proposition that colonial forces exhibited the greatest degree of conflictualism, a reflection of the magnitude of the task at hand—the 'bringing to order' of vast populations of unwilling and often resistant subject peoples, in order to profit from their human and natural resources.

The inherently exploitative and oppressive nature and method of the colonial policing task required *politically directed* policing by heavily armed patrolmen acting in groups to impose the occupying power's definition of 'peace and good order'. Irish and colonial constables were occupation police, practiced in paramilitary or semi-military modes of social control and with strict lines of disciplinary command. Often single young men, they lived and patrolled communally, their barracks fortified against the possibility of attack. While English constables could not punish those they had arrested, in Ireland and empire their counterparts could often discipline as well as detain—which prompted the archetypal historian of consensual policing to talk of the RIC's 'very defective principles'.[31] Although both Irish and colonial regulations often instructed the men not to alienate the people, this was—as with the early Met precepts—mostly aspirational.[32] How could it be otherwise in such a tough operating environment? Wedged between the duty of controlling dogs and protecting the electricity supply, for example, the Irish constable's rulebook of 1913 outlined a crucial public order task—suppressing unauthorised 'assemblies of persons for the purpose of training or drilling'.[33]

Similar instructions graced colonial rulebooks around the globe, albeit the assemblyists were generally indigenous. But were these forces modelled on the RIC? Or did they grow autochthonously out of the requirements of each colony? Or did they begin as Irish in organisation and ethos and later develop their own paths to meet local circumstances? By the end of the 1980s, debates on such questions were beginning to form. Richard Hawkins's pioneering coverage of some of the issues included a provocative rejection of the traditional linking of RIC and colonial policing, suggesting that the RIC model had no 'real common ground with forces in other parts of the world'.[34] This aspect gained little traction, for there was a great deal of evidence to indicate levels of connectivity. Moreover, controlling Ireland and controlling colonies involved similar challenges: how to impose a sufficient state of control over resistant populations to allow the metropole to control people and exploit resources. This was common enough ground, whatever the ethnicity of police or policed alike.

Some scholars, however, were uncomfortable with using Irish and English labels, believing these to be justifiable only upon production of evidence of a *direct* transfer of Irish (or English) organisational and methodological knowledge. Such a 'smoking-gun' approach risked setting up a self-fulfilling prophecy. Quite apart from loss of records, policing (or other) knowledge transfer seldom involved organisational or methodological templates. Controlling sectarian turbulence in the Irish countrywide clearly differed from suppressing shifta in the Somali desert or bandits in Burmese forests; indigenous resistance in Sierra Leone or the Sind produced differing configurations of repression to that of Sligo. The point is that, regardless of whether Irish rulebooks were studied or copied, their general organisational and operational principles of social control were well known within imperial administration and applied in very diverse circumstances.

Scholars who argued against colonial *replication* of the RIC and its predecessors certainly presented a better case than those who denied all connection. Even where Irish organisation and methods *were* instituted directly in new colonies, in fact, local conditions would invariably lead to a series of adaptations. While there had not been replication of the Irish Constabulary, then, at least not over long timespans, Irish influences were 'more than imaginary'—as a leading historian on these issues put it with reference to Canadian history.[35] Historians of colonial policing would come generally to agree that in the conflictual policing which dominated most colonies, most of the time, the RIC had, in Elizabeth Malcolm's words, undoubted 'influence in shaping [colonial] forces'.[36]

But Malcolm and others had been further complicating academic discussion by producing evidence that the RIC's ethos and operations had, at least through time, been less violently coercive than generally believed. This was an important caveat to the picture outlined, approvingly or otherwise, by traditionalists and revisionists alike. Just as Reithian principles had partly come to fruition in Britain, so too had some degree of consensualism developed in Ireland. By the present century, while the Irish police would continue to be contrasted with a gentler English model, the latter too was seen to carry with it the coercive capacity implicit in the foundational purpose of policing—the legitimated capacity to apply force to civilians. Conversely, it was becoming better appreciated that the Irish model could accommodate relatively benign policing methods. In the literature, then, the models were drifting towards each other and, in places, even converging or overlapping.[37]

EXAMINING THE IMPACT OF IRISH TECHNIQUES

However significant this trend, nonetheless, colonial policing continued to be analysed through the useful (albeit now more flexible) lens of the two-model binary. Patrolling in non-urban spaces where the RIC was cited as a model, such as the highlands of Kenya's or Canada's northwest frontiers, was clearly very different from monitoring the roads of England's or Sydney's northwest. However modified or even melded the models became, they retained an essential validity. A heavily coercive, politically directed RIC-style organisation differed in fundamentals from one considerably less coercive and less overtly politicised, with the operational mores of the one inflicting far more damage on, and instilling far more fear in, the subjects of the empire than the other.

No colonial state machine was established in a territory without bringing a raft of beliefs, assumptions and methods with it, although of course each needed to deal with order imposition within the broad parameters presented by the land and its peoples. Voices of imperial and colonial administrators all over the world, as they have come down to us on paper and, sometimes, in oral testimony, indicate very clearly that, at the beginning in their search for something that would fit the grave problems of securing the colony that generally faced them, they first looked to imported models and principles. They often chose to do so within the broad principles of control worked out in Ireland. Colonial officials establishing a new colony might not be appraised of the details of how the RIC operated, but they knew of its reputation for containing unrest and quelling opposition, and that this rested on the its coercive formation and orientation towards the public. They knew that keeping a lid on disorder in Ireland depended on surveillance patrols by bodies of heavily armed and militarily drilled policemen, on the harsh discipline wielded by the stranger from other parts, a man insulated by barracks life from the people—and therefore able to crack heads without hesitation when ordered to.

In colony after colony political and police authorities systemically implemented their understandings of the broad principles of this type of policing.

Many colonial governors and their officials, in fact, knew far more than the broad outlines of coercive policing. Large numbers had served in the military or police in Ireland, and some, such as the colonial troubleshooter George Grey, had intimate knowledge of Irish rules, organisation, and practices. Those who were not acquainted with the RIC's aims and methods were generally surrounded by those who did, and information on structures, weaponry, patrolling, and the like was often sought from the colonies.

This was at least the case until the colony was sufficiently stabilised to allow the beginning of a police civilianisation (or demilitarisation) process. That being said, colonial officials generally continued to monitor developments in their 'home' forces at the same time as adapting their templates and ideals to the situations they had inherited (or created). Even in late colonial times, then, even after its demise, the RIC was endemically invoked for both its broad control principles and its organisational and operational details; and with its disbandment in 1922 Irish policemen transferred en masse to colonies. Although colonial forces quickly adapted to the autochthonous challenges of terrain, people, objectives, and exigencies, examination of the records of many a colonial force indicates continued convergences of method, style, and organisational principle between Irish and colonial constabularies. In the colonial state's quest to control people and exploit their resources, the paramilitary patrol of the Irish countryside provided more useful guidelines for policing the vast spaces of the empire than the lightly armed, timed urban beats of the Met. Here the RIC remained the most useful example of a successful force in the empire—one sometimes touted as the best in the entire world.[38]

Its principles were complemented by practical advice, such as that relating to the importance of surveillance over place and people as a prerequisite for effective coercive control. When a constable arrived to take up a position at a new station, for example, it was 'of the utmost importance' that he took

> every pains to inform himself of the several roads, residences, and characters in his immediate neighbourhood, so that he can immediately detect any stranger who may arrive, and also to be able to bring forward at once any offender against the laws. Their local information and general intelligence will, in most cases, be more useful than their personal exertion[.][39]

Such practical details reflected the needs of small paramilitary detachments which were frequently on the move in potentially hostile environments. Colonial patrolmen were thus instructed to behave as Irish constables. They were

> not to go out on stated nights or at particular hours, but shall do so at irregular periods, and are always to visit suspected places and observe suspicious house and persons. They will not confine their attention only to the main lines of roads, but will occasionally proceed through the

bush, calling at the houses of the settlers to find out what is going on, and ascertain if their assistance is needed.[40]

The Irish rules contained a wealth of explicit advice on keeping the men alive and the opposition down:

> When on patrole, either with military or by themselves, they must use great caution and discretion in case they should meet armed parties by night . . . On all occasions, but most especially when small detachments occupy new stations, an immediate arrangement should be made of every article belonging to the men. Their clothing and necessaries on retiring to rest, should be so disposed of as to enable them to dress in the dark if required, in the shortest period of time. The arrangement of their arms and appointments is equally important[.][41]

Such regulations were as necessary in desert tents and jungle huts as in Irish camps. Colonial officers imported them and copied them, and they read these regulations to those of their men who were, as so often was the case, illiterate. Significant portions of the rules and regulations of Irish policing were in fact incorporated virtually word for word into colonial policing manuals. Former Irish policemen or men trained in Irish methods were frequently taken on in senior colonial positions, including in settler colonies where sometimes they were needed to suppress unruly whites as well as resistant indigenes. St John Branigan, who became the most influential policeman in nineteenth-century New Zealand, served in Ireland, Cape Colony, Victoria, and New Zealand's Otago Province before becoming head of that colony's Irish-influenced Armed Constabulary (NZAC).[42]

In pacification forces operating in conquered and turbulent zones, the tight discipline the Irish police exemplified was a necessity. This had two facets: each policeman needed to be acutely aware that he was but a link in a strict military-style chain of command. But equally, he was to be more than a soldier automaton. As the constables could well be operating in small groups, a junior member might find himself in charge of a confrontational interaction in which he needed to be able to combine his knowledge of quasi-military social control techniques and his ability to wield the discretionary powers of the constable. In this respect, the peeler was closer to the bobby than to the private.

These two factors were stressed when Victoria turned to Irish policing principles to cope with the colony-wide turmoil brought on by the opening of its goldfields. Its *Manual of Police Regulations* of 1856 declared that

> [e]very inferior [member of the Force], whether officer or otherwise, is to receive the commands of his superior with deference and respect, and to execute them without question or comment to the best of his power . . . The obedience and respect which are here required must be

observed throughout the force generally, and not be understood in any partial or confined sense . . . Every officer and constable must understand that it is an invariable rule in discipline that in the absence of a superior, the whole of the duty or charge which was entrusted to that superior devolves upon the next in rank, so the chain of responsibility may continue unbroken.[43]

This was almost an exact copy of the wording and grammar of the 'discipline' section of the consolidated *Rules and Regulations of the Constabulary Force of Ireland* published in Dublin in 1837.[44]

Similar borrowings had previously occurred in New Zealand policing regulations, having been introduced in the context of controlling dissident Maori from the mid-1840s, and then later adapted for use in the first colony-wide police regulations in 1852.[45] Their words and concepts were further moulded to local conditions by provincially controlled armed police forces. Those charged with controlling disorderly goldfields utilised Branigan's Otago rules—and therefore those of Ireland, as evolved through both Victorian and New Zealand experience.[46] When Branigan became commissioner of the NZAC in 1869, he adopted almost exactly the same wording, even though he was tasked with its 'demilitarising'—a relative term in colonies.[47] These regulations lasted until a civilianised force was established in 1886 (headed before long by a police chief imported from the Met), and even then its Met-influenced rules retained many an Irish resonance.[48]

Colonial officials, then, faced with controlling huge numbers of people disposed to reject their authority and the exploitation they presided over, needed both initial and regular injections of guidance on precedents and principles. They especially sought it from Dublin, sometimes via the policing experts in London or large colonial cities such as Cape Town. Their policing officials were often versed in the (developing) rules and regulations of Ireland, where a significant number had served, and in their application. Quite apart from the pull factor, moreover, case studies indicate a propensity by the imperial centre to instruct colonial officials to look to Ireland for guidance on social and racial control. While this was especially so upon setting up colonies, it remained a continuing refrain—and training for colonial officers was eventually established at the RIC depot in Phoenix Park in Dublin in 1907.[49]

ADAPTATION OF THE IRISH MODEL IN COLONIES

Localised colonial use and adaptation of the RIC model often stressed the most extreme aspects of the coercion which underpinned its modus operandi. Camel patrolling out of Aden or foot patrolling out of Apia might both share characteristics with horse patrolling in Antrim, but they tended to use far more violence. The British had attempted to ensure that, despite the coercive nature of the RIC, its constables observed both the law and their own regulatory cautions about excessive force:

> In apprehending and escorting prisoners, the men will never use more force or violence than is absolutely necessary for their security, and every attention must be paid to the comfort of the prisoners consistent with their safety ... and if there be reason to apprehend a rescue, the Person may be hand-cuffed[.] [I]f it should be necessary to resort to force, it must be done with great caution, at the same time with firmness and resolution ... always considering, that in the eye of the law, all prisoners are considered innocent until convicted of the offence charged.[50]

Colonial adaptations of the RIC rulebook were usually more coercive in ethos. There was often a deliberate vagueness over what matters were proscribed by law, for example, with paramilitarised constables able to arrest and flog a subject for doing or saying anything that implied disrespect for the colonial regime. Although this was most pronounced in plantation and other colonies where the extractive motive was at its most overt, even settler-colonial governments hardened the formal law of Ireland. Thus, Australasian police manuals dropped the word *lawful* when otherwise copying RIC instructions that constables obey 'lawful commands'.[51]

All the same, most colonial forces retained safeguards against oppressive behaviour in the formal rules—something which most subjects of the empire in Africa, Asia, or Australia would have been surprised to hear of, as policing was generally deployed with little regard to these: the tasks facing colonial governments were so huge that there could be little room for legal niceties. The demands of exigency overrode the much-touted British 'civilising mission' to the indigenes of the empire. Retributive descents on villages, for example, with targeted or random killing of inhabitants and destruction of homes and crops, were normal practice in many parts of the empire. In effect, as has been cogently argued, colonies constituted a vast 'state of exception' to the rule of law.[52]

The capacity to mete out exemplary punishment at will was assisted by multiple and overlapping legal systems in numerous colonies—laws transferred from other colonies deemed similar, ordinances decreed from the colonial or metropolitan capitals, customary tribal laws seen to be useful by the colonial government, and religious laws such as the sharia which could be used for social control purposes. Given such a smorgasbord of law and custom, of liminality and uncertainty, the police could generally with impunity detain or discipline any indigenes they wished. In fact, the gap between imperial police (including Irish) theory and colonial practice widened as colonial mellowing failed to keep pace with that of the RIC.

RIC methods, then, harsh as they were compared to those of consensual policing, could be extended to impose disciplinary regimes far beyond anything initially envisaged in Ireland (that is, until the savageries inflicted by the restructured RIC as the 'internal colony' drew to a close).[53] All along, the Irish model had become more and more attenuated as a set of colonial practices. Sometimes all that remained were its principles of social control, its basic methods of patrolling and surveilling, and its capacity to apply main force. But reiteration of the wisdom encapsulated within the RIC model and its continued take-up, in, however, modified a form, remained, among other things, a legitimating device for *endemic* coercion.

By extension, incantation of Irish principles also legitimated the use of *extreme* force when this was deemed to be necessary. If suppressive techniques needed to be applied to a white people so close to the heart of the empire, the violence needed to control resistant indigenes was surely justifiable, given that these were deemed to be located much lower on the evolutionary scale. Bureaucrats in colonial capitals, and policemen patrolling desert or jungle, mountains or plains, could take shelter beneath the Irish model whatever their level of understanding of its operating modes. While the coercion inherent in Irish methods or mission is now often condemned, one can at least acknowledge that it provided an expert and effective service to the imperial state and its colonial regimes. Moreover, those who applied RIC principles and procedures to colonial situations generally adapted them efficiently in terms of their brief to secure and hold onto imperial territory. In utilising the RIC model, they were well aware that it had developed for the instrumental purpose of defence of the political economy—if that purpose, in its colonial manifestation, required modifying, supplementing or outgrowing the model, so be it.

RECONTEXTUALISING THE MODELS ON A GLOBAL CONTROL CONTINUUM

While policing practitioners undoubtedly utilised the RIC model, the question remains as to its usefulness, from an *academic* perspective. Can a model that was expanded, extruded, attenuated, distorted, and diffused make much sense? Do the words *Irish Constabulary* meaningfully encapsulate diverse modes of colonial policing—suppressing peasants in West Bengal as well as in Waterford, or surveilling the 'criminal tribes' of India and the criminal gangs of Asia?

Given that there are broad principles of controlling, regular techniques of patrolling, and tactical modes of deployment (such as subduing 'rioters') which have exhibited empire-wide validity, in one sense the question can be answered in the affirmative. Most of these, in the English-speaking world at least, were first and most comprehensively typologised in Ireland, albeit supplemented by the high-vigilance, minimal-force beats of the Met and other urban spaces 'at home'. However much we may interrogate and deconstruct them, the Irish and English models had meaning to their wielders and those who instructed them, and we neglect that at our intellectual peril.

On the other hand, further interrogation and complexification is needed, both to maximise their academic application and to take into account their attenuating journeying through time and space. Remodelling the models can be assisted by a recent escalation of interest in empire which indicates (among other things) that 'webs of empire' were far more widespread in policing than generally believed.[54] Added to this, scholarly attention on the policing of non-British colonies has been growing, and there is now some incipient scholarship on comparative policing within and between colonies.

Case studies under investigation by the present author for an international comparative project indicate that transfer of policing knowledge within and across colonial and imperial boundaries was frequent and sometimes systemic; that, indeed, the proposition of an incipient globalisation in policing theory and practice by the nineteenth century can now plausibly be mounted. Recontextualising the Irish and English models in global terms makes them appear less 'Irish' or 'English'. First, not only do they often contain elements of the other but also elements of others, including indigenous policing practices—so much so that some approach hybridised formations whose original models serve merely as a guide or provide a patina. Second, and even more significantly, many of their overarching characteristics are seen to align with broadly conflictual or consensual models in other empires (which themselves need scrutinising in terms of their mutual exclusivity or otherwise).[55]

Taking these two key points together adds strength to a contention that, while revisionist blurring of the boundaries between the models was *necessary*, it was not *sufficient*. While the two models should not be discarded, because they were used historically and remain useful, a conceptual device that both endorses their essential utility and accounts for their hybridised and autochthonist tendencies and provides interpretational flexibility can better assist our understanding of the imperial policing past. This requires envisaging a strategic coercive continuum of policing methodology by which the social control of any part of the empire at any given time can be characterised by its positioning on the continuum. Any strategic situation is in effect the sum of the parts of a cluster of policing principles and mechanisms, themselves a response to the scale and nature of the opposition to the imperial power and its colonial state machinery. The models can be seen as occupying different positions on the continuum, the English/consensual tending towards the benign pole and the Irish/conflictual towards the condign pole: that of violence and maximal force.[56] But the continuum adds value by allowing for strategic repositioning, and tactical departures from strategy, in a way that the traditional use of models tends to obscure.

Policing was situated at or near the condign pole at times of potential or actual threats to the security of the state and the interests it privileged. This was especially so given resistance of mass and resilient nature and, more especially, when such developed into potential or actual armed resistance. Political and police responses to such challenges particularly large-scale organised struggle, usually entailed severe coercion. Here, policing and soldiering often segued into each other; mass killing, repressive incarceration, exemplary mutilation, or targeted torture, all of these and much more might be practiced routinely and without compunction in such environments, often making use of indigenous police and indigenous methods.[57]

At the other extreme, 'friendly' constables policed communities where most people had internalised the required forms of behaviour (including productive rhythms) most of the time. With most people generally self-disciplined, police discipline could thus be geared mostly to subduing *individual* offenders, but this was not applicable in most colonies, except in pockets and from time to time. For the challenge to the colonial order did not necessarily involve armed rebellion, or even be 'well-formed or explicit'.[58] Rather, it more often involved actions or non-actions reflecting an inchoate unwillingness to cooperate with outside invaders and controllers, and so required a more discipline-based approach.

On the other hand, when sociopolitical threat lessened, Irish-influenced forces would move in a benign direction on the continuum, as the home model itself had done, taking on some characteristics of the consensual force. As both colonies and Ireland stabilised, then, the Irish model would lose some of its coercive punch. However, the force retained the capacity to move in a coercive direction again whenever necessary, whether tactically or strategically. The continuum allows for strategic repositionings in a way that the traditional use of models tends to obscure. Conversely, the English model retained the capacity to return to the extreme coercion which underpinned the policing role, when the political economy and its desired state of order was under threat. In doing so it may well 'borrow' methods from the forces applying condign power, as well as indigenous personnel and customs.

PLACING IRISH POLICING ON THE COLONIAL CONTROL CONTINUUM

All that being said, the two broad models continued to occupy quite different strategic locations on the continuum. The African soldier policeman, the *askari* (a word covering either or both functions), differed enormously in ethos and operation from the rural bobby bicycling around an English village or the lone constable patrolling an antipodean suburb, although all swore a similar oath and had the same ultimate function of imposing and preserving peace and good order as defined by the state. With most colonial populations remaining to a greater or lesser degree resistant, their authorities necessarily used tools and techniques, strategies and tactics, that were arrayed more towards the condign/Irish pole than that of minimal coercion. As the RIC model widened in application it gained new names—'Palestinian' or 'Ceylonese', 'Canadian Mounties' or 'Branigan's Troopers'. In modern analysis it is more useful to typologise different subsets of Irish policing, such as paramilitary, quasi-military, semi-military, militarised, or military policing, which can take into account autochthonisation, hybridisation, and other processes.

Whatever the nomenclature, however, one can say with confidence that the general colonial typology was Irish-strategic policing, a catch-all for the ethos and operation of forces positioned closer to the violent than to the benign pole on the social control continuum. As a result of temporal, spatial, situational, and many other factors, policy and practice in a colony shifted and reconfigured within each model, taking on aspects of other western models and indigenous methods. Supposedly benign models would revert to so-called Irish methods: when 'native rebellions' needed crushing, for example, or—as the requirements of colonial political economies changed in the twentieth century—strikes and other labour-based threats to metropolitan and colonial profit were suppressed.[59]

On the other hand, strategic positioning tended to move away from extreme violence though time, with one major exception—from the 1930s, and especially after 1945, when decolonisation pressures often led to a remilitarisation of policing.[60] Meanwhile Irish-styled police—like Irish police themselves—had tended to develop a higher respect (or, perhaps, lesser disrespect) for legal rights. A continuum-based analysis takes into account such long term strategic movement of policing modes, as well as sharp tactical movements and the strategic reversionary violence meted out to subject peoples fighting for their liberation—as by the RIC itself at the time of its own endgame.

Such episodes of extreme repression bring us back to the raison d'être of policing—the 24/7 capacity to deter, detain, and discipline on behalf of the state and its interests. Whatever the models or their variations, in other words, their fundamental underpinnings were the same. These might be summed up in the first page of a notebook kept by a probationer constable in a force that had moved from conflictual towards consensual in ethos. His task was to secure 'a rule of civil conduct, prescribed by the State, commanding what is right, and preventing what is wrong'.[61] Given that the amount of violence in doing so was greater in Ireland and colonies, the traditional reason for conflating Irish with colonial policing is appropriate—alien controllers of unwilling populations needed to be discipline-orientated. Although less condign methods were desirable for many reasons, not the least being cost, virtually no violence was too extreme if needed to defend the imperial state and its colonial interests. If this meant harsh or ignored laws and police regulations which contradicted the civilising mission, such was the price to be paid for the effective running of the colony and the empire.

CONCLUSION

Most colonial policing in the British Empire was, at very least, Irish-influenced; most of it involved a high degree of violence perpetrated against colonial subjects, especially the indigenes of the empire. Given what we now know about colonial operating environments, the imperial world view and the crucial role of policing in imposing and maintaining 'peace and good order', this is logical enough. Police were of necessity complicit with, indeed central to, inflicting the lawful oppression and the extra-legal savagery embedded in colonial regimes. Fully understanding why and how involves more than taking on board revisionist history on police models, however. It entails situating, at any given time in any given colony, the dominant and secondary policing models on a strategic continuum of social control measures which range from extreme and exemplary to mild and targeted violence. The continuum is universally applicable in empires; the labels Irish and English are paralleled by similar labels in non-British Empires.

But the fact remains that it was the Irish policing mantra which was evoked throughout the largest empire in the world. This was a complex set of processes. The cachet of the RIC, for example, was as useful for legitimating harsh coercion as for its providing techniques of policing control, if not more so. Given the permeability of boundaries between conflictual and consensual policing models, moreover, English policing gained greater colonial significance once colonial populations had been 'tamed' or 'tranquilised' (to use typical colonial police parlance)[62]—at least until end-of-the-empire violence. Whatever model was being applied, too, colonial governments adapted their imported policing templates and practices to local circumstances so that the Irish model became greatly attenuated. But in an era when violence and policing were virtually synonymous, the precepts underpinning the RIC had provided the most useful basis from which to develop efficient action to control the vast indigenous spaces of the empire. The Irish policing model, put simply, was the touchstone for effective principles and techniques of colonial control in the British Empire, and the RIC ethos had global resonance.

NOTES

1. I wish to thank the anonymous reader who made some most helpful suggestions on historiographical and other matters.
2. This proposal can be applied to other binarised ways of viewing policing, among them rural versus urban and community versus imposed; see too W. Miller, *Cops and Bobbies* (Chicago: University of Chicago, 1973).
3. These principles were exported and paralleled elsewhere in England and Wales during a quarter century of reform: D. Philips and R.D. Storch, *Policing Provincial England 1829–1856* (London: Leicester University Press, 1999).
4. For a typical formulation of the principle, see M.S. Pike, *The Principles of Policing* (London: Macmillan Press, 1985), p. 120.
5. For endorsing the model, see the various works of C. Reith including *The Police Idea* (London: Oxford University Press, 1938).
6. 'C.C.', Foreword, *Surrey Special Constabulary Magazine*, n.d., copy located in BLET 1/6, Churchill Archives Centre, Churchill College, Cambridge University.
7. 'Instruction Book for the Use of Candidates and Constables of the Metropolitan Police Force', MEPO 4/36, p. 10, The National Archives, London; for a

colonial example, R. Haldane, *The People's Force* (Melbourne: Melbourne University Press, 1986), p. 30.
8. G. Broeker, *Rural Disorder and Police Reform in Ireland, 1812–36* (London: Routledge & Kegan Paul, 1970), p. 188.
9. C.J. Jeffries, *The Colonial Police* (London: Parrish, 1952), pp. 30–32 and passim.
10. This was cemented into place in W.L.M. Lee, *A History of Police in England* (London: Methuen & Co, 1901), and most famously later developed by Charles Reith. See, for example, among his several works, *A Short History of the British Police* (London: Oxford University Press, 1948). See, too, T.A. Critchley, *A History of Police in England and Wales* (London: Constable, 1967).
11. For typical use of the concept of 'willing cooperation', see former British home secretary J. Chuter Ede's foreword to [A.J. Durrant], *A Short History of the Surrey Constabulary, 1851–1951* (Guildford: Biddles Ltd, 1951), p. vii.
12. For the foundational (and approving) account of the RIC, see R.H. Curtis, *The History of the Royal Irish Constabulary* (Dublin: McGlashan & Gill, 1871).
13. C. Reith, *A New Study of Police History* (Edinburgh: Oliver and Boyd, 1956), pp. 135–36.
14. This is in their incarnation as Principles 2 and 3 of 'The Nine Principles of Police': Reith, *New Study*, p. 287.
15. A.D. Silver, 'The Demand for Order in Civil Society', in D.J. Bordua (ed), *The Police: Six Sociological Essays* (New York: Wiley, 1967), pp. 1–24; R.D. Storch, 'The Policeman as Domestic Missionary', *Journal of Social History*, 9 (1976), pp. 481–502; D. Philips, *Crime and Authority in Victorian England* (London: Croon Helm, 1977). For later work, see, for example, C. Steedman, *Policing the Victorian Community* (London: Routledge & Kegan Paul, 1983); and Philips and Storch, *Policing Provincial England*. For defining police by their capacity to use force, see E. Bittner, *The Functions of the Police in Modern Society* (Rockville, MD: National Institute of Mental Health, 1970).
16. This represented a logical development in Whiggish police history; see E. Cumming, I. Cumming, and L. Edel, 'Policeman as Philosopher, Guide and Friend', *Social Problems*, 12:3 (1965), pp. 276–86.
17. R. Reiner, *The Politics of the Police* (Brighton: Wheatsheaf Books, 1985).
18. S.H. Palmer, *Police and Protest in England and Ireland, 1780–1850* (Cambridge: Cambridge University Press, 1988).
19. See, notably, C. Emsley, 'The English Bobby: An Indulgent Tradition', in R. Porter (ed), *Myths of the English* (Cambridge: Polity Press, 1992), pp. 114–35.
20. See, for example, several of Clive Emsley's works: *Policing and its Context, 1750–1870* (London: MacMillan Press, 1983); *The English Police: A Political and Social History* (New York: St Martin's Press, 1991); *Gendarmes and the State in Nineteeth-Century Europe* (Oxford: Oxford University Press, 1999); *The Great British Bobby: A History of British Policing from the 1829 to the Present* (London: Quercus, 2009); 'A Typology of Nineteenth-Century Police', *Crime, History and Societies*, 3:1 (1999), pp. 29–44; and 'Marketing the Brand: Exporting British Police Models 1829–1950', *Policing*, 6:1 (2012), pp. 43–54.
21. See, for example, G. Sinclair and C. A Williams, '"Home and Away": The Cross-Fertilisation between "Colonial" and "British" Policing, 1921–85', *Journal of Imperial and Commonwealth History*, 35:2 (2007), pp. 221–38.
22. Jeffries, *The Colonial Police*.
23. For example, M. Finnane, 'The Varieties of Policing: Colonial Queensland, 1860–1900', in D.M. Anderson and D. Killingray (eds), *Policing the Empire* (Manchester: Manchester University Press, 1991), pp. 33–51.

Policing Ireland, Policing Colonies 79

24. This was powerfully expressed by M. Brogden, 'An Act to Colonise the Internal Lands of the Island: Empire and the Origins of the Professional Police', *International Journal of the Sociology of Law*, 15 (1987), pp. 179–208. This article can also be conveniently found in G. Sinclair (ed), *Globalising British Policing* (Farnham: Ashgate Publishing, 2011), pp. 29–58.
25. Reith, *A Short History*, p. 79.
26. The Sydney Police Act of 1833 was partly modelled on Peel's Metropolitan Police Act: B. Swanton, *A Chronological Account of the Police of Sydney 1788–1862* (Canberra: Australian Institute of Criminology, 1983), p. 40.
27. G. Karskens, *The Colony* (Sydney: Allen & Unwin, 2009).
28. R.S. Hill, *Policing the Colonial Frontier* (Wellington: Government Printer, 1986), pp. 95, 536ff.
29. R. Clyne, *Colonial Blue* (Adelaide: Wakefield Press, 1987), p. 83.
30. Reith, *A New Study*, p. 287.
31. C. Reith, *The Blind Eye of History* (Montclair, N.J.: Patterson Smith, 1975; first published 1952), p. 147.
32. *Standing Rules and Regulations for the Government and Guidance of the Constabulary Force of Ireland* (Dublin: George and John Grierson, 1837) p. 2.
33. Sir A. Reed, *The Irish Constable's Guide* (Dublin: Alex. Thom & Co., 6th rev. ed., 1913), p. 186.
34. R. Hawkins, 'The "Irish Model" and the Empire: A Case for Reassessment', in Anderson and Killingray (eds), *Policing the Empire*, pp. 18–32.
35. G. Marquis, 'The "Irish Model" and Nineteenth-Century Canadian Policing', *Journal of Imperial and Commonwealth History*, 25:3 (1997), pp. 193–218, 213.
36. E. Malcolm, *The Irish Policeman, 1822–1922: A Life* (Dublin: Four Courts Press, 2006).
37. An important precursor to Malcolm's *The Irish Policeman* was W.J. Lowe and E.L. Malcolm, 'The Domestication of the Royal Irish Constabulary, 1836–1922', *Irish Economic and Social History*, 19 (1992), pp. 27–44. For an earlier perspective see C. Brady, *Guardians of the Peace* (Dublin and London: Gill &Macmillan, 1974). G. Sinclair and C.A. Williams have made an important contribution to the debate on such matters in recent times, in both 'Home and Away' and other contributions.
38. Hill, *Policing the Colonial Frontier*, p. 384.
39. *The Standing Orders and Regulations for the Conduct and Proceeding of the Chief Constables, and other Constables of the County* (Dublin: His Majesty's Printers, 1825), pp. 14–15.
40. *Manual of Police Regulations for the Guidance of the Canterbury Constabulary Force* (Christchurch: Ward and Reeves, 1862), p. 81.
41. *Standing Orders and Regulations*, pp. 19–20.
42. R.S. Hill, 'Branigan, St John, 1823–4?-1873', *The Dictionary of New Zealand Biography, Volume One, 1769–1869* (Wellington: Allen & Unwin/Department of Internal Affairs, 1990) pp. 36–38.
43. *Manual of Police Regulations for the Guidance of the Constabulary of Victoria* (Melbourne: John Ferris, Government Printer, 1856), p. 7.
44. *Standing Rules and Regulations for the Governance and Guidance of the Constabulary Force of Ireland* (Dublin: George and John Grierson, 1837), p. 5.
45. *Rules and Regulations of the Constabulary Force of New Zealand* (Wellington: Civil Secretary, 1852).
46. *Supplement* to *Otago Government Gazette*, No.417 (Dunedin: Otago Provincial Government, 24 April 1866), p. 89.
47. *Manual of the Rules and Regulations for the Guidance of the Armed Constabulary Force of New Zealand* (Wellington: Government Printer, 1869) p. 9.

48. *The Police Act, and Regulations for the Guidance of the Police Force of New Zealand* (Wellington: Government Printer, 1887); R. S. Hill, *The Iron Hand in the Velvet Glove* (Wellington: Dunmore Press, 1995).
49. Hawkins, 'The "Irish Model" and the Empire', p. 19.
50. *Standing Orders and Regulations*, pp. 18–19.
51. This remained the case until civil forces emerged. See, for example, *Manual of Rules and Regulations for the Guidance of the Armed Constabulary Force of New Zealand* (Wellington: Lyon & Blair, 1881).
52. The longstanding state of exception theory was further developed in the twentieth century in C. Schmitt, *Political Theology: Four Chapters on the Concept of Sovereignty* (Chicago: University of Chicago Press, 2005; first published 1922). See, too, G. Agamben, *State of Exception* (Chicago: University of Chicago Press, 2005); and, for a colonial extension, M. Hardt and A. Negri, *Empire* (Cambridge, MA: Harvard University Press, 2000); and Partha Chatterjee's 'rule of colonial difference' in P. Chatterjee, *Nation and its Fragments* (Princeton, NJ: Princeton University Press, 1993).
53. Of course, policemen suffered too; see, for example, R. Abbott, *Police Casualties in Ireland, 1919–1922* (Cork: Mercier Press, 2000).
54. For 'webs of empire' see Tony Ballantyne's pioneering 'Race and the Webs of Empire', 2001, reprinted with other relevant material in T. Ballantyne, *Webs of Empire: Locating New Zealand's Colonial Past* (Wellington: Bridget Williams Books, 2012), pp. 24–27.
55. Both Georgina Sinclair and Chris. A. Williams have made an influential contribution to scholarship on such matters, in their co-authored 'Home and Away' and elsewhere.
56. The continuum approach underpins R. S. Hill's contributions to 'The History of Policing in New Zealand' series: *Policing the Colonial Frontier* (see, for example, p. 1), *The Colonial Frontier Tamed* (Wellington: Historical Branch, 1989) and *The Iron Hand in the Velvet Glove*. This approach has resonance with other works dating from the revisionist 1980s, such as that of Brogden, most especially his 'An Act to Colonise'.
57. Quite apart from the strategic policing locus on the continuum, the colonial police—all-purpose agents of the state—would also carry out tactical interventions which might take them far from their strategic orientation. Even in a 'quiet' colony with a relatively non-coercive force, for example, extreme violence might be needed from time to time, to deal with such matters as rebellion.
58. J. Mooney, 'A Tale of Two Regicides', *European Journal of Criminology*, 11:2 (2014), pp. 228–50, 246.
59. M. Thomas, *Violence and Colonial Order* (Cambridge: Cambridge University Press, 2012).
60. D. Anderson and D. Killingray (eds), *Policing and Decolonisation* (Manchester: Manchester University Press, 1992); G. Sinclair, *At the End of the Line: Colonial Policing and the Imperial Endgame 1945–80* (Manchester and New York: Manchester University Press, 2006).
61. 'The Definition of Law', in Notebook of James F. Cleary, Mount Cook Police Station, Wellington, New Zealand, 22 November 1905 (in author's possession).
62. See, for example, J. Breman, *Taming the Coolie Beast* (Delhi: Oxford University Press, 1989).

4 'From beyond the Sea'
The Irish Catholic Press in the Southern Hemisphere

Stephanie James

Statistics of approximately 8 million people leaving Ireland between 1801 and 1921[1] summon up stories of scattered Irish communities across the globe. In such diaspora communities, many Irish migrants and their descendants actively sought connection with, and ongoing knowledge about, their homeland. Newspapers provided one crucial mechanism supplying both the link and the demand for information. More-affluent migrants sourced publications from Ireland,[2] but locally produced newspapers, typically associated with the Catholic Church, provided a more common conduit for Irish Catholics maintaining homeland attachments and wanting news. This chapter represents a preliminary examination of the role of the Irish Catholic press in the southern hemisphere, a role argued here as critical, and predominantly orchestrated by Irishmen. How did a variety of newspapers in different locations foster and encourage a sustained identification with Ireland, for original migrants and ongoing generations?

The discussion largely focuses on Australasia (with a brief glance at Argentina), and adopts a definition of diaspora as a 'triangular dialogue between the homeland and ... new communities [and] a consciousness of being part of an international community'.[3] The Irish American press has understandably received closer attention than Southern Hemisphere publications,[4] given the vastly greater numbers of Irish migrants to the United States—4,905,083 according to Donald Harman Akenson in comparison to 340,640 to Australasia.[5] However, the Irish outflow contributed one-quarter of Australia's 1911 population and this underlines the importance of examining the antipodean Irish Catholic press. Despite Alan O'Day's dismissal of the 'Southern hemisphere lands' as 'too distant' for inclusion in his discussion of the significance of overseas visits by prominent Irishmen,[6] coverage of Irish missions to Australasia in the Irish Australasian press documents the importance, strength, and interconnectedness of these remote newspaper networks.[7]

Before presenting an overview of the newspapers discussed here, comment is made on the apparent neglect of Irish Catholic newspapers as a transnational focus for historians. The system of newspaper 'exchanges' used by all editors (i.e., interchanging copies of publications, with subsequent printing of extracts) is then examined and the impact of the editors' relationships to the Catholic Church evaluated. The chapter concludes by focusing on the use of Irish iconography in newspaper mastheads, and examining the ways that these newspapers reinforced a staunch Irish identity.

A TRANSNATIONAL GAP?

It is surprising that historians seem to have largely bypassed the role and significance of the Irish Catholic press, a transnational institution shadowing the Catholic Church, in enabling and reinforcing links across the diaspora. Although Sheridan Gilley's examination of the role of Catholicism in the nineteenth-century diaspora implicitly recognises that newspapers had a role 'in the international consciousness' of Irish Catholic migrants, there is no specific focus on the press.[8] He concludes that the nineteenth-century church 'performed a wide range of functions'—including community, national identity, and 'international consciousness'[9]—but without reference to the means by which this occurred. However, his point connects neatly with Benedict Anderson's concept of 'imagined community' in which the role of newspapers was seminal.[10] In Kevin Kenny's discussion of the global Irish, he pinpoints the critical need to integrate comparison and diaspora. The former, he argues, provides a means of understanding symmetries between diverse Irish communities, whereas the latter 'captur[es] the fluidity, hybridity, and frequent ambiguity of transnational interactions'.[11] As a 'way of seeing' and 'a way of uncovering connections',[12] transnationalism facilitates closer examination of Irish Catholic newspapers because it 'seeks to understand ideas . . . people and practices which have crossed national boundaries'.[13]

Enda Delaney argues persuasively for mapping out 'an alternative history of late modern Ireland that integrates the diaspora within Irish historical writing'.[14] His discussion of possible directions for this transnational approach includes topics for analysis such as class, power, material culture transfer, and religion.[15] But despite listing the exchange of ideas, Delaney does not include the revolving transnational wheel of newspaper connections across the diaspora, from Ireland to many locations and back, and also between diaspora sites. Heather McNamara's study of the *New Zealand Tablet* therefore represents an important beacon in this field. Lamenting in 2003 that 'almost no attention has been devoted to the interplay of institutional ties and individual relationships that facilitated the ongoing exchange of information between organs of the Irish Catholic and secular immigrant press' in the diaspora,[16] McNamara claimed her work as a 'first':

> [T]he *New Zealand Tablet* enjoyed international recognition as an intersection in the exchange of news and information through the Irish diaspora. It was enjoined with a host of other Irish, immigrant and

Table 4.1 Irish Catholic Newspapers: Dates, Locations, Founders, and Significant Editors and Their Backgrounds

Paper	Place	Year	Founder/s	Background	Editors	Background	Years
Freeman's Journal	Sydney	1850	Archdeacon J. McEnroe	Irish	Fr McEnroe;	Irish	1850–53
Adopted a company model in 1894					J.K. Heydon;		1857–60
					R. Sullivan;	English	1866–69
					T. Butler;	Irish	1869–96
					E. O'Sullivan;	Irish–Aust;	1898–99
					J.D. Fitzgerald;	Irish–Aust;	1899–1904
					J. Blakeney	Irish–Aust;	1904–14
Advocate	Melbourne	1868	S. Winter; C. Gavan Duffy; M. O'Grady;	Irish–Aust; Irish	W.H. Gunson; J. Grattan Grey; ?. J. Winter	Irish Irish Irish–Aust;	1868–1901 ?1902–04 1904–12
A family company until 1919 purchase by Dr Mannix			Fr J. Dalton S.J; Fr I. Moore S.J.		T.C. Brennan; T. Shorthill; Fr W. Collins	Irish–Aust; Irish–Aust; Irish	1912–17 1917–1920 1920
Tablet	Dunedin	1873	Bishop Patrick Moran	Irish	Bishop Moran; J.F. Perrin;	Irish Irish	1873–1881 1881–1895

(*Continued*)

Table 4.1 (Continued)

Paper	Place	Year	Founder/s	Background	Editors	Background	Years
Registered as commercial company in 1874, then public company in 1886.					Fr H.W. Cleary;	Irish	1898–1910
					J.A. Scott;	English	1910–16
					Fr J. Kelly;	Irish	1917–32
Catholic Record	Perth	1874	Fr M. Gibney	Irish	J.T. Reilly & J. Roe;	Irish	1874–79
Fully acquired by the church in 1923					Fr J. O'Reily;	Irish	1879–87
					Fr W.B. Kelly;	Irish–Aust;	1888–97
					J.F. Perrin;	Irish	1898–1903
					J. Grattan Grey:	Irish	1904–5
					Fr T. O'Grady	Irish	1914–18
Southern Cross	Buenos Aires	1875	Canon P. Dillon	Irish	F.H. Mulhall	Irish	1875–?
					W. Bulfin	Irish	1896–1910
Southern Cross	Adelaide	1889	Archbishop Reynolds;	Irish	J.V. O'Loghlin;	Irish–Aust;	1889–96;
Limited Liability Company			Archdeacon P. Russell;	Irish	W.J. Denny;	Irish–Aust;	1896–1903;
1889–1937			F.B. Keogh;	Irish-Aust	F.M. Koerner	Irish–German;	1903–34;
			J.F. Murphy;	Irish–Aust;	Fr M.L. Dunne	Irish;	1934–46

Catholic Press Limited Liability Company	Sydney	1895	Miss E. Baker Fr J. Bunbury; Dean Slattery; Fr J.P. Moynagh; A.M. Kavanagh	English Irish Irish Irish Irish	Fr P.P.Kelly J.F. Perrin Tighe Ryan; P.S. Cleary	Irish-Aust: Irish Irish Irish–Aust	1946–59 1895–97 1897–1922 1922–41
Catholic Advocate Board of Directors, clerical chair	Brisbane	1911	F. McDonnell; committee of businessmen; Mgr J. Byrne	Irish Irish	L. O'Dwyer; J.L. McArdle; L. J Keating;	Irish–Aust; Scottish–Aust; Irish–Aust;	1911–14 1915–? 1925–?

86 *Stephanie James*

Roman Catholic newspapers in a complex circuit that linked the Irish homeland with millions of men and women of Irish birth or descent worldwide, and also maintained independent connections between the diaspora destinations themselves.[17]

Delaney presents a compelling case for a transnational history of Ireland, but in the decade following McNamara's case study of the transnational network within which the *Tablet* flourished, her analysis awaits further attention from historians of the diaspora.

Within Australasia some historians have acknowledged the significance of the Irish Catholic press. For example, Richard P. Davis's analysis of the role of Irish issues in New Zealand politics at the turn of the century foregrounds the voice of the *Tablet*.[18] And in Australia, Rosa MacGinley's analysis of the first decade of Brisbane's *Age* (forerunner of the Catholic *Leader*) provides a valuable framework for a wider discussion of Irish Catholic publications. Her classification is applicable beyond Australia. It incorporates newspapers edited by Catholics and covering 'Catholic affairs sympathetically', those 'Catholic by policy but . . . not . . . officially diocesan publications', and finally, publications including 'a group of Catholic laymen and usually several priests'.[19] Expansion to include those newspapers published under the aegis of limited proprietary companies, with or without diocesan sanction, broadens her schema's utility. This chapter's review of eight Irish Catholic newspapers (see Table 4.1) identifies how their church association initially strengthened their capacity to reinforce Irishness, but subsequently functioned as a means of controlling Catholic communities.

THE NEWSPAPER 'EXCHANGE' SYSTEM, ITS RATIONALE, AND OPERATION

Core to the argument that the transnational nature of the Australasian Irish Catholic press enabled a homeland connection and identity for Irish migrants is the widespread use of 'exchanges'. Editors dispatched their publications extensively, ensuring that contemporaries received copies consistently, and in return, received a wide range of newspapers, both Irish Catholic and secular.[20] Preliminary analysis of the eight newspapers under discussion in this chapter reveals their common receipt of many overseas publications such as the Dublin *Freeman's Journal, Boston Pilot*, the *Irish World*, the Liverpool *Catholic Times*, the American *Ave Maria*, the London *Tablet*, and *Universe*. Papers catering for larger populations sourced more 'exchanges'.

Occasionally these Irish Australasian newspapers reveal something of the exchange system's internal self-ranking system. In 1875 the Sydney *Freeman's Journal* published a *Tablet* 'exchange', an item 'clipped from the Boston Pilot*, the leading Catholic journal in America'. Describing receipt from the Antipodes of 'some of our best Catholic exchanges', the *Pilot* categorised the Sydney *Freeman's Journal* and *Advocate* as 'admirable', the *New Zealand Tablet* as 'one of the best edited and most interesting journals we read', and the *Catholic Record* as 'a remarkably handsome paper'. The final comment represented unstinting general praise from a hallowed publication: 'When the Australian mails arrive we are led to think that our co-religionists in the southern hemisphere exceed us in the taste and intelligence which characterises their publications.'[21] The positive judgement of Australasian newspapers from the *Boston Pilot*, first noted in Dunedin then echoed in Sydney, represented crucial affirmation for editors— the 'leading' diaspora publication had publicly stated their value.

The *New Zealand Tablet* editors incorporated material from Australia's Irish Catholic newspapers.[22] The reverse was also true.[23] Items covered a broad range including local church news, particularly about senior churchmen such as Bishop Moran,[24] but also about Archbishop Croke of Cashel, bishop of Auckland from 1870–74. An 1896 item in the Sydney *Freeman's Journal* reported that Croke was sent an issue of the *Tablet* which discussed a character sketch by W. T. Stead published in the *Review of Reviews* of September 1895. In challenging the content and the spirit of Stead's article (and by implication *Tablet* coverage), the archbishop revealed his sensitivity to the depiction of the New Zealand Church, and emphasised the original discussion was a conversation, not an interview.[25] Irish Australian readers also read about the ways that their New Zealand counterparts marked significant Irish events such as the Centenary of '98. In Queenstown, a conversazione atmosphere included 'lecturettes', Irish airs from the local Brass Band, and recitations, while in Opotiki 'a Requim [sic] Mass was celebrated for the repose of those who died in defence of faith and fatherland one hundred long years ago'.[26] The *Tablet* 'exchanges' also included reports of Irish delegation visits[27] and, inevitably, of local fund-raising for Ireland.[28] Frequently such fund-raising items demonstrated triangular 'exchange' traffic. An 1888 item in Sydney's *Freeman's Journal* cited the *United Ireland* of 15 September for details of remittances to Ireland, mentioning sums of £161.12.4 and £236.3.4 'from New Zealand, per John F. Perrin Esq., editor of the . . . *Tablet*.'[29]

One theme recurring across many newspapers involved the necessity of the Catholic press and the allied issue of dilatory subscribers.[30] Lapsed subscriptions certainly had financial implications, but additionally 'Irishness' and Catholicity were potentially endangered. In 1876 the *Freeman's Journal* utilised Bishop Moran's analysis of 'Catholic Newspapers' in the *Tablet*. Arguing that 'the non-Catholic press is so thoroughly saturated with prejudice against all things connected with the faith' and that 'Ireland is universally included in [this] prejudice', Moran concluded that '[t]he Catholic press alone is the friend of the Irishman. In its columns only does he meet with justice and due appreciation, and here alone does he find his nation fitly estimated, its trials considered, and its interests advocated.'[31] In the first year of the *Southern Cross*, J. V. O'Loghlin reproduced a complete *Tablet* 'exchange' clearly serving his subscription-increasing goal. Titled '"Stop My Paper": A Good [Irish] Priest Speaks As to the Value of a Catholic Newspaper', the writer deplored those cancelling *Tablet* subscriptions, insisting 'that a Catholic newspaper is more necessary than even the prayer book to a Catholic family'.[32]

In the absence of records for the Adelaide *Southern Cross*, first published in 1889, reasons for establishing an 'exchange' relationship with its namesake in Buenos Aires remain speculative. But the 1880 arrival of the Irish Sisters of Mercy from Argentina, via Ireland, and their establishment of city and rural convents and schools in South Australia, suggests a possible explanation for the connection, in addition to their parallel title.[33] Examples of the Buenos Aires *Southern Cross* 'exchanges' in 1901 included details of the murder of a priest[34] and a return visit by some sisters to Argentina to raise funds for their Adelaide expansion.[35] The 'exchange' relationship between these newspapers persisted until editorial change in Adelaide during 1960, despite the fact that Spanish had increasingly become the language of publication in Buenos Aires and that the original rationale had faded.[36]

Occasionally, editorial comment or exchanges themselves provided insight about 'exchange table' existence. In 1914 when Adelaide's *Southern Cross* reached 25 years, the editor Frederick Martin Koerner published the *Tablet*'s congratulations. The paper was 'one of the brightest, most readable, best edited . . . that comes to our exchange table'.[37] Incoming papers provided, for example, a regular digest of Irish and international church news, general overseas items, or incidental copy to fill publishing spaces. World War I disrupted this information flow. Editors were challenged in many ways including limited access to Irish exchanges because of the banning of many Irish newspapers (especially after 1916)[38] and the prohibition of some Irish American publications under the War Precautions Act (WPA).[39] Further difficulties accompanied the Irish War of Independence. In Adelaide, the editor, Koerner, commented briefly on the impact of information blockage about Ireland in mid-1919: 'We are gradually learning the truth about many [suppressed] things'.[40] Later, in an embarrassing confession about having been a victim of confused sources, Koerner also demonstrated a functioning 'exchange' relationship between the *Southern Cross* in Adelaide and the Dublin *Freeman's Journal*. He acknowledged the Irish publication's criticism of his interpretation of a cable about a supposed interview between the Irish chief secretary and the London correspondent of an American paper.[41] In Melbourne, *Advocate* editor Thomas Shorthill decried the 'poisoned source' which limited information about Ireland.[42]

The 'exchange' system was crucial for all overseas Irish communities. Assumptions of daily press bias about Ireland in London-derived material were widespread across the Irish Catholic press. In February 1868 the *Advocate*'s opening issue justified the necessity of providing 'full or *accurate* news . . . on topics of special interest' to Irish Catholics.[43] Not only was Fenianism then an acute transnational anxiety, and predominant as an item in opening issues,[44] but the *Advocate*'s existence barely preceded the March assassination attempt on Prince Alfred in Sydney.[45] Accusations of biased Irish news reports were persistent.[46] And, some months after the O'Farrell saga, W.H. Gunson's editorial, referring obliquely to the preoccupation with Fenianism, justified the exchange system:

> Our readers are chiefly of Irish race . . . The first months of our existence was . . . a period [of intensified sorrow for scattered Irish]. Ireland had then to witness the sufferings of those who loved her . . . not indeed wisely, but well enough to risk all for what they deemed her good. Those in Victoria . . . longed for *full particulars* of all that story [of the Fenian saga]; and to satisfy this longing was our simple duty. Because of this, extracts from Irish, American and English papers . . . appeared in our columns weekly, and gratified the desire . . . for *unadulterated intelligence*.[47]

In 1876, Irishman J.F. Perrin, newly associated with the *Tablet* in Dunedin (and its editor from 1881), clarified the paper's position in relation to Ireland in a circular. He argued it was 'the office of the *Tablet* to remove that veil of prejudice through which the Irish nation is regarded'.[48] Two decades later in Adelaide, J.V. O'Loghlin listed one of his paper's 'leading features' as the provision of '[f]ull *and trustworthy intelligence* . . . as to the progress of the great struggle for life and liberty now going on in the old land'.[49] Cable items about Ireland were often questioned.[50] From 1915, 'canard' (or false rumour) was increasingly employed,[51] after 1916, 'unreliable',[52] 'cable liar',[53] 'camouflaged and minimised',[54] and by 1922 from the *Advocate* during the civil war, 'Cable Fakers and anti-Catholic press'.[55] A 1919 *Advocate* reflection on the taint of prejudice over its 50-year history revealed its publishing rationale: 'The Australian daily papers, then as now, were hostile to the cause of the people of Ireland, and as far as Victoria was concerned, it was only in the pages of "The *Advocate*" that the *truth* regarding affairs in Ireland could be found.'[56]

By 1920 Koerner's total distrust of cables from the daily papers was reflected in the qualification heading all such material: 'We do not vouch for the accuracy of the following cables . . . We amend such errors as are within our own knowledge and add explanatory or corrective notes where necessary.'[57] Quoting an 'exchange' from the London *Tablet* about British violence in Ireland, he reminded readers that its pro-British conservative stance guaranteed 'it is not too highly coloured'.[58]

Perceptions of misrepresentation or the distortion of Irish affairs was general and long-standing. An 1890 correspondent wrote that he had ordered 'the [Dublin] *Freeman's Journal* for years, but I am satisfied with what I get in the *Southern Cross* now'.[59] Others suggested that a local reduction in Irish detail would require access to Nationalist publications to fill the gap.[60] An early issue of the Buenos Aires *Southern Cross* reveals Irish migrant interest in accessing Irish news; in 1875 they could choose between two sources for purchase of three weekly Dublin papers: the *Nation*, the *Weekly Freeman*, and the *Weekly News*.[61]

Despite a plethora of daily newspapers available to Irish migrants, typically cheaper than the weekly Irish Catholic publications, the choice of the latter served to reinforce connections to 'home' as well as countering local bias. If, as Kevin Molloy found for the *New Zealand Tablet*, other diaspora papers attracted six readers per copy (the 1890 correspondent mentioned earlier complained of neighbours 'who are not ashamed to come borrowing "*The Cross*" from me'), then the secular to religious newspaper price differential mattered less than content and community access for Irish-connected readers.[62] Although McNamara highlights the 'painfully slow movement of information into New Zealand' and suggested that readers were disadvantaged by non-current news (shipping delays of six weeks controlled the arrival of detailed 'News by Mail'), it can also be argued that the receipt of layered accounts in instalments, added value to Irish news. Details in the 'dailies', followed by extensive coverage in the Irish Catholic press, reminded readers of the issues and further informed them. The double effect initially reinforced British perfidy and/or Irish struggles, but from 1919 when eventually Britain acknowledged war in Ireland, the delay factor between cable news and greater, more reliable detail contributed to distress for diaspora communities.

EDITORS AND THE CHURCH

The widespread use of 'exchange' material represented one of many similarities in the Irish Catholic newspapers being discussed here. Table 4.1 shows another—two points when newspaper establishment peaked. Between 1868 and 1875 new publications appeared in Melbourne, Dunedin, Perth, and Buenos Aires, and between 1889 to 1911 when the *Southern Cross* emerged in Adelaide, both Sydney and Brisbane acquired a second Irish Catholic paper.[63] Reasons for the apparent synchronicity at these points must remain speculative. In some cases, success followed numerous failed attempts—four in Melbourne and eight in Adelaide—so the combination of determined individuals (mainly clerical), propitious timing, and effective planning, somehow coalesced in all these diaspora sites. Although Patrick O'Farrell argues that the 'continuity . . . power . . . and resources of the Church . . . gave it control of the Irish-Catholic press', he concedes generally that their leadership role met 'some tension with a laity not always docile'.[64]

Editorial instability plagued the Sydney *Freeman's Journal*[65] and *Catholic Press*, Perth's *Catholic Record*, and later Melbourne's *Advocate* for some years after the death of founding editor Gunson. Some newspapers began as registered companies while others adopted this model later. Clerical shareholders and/or company structures ensured greater church control for both the

Tablet[66] and, after 1896, the Adelaide *Southern Cross*.[67] But MacGinley's observation that, after World War I, the range of newspaper categories was replaced by 'official diocesan papers',[68] applies across most papers discussed here. The change was reflected in the Adelaide *Southern Cross* masthead in June 1927, where the founding statement of 'A Weekly Record of Catholic, Irish and General News' was replaced (without any explanation) by 'The Official Catholic Organ of South Australia'.[69] In Sydney, one justification for the 1942 amalgamation of the two Irish Catholic papers into the new *Catholic Weekly* was the impossibility of 'nam[ing] either as the official organ of the Archdiocese of Sydney'.[70]

Table 4.1 also reveals that few Irish Catholic papers were founded without guiding clerical Irish hands. Equally it shows that many editors were laymen. Within MacGinley's priests and laymen category, the early years of Sydney *Freeman's Journal* were volatile. Diocesan policies received *Freeman's Journal* support based on 'the best interest' of readers, not their official genesis.[71] Despite church mentoring, founding statements from editors of the *Advocate*, the Adelaide *Southern Cross*, and the *Catholic Press* made early and explicit statements about the limitations of their religious identification. Responding to an early challenge in Melbourne (where the *Advocate* probably straddled MacGinley's second and third categories—established by laymen and priests and Catholic by policy without official diocesan endorsement),[72] Gunson proclaimed it as 'a political and national journal'. He insisted the *Advocate* was without 'a mission to deal with religious questions' unless introduced by prejudiced opponents.[73] It is to Gunson that Patrick J. Naughtin ascribes responsibility for the *Advocate* operating as more of an Irish than a Catholic paper.[74] In Sydney the *Catholic Press* (priests establishing a company) announced that it would 'not be a religious publication, but a newspaper. Its tone . . . will be intensely Catholic'.[75] The appointment of former *Catholic Record* editor, Father John O'Reily, as Adelaide's archbishop in 1895, accelerated clerical concerns about purported theological gaps and political partiality in the *Southern Cross*, a company with official church support. Following major differences of opinion between founding editor O'Loghlin and senior clergy at the shareholder meeting of 1895, an extraordinary number of proxy votes the next year increased the number of clerical directors to equal the laymen.[76] Challenging criticism in 1895, O'Loghlin had reminded the meeting 'that it was never intended that the paper should be an exclusively religious one'.[77] The smooth combination of a company/shareholder framework with a church-fostered publication, inherently contradictory, ultimately became untenable in Adelaide. The same model in Sydney's *Catholic Press* seemed to cause fewer problems, although the difference probably lies in the ratio of clerical to lay shareholders. In 1896 there were 17 priests and four lay shareholders,[78] and in 1928, '73 bishops and priests and 96 laymen'.[79] In Adelaide, almost three-quarters of founding shareholders were laymen and -women, but by the time the company was wound up in 1937, this proportion of lay to clerical/church shareholder was reversed.[80]

Without a detailed history of the religious press in Australasia, and with very limited accounts of most newspapers under discussion, locating even a basic narrative of individual publications presents challenges. Occasional nuggets within newspaper columns are therefore of immense importance. From the *Southern Cross* 'Sydney Notes', penned by *Catholic Press* editor Tighe Ryan,[81] emerged a revealing insight about his publication's early struggles. At the paper's 1901 staff picnic, Monsignor O'Brien (chairman of the directors) announced that all liabilities, including new equipment, had now been paid off. Contrasting the current position—'on velvet'—with the 'indescribable difficulties' of the first two years, he said, 'At times the situation was so desperate that hurried meetings of priests needed to be called in order to raise funds to bring out the next issue'.[82] The comment points to possible reasons for the disappearance of J. F. Perrin as editor. His departure from the *New Zealand Tablet* (where he had followed Bishop Moran as editor) was greatly regretted. In response to Perrin's resignation, Dunedin's administrator wrote that 'simple truth compels me to say that New Zealand loses and Australia gains a devoted Catholic, a true-hearted Irishman, and a scholarly and uncompromising Catholic journalist'.[83] Perrin was with the *Tablet* for two decades; despite the publicity surrounding his arrival and role in Sydney, he barely lasted 18 months. Was his departure related to the 'indescribable difficulties', or was it church and editor tensions? The cause has yet to be located.[84]

Clearly church and editor tensions did exist in some newspapers. Whether they also followed Perrin to Perth where he edited the *Catholic Record* for five years remains unclear.[85] His sudden and unexplained departure from that paper at the end of 1903 could suggest some offence against hierarchical sensibilities.[86] T. C. Brennan, *Advocate* editor in 1917, retired to concentrate on his legal practice following Archbishop Mannix's objections to the paper's pro-conscription leaning.[87] O'Loghlin, Perrin, and Brennan were all lay editors, a fact which seems of significance here. As editor of the *Catholic Record* in Perth from 1914 to 1918, Irishman Fr T. R. O'Grady served under Irish Archbishop Clune, a vigorous proponent of recruiting. Yet in three 1915 editorials when Fr O'Grady 'announced his total and unalterable opposition to conscription',[88] there were no apparent consequences; presumably his clerical status offered some protection.[89]

Remaining tensions between editors and the hierarchy were resolved by progressive church takeover of newspapers, the pattern suggested earlier by MacGinley. For example, Archbishop Mannix acquired the *Advocate* by 1919,[90] Archbishop Clune the *Catholic Record* in 1923,[91] and Archbishop Killian the Adelaide *Southern Cross* in 1937.[92] Earlier, in 1928, Brisbane's Archbishop Duhig 'declared the [struggling] *Age* as the official diocesan organ'.[93] Duhig's biographer shows him as a former contributor to Sydney's *Catholic Press* and claims his move into 'the Catholic newspaper business' was deliberate. His intention was 'to form public opinion'. Duhig was unhappy with the *Age* and the *Catholic Advocate*'s 'continual backward glancing . . . policy of Irish identification'. Thus, the *Catholic Leader* replaced the *Age* in 1930, and Duhig allowed the *Catholic Advocate* to fade away.[94] In Sydney, Australian-born Archbishop Gilroy (with Irish forebears) amalgamated the *Freeman's Journal* and the *Catholic Press* as the *Catholic Weekly* in 1942. According to the *Freeman's Journal*, the recently deceased Irish Archbishop Michael Kelly 'was always anxious that the two Catholic papers should be reduced to one . . . [and] it was among . . . [his] last wishes'.[95] Within the first few decades of the twentieth century, then, these Irish prelates shared an objective where the Catholic component of Irish Catholic newspapers required elevation beyond the more flexible earlier framework. Previously many editors promoted an Irish identity in conjunction with explicit church identification. O'Farrell emphasises the importance of Catholicism in sustaining these publications, 'thus enabl[ing] Irishness to retain its voice as a facet of continuing Irish Catholic identity'. But his subsequent point that this 'survival . . . [was] a partly artificial construct', helps explains why the shared identity became less important. The newspaper model moved towards total clerical control in which both the explicit Irish identification and the lay/clerical partnership style evident previously in Irish Catholic publications became increasingly redundant.

THE IRISH CATHOLIC PRESS AND IRISH IDENTITY

The Irish handprint appeared throughout these papers, but its visibility faded over time. Evident in the publication rationale for all these newspapers, the dual role of Irish Catholic newspapers was voiced in Canon Dillon's 1875 announcement that the Buenos Aires *Southern Cross* would 'supply the wants of an Irish and Catholic organ'.[96] Founding principles for the *Advocate* and Adelaide's *Southern Cross* have already been discussed; the *Catholic Press* also endorsed 'the sacred cause of Ireland's freedom'.[97] In their early decades, all newspapers reflected self-conscious but powerful bonds with Ireland. Layouts typically included 'News from Ireland' in the opening pages. In addition to church items, much of it Irish, the selection of news reflected a consistent focus on English policies and their Irish impact. Parliamentary coverage, Irish Parliamentary Party (IPP) activities, political activity in Ireland as well as historical event marking, and significant deaths, all added up to many columns in these papers.

Significantly, some businesses integrated Irish cues or greetings to emphasise their connection to potential customers. For example, in the Buenos Aires *Southern Cross*, an 1896 advertisement for 'The Gladstone, Dublin Boarding House' made a clear statement about potential customer expectations.[98] In April 1916 its front page displayed John Keenan's wares under the heading of 'Irish Manufactures', listing 'Tweeds . . . Linen Suiting, Damask . . . Direct from the manufacturers'.[99] From its Adelaide namesake, two examples will suffice. From the first issue in July 1889, Patrick Whelan took advantage of the editorial page to advertise 'Shin Fane. Shin Fane. Support Irish Manufacture by Wearing the Celebrated Blarney Tweeds to be had from the only Direct Importer in South Australia'.[100] In 1900, a boot maker and a butcher both used 'CEAD MILLE FAILTHE' to advertise their totally different goods.[101] In Melbourne, Richmond's Galway Bakery and the Shamrock Dairy at Collingwood provide two further examples of businessmen deliberately utilising Irish links to attract custom.[102]

The lure of Home Rule preoccupied the Irish Catholic press in the Southern Hemisphere for almost 25 years, providing an important gauge of ongoing identification with Ireland. *Advocate* coverage in 1886, 1893, and 1912 demonstrates not only the extent of editorial focus on the issue[103] but also its comprehensive provision of details about the measure's complex parliamentary journeys and Irish Victoria's engagement with this reform.[104] While Irishman Gunson was editor for the first two attempts, his probable successor in 1912, Irish Australian T.C. Brennan, retained the same level of coverage. Accompanying fulsome details of the tactics and twists associated with Prime Minister Gladstone's 1886 attempt[105] were letters to the editor as well as accounts of local Home Rule meetings.[106] Both layers of response from Irish Australians demonstrated close involvement with the issues, and the ongoing Irish connection of many migrants. In 1893, although coverage levels were similar,[107] some correspondents criticised the delay in organising a large public meeting, arguing diaspora support was vital for Gladstone.[108] While reports from country towns continued to show local Irish interest,[109] editorial comment on 8 April reinforced disappointment that Melbourne's 'Great Meeting' was not organised before 11 April.[110] In 1912 the local impact of Westminster manoeuvring was intensified by the presence of the fifth IPP Mission to Australasia. IPP leader John Redmond's son was one of three touring 'Home Rule' delegates. Jubilation characterised *Advocate* response to the successful first reading of the bill in the House of Commons.[111] The nature of Irish Australian readers, and indeed of Irish Australian newspaper style, had evolved since 1886, but editorial perceptions of the issue's importance to their audience remained visible.

Close relationships between Australasia's Irish Catholic editors and IPP figures sustained and reinforced direct identification with Ireland. Dating from June 1881 when J.W. Walshe, the first IPP delegate, somehow located *Advocate* proprietor, Joseph Winter, in Melbourne after his anonymous arrival,[112] he subsequently related that IPP members had been unable to provide him with any Australian contacts.[113] From that point the *Advocate* office became central to all communication with Ireland—especially financial—and Winter managed the subsequent tours for the Redmond brothers, John Dillon, and Michael Davitt. His front-line role facilitated the function of the Australasian Irish Catholic newspaper network as the fulcrum for all further visits of Irish delegations. The Australasian Convention of 1883 was one important outcome of these Irish and Irish Australian newspaper links which were reinforced by regular contributions from both John Redmond and Davitt to some Irish Australasian newspapers and frequent reference to their views in others.[114]

Pleas for financial assistance to Ireland, one cause motivating Irish delegations, persisted in all Irish Catholic newspapers. Calls for Irish Australasian generosity to the 'Old Land' came in many forms. Immediate crises, such as that of 'The Distress in Ireland' during 1898, revealed, for example, the dedication of South Australia's Irish National Federation (INF) in sending sums to Dublin. Publication of two grateful, semi-personalised letters from Dublin's Archbishop Walsh in the *Southern Cross*, thanked 'friends in Adelaide' for their 'generous contribution' and reminded them they 'had good reason to thank God that they are not . . . living in Ireland'.[115] A Dublin Appeal for Evicted Tenants, dated St Patrick's Day 1899, incorporated reference to a less than totally generous 'home response' precipitating the exhortation 'with every confidence to our countrymen abroad'.[116] The same constituency was also prevailed on to support building projects in Ireland. Irishmen, typically clerical, toured diaspora communities appealing to their Irish generosity for major restoration projects; in 1870, according to the Sydney *Freeman's Journal*, an Irish Canon garnered £3,000 in the colonies for the Queenstown Cathedral.[117] But the Irish Catholic newspaper networks allowed for less personal, more manipulative appeals to 'the love of the scattered sons of St Patrick for faith and fatherland'. Contained in Irish Cardinal Logue's 1899 'Appeal to the Irish Catholics of America and Australia' to 'make perfect' the National Cathedral of St Patrick at Armagh, this emotive request was widely publicised.[118] Resistance to such pleas must have been difficult for many across the diaspora, given the close relationship between many Irish, their clergy, and the church hierarchy. Many offerings in subscription lists were described as 'mites'.[119]

Nevertheless, persistent negative newspaper discourses about the adequacy of Irish Australasian generosity towards Ireland reflected differing views about colonial levels of Irish identification.[120] Focus on the Adelaide *Southern Cross* of 1890 reveals correspondents questioning the level of local commitment to the Irish National League (INL). Their challenge to local Irish patriotism raised the issue of donations to the Evicted Tenant's Fund, figures of £6,500 in Queensland compared to 'about as many pounds' in South Australia.[121] A later correspondent urged greater generosity, asking whether 'the Irish priests and the people of the colony [are] working unitedly in securing in their own comparatively powerful way that assistance to the Irish cause which may be fairly expected of them'?[122] Evidence of this critical strand persisted, demonstrating that Irish migrants and their children occupied different positions in relation to Ireland. The actions of Adelaide's Archbishop O'Reily in directing the proceeds of 1896 St Patrick's Day away from Ireland and towards defraying diocesan debt represented further evidence of this dichotomy.[123] His insistence, something greatly distressing many INF stalwarts,[124] prefigured the subsequent move away from that previously discussed shared church/Irish focus, towards a more uncompromising clerically controlled stance.

Particular events in Ireland attracted newspaper attention. The 1896 convention in Dublin, for example, an occasion fervently promoted by Michael Davitt following his return from Australasia earlier that year, represented a conciliation attempt for the warring IPP factions. Davitt sent personal invitations to Australasian Irish nationalists, including J. V. O'Loghlin in Adelaide. O'Loghlin's response urged unity. Arguing that without this, 'the Irish cause . . . would be once again be like a dead body on a dissecting table', his letter made front-page news in the Dublin *Freeman's Journal*. In Buenos Aires, the *Southern Cross* convention coverage did not quote sources, suggesting the attendance of an Irish Argentine correspondent.[125] The paper's subsequent interpretation quoted non-dated 'exchanges' from the Dublin *Freeman's Journal* and *Boston Pilot* and pronounced disappointed judgement.[126]

The '98 Centenary celebrations two years later symbolised a great occasion across the diaspora. Most Australasian editors were Irishmen for whom the event had a particular resonance.[127] Newspaper focus was multidimensional. Reports of specific Irish events such as masses performed to mark 'The Dawn of '98',[128] May 'Celebrations in Wexford and at Vinegar Hill',[129] and a major excursion to 'Wolfe Tone's Grave' at Bodenstown, all sites of original importance, were provided.[130] In addition, detailed historical background and rebel profiles[131] helped educate the younger generations, while news of an American Irish pilgrimage[132] and reported New Zealand celebrations, all constructed more detailed layers of understanding about the year's significance to the Irish everywhere.[133]

Local markings of this centenary, so significant in the troubled saga of the Irish struggles for independence, probably had a more immediate impact on Irish Australian identification with Ireland. In Adelaide, for example, the INF organised a lecture at the Trades Hall. The speaker, a local priest, offered no apology for the men of '98 as 'he was there to praise their lives and deeds, their aims and objects'.[134] Negative daily paper publicity around Archbishop O'Reily's presence ('in the large and enthusiastic audience') merely presented him with an opportunity to write to the *Advertiser* traversing '98 history in political rather than the critic's religious agenda.[135] Editor Denny summarised Sydney's 'Unique Ceremony' for the May reburial of 'Wicklow Chief', Michael Dwyer, and included an artist's sketch of the planned £2,000 memorial.[136] In December the INF held a social to conclude Adelaide's centenary year and to revisit the twin identity themes of 'remembering those brave but unfortunate men', as well as the possession by the 'people of Australia [of] the power to make laws for themselves'.[137]

In both Sydney and Melbourne, reflecting their larger Irish Australian populations, the *Freeman's Journal, Catholic Press*, and *Advocate* devoted fuller attention to plans for reburying the '98 rebel who was transported to New South Wales for his role in the rebellion. Reports of regular committee meetings (including women's groups in both cities), burial site negotiations, fundraising, plans for the disinterment, blessing, and burial procession to the Waverly Cemetery contributed to an intense Irish Australian focus on 22 May in Sydney. The *Advocate*'s three-page account included Cardinal Patrick Francis Moran's address, and estimated the crowd at 100,000. It proclaimed the event was

> the most imposing demonstration of a national kind ever held in Australia ... it was the largest in the number of people who witnessed it; in a historical sense it had a meaning of deepest importance to the whole people of a scattered, but virile race, who are persistently struggling for the great principle for which the men of '98 so bravely fought and fighting fell.

While Victorian INF president Nicholas O'Donnell's speech argued that the event 'is proof that the spirit of Irish patriotism is alive in Australia',[138] Irish Cardinal Moran had strongly opposed the exhumation and reburial plans. According to O'Farrell, Moran's vision for Irish Australia did not allow the revival of 'these rebels or their traditions'.[139] Following 'bitter criticism', a diplomatic change of mind permitted Moran's participation in the seminal occasion. However, the force of hierarchical power was already evident in his restructuring of St Patrick's Day from 1895.[140] Non-clerical promoters of Irish identity in Adelaide and Sydney were under notice from senior Irish churchmen that this was now church territory. As has already been shown, the process of church newspaper acquisition after World War I resulted in even greater erosion of overt Irish identification.

The overwhelmingly Irish character of the Australasian church into the early twentieth century facilitated editorial partnering of Irish and church matters.[141] For example, in January 1890, under 'Irish News (From the Home Papers)', O'Loghlin reproduced a letter from Archbishop Croke of Cashel. The Dublin *Freeman's Journal* 'exchange' showed Croke, who had visited eastern Australia in 1872, writing in support of the Irish Tenant's Defence Association. His endorsement as a senior Irish churchman facilitated the local collection of subscriptions. Following the Easter Rising of 1916, any Irish Catholic press generated and promoted subscription to Irish causes moved towards unacceptable Irish identification. In Buenos Aires, the *Southern Cross* quickly announced a fund 'for the poor of Dublin who have suffered by the rising', and letters reveal that many Irish Argentines were proud of 'those brave men who gave up their lives for the old mother land'.[142] Irish Australian communities responded to church organised Irish distress appeals, a wartime activity which alienated many other Australians.[143] Authorities in both countries perceived Irish Catholic publications as both a useful source of information about disloyal Irishmen and a wartime security risk after 1916. In 1919 the Buenos Aires editor referred to 'stress and trials' including censorship, pro-German accusations, and Secret Service Activities;[144] in Dunedin, Father James Kelly, *Tablet* editor from

1917, was a security target.[145] Australian surveillance files reveal the monitoring of editors. Both Fr O'Grady in Perth and Koerner in Adelaide were under surveillance. In Melbourne the *Advocate* proprietor and editor were charged over censorship violations.[146] The impact of the Great War, in conjunction with events in Ireland, heralded changes for diaspora communities, changes reflected in the evolving nature of the Irish Catholic press.

But as these changes were unfolding—typified by the sale of the *Advocate* to the church in early 1919—the development of the War of Independence, presented a new and polarising chapter of Irish Catholic identification with Ireland. All Irish Catholic papers included graphic details of British conduct from multiple sources, among the most important of which were testimonies from visiting hierarchical figures. Many sources documented widespread violence—'awful times—nothing but shootings and burnings'.[147] These included accounts of a family member's treatment as an internee,[148] and regular use of confronting titles for weekly Irish news: 'Raids, Robberies and Murders',[149] and 'On the Irish Front'.[150] But following the 1920 or 1921 visits of numbers of Australasian Irish prelates to Ireland en route to or from Rome, their reactions and accounts received unprecedented prominence in the Irish Catholic press, within and beyond their dioceses.[151] When Archbishop Spence was welcomed back to Adelaide at the Cathedral in February 1921, he proclaimed 'the state of Ireland as too awful' to mention 'in God's house'.[152] However, both during and following the trauma of Ireland's civil war, it was not only the network of personal ties and shared Irish ideals which disintegrated, but the closely woven texture of Ireland and church which previously characterised the Irish Catholic press, increasingly frayed.

Few editors had backgrounds other than Irish or Irish descent. The uniformity in terms of Irish birth was most striking in the *Advocate* and the *Tablet*, whereas the history of Adelaide's *Southern Cross* shows second-generation Irish Australians guided its first 45 years. That this mattered little in their representation of Irish issues was suggested firstly by W.J. Denny, who in 1939 described his predecessor, O'Loghlin, 'as very pro-Irish . . . more Irish than the Irish themselves—he was certainly a great student of Irish history'.[153] Then, following the retirement of third editor Koerner in early 1934, when Adelaide's Irish National Association (INA) and the Irish Pipers combined to make him a presentation, they declared that 'In him Ireland and the friends of Ireland had a learned supporter'.[154] Koerner's response explained the genesis and strength of his Irish connection: 'With an Irish mother and the strength of such exiles [as Sir Charles Gavan Duffy, Sir John O'Shannassey, Michael O'Grady and Peter Lalor] before his eyes [in Victoria], it was only natural that he should have sympathised with the Irish National cause'.[155]

Previously, Koerner's reminiscences had disclosed that 'Archbishop [O'Reily] often dropped into the office informally to speak with me on some subject to which he desired attention to be called in the paper'. Such unofficial interaction clarified the subtlety of mechanisms allowing greater church

'From beyond the Sea' 99

control, and ultimately the reduction of the previous Irish association.[156] In Melbourne, church ownership from 1919, followed by an Irish clerical editor, while not reducing Irish coverage per se in the *Advocate*, in the short term at least, limited its scope to matters consistent with Archbishop Mannix's position.[157] For the Irish Catholic press, the 'advocacy of Irish and Catholic interests' was no longer synonymous; church leadership had reversed the order, claiming defining rights.[158]

MASTHEADS AND IRISH ICONOGRAPHY IN THESE NEWSPAPERS

It is significant that most publications examined here utilised Irish symbols as a visual mechanism for reinforcing Irish identity and a sense of shared community. The most senior Australian publication, the *Freeman's Journal*, and the twentieth-century *Catholic Advocate* present a striking founding contrast, the former appearing without any visible Irish cues in 1850,[159] and the latter incorporating in 1911 Irish symbols only: the round tower, Celtic cross, and shamrocks (see Figure 4.1). Although the *Freeman's Journal* introduced masthead changes in 1870, 1884, and 1895 (probably in response to the emergence of local competition in the *Catholic Press*), it was not until 1900 that symbols were added—some shamrocks and other floral items, possibly Australian.[160] Further changes in 1912 clarified masthead appearance: it now presented a more identifiable shamrock and wattle and added 'Australasia's Oldest Catholic Paper' and 'For Sixty-Two Years the Recognised Catholic and Irish-Australian Organ'.[161] In 1915, masthead wording reflected a shift in focus with the addition of 'Official Organ of the Hibernian Australasian Catholic Benefit Society. 50,000 Members in the Commonwealth' to the existing template (see Figure 4.2). Changes in 1923 simplified masthead symbolism further. Retaining a small shamrock and wattle focus, it added a garland emphasising its 73 years' establishment.[162] Explanations of the various transitions outlined here await further research.

Of the newspaper cluster appearing between 1868 and 1875, three were initially published without Irish masthead cues. This was true for the *Advocate* until July 1869 when intertwining shamrocks were matched by a branch of gum leaves and nuts on the opposite masthead side.[163] Such early blending of Irish and Australian iconography possibly represents a colonial first. Unusually, the *Tablet* masthead in Dunedin never included any visual reference to Ireland or New Zealand, incorporating the title only until 1900.[164] The title was derived from handwritten medieval script, a feature used throughout the early paper. Changes in 1906 removed this script, using more conventional type, and adding a cross with radiating lines. In 1907, 'The Sole Organ of the Catholic Body in New Zealand' became part of the masthead.[165] For its first 14 years, after 1874, the Western Australian *Catholic Record* masthead was small but striking. It consisted of a Celtic

100 *Stephanie James*

Figure 4.1 Masthead of Australia's *Catholic Advocate*, 24 June 1911, showing round tower, shamrocks, and Celtic cross

Source: Courtesy of *The Catholic Leader*.

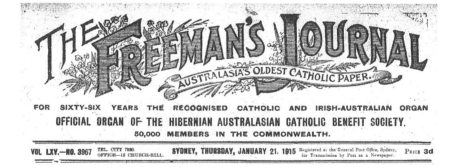

Figure 4.2 Masthead of Australia's *Freeman's Journal*, 21 January 1915, with shamrocks and wattles intertwined.

Source: Courtesy of the Sydney *Catholic Weekly*.

cross with radiating rays above a single shamrock, but this disappeared in July 1888 under Irish Australian editor, Fr W. B. Kelly.[166] While the removal indicates that his perspective differed from his Irish predecessors, Kelly left no elucidation of his decision. Like the *Tablet*, the early years of the Buenos Aires *Southern Cross*, did not involve any Irish iconography in the masthead; its title lettering was also medievally based. By 1916, however, the masthead incorporated two Celtic-derived frames on either side, one encasing an Irish harp and the other two hands holding a flaming torch. Within the paper, opening lettering in columns was Celtic.[167] In the absence of any editorial explanation for masthead evolution in these publications, one tentative conclusion points to decisions about the value and importance of greater visibility of Irish symbolism, due perhaps to local factors, or as in the Western Australian case, some belief that reduced emphasis was necessary.

Two company publications, the Adelaide *Southern Cross* (established 1889) and the Sydney *Catholic Press* (established 1895) included no Irish iconography in early mastheads. But the former publication's first issue announced its mission as 'A Weekly Record of Catholic, Irish and General News'. Six weeks later the masthead integrated harps and shamrocks (see Figure 4.3).[168] And in November 1892, O'Loghlin explained further changes—the constellation of the Southern Cross entwined with shamrocks, a presentation which lasted until mid-1927 (see Figure 4.3). In Sydney, J. F. Perrin replaced the plain lettering of the early *Catholic Press* with a more ornate version in September 1896. From January 1899 under the direction of Tighe Ryan, the masthead incorporated the Southern Cross, a waratah (a New South Wales floral symbol), the sun, and silhouettes of dead trees to represent the Australian environment. A year later 'Organ of the Catholics of Australia' was added (see Figure 4.4), then altered in July 1901 to 'The Leading Catholic Paper of Australia'.[169] A focus on the mastheads chosen by many early editors of these Irish Catholic newspapers demonstrates very

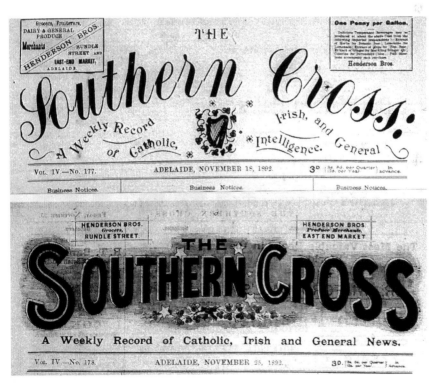

Figure 4.3 Masthead of the Adelaide *Southern Cross*, 18 November 1892, showing harp and shamrocks.

Source: Courtesy of *The Southern Cross*, Adelaide.

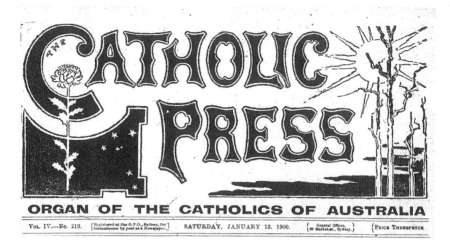

Figure 4.4 Masthead of the Sydney *Catholic Press*, 13 January 1900, with Southern Cross constellation, waratah, sun, and dead trees.
Source: Courtesy of the Sydney *Catholic Weekly*.

clearly that most not only recognised the importance of this visual impact, but increasingly integrated Irish (and, in some cases, local) symbolism, suggesting that Irish iconography was of greater apparent significance than were religious symbols.

CONCLUSION

Emigration created physical and psychological distance for millions of nineteenth-century Irish. Irish Catholic newspapers helped fill this void for many Irish migrants. Living in scattered communities in colonies remote from Catholic Ireland, and often amidst perceived anti-Irish sentiment, for migrant Irish the importance of an Irish-focused newspaper was elevated. Irish priests played dominant roles in the founding of the eight newspapers discussed here, testament to Church recognition of the need for a tangible focus for their 'imagined communities'. Clerical perceptions were stark—to be a good Irish person was to be a good Catholic and vice versa[170]—thus securing a Catholic paper provided a bulwark in colonies that were English and Protestant. Editors were Irish or of Irish descent; their publications were associated, formally or informally, with a local church of overwhelmingly Irish characteristics and personnel; and revealed an equally overwhelming emphasis on Irish affairs, both religious and sociopolitical. All editors implemented the 'exchange' system which allowed them to promote their own publication, extract content from Irish Catholic and Irish American newspapers, and then publish selected material. Newspaper readers could easily connect with matters Irish, whether they were migrants struggling with distance or their children were living between two worlds as hyphenated Irish.

Irish Catholic newspapers thus played a crucial role in reinforcing Irishness and were probably the most powerful conduit of its transmission in the diaspora. The content range enabling this was extensive, moving from the masthead, its symbols and wording, through to local advertisements, to 'News from Ireland' and, often, local church news. Updated Irish church news, English policies and Irish responses, cultural news, and insights featured in all newspapers discussed and constantly the Irish nation was represented as waiting for reform. As residents enjoying political rights and freedom denied those 'at home', Irish migrants decried the discrepancies and insisted that Ireland and England would prosper when such changes were implemented in Ireland. Financial support for Ireland, whether for immediate crises, Irish Party funds, or cathedral reconstruction plugged the diaspora Irish visibly and economically into Ireland. These newspapers reveal that the diaspora Irish believed their contributions empowered a voice and some role at the centre, a voice increasingly critical of Irish divisions and disharmony. Significant Irish visitors can be located through the pages of Irish Catholic newspapers; these Irishmen observed a community with rights, and relayed some practical understanding of the diaspora Irish back to Dublin, and friendships made on missions threaded all subsequent communication between Ireland and Australasia. It can truly be claimed that the Irish Catholic press operated as the paper glue holding the far-flung Irish together as a functioning, if 'imagined', community.

NOTES

1. D. Fitzpatrick, *Irish Emigration 1801–1921* (Dundalk: Economic and Social History Society of Ireland, 1984), p. 1.
2. See R. B. Walker, *The Newspaper Press in New South Wales, 1803–1920* (Sydney: Sydney University Press, 1976), p. 154.
3. E. Delaney, K. Kenny, and D. M. MacRaild, 'The Irish Diaspora', *Irish Economic and Social History*, 33 (2006), p. 58.
4. See P. Rodechko, *Patrick Ford and his Quest for America: A Case Study of Irish-American Journalism, 1870–1913* (New York: Arno Press, 1976); S. M. Miller (ed), *The Ethnic Press in the United States: An Historical Analysis and Handbook* (New York: Greenwood Press, 1987).
5. See D. H. Akenson, *The Irish Diaspora: A Primer* (Toronto: P. D. Meany Company, 1996), p. 56. His figures cover 1825 through 1920 and although indicating that Australasia only attracted 10 per cent or more of Irish migrants between 1861 and 1880, the total remains significant.
6. See A. O'Day, 'Imagined Irish Communities: Networks of Social Communication of the Irish Diaspora in the United States and Britain in the Late Nineteenth and Early Twentieth Centuries', in E. Delaney and D. M. MacRaild (eds), *Irish Migration, Networks and Ethnic Identities Since 1750* (London and New York: Routledge, 2007), p. 267.

7. Major visits were J.W. Walshe (1881), the Redmond Brothers (1883), John Dillon, Sir Thomas Esmonde and John Deasy (1889), Michel Davitt (1895), Joseph Devlin and John T. Donovan (1906), W.A.K. Redmond, Donovan and Richard Hazelton (1911–12). The Redmond tour has attracted most research interest; see M. Campbell, 'John Redmond and the Irish National League in Australia and New Zealand, 1883', *History*, 86 (2001), pp. 348–62; J. Kildea, 'The Redmond Brothers Tour 1883: A Narrative Account', www.jeffkildea.com (accessed 1 June 2014).
8. S. Gilley, 'The Roman Catholic Church and the Nineteenth Century Irish Diaspora', *Journal of Ecclesiastical History*, 35:2 (1984), p. 189.
9. Ibid., p. 206.
10. See B. Anderson, *Imagined Communities: Reflections on the Origin and Spread of Nationalism* (London: Verso, 1983), p. 9.
11. K. Kenny, 'Diaspora and Comparison: The Global Irish as a Case Study', *Journal of American History*, 90 (2003), pp. 161–62.
12. S. Beckett, 'AHR Conversations on Transnational History', *American Historical Review*, 111 (2006), p. 1459.
13. A. Curthoys and M. Lake (eds), *Connected Worlds: History in Transnational Perspective* (Canberra: ANU E Press, 2005), p. 5.
14. E. Delaney, 'Our Island Story? Towards a Transnational History of Late Modern Ireland', *Irish Historical Studies*, 37:148 (2011), p. 601.
15. Ibid., pp. 612–18.
16. H. McNamara, 'The *New Zealand Tablet* and the Irish Catholic Press Worldwide, 1898–1923', *New Zealand Journal of History*, 37:2 (2003), p. 153.
17. Ibid., p. 167.
18. See R.P. Davis, *Irish Issues in New Zealand Politics 1868–1922* (Dunedin: University of Otago Press, 1974), pp. 35–37, 56–57, 60–61, 64–66, 86–88, 91–92, 96–97, 100–2, 112–14, and 123–24.
19. R. MacGinley, 'The *Age* 1892: An Early Brisbane Catholic Newspaper', *Proceedings of Brisbane Catholic Historical Society*, 10:1 (2005), pp. 10–11.
20. McNamara, 'The *New Zealand Tablet*', p. 157.
21. Sydney *Freeman's Journal*, 14 August 1875.
22. McNamara, 'The *New Zealand Tablet*', pp. 156, 157, 160.
23. See Sydney *Freeman's Journal*, 16 September 1876, 28 July 1883, 12 January 1895, and *Catholic Press*, 10 April 1897, 29 March 1902.
24. See Sydney *Freeman's Journal*, 27 February 1875 on 'Temperance' and 12 January 1895 on 'Irish Politics'.
25. Ibid., 14 March 1896. Croke's letter was dated 5 January 1896.
26. Ibid., 10 April 1897 and 7 January 1899; the latter described the Invercargill Commemoration as 'The Nearest to the South Pole'.
27. Ibid., 3 November 1883; for *New Zealand Tablet* (hereafter *NZ Tablet)* see 20 October 1883.
28. See Sydney *Freeman's Journal*, 4 May 1889 (£658.4 for Parnell Defence Fund), 8 June 1889 (£274.19 sent to *Nation* for National Indemnity Fund).
29. Ibid., 3 November 1888.
30. Ibid., 8 September 1888, using a *Tablet* 'exchange' from 24 August 1888; and the *Southern Cross*, 11 July 1890, for a letter from Bishop O'Reily (of Port Augusta), and discussion at shareholder's meetings in issues 1 November 1889, 8 August 1890 (£800 was owed), 7 August 1891, and 4 August 1893.
31. Sydney *Freeman's Journal*, 16 September 1876.
32. See *Southern Cross*, 13 June 1890, for the *NZ Tablet* item.
33. M. Press, *From Our Broken Toil: South Australian Catholics, 1836–1905* (Adelaide: Archdiocese of Adelaide, 1986), pp. 204–10.
34. *Southern Cross*, 4 October 1901.
35. Ibid., 2 August 1901.

36. Personal Communication between P.R. Wilkinson (Adelaide *Southern Cross* editor, 1960–1977) and Stephanie James, 29 August 2013. See Buenos Aires [hereafter BA] *Southern Cross*, 2 December 1921, for items using 'exchanges' from both the Adelaide *Southern Cross* and the *Catholic Record*.
37. *Southern Cross*, 14 August 1914.
38. National Archives of Australia: D1915, SA29, Pt. 1, 30 May 1918. Koerner's response to a letter wanting greater Sinn Fein coverage outlined his greater reliance on the Dublin *Freeman's Journal*, the *Irish Catholic*, and the Liverpool *Catholic Times* because so many Irish and American papers were banned.
39. Introduced in late September 1914, and adjustable by proclamation rather than parliament, the WPA was not repealed until December 1920.
40. *Southern Cross*, 27 June 1919.
41. See *Southern Cross*, 13 June 1919 (for Koerner's denunciation) and 20 September 1919 for the *Freeman's Journal* correction.
42. *Advocate*, 8 September 1919.
43. Ibid., 1 February 1868. Emphasis is mine.
44. See *Advocate*, 1, 8, 15, 22, and 29 February and 7 and 14 March 1868.
45. On 16 March 1868 Irishman Henry O'Farrell shot at the Duke of Edinburgh at a Sydney picnic. Arrest led to a speedy trial and his execution amidst widespread scenes of anti-Irish hostility.
46. See *Advocate*, 14 March 1868. This editorial describes the paper's duty as seeking 'the antidote to this poison [of biased home news], to set these facts right, and to shatter these fabrics, in order that our people may no longer be deluded as they have been'.
47. *Advocate*, 18 July 1868. The editorial was titled 'Our Extracts'. Emphasis is mine.
48. See *NZ Tablet*, 11 February 1876. Perrin was named as secretary for the *Tablet* Company; the issue of 21 April 1876 describes him as 'Manager'.
49. *Southern Cross*, 5 July 1889. Emphasis is mine.
50. See *Advocate*, 10 May 1902 and 14 June 1902, for use of term *cable crammer* to identify cables where truth was of no consequence. The latter issue pointed to different coverage in the Melbourne *Age* and Sydney *Freeman's Journal* over reasons for the jailing of an Irishman in Dublin.
51. *Advocate*, 9 February 1915.
52. See *Southern Cross*, 16 May 1919, and *Advocate*, 24 June 1920.
53. See *Southern Cross*, 31 October 1919. The comment was in the editorial.
54. Ibid., 2 February 1920.
55. *Advocate*, 27 July 1922.
56. Ibid., 1 March 1919. Emphasis is mine.
57. *Southern Cross*, 9 January 1920.
58. Ibid., 6 February 1920.
59. Ibid., 4 July 1890.
60. See ibid., 9 August 1889 and 9 August 1895; the second correspondent also complained about 'borrowers'.
61. See BA *Southern Cross*, 21 January 1875. Wm. P. Daws Foreign Newspaper Agency, and E.S. Bowring & Co.
62. K. Molloy, 'Victorians, Historians and Irish History: A Reading of the *New Zealand Tablet*, 1873–1903', in B. Patterson (ed), *The Irish in New Zealand: Historical Contexts and Perspectives* (Wellington: Stout Centre for New Zealand Studies, 2002), p. 155.
63. Although the 1900 *Tribune* is not included in this discussion, its emergence as Melbourne's second Irish Catholic paper also fits into this period.
64. P. O'Farrell, *The Irish in Australia* (Sydney: New South Wales University Press, 1988), p. 108.

65. See T. L. Suttor, *Hierarchy and Democracy in Australia 1788–1870: The Formation of Australian Catholicism* (Melbourne: Melbourne University Press, 1965), pp. 147–208 passim; and Walker, *The Newspaper Press*, pp. 150–5.
66. H. McNamara, 'The Sole Organ of the Irish Race in New Zealand? A Social and Cultural History of the *New Zealand Tablet* and its Readers 1898–1923' (MA thesis, University of Auckland, 2002), pp. 19–20.
67. See *Southern Cross*, 7 August 1895 and 2 August 1896, for reports of annual shareholder meetings where senior clerics and the new, journalistically experienced, Archbishop O'Reily challenged founding editor J. V. O'Loghlin.
68. MacGinley, 'The *Age* 1892', p. 19. She notes a comparable process in the United States.
69. *Southern Cross*, 3 June 1927.
70. See *Catholic Press*, 12 February 1942, and *Freeman's Journal*, 19 February 1942.
71. P. O'Farrell, *The Catholic Church and Community: An Australian History* (Sydney: New South Wales University Press, 1985), pp. 117, 119, 121–22.
72. Patrick Naughtin, 'The Melbourne *Advocate*, 1868–1900: Bastion of Irish Nationalism in Colonial Victoria', p. 224, in C. Breathnach and C. Lawless (eds), *Visual, Material and Print Culture in Nineteenth Century Ireland* (Dublin: Four Courts Press, 2010), describes 'loss of episcopal patronage' as a determining factor in the collapse of the *Advocate*'s forbear, the *Victorian*, in 1863.
73. *Advocate*, 7 March 1868.
74. Naughtin, 'The Melbourne *Advocate*', p. 225.
75. *Catholic Record*, 9 November 1895.
76. See *Southern Cross*, 7 August 1896. In contrast to other years when proxy numbers were small, in 1896 more than 100 were registered; 16 shareholders were present.
77. See *Southern Cross*, 2 August 1895. O'Loghlin referred to the 1889 prospectus which stated Catholic interests were to take first place, 'Irish matters next, and colonial politics were not to be omitted'.
78. See Walker, *The Newspaper Press*, p. 159.
79. *Catholic Press*, 13 September 1928.
80. State Records of South Australia, Adelaide, GRS 513/3/31, File 20/1889, *Southern Cross* Printing and Publishing Company. By 1915 the archbishop had inherited a significant bundle from priests' estates, and in 1922 these were vested in the Church Endowment Society which shared an address with the archbishop. As this holding increased, and priests also held shares, lay impact was further reduced.
81. See *Southern Cross*, 28 July 1939, for former editor W. J. Denny's comment about the Sydney correspondent's identity.
82. *Southern Cross*, 8 November 1901.
83. *Catholic Press*, 7 December 1895.
84. Ibid., 30 March 1911. In 'Mr Tighe Ryan Farewelled', a report of a 'send off' prior to Ryan leaving for Europe, he mentioned being 'offered the editorship of the *Press*.' This could either suggest Perrin's removal by clerical directors, or his own initiation of the change. See Sydney *Freeman's Journal*, 20 August 1898, for comment that Perrin was 'greatly missed' in Sydney.
85. Further research is required to clarify Perrin's short-term editorial role in Sydney (December 1895 to July 1897), and the process of his becoming editor in Perth.
86. The offence theory is supported by Perrin's exclusion from the 'Editors of the *Record* Newspaper' file at the Archives, Roman Catholic Archdiocese of Perth.
87. *Advocate*, 21 April 1917.

88. M. McKernan, *Australian Churches at War* (Sydney and Canberra: Catholic Theological Faculty and Australian War Memorial, 1980), p. 91.
89. See *Catholic Record*, 9, 16, and 23 October 1915.
90. *Advocate*, 8 March 1919. By 1924 the clerical managing editor of the *Tribune* (*Advocate* competitor), was forced to relinquish his shares, and Mannix assumed control.
91. *Catholic Record*, 8 February 1923.
92. *Southern Cross*, 25 June 1937.
93. T.P. Boland, *James Duhig* (Brisbane: University of Queensland Press, 1986), pp. 215–16.
94. Ibid.
95. Sydney *Freeman's Journal*, 26 February 1942.
96. See *Dictionary of Irish Latin American Biography*, www.irishargentine.org/dilab_dillonpj.htm (accessed 5 May 2010).
97. *Catholic Press*, 9 November 1895.
98. BA *Southern Cross*, 2 October 1896.
99. Ibid., 21 April 1916.
100. See *Southern Cross*, 5 July 1889.
101. Ibid., 12 January 1900.
102. *Advocate*, 29 January 1898 and 3 August 1901.
103. Ibid., 18 and 25 February 1893, 11 and 25 March 1893, and 1, 8, 15, and 29 April 1893.
104. Ibid., 6, 13, 20, 27 January 1912; 3, 10, 17, 24 February 1912; 2, 9, 16, 23, 30 March 1912; and 6, 13 April 1912.
105. Ibid., 1, 8, 15, 22, 29 May 1886 and 5, 12, 19 June 1886.
106. Ibid.; see 15, 22 May 1886 and 5 June 1886, for examples of letters; 8 and 15 May 1886 for meetings at Cootamundra and Warrnambool; and 19 June 1886 for Melbourne's 'Monster Mass Meeting'.
107. Ibid., 18, 25 February 1893; 4, 11, 18, 25 March 1893; 1, 8, 15, 22, 29 April 1893; and 6, 13, 20, 27 May 1893.
108. Ibid., 4 March 1893.
109. Ibid., 1, 8, 15, 22 April 1893 for mention of 21 Victorian towns, 17 of which held meetings addressed by Rev W. Currie of Melbourne.
110. Ibid., 8 and 15 April 1893. The latter issue provides a three-and-a-half page meeting report.
111. Ibid., 20 April 1912.
112. See Sydney *Freeman's Journal*, 19 April 1884, for Walshe's account: 'For four days he wandered about Melbourne without a friend till he met Joseph Winter, the patriotic Irish editor'.
113. Ibid., 3 May 1884. Walshe was speaking at a gathering welcoming his two sisters to Australia.
114. Ibid., 7 February 1885, for *Tablet* item about organising a monthly letter from J.E. Redmond on 'Irish Affairs'. See C. King, 'Always with a Pen in his Hand . . . Michael Davitt and the Press', in Breathnach and Lawless (eds), *Visual, Material and Print Culture in Nineteenth Century Ireland*, p. 189. See *Southern Cross*, 24 October 1890, for letter from Davitt regarding land holdings to the Dublin *Freeman's Journal*.
115. See *Southern Cross*, 30 September 1898 (for Walsh's letter of 20 August) and 30 January 1899 (for his letter of 10 December).
116. See *Southern Cross*, 19 May 1899. Signatories included John Dillon, John Redmond, T.D. Sullivan, and Alfred Webb, all IPP figures known to Irish Australians.
117. See Sydney *Freeman's Journal*, 24 December 1898, for a report of his success.
118. See ibid., 7, 14, and 21 October 1899; 9 December 1899; 13 and 20 January 1900; and 3 and 10 February 1900.

119. See, for example, *Southern Cross*, 24 June 1898.
120. Ibid., 11 October 1889, 17 January 1890, 27 June 1890, 25 July 1890, and 31 October 1890.
121. Ibid., 1 August 1890.
122. Ibid., 31 October 1890.
123. Ibid., 7 February 1896.
124. Ibid., 14 and 21 February 1896. Some members wanted to challenge the archbishop, but ultimately discretion prevailed.
125. BA *Southern Cross*, 2 October 1896.
126. Ibid., 9 October 1896.
127. Gunson, Tighe Ryan, Fr Cleary, and Perrin were Irishmen, while Denny and E.W. O'Sullivan were Irish Australian.
128. *Catholic Press*, 19 February 1898.
129. Sydney *Freeman's Journal*, 16 July 1898.
130. See *Southern Cross*, 3 June and 5 August 1898, and Sydney *Freeman's Journal*, 27 August 1898.
131. See Sydney *Freeman's Journal*, 19 February 1898, for first in a series 'The Story of Ninety Eight'.
132. Ibid., 12 February 1898; *Catholic Press*, 14 May 1898; and *Southern Cross*, 3 June 1898.
133. See Sydney *Freeman's Journal*, 27 August 1898, for report of Waimate 'Demonstration', and *NZ Tablet*, 20 October 1898, for accounts of events at Queenstown and Opitiki.
134. See *Southern Cross*, 24 June 1898.
135. See *Advertiser*, 18 June 1898, for the critical letter; O'Reily's reply appeared on 21 June 1898.
136. *Southern Cross*, 27 May 1898.
137. Ibid., 6 January 1899.
138. *Advocate*, 28 May 1898.
139. See O'Farrell, *The Irish in Australia*, pp. 239–40.
140. Ibid., pp. 181–84, 235–36.
141. See McKernan, *Australian Churches at War*, p. 18, for figures of around 800 of Australia's priests as Irish-born in 1914.
142. BA *Southern Cross*, 5 and 12 May 1916.
143. See *Advocate*, 24 September 1916, and *Southern Cross* of 22 September 1916. Melbourne's appeal raised £8,000 while Adelaide's total was £1035. See Boland, *Duhig*, p. 135.
144. BA *Southern Cross*, 3 January 1919.
145. See McNamara, 'The Sole Organ', p. 62.
146. See *Advocate*, 1 and 22 December 1917.
147. *Advocate*, 9 June 1921. The writer was in Listowel, Kerry, and her sister was in Victoria.
148. See *Southern Cross*, 17 September 1920.
149. Ibid., 19 March 1920.
150. See *Advocate*, 10, 17, and 24 June 1920 and 1 July 1920.
151. In 1920 at least 12 Australian prelates visited Ireland en route to or from Rome. See *Southern Cross*, 7 May 1920 (Hobart's Bishop Barry), 24 September 1920 (Brisbane's Archbishop Duhig), and 10 December 1920 (Sydney's Archbishop Kelly).
152. *Southern Cross*, 25 February 1921.
153. Ibid., 28 July 1939.
154. The INA, a radical organisation which increasingly viewed Ireland's solution as beyond the British Empire, was founded in Adelaide in August 1918, while the Irish Pipers were formed during 1910.

155. *Southern Cross*, 26 October 1924. Koerner described observing the participation of three Irishmen in adjacent parishes: Duffy, a leader in Ireland's '48 rebellion and subsequently a minister, premier, and Speaker in Victoria's parliament; O'Grady, who held ministerial positions in Victoria; and Lalor, who was a key participant in the Eureka rebellion.
156. *Southern Cross*, 13 November 1936.
157. M. P. Jageurs to John Dillon, 21 October 1924, Letter, Trinity College Dublin, MS6849/2966, Dillon Papers. Jageurs, a long-term IPP supporter and pro–Free State, refers to the local Irish Catholic press as 'completely muzzled'.
158. *Advocate*, 4 March 1893. This was from a correspondent congratulating the paper on its first 25 years.
159. Sydney *Freeman's Journal*, 27 June 1850.
160. See Sydney *Freeman's Journal*, 1 January 1870, 5 January 1884, 5 January 1895 (adding 'The Oldest Established Weekly Newspaper in the Australian Colonies), and 6 January 1900.
161. *Freeman's Journal*, 8 February 1912.
162. *Freeman's Journal*, 29 March 1923.
163. See *Advocate*, 1 February 1868 and 3 July 1869.
164. See *NZ Tablet*, 4 January 1900. The change involved noting the length of *Tablet* publication as well as issue details in larger print.
165. See *NZ Tablet*, 4 January 1906, 29 March 1907, and 5 April 1907. See McNamara, 'The Sole Organ', p. 47, for Bishop Cleary's 1917 campaign to have this removed when he opposed his successor's position on Ireland.
166. See *Catholic Record*, 7 August 1874 and 19 July 1888.
167. See BA *Southern Cross*, 14 January 1875 and 21 April 1916.
168. See *Southern Cross*, 5 July 1889, 9 August 1889.
169. See *Catholic Press*, 26 September 1896, 7 January 1899, 13 January 1900, and 6 July 1901.
170. See *Southern Cros s*, 16 August 1899, for Irish Cardinal Logue's comments from the Dublin *Freeman's Journal*, titled here 'A Good Irishman Is a Good Catholic'.

5 'In Harmony'
A Comparative View of Female Orangeism, 1887–2000

Patrick Coleman

> The Orange cause is booming strong
> Since Ladies' joined the Order, O!
> They gain large numbers all along
> From centre to the border, O!
> Long live the lasses, O!
> Long live the lasses, O!
> Our English girls shine bright as pearls,
> Arrayed in Blue and Orange, O![1]

The welcoming of the ladies' lodges to the Orange cause as announced in this stirring song from England belies the difficulties that Orangewomen endured to join in with their fellow Orangemen. This was one of only a handful of Orange songs such as 'The Orange Grand Mistress',[2] 'The Orange Maid of Sligo', and 'The Young Orange Bride' that specifically referred to Orangewomen.[3] They celebrated the attributes of Orangewomen and 'The Orange Grand Mistress' even suggested a rebuttal to any men who suggested they be excluded: '[W]hy should those Orange-men, our sex one and all, Shut out from their secrets, when Mary was founder?'[4] The ladies' lodges in their various forms throughout the global Orange world helped to bring a softer side to the turbulent and sometimes violent public face of Orangeism.

Orangeism, with its pro-monarchist, pro-Protestant ideals, coupled with Masonic-style rituals and structure, has since its founding in Ireland in 1795 been exported to the farthest reaches of the British World. Newspapers throughout the nineteenth and early twentieth centuries were filled with stereotypes of mostly Northern Irish Protestant men marching, fighting, and verbally assaulting their predominantly Irish Catholic coreligionists.[5] This media creation, which is equally unjustified and self-inflicted, has obscured and often marginalised the role of women in Orangeism. The Association of Loyal Orangewomen of Ireland (ALOI) was founded in Dublin in 1887 and just one year later the first ladies' Orange Lodge was formed in Wellington, New Zealand. Other Orange jurisdictions in Australia, England, Canada, Scotland, and the United States had already formed associations, revived dormant ones, or initiated new ladies' lodges. Initially the 'Ladies' purpose was seen (often derisively by their male counterparts) as one of tea and scone makers, but eventually their role changed.

To assist in identifying the factors that influenced and helped change the role of Orangewomen in the Orange Order, comparisons are made between the New Zealand experience and other Orange jurisdictions in Britain, North America, and Australia. Elaine McFarland and Graham Walker have both pointed to the important role of women in Orangeism in Scotland but did not utilise archival material.[6] Research undertaken by D.A.J. MacPherson and Donald MacRaild, who both benefitted from access to Orange archival material, has produced insights into the workings of female Orangeism in the north of England while MacPherson has undertaken the same for Scotland.[7] MacPherson, in particular, has focused on the working-class nature of Scottish female Orangeism with its Irish Protestant roots and involvement in wider public activism. He further articulates the Scottish Orangewomen's support for other members in the migration process using the phrase 'diaspora consciousness'.[8] The *Belfast Weekly News* is emphasised as a conduit for this process of shared 'diasporic identity' across the Orange diaspora.[9] MacRaild called the *Belfast Weekly News* a 'kind of chatroom' and painted a picture of Orangemen across the world reading it and joining in a kind of transnational network.[10] Both MacPherson and MacRaild posit an Orange World that was globally linked.

This chapter examines the influence of female Orangeism not only across borders but also regionally and locally within their communities scattered across the world. Yet in acknowledging differences between nations, it also adopts a comparative framework to explore two central questions: Did women look to Ireland or the Orange diaspora for the origins and subsequent growth of their ladies' lodges? Did uniformity or diversity characterise their ritual instruction and practice? To address these questions in a transnational and comparative context, this chapter draws on, where available, annual proceedings, minute books, and ritual and rule books from across the Orange World.[11] Contemporary newspaper accounts are also used to highlight activities and events that are in the public sphere. The source material that originates from Orange archives or Orange members is crucial to developing a fuller understanding of female Orangeism. It often provides information that is not covered in newspapers such as insights into ritual and practice. Nevertheless, these Orange sources should be read with caution given their biased nature. Newspaper sources likewise need to be used carefully as the editorial bias often swung from being favourable to being hostile depending on the editor or the newspaper. They are, however, helpful in further contextualising the female Orange world.

ORIGINS AND GROWTH: INFLUENCES FROM IRELAND OR THE ORANGE DIASPORA?

Ireland

The masculine form of Orangeism unquestionably originated in Ireland and has continued to thrive there over the centuries despite a significant numerical drop in the present day. Therefore, it is natural that Ireland, particularly Northern Ireland, is seen as the homeland of Orangeism. This is also the case with Orangewomen as Ireland provided the first ladies' lodges with eight being active in Dublin in 1801.[12] Yet their beginnings were far from smooth. Christi McCallum has argued that '"ladies" lodges were not long-lived in the nineteenth century; they were opened and active for a few years before dying out.'[13] She argues that Orangewomen were still active in events like parades, but this still does not answer why these lodges became defunct. Her explanation for the failure of these early lodges points to government and nationalist opposition to Orangeism.[14] Unfortunately, very little in the way of records survive. The only extant warrant is No. 8 Ladies' Orange Lodge from Bray, which was very close to the other Dublin-based female lodges.[15] The lack of a documentary record speaks volumes about the true place of Irish Orangewomen. It may well have been a lack of support and a lack of focus that meant these early lodges failed to survive.

The impetus for the nineteenth-century push for women to become more involved in Orangeism can be linked to women's participation in other movements worldwide. The temperance movement, for instance, figured prominently in the lives of Protestant women who were likely recruits for ladies' lodges. Many temperance societies that had been founded in England or the United States around the 1830s spread rapidly, particularly across the English-speaking world. With names like the Band of Hope, Rechabites, and Sons and Daughters of Temperance, they flourished and often worked in tandem with Protestant churches such as the Baptists, Methodists, and Presbyterians.[16] Even more influential was a later temperance movement, the Women's Christian Temperance Union (WCTU). Ellen Carol DuBois has emphasised the role of the World's WCTU that grew out of the American WCTU founded in 1874. This movement engaged with more than temperance as it moved swiftly into the realm of women's suffrage. Their message was spread by American organisers to countries such as Australia and New Zealand in the mid-1880s.[17] Across the English-speaking world women in the nineteenth and early twentieth centuries increased their presence in the public sphere. From clubs, philanthropic societies, and guilds, women's involvement in wider society became more pronounced. Some of these groups were exclusively religious such as missionary societies or fraternities, but others had a civic function of improving society through helping the needy such as orphans, 'fallen women', or prisoners.[18]

Against this backdrop of burgeoning female activism, female Orangeism in Ireland tried to revive itself in 1887 with an Orange Women's Association that held strident unionist views. It was founded by Lady Helena Saunderson and sanctioned by the Grand Lodge of Ireland, but within a short time was inactive.[19] A lull in the Home Rule debate and the advent of the South African War (1899–1902) are suggested as possible explanations for the ALOI collapsing. That other female unionist bodies, including the Women's Unionist Association (WUA), also collapsed does give some credence to this view.[20] Maybe it was the lack of a crisis or other external events that precipitated the collapse of the ALOI.

Pope Pius X's decree on mixed marriages, *Ne Temere*, helped spur the revival of female Orange lodges in Ireland from the early twentieth century.[21] In particular, the McCann case caused an uproar in the Protestant community.[22] This was the case concerning the Catholic Alexander McCann and his Presbyterian wife Agnes. They were married in 1908 and later had two children. In 1911 the local priest wanted them to validate the marriage in the Catholic Church. Agnes refused so Alexander left her and took the children with him. At the same time, Mary Elizabeth Johnstone, a former member of the defunct ALOI, wanted to revive her former Orange lodge to dissuade young Protestants from marrying Catholics.[23] The McCann case prompted her request to the Grand Lodge of Ireland for consent to revive her lodge.[24] Although the ALOI was reborn in Dublin in February 1912, the first warrant No. 1 went to Sandy Row in Belfast. The granting of the warrant to Belfast is significant, because although there were ladies' lodges in Dublin (the base of the ALOI), this changed with the revived organisation. Now Belfast became the centre of female Orangeism.

The year 1919 saw the existence of 10 female Orange lodges in Belfast compared to only three in Dublin.[25] The growth of the ALOI did not gain momentum until after 1921, the year when partition divided the north from the south of Ireland. A stimulus to this growth was the increase in women's rights, notably through the suffrage movement. The creation of the state of Northern Ireland bolstered growth and the formation of Orange lodges provided networks and unified Irish Protestants in the early years of the new state. As can be seen in Figure 5.1, numbers continued to climb steadily including over the war period. After this there was a sharp rise in numbers from 6,206 in 1946 to a peak at 8,448 in 1951. This high point of the AOLI has been described by McCallum as being the result of a number of external political factors. A Labour government taking power in the United Kingdom in 1945 provoked fears among the more conservative members that this would continue the decline of the British Empire. The declaration of an Irish Republic in 1948 also stimulated fears of a takeover from the south. This fear was felt by both Orange and Unionist members and supporters.[26] Just as a crisis resulted in a revived ALOI, so did a crisis bolster membership. After the mid-twentieth century, membership fell quite dramatically to 2,544 in 2013.[27] Eric Kaufmann has provided insightful reasons for the decline of Orange membership, both male and female. He concludes that 'the most important determinants of membership are anchored in less sexy, slowly changing socioeconomic trends related to geographic mobility and

114 *Patrick Coleman*

Figure 5.1 ALOI membership in Ireland, 1919–67
Source: C. McCallum, *Orangewomen Show Their True Colors* (Southern Illinois: University of Carbondale, 2011), p. 327.

changing cultural practices'.[28] Close-knit communities, which previously had been fairly static in their movement, became more mobile as road networks were expanded. The resulting mobility, according to Kaufmann, was a factor in reducing stable Orange membership.

England

The uneven nature of female Orangeism in Ireland may well have led to other Orange jurisdictions looking to the Orange diaspora rather than to Ireland for inspiration. While Orangewomen in Ireland may lay claim to having the first ladies' lodges, England had a greater degree of stability. This was not apparent at first as there is little evidence for ladies' lodges in England before 1836. A year earlier, the Orange Order was dissolved as a result of a House of Commons Select Committee Enquiry into the Orange Order's alleged involvement in a plot to put the Duke of Cumberland on the British throne. English female Orangeism grew out of this uncertain phase of Orangeism. James Worral Sylvester (1794–1857), an Orangeman who did not want to see the movement disintegrate, formed the Grand Protestant Confederation in response to the dissolution. He managed to gather the remnants of Orange lodges and formed loose links with other Orange societies. By 1844 the Confederation had become the Grand Protestant Association of Loyal Orangemen (GPALO). This rather gender exclusive name did not seem to deter the formation of ladies' lodges. The reports of the GPALO in 1850 record 24 female lodges although No. 8 and 9 were dormant. Most were in Sylvester's heartland of Lancashire, but four were in

Wales, an area not normally seen as a powerbase of Orangeism. These early female lodges met in hotels or inns.[29] The Loyal Orange Institution, which laid claim to being the original Orange body in England, merged in 1876 with the GPALO to become the Loyal Orange Institution of England.

The GPALO had numerical superiority after 1836 and this included the number of female lodges. The earliest list of lodges for the GPALO from 1850 show they had 269 lodges over a wider region including Scotland.[30] Early lodge lists for the Loyal Orange Institution from 1854, by contrast, show they had 57 lodges with 85 per cent of membership based in Liverpool.[31] However, by the time the two organisations amalgamated in 1876 the Institution had 313 lodges and the GPALO 320 lodges.[32] Amalgamation seemed to have stunted the growth of the ladies' lodges as the earlier GPALO had large numbers of female lodges and membership. As noted earlier, the GPALO had 24 female lodges in 1850, and even in 1870 there was an annual report that noted 600 members belonged to the Female Protestant Association of Loyal Orangewomen, Rossendale, in Lancaster.[33] The growth of the lodges from the 1880s through to the First World War coincides with the Home Rule debates as well as the suffragette movement and the general changes in society that saw women more involved in voluntary organisations. Figure 5.2 demonstrates this steady growth. In 1910 there were 77 female lodges, and while there was a dip during the First World War, by 1938 female lodges had peaked at 91 lodges before continuing to fall. Peter Day has suggested a range of reasons for this decline for both men's and women's lodges including slum clearances and rebuilding in Merseyside in the 1950s, falling church attendance, secularisation in society,

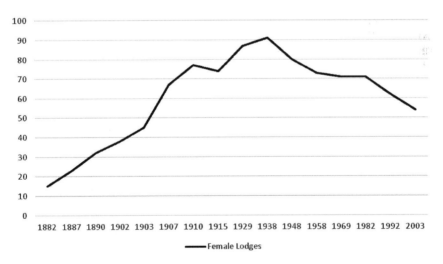

Figure 5.2 Orange female lodge numbers in England, 1882–2003

Source: Grand Orange Lodge of England Reports, 1882–2003.

and a lack of interest among young people.³⁴ MacPherson has reiterated similar reasons and, as with Day, used interviews with Orange members to gauge their views on membership decline.³⁵

Scotland

With the spread of female Orangeism, transnational and regional links developed and Scotland, the United States, and Canada provide good case studies of the establishment of female Orangeism. MacPherson has noted that there were female lodges in Scotland at least as early as the 1870s. In particular he cites the opening of lodges in Glasgow in 1872 with assistance from an English female lodge in Birkenhead called the 'Star of Progress'.³⁶ Unfortunately no records seem to have survived, but it can be established that they were under the jurisdiction of the Loyal Orange Institution of Great Britain (LOIGB) as LLOL No. 7 and 8 were both in Glasgow.³⁷ There was great hope for these lodges as in 1872 the *Belfast Weekly News* reported that 'the members of the lodge [are] promising to help forward and spread the Order in all ways possible.'³⁸ Within a short time they shut down. MacPherson is unsure what happened to these lodges. Scottish Orange archivist David Bryce proposed an explanation tied to the amalgamation of 79 lodges from the Provincial Grand Lodge of the LOIGB with the Scottish and English Grand Lodges. As a consequence, these two ladies' lodges were lost.³⁹ The reasons for the closure, however, were not given. From this point on both Grand Lodges looked after the affairs of their own areas and there were no more cross-border lodges.

MacPherson has ably recounted the various failed attempts made by the Grand Lodge of Scotland to revive female lodges, including recognition of their success in England. Nevertheless, successive motions to form female lodges were voted down. Into the mix came some determined women. In July 1908 Dorothy Wilson and her daughter Harriet made the journey south to Newcastle, England, to become initiated into Orangeism. On their return to Scotland they formed a ladies' auxiliary in Glasgow; after some pressure the Grand Lodge relented, and the first revived Scottish ladies' lodge was reborn in November 1909.⁴⁰ Harriet Wilson, later Harriet Thomson, became the first Worthy Mistress.⁴¹ This first lodge opened on 17 November 1909 and appropriately called itself Scotland's First Ladies Loyal Orange Lodge 1.⁴² Research into membership has shown that it was drawn mostly from either Irish Protestant migrants or their descendants.⁴³

Once this revived version of ladies' lodges took hold, they spread across Scotland. According to Figure 5.3, the greatest growth began in the 1920s. Some historians explain this growth as a result of women's interest in Orange ladies' lodges being influenced by their previous experience in the Primrose League.⁴⁴ Another possible explanation has been increased opportunities in employment coupled with the public activism by women in society. Instances of this activism include the suffragette movement and the political issues of Home Rule leading up to the First World War as well as

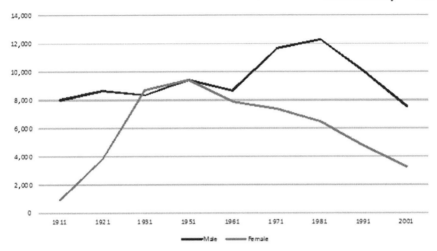

Figure 5.3 Male and female Orange membership in Scotland, 1911–2001
Source: E. Kaufmann, *Orange Order Membership Data, with a Focus on Ireland, Canada and Scotland, 1852–2002* (Colchester: UK Data Archive, 2004), SN: 4916.

the anti-Catholic politics that were prevalent in 1920s Scotland.[45] This anti-Catholic sentiment was embodied in the general assembly of the Church of Scotland in 1923 supporting a report recommending curbing Irish immigration and deporting those who needed poor relief.[46] By 1931 there were just under 9,000 female Orange members, which exceeded the men by several hundred. This growth continued up until 1951 after which time numbers continued to fall at a faster rate than the men's did. Kaufmann has suggested that changing gender roles and falling church membership by Scottish Protestants, coupled with the rise of Orange Men's social clubs, precipitated the dramatic fall in Orangewomen's membership while the men sustained a rise that lasted until the 1980s.[47] Critically, however, in both their earlier and later attempts to establish female Orange lodges in Scotland, women looked to England rather than Ireland for their inspiration and support. Despite being the same nation state, such influences can be conceived as transnational given a border crossing. They can also be perceived as regional links as members could move quite freely between countries.

United States

As with female Orange lodges in Scotland, the United States benefitted from the 'Star of Progress' female lodge in Birkenhead, England. Again, there do not appear to be extant lodge records, except references in annual proceedings and newspaper accounts. There is no doubt that this was a pioneering lodge as it helped to set up other female lodges regionally in the case of Scotland and gave 'transnational advice' to the Americans. The *Belfast Weekly*

News reported on a communication that Brother Collinson discussed in 'his application to the Grand Lodge to establish the Female Order in New York, which had been kindly granted, and he was now in communication with officers of the city for the purpose of arrangements'.[48] This was the Grand Lodge of the Loyal Orange Institution (GLLOI) of Great Britain. This was then expanded on by the GLLOI of Great Britain meeting on 2 July 1873 which decided

> [t]hat in reply to the MWGM of New York, in reference to the Female Order, he be respectfully informed that *information only* has been communicated to Bro Schofield of New York as to the working of Female Lodges in England, and this Grand Lodge being desirous of working fraternally with the Grand Lodge of New York beg to assure Bro Bond, the MWGM, that it will not give authority to anyone to interfere in any way whatever with the jurisdiction of the Supreme Grand Lodge of New York.[49]

The response indicates that while the English were happy to help they were very careful not to be seen as encroaching on another jurisdiction. It also suggests that the American Orange fraternity had close contact with their English counterparts. It was England, not Ireland, which was the point of contact because of the lack of ladies' lodges operating in Ireland at this time.

In August 1876, three years after contact with the Birkenhead lodge, ladies' Orange lodges were instituted in the city of Philadelphia, Pennsylvania. This date is also significant in that only a month earlier in the same city, a group of women from the National Woman Suffrage Association had interrupted centennial celebrations to present their own Women's Declaration of Rights.[50] It was within this female activist climate that Margaret Thompson (1839–1896) founded the Loyal Orange Ladies' Institution of the United States, having gathered 11 women and four men from among her friends to establish the lodge. This lodge took the name Daughters of Zion, LOLI No. 1. At the first meeting, Thompson became not only the Worthy Mistress but also the Supreme Grand Mistress.[51] Why, however, did Philadelphia manage to establish a ladies' lodge before New York, given the earlier overtures from New York towards the English Grand Lodge? A possible explanation may lie in the stronger Irish Protestant community in Philadelphia. Cecil J. Houston and William J. Smyth have argued that Pennsylvania, with Philadelphia and Pittsburgh 'made up the core of Orange America.'[52] This could then explain the natural rise of ladies' lodges as there was a membership base in these two cities to facilitate them. Membership was drawn mostly from the Irish and the Scottish Protestant community. Sometimes they were Americans who married into this community.[53]

The ladies' lodges in the United States did experience some growth as seen in Figure 5.4 with 127 lodges in 1927, which was the peak of American Orange ladies' lodges growth, but numbers continued to freefall to just

Figure 5.4 Orange ladies' lodge numbers in the United States, 1911–2008

Source: Loyal Orange Institution of the United States of America Official Directory (United States: The Supreme Grand Lodge of the United States, 1911–2008).

10 lodges by 2008.[54] This fall, which was earlier than all the other parts of the world, was mostly due to internal issues rather than to external ones. There were tensions from the turn of the twentieth century with two lodges in Pennsylvania and in Ohio, both claiming Supreme Grand Lodge status. The 1920s saw the split in American Orangeism widen as the Pennsylvanian group renamed itself 'The International Orange Association' in 1926. Orange historian Samuel Ernest Long insightfully noted that '[o]ne of the incontrovertible facts of Orange history is that the injuries of this division made the institution in America incapable of recovering its original vitality'.[55] This division meant that some lodges split and other became dormant. Although the two branches of American Orangeism joined in 1930 the damage had been done.

Canada

In Canada the present-day Ladies' Orange Benevolent Association (LOBA) acknowledges the indefatigable Mary Cullum (1859–1934) as its founder. She was the daughter of County Longford Irishman Crofton David Cullum.[56] She sent out a letter to LOL 286 Hamilton, Ontario, to request the presence of lodge members' wives and daughters to attend a meeting on 12 December 1888.[57] Until they gained approval from the Grand Lodge they decided to not use the word *Orange* and so were initially called the 'Ladies' Protestant Association'.[58] They petitioned all the primary, district, county, and provincial lodges that all approved except for the Grand Lodge. A special delegation met and Mary Cullum made a compelling argument for their application. This was ratified in 1891 and the LOBA was born. The push for female lodges by Cullum mirrors a similar situation with the Scottish Orangewomen who wanted to revive their lodges. It also demonstrates a shift in gender roles whereby women's voices were being heard and their opinions mattered.

While the LOBA was busy establishing itself, the United States LOLI made a foray into Toronto, Canada, in 1890 and set up the Queen Victoria Ladies' Loyal Orange Lodge No. 26. Its charter was issued from Boston, Massachusetts.[59] This cross-border activity echoes the English–Scottish situation. The American Orangemen even appointed a Bro F.H. Wright in London, Ontario, as organiser for the Loyal Orange Ladies' Institution of the United States in the Dominion of Canada. However, once it learned about the LOBA, the United States Supreme Grand Lodge discontinued its efforts. The Supreme Grand Lodge of the Loyal Orange Ladies' Institution met in Boston, Massachusetts, in August 1890 in response to communication from Brother R. Newman of Canada, representing the LOBA, and decided that the two U.S. Lodges chartered and existing in Canada would be permitted to amalgamate with the Canadian Association.[60] This is a good instance of national interests taking precedence over any transnational interests as any hint of competition was quickly extinguished.

The rapid progress of the LOBA drew comment from as far away as Sydney, Australia. Writing in the Sydney-based *Watchman* in 1924, a 'Scottish brother' claimed that the LOBA's growth was attributed to the combined efforts of Mary Cullum and 'Mrs John Tulk'. Canada now had more than 500 female lodges with 15,000 members who were 'a magnificent force,

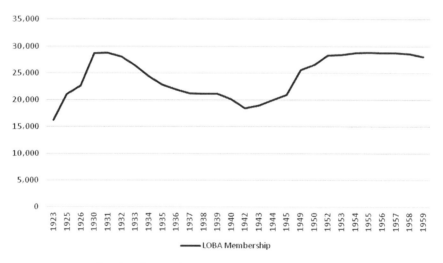

Figure 5.5 Membership figures for LOBA, Canada, 1923–59

Source: Eric Kaufmann, *Orange Order Membership, with a Focus on Ireland, Canada and Scotland, 1852–2002* (Colchester: UK Data Archive, 2004), SN: 4916.

whose purpose, like that of their brethren, is the defence of the Protestant religion and the preservation of British ideals in the Dominion.'[61] Often members of the Orange Order are accused of exaggerating figures, but in 1923 there were 16,172 members in the LOBA. By 1925 it had reached 21,031.[62] The *Watchman*, although it was sympathetic to the Orange cause, was fairly accurate in this instance.

As with other Orange Ladies' lodges, some of the reasons for the growth reflected changes in society with women taking a prominent role in civic and religious organisations. The ethnic make-up of the LOBA would have been reflected in many members being the wives and daughters of male members. Given that the early impetus for Canadian Orangeism came from Irish Protestants and then to a lesser degree from English and Scottish migrants, the women were also most likely Irish-born or of Irish descent.[63] Further research still needs to be undertaken to confirm this assumption. The LOBA grew rapidly after the First World War but, as can be seen in Figure 5.5, fell during the period of the Great Depression to reach a low of 18,412 in 1942. After this period, membership continued to rise and peaked in 1955 at 28,851 before levelling off.[64] This drop in numbers by both Canadian Orangemen and Orangewomen does seem to mirror the 'Putnam effect.' This is the collapse of 'social capital' associated with clubs and fraternities in the United States since the 1960s.[65] The LOBA followed their male counterparts in membership increases and decreases, which suggests close family links as where the men went the women were there as well.[66]

New Zealand

Like Canada, New Zealand established male Orange lodges early. The first was created in 1843, but it was not until 1888 that the first ladies' lodge was formed.[67] At this time there were two Grand Lodges: one for the North Island and one for the Middle Island (South Island). The North Island formed the first ladies' lodge in Wellington, called Orange Lily No. 1, and the newspapers cheerily reported that 'all the officers are women, and there is no doubt that they will perform their various duties ably, and this Lodge will prove a useful auxiliary to the Order.'[68] The president of the newly formed lodge was Mary Linnell.[69] She remained president for some years and was noted as someone 'who has during a very long residence in Wellington always taken an active interest in the Orange cause.'[70] Just like their Canadian, Scottish, and American sisters, the presence of a founding individual or small group of Orangewomen helped to maintain early stability.

It is notable, however, that the ladies' lodges appear as an 'auxiliary' to their male counterparts, and this was reflected in these lodges being attached to the men's lodges. It took some time before the women in the New Zealand lodges were able to exert their independence. While 1923 saw the advent of the Ladies' Conference, ultimate control was still in the hands of the all-male Grand Executive.[71] The New Zealand Orangewomen had their own conference and could run their own affairs fairly independently except

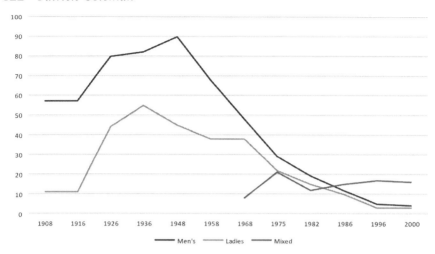

Figure 5.6 Male and female Orange lodge numbers in New Zealand, 1908–2000
Source: Grand Lodge of New Zealand Annual Reports, 1908–2000.

for the fact that they had no real power overall. It took until 1982, when the Grand Lodge became mixed, for men to start nominating women to join the Grand Lodge.[72] Finally women could send delegates, and in 2000, in a first for the Orange World, the first grand master of New Zealand was a woman from Christchurch.[73] The change in structure for New Zealand Orangeism reflected not just transformations in society but also quite simply a fall in numbers. Fewer members meant modifications had to be made or their organisation would die.

Prior to the formation of New Zealand ladies' lodges, temperance missionary Mary Clement Leavitt of the WCTU of America arrived in 1885 and helped to initiate the start of this very influential women's movement. Given that membership was drawn from the same churches that the Orangewomen went to it is not surprising that advocacy for a ladies' Orange lodge came about. Organisations such as the WCTU helped women gain more confidence, but the inspiration for ladies' lodges in New Zealand came from abroad. Earlier that same year the Christchurch Orangemen had a special meeting, which put forward the motion of forming ladies' lodges. Again, it was not to Ireland that the brethren looked for inspiration, but to the United States. A past grand master of the Middle Island, Irish-born J. W. Anderson, emphasised 'the success these Lodges had achieved in the United States of America, and he had no doubt that, properly introduced, they would be a power for good in the Middle Island.'[74] This nod to the Orange diaspora may well have been borne out of reports of the success of the Americans who were also targeting a similar demographic of diasporic Protestant women across denominations and social class rather than the elite-orientated Irish in Dublin. Also the AOLI had only begun in 1887 and therefore was not the model to aspire to whereas the Americans had been in existence for about a decade and had large numbers of lodges.

Despite the rhetoric and local efforts to begin opening ladies' lodges in New Zealand, it took some time to gather any sustainable numbers. As membership data is not available, lodge numbers are the next best indicator of growth. Interestingly, the time period of most growth after 1916, as noted in Figure 5.6, was also the time that New Zealand Orangewomen called for greater representation within New Zealand Orangeism. The peak of lodge growth came early with 55 lodges in 1936 before numbers fell dramatically to only three lodges by 2000.

Australia

In a nod to the New Zealand situation, Orange male lodges were established early in Australia with women's lodges lagging behind. Female lodges in Australia had a rather complex beginning as each state had its own Grand Lodge and therefore the spread of Orangeism throughout the country was different. The same rise of the temperance movement across the English-speaking world also had an impact on Australia. The American WCTU advocates did the Australasian tour so the various Australian states heard the same message. Queensland was an early starter for ladies' lodges as Protestant women in the state lobbied for some years to open a women's lodge. Permission was finally granted in 1889. The first female lodge was opened in August 1890 at Gympie, a gold mining town north of Brisbane, 'with great promise of usefulness.' The lodge in Gympie did not last long, and by 1906 Orange Lily No. 2 Brisbane lodge changed its number to No. 1 under a new warrant.[75] By 1912 the number of ladies' lodge had increased to 18 and climbed to about 40 by 1932.[76]

New South Wales echoed the Queensland situation with Protestant women clamouring for their own ladies' lodge. Eric Turner has recounted various attempts in 1874 and 1877 by individual women to start lodges, but their efforts were rebuffed by the Grand Lodge.[77] In October 1894 the Grand Lodge of New South Wales finally succumbed to pressure and allowed ladies' lodges.[78] The argument was an intriguing one, with one member claiming,

> As the maintenance of civil and religious liberty at the present day did not so much depend upon physical force for its existence as upon moral and intellectual power, so did the qualification for membership become varied; and instead of Orangemen now being exclusively males, it was found permissible to admit Ladies' to the privilege and obligations of the order.[79]

This switch from a clearly masculine view of Orangeism to a more refined, almost feminine one certainly reflects a change in society. The first female lodge founded in Sydney in December 1894 was called Daughters of Derry Loyal Orange Lodge No 301. Comparison was also made with New Brunswick, Nova Scotia, Canada, and other parts of North America as good role models for successful ladies' lodges. As was the case in New Zealand, Ireland was never mentioned.[80] Once again it was the Orange diaspora that inspired and provided a ready model for the Australian Orangewomen to emulate. While the Grand Lodge was deciding whether to start a ladies' lodge, male membership was on a downturn, especially between 1892 and 1895, so the ladies' lodges provided a boost to overall membership. The newly formed women's lodges went from strength to strength and by 1911 had 104 lodges in New South Wales.[81]

The other Australian states followed in quick succession with Tasmania having its first women's lodge opened in January 1901 in a small town called Zeehan under the name Federal LOL, No 1, Tasmania.[82] Richard Davis in his excellent study of Tasmanian Orangeism briefly noted the early stages of ladies' lodges with their focus on 'boiling the kettle' to playing a prominent role in the social life of the lodges.[83] Their growth was never spectacular and Orangeism in Tasmania was defunct by 1967.[84]

A few months later South Australia opened its first female lodge in yet another small town, Auburn.[85] By 1903 there were five female Lodges with numbers increasing to a peak in about 1914 with more than 40 lodges and about 2,000 members.[86] However, by 1991 only the Grand Lodge and a single private Lodge remained.[87] David Fitzpatrick, having access to a rich vein of Orange archival sources, noted that South Australian Orangeism never matched the growth of New South Wales or Victoria. He did note that the Depression and two world wars took their toll, but maybe poor growth was due to a lack of Irish-born residents in the region. South Australia never had large numbers of Irish-born Protestants and therefore membership came from elsewhere, but not in any significant amounts.[88] This situation may have accounted for Orangeism, either male or female, never taking a firm hold. Other parts of Australia, notably New South Wales and Victoria, had large influxes of Irish, both Catholic and Protestant. In Victoria in 1871 one in four (100,468) were Irish-born.[89] The Orange Order in that state relied heavily on Irish Protestants for membership.[90] In 1846 New South Wales had almost as many Irish-born (47,547) as English-born (58,011). Just like Victoria, New South Wales continued until the early twentieth century to have large numbers of Irish-born migrants who also initiated and filled the membership of the Orange Order in that state.[91]

Two years later the first ladies' lodge was opened in the mining town of Coolgardie in Western Australia.[92] The state of Victoria also opened its first ladies' lodge in the same year. It experienced a high success rate with 36 female lodges opening the first year.[93] Tas Vertigan's history of Victorian Orangeism only devoted a page and a half to Orangewomen and proclaimed that their admission into Orangeism 'marked the beginning of a new era for Orangeism in Victoria' by which he meant their leadership qualities, including wider community work.[94] The Australian experience highlights the initial transnational

Figure 5.7 Members of the ladies' and junior lodges, Twelfth of July Parade, Christchurch, circa 1950s

Source: Reproduced with the permission of Colin Buist, Christchurch.

inspiration for ladies' lodges as these lodges subsequently opened up across all the Australian states. They also reveal the broad patterns of growth that occurred in migrant destinations such as Canada as areas of high Irish Protestant migration tended to reflect initial growth in Orange membership.

RITUAL: UNIFORMITY OR DIVERSITY?

The Orange parade, sometimes referred to as a ritual parade, was the main feature of Orangeism that had a public face. The ritual parade has also featured in a number of studies mainly focusing on Ireland, but excluding consideration of Orangewomen.[95] Part of the reason is that the time period analysed generally predates active female Orangeism. Additionally, until 1990 the Grand Orange Lodge of Ireland did not officially allow women the right to walk during marching season.[96] Many of these studies expound either an anthropological or a sociological stance on parades. Similarly, the various rules and regulations throughout the Orange world do not focus on parades and tend to only mention the anniversaries such as the Fifth of November, or double fifth with its dual celebration of the Gunpowder Plot and the landing of William III at Torbay, and the Twelfth of July celebration of the Battle of the Boyne. Attending divine service on these dates was stipulated, but having a parade was not.[97]

Nevertheless, Orange parades are a well-documented feature of Orangeism with male participation predominating. Yet this gender divide developed quite differently in other parts of the Orange diaspora. While acknowledging that Orangewomen did march throughout the Orange world from Auckland to Toronto, a few examples are worth mentioning. In England, as early as 1852, the GPALO included Orangewomen. At the Black Dog Inn, Newchurch, in Rossendale, Lancashire, Orangewomen celebrated their own anniversary by attending church and then walking in procession to Booth-fold and Stacksteads. Their celebrations included songs, recitations, and some 'airs from the band'.[98] This gender inclusive parading and revelry demonstrates a family atmosphere. By 2013 there were upwards of 6,000 people taking part in Orange parades in Liverpool and Southport.[99] These parades always featured families with children often dressed as William and Mary, a feature of Liverpool parades for many years.[100] So whether in small celebrations or larger occasions the English Orangemen and Orangewomen were united in the way they celebrated their anniversaries of lodges or King William's exploits at the Battle of the Boyne.

Another example originates from New Zealand, where in the early years Orangewomen did not march but assembled at the church, where they preceded the men inside. No reason is given as to why the women did not march, but in later years women did march in their respective lodges.[101] Again the reason, at best speculative, may have been the change in the wider culture or following the overseas model of Canada or the United States, where women did march. Whether the women marched or not, their preparations for any concerts or festivities associated with 12 July remained constant. This was more of a chore than a ritual. Preparations were usually noted in the minutes, such as this example from LLOL No. 14 'Loyal Primrose', Ashburton, which recorded that a 'letter of thanks for assistance at July celebration was received from the 23rd', that is the LOL No. 23, 'Star of Ashburton'.[102] The sphere where Orangewomen were not as dependent on the men was in use and experience of ritual in their own lodge meetings.

The apparent dullness of the lodge meetings provided a sense of order, which is symptomatic of reformation Protestantism. It meant members learnt as much about meeting procedures as they did about ritual. The differences between the men's and women's rituals occurred in the second degree. Both had the Orange degree as their first ritual degree, but the second differentiated the men from the women. While the men had the Royal Arch Purple, the women had the Blue degree or simply the Second Degree.[103] The use of passwords and the set-up of lodge rooms have a Masonic influence. However, the reciting of set words is heavily influenced by biblical passages. For instance, the Second Degree in the Scottish ritual centres on the story of Ruth and her link to her mother-in-law, Naomi. It focuses on the bond between the two as they left the land of Moab and travelled back to Bethlehem. The ritual, in which the initiate and members recited scripture and role-played, evokes a female bonding that emphasises a sisterhood of believers.[104]

An aspect of Orangeism that has often been derided was the use of ritual in ceremonies. Having borrowed the use of passwords, degrees, and other visual signs from Masonic lodges, Orangeism always had critics not just from the Catholic quarter but also from other Christian denominations that saw anything Masonic as stemming from the devil. Melbourne-based former Orangeman Edward Lewis, writing in 1899, claimed in his pamphlet 'Orangeism Exposed' that the various ceremonies carried out to initiate new candidates were an 'abominable farrago of blasphemous and idiotic fooling'.[105] Henry Cleary (later bishop of Auckland) in his much reprinted *The Orange Society* documented the activities of Orangemen and made some rather pointed comments about 'practices' that had to be revised as they were 'offensive even to common decency.'[106] Notwithstanding these polemical comments, having rituals gave Orangeism an appeal as being a part of something special. However, there were penalties, which included the prospect of being expelled if women 'divulge the secret work of a Lodge.'[107] This was standard for most rules across Orange jurisdictions, and it helped to heighten the uniqueness of the rituals as being something requiring guarding.

The Scottish ladies' lodges, although they gained their impetus from England, looked to Canada for guidance in their ritual. In fact, the founder of the LOBA and then Grand Mistress, Mary Cullum, in 1909 gave the Scottish women instructional advice about the various rituals and the lectures for their lodges.[108] This transnational link may well have come from other Scottish Orangewomen who migrated to Canada. The nineteenth and early twentieth centuries had seen a large exodus of Scots to Canada. Between 1919 and 1938, a recorded 197,325 Scots migrated to Canada and 62,725 returned during the same period.[109] Some of these new migrants may have been impressed by the style of ritual that the Canadian Orangewomen offered. It is not, therefore, surprising that they sought practical advice from the head of the LOBA.

These transnational links continued as in April 1920 eight members of the Women's Orange Association of Ireland and England visited Scotland. They were not, however, permitted at lodge meetings as visitors while ceremonial work (such as the initiation) was being conducted, because they did not follow the same ritual as Scotland.[110] This demonstrates the mystery and exclusivity that only initiated members can partake in a ritual. The result of the visit was that in October that year Margaret Drennan (later Grand Mistress) 'had by arrangement been initiated in Scotland's First Lodge, with the object of introducing our ceremonial work into the Women's Orange Association of Ireland.' There were other Irish women present, and they were impressed.[111] By 1920 the Grand Lodge of Ireland had sent for copies of the Scottish ladies' rules and ritual to see if they could be adopted.[112] Whatever was adopted proved to be sufficient enough for the Scottish ladies to never raise the issue again and therefore the Irish Orange women were now 'proper Orangewomen'.[113] This provides an instance of the Orange diaspora influencing Ireland. While a transnational tie is evident here, it

Figure 5.8 Margaret and William R. Norris Memorial LLOL No. 228 marching in the Annual Twelfth of July celebrations, Bath Street, Glasgow, 1976

Source: Reproduced with the permission of the Grand Orange Lodge of Scotland.

also demonstrates that although Ireland may have been the birthplace of both male and female Orangeism, it did not have the monopoly on ritual development.

In South Australia the Orangewomen had in their early years to use the same ritual as the men.[114] This arose as a result of the Grand Committee in 1905 ordering all female rituals be returned and replaced by the men's ritual. It was not until 1913 at the Loyal Orange Grand Council of Australasia that a new female ritual was implemented.[115] A transnational uniformity was being enforced as this ritual was to be used not just in the Australian states, but also in New Zealand. The use of ritual in ladies' lodges while forming part of the mystery of lodge life was not as malevolent as outsiders may have imagined. The standard lodge meeting involved opening and closing prayers, reports, ballots, propositions, and nominations.[116]

The local Orangewomen in New Zealand also found that Scotland, not Ireland, was the place to look for guidance in their ritual. This was well illustrated in the example of a newly arrived member from Glasgow called Sister Wyne:

> In conversation with our sister, we found that there was little, if any, uniformity in ritual, passwords, etc., between Scotland and Australasia. Ladies' Lodges in Scotland have reached a high degree of perfection in initiation and Second Degree working in the lodges there. The general opinion seems to be that nothing can be learned from Ireland concerning the higher phases of Orange ritual. This opinion is well borne out by visits paid to several Irish lodges.[117]

This comment neatly illustrates the lack of influence of the Irish Orangewomen and that the Scottish Orangewomen proved to be one of the mentors for the Orange diaspora. It also foreshadowed later events when Orange women from around the world met and compared these same issues in regards to ritual.

Differences between the ALOI and the other Orange women's organisations became pronounced at the Triennial Orange Council of the World in Glasgow July 1937. The Ladies' Loyal Orange Institution, USA; the International Ladies' Orange Association, USA; and the Ladies' Orange Association of Scotland held a special meeting where they outlined their activities. The other organisations wanted to use the same ritual work that everyone used. The ALOI refused to change. The same thing happened again in the 1950s with this steadfast refusal. The Grand Mistress in Ireland made the pointed statement that they were the only Grand Lodge that made all their own decisions and were not under the direct rule of their male counterparts.[118] This was probably a show of strength in that they made their own decisions and while not actually relevant to the ritual debate, it was their way of deflecting any criticism.

This stance over ritual leads to the question of what distinguished rituals in Ireland from those in the Orange diaspora? In essence it was that the other women's associations had a more complex ritual, which involved all officers playing a role in the various rituals. The Irish one was far simpler. McCallum makes an important observation that sums up the differences: 'the ritual that the international sisters wished the ALOI would adopt was less authentic in many ways with fewer gritty sectarian undertones and more mystery and ceremony.'[119] This is what separates Ireland from all the other jurisdictions as the Orange diaspora wanted uniformity, but lodges in Ireland wanted to be different. Orange women in Ireland could be seen not as simply being defiant, but reactionary. After all there is not a lot of difference from the militant style of the original 1801 warrant and the current Irish ritual.[120] This simplicity is corroborated by former New Zealand Deputy Grand Master Beverley Buist, who recalls having seen different floor work, which is the processional ceremonial part in other Orange lodges. In contrast to the Australian and Scottish lodges, ceremonies in Ireland were practically non-existent. She claimed that 'in Ireland there is no floor work as they just sit around the table'. The differences in New Zealand may have been due to early Masonic influence in Orange ceremonies.[121] Former Grand Master Patricia Ellis has also noted that even at the local level all of the lodges in the South Island of New Zealand work on the same ritual but do it differently. She states that although the ritual is printed and is in front of you, the way the lodge room is set out and the way officers do floor work were different.[122] Uniformity is shown in the English ladies' lodges who use the same rule books as the men. With regard to rituals, the book form was discontinued a long time ago and all rituals and ceremonies are now learned verbally, using qualified lecturers in classes.[123]

CONCLUSION

The numbers of Orangewomen today have fallen from the larger numbers of the 1930s and 1950s. This is symptomatic of all community-based groups going through a cycle of initial set up, increase in numbers and influence and then the decline as the focus is no longer relevant. Although there are still Orange women around the world meeting and taking part in the ritual and social life of their lodges, they struggle to attract new members or be seen as relevant. Mothers used to encourage daughters to join, but the generational links are no longer there. Present-day members are ageing, and ongoing issues of how to attract new members remain problematic.

Nevertheless, as this chapter has shown, female Orangeism provided a network of cultural and social activities for Protestant women of the reformed faith. They wanted their own expressions of belief that they saw their fathers, husbands, and brothers have. Their numbers did help to bolster Orangeism overall, but they wanted to be more than mere auxiliaries or tea and scone makers. The development of female Orangeism has seen members prepared to work transnationally as well as regionally in order to help their fellow sisters. While there are differences with Ireland refusing to join a uniformity of ritual, these Orange sisters, although seemingly dysfunctional on the surface, have, like many families, tried to maintain a sense of harmony over the years.

The comparative approach adopted in this chapter reveals that female Orangeism has had a patchy record in the annals of Orangeism with lodges begun with good support in England whereas the Orangewomen in Scotland had to fight to get their own lodges started. Lodges in Ireland seemed haphazard at first, but managed to find a stable base and continue. Ireland, although providing a basis for Orangeism, did not seem to produce the dynamism of female lodges elsewhere in terms of regular participation in parades and having a distinctive ritual. Orange female lodges in Scotland and Canada were seen as the movers and shakers in terms of ritual whereas the English and the Canadians were pioneers in other Orange countries looking to set up ladies' lodges. Irish Protestant women, including those with Irish parents such as the Wilsons in Scotland and Cullums in Canada, seemed to have a part to play in any set up. Yet Englishwomen were also just as active as well. The fact that overseas women looking to set up or even get help with Orange ritual never looked to Ireland demonstrates that the Orangewomen in Ireland, while claiming to be more independent than the others, showed their reactionary streak.

Although examining comparisons between nations, this chapter also highlights the transnational impulse of female Orangeism to reveal a global picture of the interactions and activities of this understudied group. The key finding that this approach has highlighted is how different the Orange diaspora is compared to the home of Orangeism—Ireland.

ACKNOWLEDGMENTS

A special note of gratitude goes to Charles Ferrel, Past Imperial Grand Master of New Zealand; David Bryce, Orange Archivist, LOI of Scotland; and Michael Phelan, Orange Archivist, LOI of England, for access to their knowledge and source materials. I would also like to thank the anonymous referee of this chapter for the helpful suggestions.

NOTES

1. W. Peake (compiler and arranger), *A Collection of Orange and Protestant Songs* (Belfast: Offices of the "Belfast News-Letter", 1907), p. 54.
2. *A Collection of Loyal Songs, as Sung at all the Orange Lodges in Ireland* (Dublin: W. M'Kenzie, 1798).
3. W. Archer, *The Orange Melodist: Original Orange Songs, with Occasional Verses, and an Appendix Containing Copius Explanatory Notes* (Dublin: J. Kirkwood, 1852).
4. *A Collection of Loyal Songs*, p. 43.
5. Newspapers often printed provocative headlines like 'Riot between Orangemen and Irishmen in Liverpool', *Manchester Times*, 17 July 1850; 'Religious Riots in Toronto: Fight between a Catholic Procession and Orangemen', *New York Times*, 4 October 1875; 'Rioting in Ulster: Orangemen Attack Catholics', *Geraldton Guardian*, 17 July 1913.
6. E. McFarland, *Protestants First: Orangeism in Nineteenth-century Scotland* (Edinburgh: Edinburgh University Press, 1990); G. Walker, 'The Orange Order in Scotland between the Wars', *International Review of Social History*, 37 (1992), pp. 177–206.
7. D.A.J. MacPherson and D.M. MacRaild 'Sisters of the Brotherhood: Female Orangeism on Tyneside in the Late Nineteenth and Early Twentieth Centuries', *Irish Historical Studies*, 35:137 (2006), pp. 40–60; D.A.J. MacPherson, 'Migration and the Female Orange Order: Irish Protestant Identity, Diaspora and Empire in Scotland, 1909–40', *Journal of Imperial and Commonwealth History*, 40:4 (2012), pp. 619–42; D.A.J. MacPherson, 'The Emergence of

Women's Orange Lodges in Scotland: Gender, Ethnicity and Women's Activism, 1909–1940', *Women's History Review*, 22:1 (2012), pp. 51–74; D.A.J. MacPherson, 'Personal Narratives of Family and Ethnic Identity: Orangewomen in Scotland and England, c. 1940–2010', *Immigrants and Minorities*, 32:1 (2014) pp. 1–25.
8. MacPherson borrows this term from MacRaild who took it from Donna R. Gabaccia, *Italy's Many Diasporas* (Seattle: University of Washington Press, 2000).
9. MacPherson, 'Migration and the Female Orange Order', p. 620.
10. D.M. MacRaild, *Faith, Fraternity and Fighting: The Orange Order and Irish Migrants in England, c.1850–1920* (Liverpool: Liverpool University Press, 2005), p. 308.
11. The archival records that have survived are fragmentary across the Orange world. Fire, water damage, deliberate destruction, and even negligence have contributed to the loss of Orange documentation. The efforts of energetic volunteers within and outside Orangeism have been the reason why some records still remain.
12. MacPherson, 'Migration and the Female Orange Order', p. 623.
13. C. McCallum, 'Orangewomen Show their Colors: Gender, Family, and Orangeism in Ulster, 1795-Present' (PhD dissertation, Southern Illinois University Carbondale, 2011), p. 25.
14. Ibid., p. 30.
15. Ibid., pp. 35, 40. This warrant only came to light in recent years having been discovered in a shoebox in the attic of an Englishwoman's home.
16. P. Grimshaw, *Women's Suffrage in New Zealand* (Auckland and Oxford: Auckland University Press/Oxford University Press, 1987), p. 22.
17. E.C. DuBois, 'Woman Suffrage around the World: Three Phases of Suffragist Internationalism', in C. Daley and M. Nolan (eds), *Suffrage and Beyond: International Feminist Perspectives* (Auckland: Auckland University Press, 1994), pp. 256–57.
18. S. Morgan, *A Victorian Woman's Place: Public Culture in the Nineteenth Century* (London and New York: Tauris Academic Studies, 2007); L.D. Ginzberg, *Women and the Work of Benevolence: Morality, Political and Class in the Nineteenth Century* (New Haven, CT: Yale University Press, 1992).
19. Saunderson was the wife of Colonel Edward Saunderson who was the Conservative member of Parliament for North Armagh.
20. McCallum, 'Orangewomen Show their Colors', p. 131.
21. E. de Bhaldraithe, 'Mixed Marriages and Irish Politics: The Effect of "Ne Temere"', *Studies: An Irish Quarterly Review*, 77:307 (1988), pp. 284–99. The decree came into force in 1908 on Easter Sunday without anyone realising the consequences of it. The contentious aspect of the decree was that marriages between Catholics and Protestants were only valid if performed by a priest.
22. D.A.J. MacPherson, '"Exploited with Fury on a Thousand Platforms": Women, Unionism and the Ne Temere decree in Ireland, 1908–1913', in J. Allen and R.C. Allen (eds), *Faith of Our Fathers: Popular Culture and Belief in Post-Reformation England, Ireland and Wales* (Newcastle: Cambridge Scholars Press, 2009), pp. 157–75.
23. Johnstone became the first Grand Mistress (1912–23).
24. K. Haddick-Flynn, *Orangeism: The Making of a Tradition* (Dublin: Wolfhound Press, 1999), p. 366.
25. McCallum, 'Orangewomen Show their Colors', p. 145.
26. Ibid., p. 239.
27. RSM McClure Watters, *A Report on the Socio-Economic Impact of the Traditional Protestant Parading Sector in Northern Ireland* (Belfast: Grand Orange Lodge of Ireland, 2013), p. 2.

28. E. P. Kaufmann, *The Orange Order: A Contemporary Northern Irish History* (Oxford: Oxford University Press, 2007), p. 284.
29. *List of Warrants held under the authority of the Honourable the Grand Lodge of Great Britain, and the sanction of the MW Grand Master the Rt. Hon. the Earl of Enniskillen, with the names of the Districts, Times and Places of Meeting* (England: Thomas Gibson, 1850).
30. *Lists of Warrants.*
31. *Loyal Orange Institution of Great Britain. Proceedings of the Grand Lodge held at the Green Man Inn, Bacup, 3rd 1854* (Liverpool: Bro. T. Davies, 1854).
32. *Report of the Proceedings of the Grand Lodge of the Loyal Orange Institution of Great Britain, at the annual meeting held at Durham, 7th July 1875; Grand Protestant Association of Loyal Orangemen of England. Report of the Proceedings of the Association in Extraordinary Grand Lodge, and afterwards in Ordinary Grand Lodge assembled, on Thursday 1st July 1875 in St James Room, New Brighton* (Bradford: Squire Auty & Son).
33. *Grand Protestant Association of Loyal Orangemen of England. Report of the Proceedings of the Association in Ordinary Grand Lodge assembled, on Friday 1st July 1870 at the Cardiff Castle, Aberdare* (Bradford: Squire Auty and Son).
34. P. Day, 'Pride before a fall? Orangeism in Liverpool since 1945', in M. Busteed, F. Neal, and J. Tonge (eds), *Irish Protestant Identities* (Manchester and New York: Manchester University Press, 2008), pp. 277–81.
35. MacPherson, 'Personal Narratives of Family and Ethnic Identity', pp. 1–25.
36. MacPherson, 'Migration and the Female Orange Order', p. 623.
37. *Report of the Proceedings of the Grand Lodge of the Loyal Orange Institution of Great Britain, at the annual meeting held at Warrington, 3rd July 1872* (Liverpool: W. Williams, 1872). They were noted as 'Female Orange Associate Lodges' under a list that included their English counterparts.
38. *Belfast Weekly News*, 30 March 1872.
39. David Bryce, *The Undaunted: A History of the Orange Order in Scotland from 1799 to 1899* (Scotland: David Bryce, 2012), p. 64.
40. MacPherson, 'The Emergence of Women's Orange Lodges', pp. 3–4.
41. *Ladies' Orange Association of Scotland Centenary Celebrations 1909–2009* (Glasgow, 2009), p. 4.
42. Ibid.
43. Kaufmann, *The Orange Order in Ontario*, pp. 56–7; McFarland, *Protestants First*, pp. 103–6; MacPherson, 'The Emergence of Women's Orange Lodges', pp. 15–17.
44. G.A. McCracken, *Bygone Days of Yore: The Story of Orangeism in Glasgow* (Glasgow: Orange Heritage for the County Grand Orange Lodge of Glasgow, 1990), p. 38.
45. MacPherson, 'The Emergence of Women's Orange Lodges', pp. 8–9.
46. T. Gallagher, 'Protestant Extremism in Urban Scotland 1930–1939: Its Growth and Contraction', *Scottish Historical Review*, 64:178 (1985), pp. 145–46.
47. E. P. Kaufmann, 'The Orange Order in Scotland since 1860: A Social Analysis', in M. J. Mitchell (ed), *New Perspectives on the Irish in Scotland* (Edinburgh: Birlinn, 2009), p. 177.
48. *Belfast Weekly News*, 20 July 1872.
49. *Report of the Proceedings of the Grand Lodge of the Loyal Orange Institution of Great Britain, at the annual meeting held at Greenock, 2nd July 1873* (Liverpool: W. Williams, 1873).
50. *New York Times*, 5 July 1876.
51. Loyal Orange Ladies' Institution United States of America, *History of the Loyal Orange Ladies' Institution United States of America* (Philadelphia: Pennsylvania, 1944). This was a role Thompson held from 1876 to 1887.

52. C.J. Houston and W.J. Smyth, 'Transferred Loyalties: Orangeism in the United States and Ontario', *American Review of Canadian Studies*, 14:2 (1984), pp. 203–4.
53. Information supplied to author by Walter C. Wilson, Grand Secretary LOI-USA, 14 May 2014.
54. Loyal Orange Institution of the United States of America. *Official directory recognized and constitutional lodges of the Loyal Orange Institution U.S.A., Inc. and the Loyal Orange Ladies Institution, USA, Inc.* (United States: The Supreme Grand Lodge of the United States, 1911–2008). Walter C. Wilson, Grand Secretary LOIUSA, kindly provided access to lodge figures.
55. S.E. Long, *A Brief History of the Loyal Orange Institution in the United States of America* (Dromara, Northern Ireland: S.E. Long, 1979), pp. 24–25.
56. According to Canadian census records Mary Cullum was a dressmaker by trade and a Church of England adherent. She is also noted as being single in all subsequent censuses from 1901 to 1920.
57. *The Ladies' Orange Benevolent Association had its Birth in Hamilton*, http://canadianorangehistoricalsite.com/TheFirstLOBA.php.
58. *Souvenir Program—Meetings of the Imperial Grand Orange Council of the World, Grand Orange Lodge of British America, Grand Black Chapter of British America, Grand Orange Lodge of the Ladies' Orange Benevolent Association, Winnipeg, July 1923*. This source is online at https://www.facebook.com/pages/Imperial-Grand-Orange-Council-of-the-World-1923-Souvenir-Programme/301608763256740.
59. *Toronto Daily Mail*, 27 June 1890.
60. Loyal Orange Ladies' Institution United States of America, *History of the Loyal Orange Ladies' Institution United States of America* (Philadelphia: Loyal Orange Ladies' Institution United States of America, 1944).
61. *Watchman*, 21 August 1924.
62. E. Kaufmann, *Orange Order Membership Data, With a Focus on Ireland, Canada and Scotland, 1852–2002* (Colchester: UK Data Archive, 2004), SN: 4916, http://dx.doi.org/10.5255/UKDA-SN-4916-1.
63. C.J. Houston and W.J. Smyth, *The Sash Canada Wore: An Historical Geography of the Orange Order in Canada* (Toronto: University of Toronto Press, 1980). See chapter 5 for an analysis of male Orange membership.
64. Ibid.
65. See R.D. Putnam, *Bowling Alone: The Collapse and Revival of American Community* (New York: Simon & Schuster, 2000).
66. E.P. Kaufmann, 'The Orange Order in Ontario, Newfoundland, Scotland and Northern Ireland: A Macro-Social Analysis', in D.A. Wilson (ed), *The Orange Order in Canada* (Dublin: Four Courts, 2007), p. 55.
67. P.J. Coleman, 'Transplanted Irish Institutions: Orangeism and Hibernianism in New Zealand 1877–1910' (MA thesis, University of Canterbury, 1993). See chapter 2 which outlines the initial growth of Orangeism in New Zealand.
68. *Evening Post*, 20 October 1888.
69. Ibid., 12 October 1888.
70. Ibid., 10 November 1891.
71. *Report of Proceedings of the Fifteenth Annual Session of the Grand Orange Lodge of New Zealand, Dunedin, March 31st, April 2 and 3, 1923*, p. 9.
72. *Report of Proceedings of the Fifty Fourth Session and 39th Session of Ladies' Conference of the Grand Orange Lodge of New Zealand, Wellington, April 4, 5 and 7, 1980. Report of Proceedings of the Fifty Fifth Session and 40th Session of Ladies' Conference of the Grand Orange Lodge of New Zealand, Hastings, 9–12 April, 1982*.
73. *Report of Proceedings Wellington Grand Lodge 64th Sessions, 2000*. Patricia Ellis was made Grand Master (2000–2004).

74. *Press*, 11 February 1889. John William Anderson (1834–1898) was born in County Monaghan, Ireland. He was a publican and was grand master of the Middle Island (1875–1876). See *Press*, 5 December 1898.
75. A. S. Russell, *Loyal Orange Institution of Queensland History 1865 to 1932* (Brisbane: Loyal Orange Institution of Queensland, 1933).
76. *Ibid.*, and *Watchman*, 12 September 1912.
77. E. Turner, '"Not narrow minded bigots": Proceedings of the Loyal Orange Institution of New South Wales, 1845–1895' (PhD dissertation, University of New England, 2002), pp. 209, 211–13.
78. *Sydney Morning Herald*, 3 June 1895. While they were not technically a ladies' lodge in the general sense of other Orange lodges, New South Wales did have Orange Ladies lodges that were benefit lodges. One such lodge was the Orange Lily (Ladies) Lodge No. 11, LOBS of Australasia which formed in 1883. See *Evening News*, 1 August 1883.
79. *Sydney Morning Herald*, 5 June 1895.
80. Ibid.
81. Turner, '"Not Narrow Minded Bigots"', p. 420.
82. *The Mercury*, 10 January 1901.
83. R. P. Davis, *Orangeism in Tasmania 1832–1967* (Co. Antrim: Institute of Ulster-Scots Studies, 2010), p. 55.
84. Ibid., p. 73.
85. *The Advertiser*, 16 March 1901. By 1903 there were five ladies' lodges: Queen Victoria, No. 1 (Auburn); Loyal Duchess of York. No. 2 (Port Adelaide); Princess May, No.3 (Wallaroo); Lady Symon, No. 4 (Kadina); and Loyal Queen Alexandra, No. 5 (Adelaide).
86. D. Fitzpatrick, 'Exporting Brotherhood: Orangeism in South Australia', *Immigrants & Minorities*, 23:2–3 (2005), p. 302, footnote 39.
87. Ibid., p. 284.
88. Ibid., p. 285.
89. Australian Bureau of Statistics, Australian Historical Population Statistics, Data cube Excel spreadsheet (Canberra, 2008), cat. no. 3105.0.65.001, found online at http://www.abs.gov.au/AUSSTATS/abs@.nsf/DetailsPage/3105.0.65.0012008?OpenDocument (last accessed 14 May 2014). The Irish-born were the second-largest ethnic group from 1871 to 1891.
90. See T. Vertigan, *The Orange Order in Victoria* (Melbourne: Loyal Orange Institution of Victoria, 1979).
91. See Turner, '"Not Narrow Minded Bigots"', especially appendices 5 and 18, for information about Orange membership in New South Wales.
92. *Kalgoorlie Miner*, 31 October 1903.
93. *Watchman*, 27 March 1924.
94. Vertigan, *The Orange Order in Victoria*, pp. 99–100.
95. D. Bryan, *Orange Parades: The Politics of Ritual, Tradition and Control* (London: Pluto Press, 2000); J. Edwards and J. D. Knottnerus, 'The Orange Order: Parades, Other Rituals, and their Outcomes', *Sociological Focus*, 43:1 (2010), pp. 1–23; L. A. Smithey and M. P. Young, 'Parading Protest: Orange Parades in Northern Ireland and Temperance Parades in Antebellum America', *Social Movement Studies: Journal of Social, Cultural and Political Protest*, 9:4 (2010), pp. 393–410; T. G. Fraser (ed), *The Irish Parading Tradition: Following the Drum* (Basingstoke: Palgrave Macmillan, 2000).
96. McCallum, 'Orangewomen Show their Colors', p. 48.
97. Reading any set of rules and regulations across the Orange world, all have the stock phrases about anniversaries and their attendance.
98. *Preston Guardian*, 17 April 1852. Newchurch is a village in the Borough of Rossendale, Lancashire.
99. *Liverpool Echo*, 16 July 2013.

100. Day, 'Pride before a Fall?', pp. 276–77.
101. See P. Coleman, 'Orange Parading Traditions in New Zealand 1880–1914', *Australasian Journal of Irish Studies*, 10 (2010), pp. 81–104.
102. LLOL No. 14 'Loyal Primrose', Minute Book December 1954-October 1970, 11 August 1955.
103. The term *degree* is a masonic term and simply refers to the secret rituals which involve a mixture of set spoken words and actions that were either written down in ritual books or memorised.
104. Grand Orange Lodge of Scotland, *Ladies Loyal Orange Association: Ritual of Introduction/Ritual Second Degree* (Glasgow: George Watt, Printers, 1955).
105. E. Lewis, *Orangeism Exposed* (Melbourne: Advocate Office, 1899), p. 17. Lewis was the Assistant Chaplain of Loyal Orange Campbell Lodge, Collingwood, No. 130 in Melbourne.
106. H. W. Cleary, *The Orange Society* (London: Catholic Truth Society, 1913), p. 118.
107. *Loyal Orange Institution of N.S.W. Rules for the Establishment, Regulation and Control of Women's Loyal Orange Lodges* (Sydney: F. W. White, 1903), p. 7.
108. Grand Orange Lodge of Scotland, *The Future is Orange and Bright* (Glasgow, Scotland: n.d.), p. 34.
109. M. Harper, *Emigration from Scotland between the Wars: Opportunity or Exile?* (Manchester: Manchester University Press, 1998), p. 7.
110. 10 April 1920, Grand Lodge Committee 'Half Yearly Meetings of Ladies' Representatives with the Members of Grand Lodge Committee' minute book, 1920–23.
111. 9 October 1920, in Ibid.
112. 9 April 1921, in Ibid.
113. Information supplied to author by David Bryce, 18 May 2014. Also there is nothing on record to show that a Scottish ladies conference ever formally approved changes to any new Irish Ladies' ritual.
114. Fitzpatrick, 'Exporting Brotherhood', p. 286.
115. Ibid., p. 301.
116. Loyal Orange Grand Council of Australasia, *Ritual–Female–for the Installation of Officers and Inauguration of Lodges* (Brisbane: 'QP' Printing Co., 1913), p. 12.
117. *Nation*, 10 April 1925.
118. McCallum, 'Orangewomen Show their Colors', pp. 229–33.
119. Ibid., 232.
120. Ibid.
121. Interview of Beverley Buist by Patrick Coleman, 11 January 2005.
122. Interview of Patricia Ellis by Patrick Coleman, 19 January 2005.
123. Information supplied to author by Lillian Hall, Grand Mistress of England, 1989 to present, 26 March 2014.

6   An Irish Landlord and His Daughter
A Story of War and Survival in America and Ireland

Philip Bull

Monksgrange, in the parish of Killan, in County Wexford, was built by Goddard Richards between 1759 and 1769 on the site of an outpost of a medieval Cistercian monastery, probably that of Graigue na Managh (see Figure 6.1). Goddard Richards was a descendent of the Cromwellian soldier and onetime governor of Wexford Solomon Richards. The house was originally named Grange, but the allusion to its monastic origins was added in the 1880s. The house itself tells its own remarkable story. Twice scheduled by rebels to be burnt down, it was both times saved by rebel leaders who because of personal loyalty to the Richards family manoeuvred their followers away from their intention. In 1798 this rebel leader was none other than John Kelly, the subject of the ballad 'Kelly the Boy from Killann', a 1798 hero to whom a statue now stands in Wexford Town. In 1923, during the course of the Irish Civil War, it was Myles Fenlon, a leading Republican irregular. What was it about this family that secured such loyalty from those pitted against their class and religion makes its history of special interest.

The history of the Richards family from the mid-nineteenth century onwards, however, was deeply influenced by remarkable experiences in the United States of America and the purpose of this chapter is to illustrate how those experiences might have influenced and changed the two individuals, Edward Moore Richards and his daughter Adela, in whose hands largely rested the future of Monksgrange. The story of this family throws some light not only on these individuals but also on the ambiguities and apparent contradictions of landed and religious relationships in Ireland. It is also a particular example—very different from the more common experiences of Irish migrants in America—involving a man from the Irish landed elite. His experiences, first in Virginia and then in Kansas, demonstrate how the values of two societies, the mid-nineteenth-century American slave economy and the frontier and the old Irish landed elite, come together in one man and create a new set of values that belong to neither of those societies but represent a composite, transnational outlook which has its own impact in the later development of the individuals involved.

Figure 6.1 Monksgrange, County Wexford
Source: Courtesy of the Irish Architectural Archive.

The sources for this chapter come from a very large archive housed at Monksgrange which has not, with one exception, previously been used by historians.[1] The archive is extremely large and because of the stage at which work on the archive has presently reached this chapter is based almost solely on the letters written home by Edward Moore Richards, in most cases to his mother. These encapsulate succinctly his experience of life in America and particularly during the time that he lived and worked in the slave based society of Virginia in the region around the city of Richmond. This is the beginning of a larger project to place these experiences both into a wider American context but also to show the ways in which Irish ideas mixed with the very different perspectives of the rawer southern and frontier American environment, which may ultimately have contributed to different approaches to the management of an Irish landed estate and to life within a changing social and political environment. The analysis of the views expressed by Edward Richards will, in subsequent work on the archive, be set more firmly in his own personal educational and family background. What his letters from America reveal is his own perception of the relationship of his new experiences to the ideas that he had brought from Ireland. The very important question of why and how he had formed ideas, both before and after his American interlude, that seem so much at variance with the general characterisations of men of his class is raised in this piece and will be developed further as research progresses.

An Irish Landlord and His Daughter

I

Edward Moore Richards (1826–1911) was the great-grandson of the builder of the house, but as a younger son had no expectation of inheriting. Accordingly, he had established himself as an engineer, initially working on the Shannon River Navigation Schemes. In May 1847 at the age of 21 he set out on a voyage to Quebec, undertaken for his health but ironically on what turned out to be one of the so-called coffin ships carrying poor and often diseased migrants fleeing the Great Famine. Thus, his initial experience of the New World was immediately juxtaposed against the multitudes of his fellow country people whose emigration was both more involuntary and deriving from very different social environments than his own. Having travelled also to New York, the idea of life in the United States increasingly appealed to him. He returned there in December 1848—enticed also by the prospects for an engineer in the age of railway building. At first he worked

Figure 6.2 Edward Moore Richards (1826–1911) in December 1849, a year after he went to America

Source: Reproduced with the permission of Mr Jeremy Hill.

on the Susquehanna River before moving in September 1849 to the state of Virginia to work on the Richmond and Danville railway. By the time he eventually returned to Ireland in 1866 there had been two major developments in his life.

His mother Dorothea Sargent recorded with anguish in her journal for 4 September 1851 the news that she had just received

> a letter from my darling Eddy . . . which has filled me with the deepest sorrow—and for some days nearly bereft me of my senses! Its disclosed to me his marriage with a young American girl without fortune—without family! . . . —I wrote to him . . . bitterly deploring the step he had taken but urging his immediate return home and promising a <u>Parents</u> reception to the one he had chosen—he has been too long already living in that uncivilized part of the world without a being to exchange an idea with—May the Lord <u>overrule</u> this apparently unfortunate step for his good.[2]

The girl he had married, Sarah Elizabeth Tisdale, was only 15 years old (he was then 24), and a baby boy was born approximately six months after the wedding date. Whether or not he revealed all this to his mother at the time, by December 1851 she records that he is to come over to Ireland in the following summer, bringing his wife and 'most probably a little <u>grandchild</u>! For she is in the family way.'[3]

The visit was deferred until December 1852 but then lasted nearly a year. During that year Dorothea devoted herself unreservedly to her new daughter-in-law and to her grandson, John Evelyn, and any horror at her son's unwise marriage dissolved in the warmth of these new relationships. After nearly a year back in Ireland Edward Richards and his family returned to Virginia, where a series of tragedies reshaped his future. In 1858 John Evelyn died of scarlet fever, although a daughter, Adela Elizabeth, had by then been born. In 1859 another daughter, Dora, was born, but within three months, both mother and baby daughter had died of diphtheria. The relationship between Edward and his only surviving child, Adela, with whom in one way or another he was to share the rest of his life, was a remarkable one.

The second major development that changed his future occurred in 1860 when he inherited Grange on the death of his elder brother. John Francis Richards had inherited Grange in 1829 when only five years old, on the death of his father Goddard Hewetson Richards. Much of the responsibility for the management of the house and estate had therefore passed to their mother Dorothea (see Figure 6.3), who in turn had remarried Richard Sargent of Waterford and had given birth to two further sons. Her life thus became increasingly divided between Waterford and Grange, and when John Francis died she became very anxious for Edward's return to

An Irish Landlord and His Daughter 141

Figure 6.3 Dorothea Sargent, the mother of 'darling Eddy'
Source: Reproduced with the permission of Mr Jeremy Hill.

take possession of his inheritance and to relieve her of responsibility, not to mention her deep personal desire to have him home—the son for whom she had a particularly deep affection. Edward, however, showed no eagerness to return and remained in America for a further six years, returning then apparently only because of his own ill health.

Before his marriage and in the years up until his wife's death Edward had worked with great satisfaction and obvious success designing and supervising the construction of railways in Virginia, most of the time on the Richmond and Danville Railroad. Although he sometimes complained about not being paid sufficiently for the level of work he was undertaking, he enjoyed both great personal satisfaction and the esteem of his superiors, the latter often giving him incentives to remain even when fellow engineers were being laid off because of economic pressures on railway construction. It was in his engagement with the professional issues relating to railway construction that his attitudes to the relative merits of America and Ireland began to take shape in his mind.

II

How did this young product of Irish landed society respond to life in America, and how did he, as revealed in these letters, measure his experiences against the influences that had shaped his childhood and youth in Ireland? Although his emigration was driven by his search for a career and to earn a livelihood, a desire for travel and adventure were important factors. He also confessed to his mother that he feared that had he remained in Ireland and been 'thrown constantly into [the] society' of a certain young woman but who was mercifully now married to someone else, he 'might perhaps have taken a decisive step' which he would have regretted.[4] In this letter he asserts what became regular themes in his letters: first, a personal determination not to marry, which, as we have seen, was not long maintained and, second, what became a lifelong hostility to the principle of the indissolubility of marriage. This urge to dodge expectations of the society in which he lived indicated a disposition to differ significantly from the normal run of his class, which characterised in many ways the rest of his life. At least until the land war of the 1880s, Edward was sympathetic to Irish national aspirations, having been a member in the 1840s of the Young Ireland Confederates. He also had very strong and not very conventional views about women and their rights, including a passionate commitment to the reform of women's dress. He did not, like most landlords, belong to the Kildare Street Club, nor did he drink and, when in Dublin, stayed at a Temperance Hotel. On religion his views reflected those of the rationalist tradition, deriving from the Enlightenment, and he listed himself in the 1911 census as a freethinking agnostic. He also had distinctive views on the rights of man in general. In what follows, his experiences of America are examined and related to how he described the attitudes he had brought from Ireland through the focus of five areas: work, nation, religion, women, and slavery.

Work

Edward Richards was fascinated by the difference in engineering practice, specifically in railway construction, between the United States and Ireland and England, acknowledging that the lower American standards were 'sufficient for the wants of the community'. He regretted that Ireland had not adopted a system more like the American:

> It is all very well in a country like England where money is so plenty and traffic so great to go to great expense in making Railways, but it

was madness to think of carrying out the same system in Ireland—had the cheap system, (such as they make use of here,) been adopted most of the Irish towns of any note might now have the benefit of steam communication.[5]

The cost difference he estimated as £4,000 per mile in America compared with £32,000 in England, or eight times as expensive.[6] A year or so later, revising his figures, he compared the £2,800 per mile cost of constructing the Richmond and Danville Railway on which he was working with what it would cost 'in <u>dear</u> Ireland or still <u>dearer</u> England'.[7] This criticism of Ireland's dependency on the way things were done in England was qualified elsewhere with praise of engineering in Ireland and England, 'the place for making an Engineer' where '[o]ne would see more of real Engineering work on 2 miles of Railway . . . than on almost any length here'.[8] This captures an aspect of his personality—a propensity always to balance negative criticism with compensating virtues.

Nation

Disenchantment with Ireland and its condition was a powerful part of Edward's perspective while in America. In the aftermath of the Famine he declared himself 'sick and disgusted with Ireland she will never mend; much as I love my native place'.[9] He was particularly ashamed of his own class and wrote after reading a speech by Isaac Butt:

> I wish the landlords joy of the prosperous state of their island. . . . I acknowledge I feel a kind of malignant satisfaction at the ruin that has come upon them. Acknowledging the evils that flowed from the Union, they never would join to repeal it, afraid their petty influences would be injured, and lo! A worse evil has come upon them, their existence as a Class is threatened, and their properties are passing away to other hands.[10]

Frequently he expressed or implied disdain for the continuing subservience of his compatriots to English rule, connecting this to the dislike the Americans had of the Irish, for which he did not blame them, because 'it is our fault that we are now a sign for the figure of scorn of the whole world to be pointed at; but for our own wretched differences amongst ourselves what might we not be, a great, free and prosperous <u>nation</u>, not a beggarly, starving miserable province'.[11] He described himself as no longer belonging to any country: 'I reckon myself as of no country—Ireland is not a nation & I will never be an American citizen'.[12]

This alienation from not only a national but also a class identity, the two things being closely connected in his thinking, reflected the ambivalence of his views about Irish labourers in Virginia and their inability to rise to the challenge of equality that prevailed there: 'I like [the equality here] very well. I don't like to see a man talking to another, cowering and crouching with his hat off, as one may see at home. No, the manly, sturdy independence of these people is far better'.[13] He is struck at how inadequate Irish labourers are in handling this equality: 'It would not be very pleasant to sit down with a whole lot of Irish labourers tho'—and the equality seems to sit less gracefully on them than the others, they are more clannish in their manners, & often are presuming'.[14] And he gives a context for this: 'This equality is better than the vast difference in station you have at home—There is not any sneaking servility here & not the great disproportion of wealth'.[15]

But despite the vast difference in social class background between himself and migrant Irish labourers he identified with them with regard to the discrimination and disparagement they suffered. In 1855 he wrote to the *Wexford Independent* a long letter correcting the 'erroneous impression that used formerly to prevail in Ireland, viz.—that the Irish settled in America were favourably regarded by the Americans' and recommending Canada or Australia where prejudice against the Irish was not as bad as in the United States.[16] This letter embodied his most negative views of the Americans, declaring that their feeling towards themselves is 'one of the most boundless self-satisfaction and complacency' and condemning them for how they dispossessed the 'real' native Americans of their land.[17]

Edward Richards was deeply ambivalent in his attitude both to America and Ireland, and in the case of Ireland attributed its problems and the failings of individuals to subservience to England. He was proud of his recent membership of the Young Ireland confederates and deeply disparaging of some who had changed their views.[18] Excusing his mother for taking down a picture of Thomas Francis Meagher for the sake of peace on one occasion when guests were coming, he warned her that should she do so again she was 'to take down mine also' as '[t]hose that are too good and too loyal to look on his, must be also as regards mine'.[19]

Women

Edward Moore Richards had strong lifelong opinions about women and their rights and interests. At the heart of this was his relationship with his mother. Her own fondness for him manifestly exceeded what she felt for his older brother, and it is not hard to understand this when we read his letters to her. They reflect his deep affection and respect for her but, importantly, that he took her seriously enough to be direct with her on issues on which his own views were opposed to hers, most particularly on religion. By his own admission he lectures his mother on the subject of women's dress, specifically what he calls the pernicious use of stays and lacing. He described stays as 'one of the greatest curses in the world'[20] and attributed to them a range of ailments including consumption and depression. He also reported that he had made himself unpopular with local Virginian girls for asserting these views. Although, as he reminded his mother, 'an enemy I was always to the use of stays,'[21] his Virginian experience appears to have intensified his views, possibly through his disgust at the vulgar and unhealthy habits of young women there. He contrasted the painting of their faces and the wearing of stays and lacing with the much healthier mode of dress by Native American women. His objections to the 'unnatural' practices of women sprang not from any puritanical disapproval but were rooted in the rationalism that characterised his outlook on so many questions.

This issue of women's dress was no passing fad but a passionate lifelong commitment. His daughter later explained that his earlier views had been consolidated by his experience in America, and especially on the frontier in Kansas, where there was a need 'to bring a woman into some sort of proper relation to her surroundings when taking her out on the plains.'[22] Edward himself later wrote of how the female slaves employed in field work were 'little indeed encumbered by their clothing' and even in their Sunday best 'never wore the million-fold accursed stays, or in any way pinched in their waists', while the North American Indian 'women wore a short frock and leggings exactly . . . like the costume of the dress reformers of the United States'.[23] When that dress reform movement reached the British Isles Edward Richards was an avid supporter, contributing letters to journals on the subject. He always saw the connection between how women were pressured to dress and their more general rights. He recorded the visit to London of an American woman doctor, also a dress reformer, in 1866 and the hostility she faced, especially from protesting medical students, because she was also campaigning for opening the medical profession to women. He remarked that '[h]er thus "endangering the craft" was a worse sin in their eyes than her having discarded a long draggling skirt'.[24] He put his views on dress reform into practice, designing women's outfits; there are photos of his second wife, Ellen (see Figure 6.4), in clothes he had designed to conform to the principles of the rational dress movement. He applied similar principles to his own normal mode of dress, abandoning the conventional male suit, thus setting himself apart in appearance as well as in ideas from the general run of landlords and against the conventions of his time (see Figure 6.5).

In marrying Sarah Tisdale in August 1851 he was putting aside his repeated hostility to the idea of marriage, perhaps because of circumstances in which his idea of honour obliged him to marry—a sense of honour not necessarily universal in men of his class. In 1871 as his 16-year-old daughter set out on a visit to America he was to warn her about men:

> Some of them have the tongues of angels & the hearts of devils . . .
> Some gain their ends by one means some by another. The most usual is

146 Philip Bull

Figure 6.4 Edward's second wife, Ellen Aird, in clothes Edward designed to conform to the rational dress movement

Source: Reproduced with the permission of Mr Jeremy Hill.

a promise of marriage which they have no idea of keeping—999 men in 1000 believe intercourse between the sexes wrong without marriage & they despise the woman that permits & then won't marry her—Whether it really be a sin of itself is not now the question—But as a matter of prudence it is not worth the fearful penalty that the world exacts in case of discovery. The whole life of the woman is poisoned & destroyed.[25]

Leaving aside the relevance of this homily to his own experience, but noting perhaps identification of himself as the one exception, we have here a statement that tells us much about him. It captures his deep respect for women, his contempt for men who treat them badly (a recurring theme throughout his life), his distancing of himself from moral and religious attitudes and, above all, the frankness and directness of his relationship with his daughter. This connects with his rational and utilitarian approach to education, principles which he applied to his daughter, whose upbringing was very unconventional due in part to their location but also very significantly to his attitudes towards women and their interests.

An Irish Landlord and His Daughter 147

Figure 6.5 Edward Moore Richards in the outfit he regularly wore
Source: Reproduced with the permission of Mr Jeremy Hill.

Regardless of the circumstances of his own marriage, he became deeply attached to Sarah, treated her very well, showed great respect towards her, and grieved deeply when she and their infant third child died in 1860. He recorded remarks that his wife had made on her deathbed, which included the statement that 'The nine years of married life that I have spent with you have been the happiest of my life.'[26] Notwithstanding this his generally negative views on marriage persisted throughout his life,[27] perhaps affected by two unsuccessful proposals of marriage after he returned to Ireland and despite what was to be his very happy and successful marriage in later life to Ellen Aird. Deriving again from his rationalist perspective on the world he was an opponent of the concept of indissoluble marriage and lamented that he did not live in the future of which he predicted the demise of this idea.

His relationship with his mother, his wife, and his daughter, as well as his commitment to women's rights, all point to a disposition that was well ahead of his time in relation to women. His sensitivity towards women manifested itself in a letter written immediately after observing his wife give birth to their third child: 'If there is anything more than another that should make men love & cherish women better than they do, it is this unavoidable fiat of nature. If they were given all they ask, it would make but poor amends for what they have to suffer.'[28] In addition to the deep affection and respect in which he held individual women, his views were shaped in this as in other areas by a fundamental rationalism, captured in a broad spectrum that reached from his passion for dress reform to his scepticism on religion.

Religion

Opposition to women's dress reform was, in his opinion, reinforced by religion, to which he had many other objections as well. He encapsulated his views for his mother in 1859, writing,

> My thoughts have led me on a different road however than that by which yours travel—I cannot hold the orthodox Christian's belief. We are all in the hands of a Great, Good & Just Being who will do what is right irrespective of the opposing warring creeds by which the Earth is & ever has been cursed—I can no more look thro' another man's eyes as regards religious belief than I can hear with his ears & taste with his pallet.[29]

In America he encountered an extraordinary variety of religious belief, of intolerance associated with those beliefs, and of what he saw as a hypocritical contrast between declared principles and actions. He wrote that '[t]he clergymen here defend slavery on religious grounds. It seems to me that people prove whatever they like out of the bible.'[30] Foul language and excessive drink were things he came to abhor, in the latter case because of behaviour, such as the beating of women, which he saw as endemic in this purportedly Christian society. Through his wife he became familiar with the beliefs and practices of the Baptists, to which her family belonged. He showed wry amusement at the importance they attached to adult baptism. He explained to his mother:

> The principal difference between Church of England & Baptists is that the former sprinkle water over the face in baptism & the latter plunge the whole body into the water. The difference no doubt is awful, & whether a man is sprinkled in the face, or dipped altogether must no doubt have a tremendous influence on ones eternal salvation!!![31]

He continued: 'It reminds me very much of Swift's story of the people that went to war among themselves because one portion broke the eggs at the larger end & the other at the small.'[32] He gently mocked his mother's religious beliefs, as, for example, in a disingenuous argument against stays:

[Y]ou that are such a believer & adorer of God, don't you think he knows well enough how to shape women's bodies without any suggestions from the dress makers? & that if it was right & proper for women to have wasps' waists that he would have given them in the first instance himself—& don't you think he made all your backs strong enough at first to support themselves without any help from whalebone & linen?[33]

But it was in relation to slavery that his contempt for local religious belief reached its pinnacle, and here we see most clearly both his underlying principles and how his American experience consolidated and developed them.

Slavery

The year 1860 was enormously significant for Edward Richards. It was in March of that year that his wife Sarah and their three-month-old baby Dora died of diphtheria, leaving him as he wrote 'alone in this world save Adela . . . My heart is almost broken'.[34] In October of that year his brother John died, making him the proprietor of Grange, although despite his mother's pleas this did nothing to accelerate his return to Ireland. In November 1860 Abraham Lincoln was elected president of the United States with the implications of this for the future of slavery. Edward was appalled by slavery and had already determined to move from Virginia because of it. Kansas was his chosen destination as it had been incorporated into the Union as a free, non-slave state. He also judged it to be on the eventual route of the Santa Fé railway, with the possibilities that might give for employment but, perhaps more significant, speculatively for the value of the land he intended to purchase; it also marked a step towards an often expressed interest in the longer term to move farther west into the undeveloped frontier territories. Originally intending to take his whole family with him to Kansas, it was now only with his daughter Adela that he went.

Edward Richards's abhorrence of slavery had been immediate and unqualified. His daughter later described her father's motives, as recorded in his letters home, which 'breathe the greatest horror of slavery. It was the dreadful effect on the white people that struck him most . . . On one thing only was he fixed and determined: he would not live in a slave-holding State.'[35] Within a few months of arriving in Virginia he had described slavery as 'the most accursed system that any set of men were cursed with, either as masters or slaves'.[36] He commented on how poor and uneducated the white planters were and attributed their backwardness, their sloth, and their ignorance to slavery. He noted that in America '[h]ard work is the order of the day, except in the slave states—there the white men work little, I mean the planters'.[37] Two things that particularly appalled him were the instances of lynching that came to his attention and the laws against teaching a negro to read or write: 'The Slaves are the most totally debased & ignorant beings

I ever saw. It is a high crime punishable by <u>long imprisonment to teach one of them to read</u>.'

His abhorrence of slavery came together with his rejection of religion. In a letter to his aunt he wrote:

> It is a sick farce to hear the Southern clergymen talking about sending out missionary men to convert the New Zealanders & Sandwich Islanders, when they have at home 3,000,000 of human beings sunk in a state of the deepest moral debasement—Yet all these clergymen stand up for Slavery and call it a blessed institution, no wonder for many honest men to reject religion in toto when they see men professing to be its ministers so blinded by self interest as to uphold a state of society that has for its basis the degradation of these millions of men, for they dare not educate the blacks, if once they knew their own power, good bye to Slavery.[38]

In June 1851 after a visit to Richmond he wrote of Virginia:

> Of all the drunken countries I ever was in this beats them—every second man is almost dead from drink—& the brutes without exception horsewhip their wives—I never could account for the regular systematic flogging of the women that prevails here among the drunken families, till the other day, it is the constant whipping of the negroe women that so familiarises the men with the use of the scourge, that whenever they get drunk they apply it to the bottoms of their fair spouses. One would pity the women more were it not that they beat the slaves themselves, & it seems a just judgement on them—Mind of course I only speak of the "<u>ladies</u>" in the country, for the fine "<u>ladies</u>" in the towns, don't whip niggers, they only get others to do it for them!!!'[39]

Treatment of women, drinking, subjection of people by class, religious hypocrisy, slavery—these are the great evils that bring to the fore the principles that Edward Richards appears to have consolidated through his American experiences. Evident always is an extraordinary sense of fairness that caused him to balance the virtues of people against the evils of which they were part. Irishmen may be badly treated in America, but in a sense they deserve it. Slavery is an evil, but many of the slave owners treat their slaves humanely. Southern whites may be crass, ignorant, and dependent on slavery, but they are also open and generous to strangers, more so than their Northern compatriots.

III

In locating himself not only in the state of Virginia but in the region around Richmond, Edward Richards had put himself at the heart of events that were to change America forever. The historian William G. Thomas has drawn attention to the importance of Richmond in the civil war that was to ensue after Lincoln's election. Richmond was one of the largest manufacturing cities in the United States and by far the largest in the South, forming the heart of an international trading network especially with Brazil and Latin America. That included being 'the central point in an extremely lucrative and robust slave trade market', the location of the largest number of slaves anywhere in Virginia and with large-scale use of slaves in manufacturing industry, including railway building.[40] Edward must have extensively and closely experienced slavery. Indeed, in May 1852 he took Sarah and their infant son for a holiday to the seaside and had to hire a 14-year-old slave girl to help Sarah with the baby, explaining that if someone needed a servant it was a case of employing slaves or having 'none at all'—but 'I would not own one for anything'.[41]

By the time the American Civil War had begun he no longer lived in Virginia, having moved with Adela (see Figure 6.6) from Virginia to the then sparsely settled Kansas prairie to take up land on the edge of European settlement. Its incorporation as a free state of the Union ended the struggle between pro- and anti-slavery elements which had characterised it previously and earned it the sobriquet of 'Bleeding Kansas'. His response to the civil war when it came was both unusual and characteristic of him. While the war was fought principally over the issue of slavery, as one historian has shown the opposition to slavery was not by any means solely on moral grounds or on the rights of blacks but embodied many more issues of individual and economic interests and of regional identity.[42] But for Edward it was primarily a deep moral issue about the nature of human society, and when the time came, despite as a non–United States citizen not being liable to conscription, he volunteered to fight on the Union side, was accepted into a local unit of the mounted infantry militia, and was duly called out to fight. In doing this he was leaving behind, to her consternation, his nine-year-old daughter who, with her governess, was to assume significant responsibilities, with other neighbours relying on them for leadership.

The most remarkable consequence of this arose from instructions given to Adela by her father as to how an evacuation of the local people was to be carried out in the event of a Confederate victory in the area. While hostilities were raging she set out by horse on a hazardous scouting excursion to ascertain whether there was danger of a Confederate advance, with a number of neighbouring people attaching themselves to her on her return because of their confidence in her father's capacity to lead them to safety.[43] A significant defeat for the Confederates by the advance of a regular company of Union soldiers brought the immediate danger to an end.[44] In the aftermath of victory Edward and his daughter assisted in looking after the wounded, but characteristic of his sense of fairness, he insisted that they care for the Confederate wounded, given that others on the victorious side were caring only for their own. These were experiences for his daughter that would

Figure 6.6 Edward's daughter Adela, 'the young emigrant', age five-and-a-half years

Source: Reproduced with the permission of Mr Jeremy Hill.

shape much of her future and not least her association with her father. As she later wrote, referring also to the grief that underlay her father personally during these years:

> it was my unconscious mission to bring back once more to hope and interest in life my father, then in the prime of life, but stricken to earth by the deaths, in the short space of three years, of all the rest of his family . . . it made the bond between us extraordinarily close. Father, mother, playmate, friend, he always was to me, especially during those Kansas years, when my need was greatest; and the influence of his training has remained strong throughout my life.[45]

This was a remarkable background for a future Irish landlord and his American experience enabled him to apply very different perspectives to his management of his estate and to his role within Irish society. It was also a profoundly different upbringing for his daughter Adela, reflecting her father's views of the capacity and educative principles that were applicable for women and giving her a distinctive perspective that in due course influenced her as the inheritor of Grange, by then renamed Monksgrange. That house became the focus of considerable creative activity right up to recent times and the extent to which this nineteenth-century experience contributed is worthy of investigation. The history of Monksgrange and its occupants must be set at least in part within the context of this American episode.

IV

Adela Richards (by then Adela Orpen) was later to chronicle her extraordinary life as a child in the United States both in a novel[46] and in a volume of memoirs.[47] Their eventual return to Ireland, Edward in 1866 and Adela in 1867, was to a country again in the throes of political turbulence, and the question arises as to how Edward now connected this with his own and his family's past political opinions. Little evidence has been found yet of his view of the Fenians, but this would be of interest given his family's past. In her journal in 1849 his mother recorded receiving 'a most touchingly beautiful letter from that noble gifted being' Thomas Francis Meagher, the Young Irelander, referring ironically to the sentence of transportation being meted out to him and others by the '<u>merciful</u> English for their attempts to emancipate their country from slavery and oppression' and regretting that 'such a glorious fine creature should be lost to his country he loved so well!!'[48] Her late husband and Edward's father, Edward later wrote, 'was as might have been expected, in favour of removing the disabilities of the Catholics' during the Emancipation Campaign although, significantly, in the last year of his life he began to qualify this, dreading 'the use the priests would make of their newly acquired powers'.[49] This points to the line of distinction in the family's views on politics. They were not, at least until the 1880s, particularly attached to British government of Ireland nor to Protestant ascendancy but, not surprisingly, they sought to keep intact the role and responsibilities of the landowning class. Edward's father's support for Catholic emancipation was predicated on the assumption that landlords would retain their social standing and influence; thus his disquiet that in the latter part of O'Connell's campaign the Roman Catholic priests had acquired a power that seriously threatened the traditional landlord hegemony.

Edward's political views as a young man he articulated later in life, writing that he 'looked with somewhat of a favourable eye on the Repeal Movement, or rather the Young Ireland wing of it'.[50] According to Edward, 'Tom Davis's poetry, John Mitchell's prose and T. F. Meagher's burning eloquence completed my conversion, and in the early part of . . . [1848] I formally joined the Irish Confederation, an association having for its object the separation of Ireland from Great Britain'.[51] Subsequently, during the Land War of 1879–82, he became deeply hostile to Charles Stewart Parnell and the Land League. This was consistent with his and his family's interests as landlords and reflected his distress at the threat to the financial viability of his estate posed by the anti-rent campaign. His view of the place of landlords in Irish society connected with a line of thinking within Fenianism, characterised, for example, in John O'Leary, and hence, perhaps his hostility to them may have been less than that towards the Land League.

Edward Moore Richards's views on religion signify a continuing distinctiveness in his outlook. He alludes to his own view of religion by reference to those of his father, whom he describes as 'a radical in politics, and more or less of a Free thinker in religion'.[52] He discovered his father's views on religion only in 1861 when he expressed his own opinions to an aunt who reacted with 'Oh . . . that is just the way your father used to talk.'[53] He recorded in 1897 that he had not since a visit in 1848 ever returned to the house of one branch of his family as they would have 'shudder[ed] at the idea of an acknowledged anti-Christ, as I am, lodging under their roof'.[54] This earlier scepticism as well as his reaction and behaviour in America continued throughout his life, and by 1911 he had designated himself an agnostic in the census of that year. Privately at least, he rejected the doctrinal beliefs of the Christian Church while adhering generally to a broad deism. This did not compromise his general commitment to the Church of Ireland and in particular his support morally and financially of the local Killann church. Alongside this was a continuing friendship with Catholic priests in the area, including financial support for their work.[55]

A range of other interests singles him out as a nineteenth-century landlord with progressive ideas and interests, some of them in line with new ideas that were part of a contemporary global discourse. Astronomy was a particular interest and he used his engineering skills to design and construct an observatory at Monksgrange from which he observed the Transit of Venus on 6 December 1882.[56] More unusually, he continued to be a strong advocate for reform of women's dress, contributing to dress reform journals and using his drawing skills to design outfits. Although he connected his commitment to reform of women's dress to the cycling movement he made it clear that he saw cycling as a vehicle for his campaign and not the reason for it. As has been shown, these ideas had their origins in his observation of how Native American women and slave women dressed and had been encouraged by the dress reform movement which was much more advanced in the United States than in Britain and Ireland. This also reflected a deep and abiding concern for the interests and rights of women, contemporaneously with new cosmopolitan principles of women's role and rights. Arguably this was significantly influenced by the two most important and very strong women in his life, his mother, Dorothea, and his daughter Adela.

His relationship with his mother was an exceptional one. The warmth that comes through in their correspondence and the devotion recorded in her journal appears exceptional for a Victorian-era relationship and can be juxtaposed against her much lesser feelings for her older son, John, the inheritor of the estate. After his marriage Edward responded to a sense that his mother might fear a lessening of his affection for her, writing that 'you need not be afraid of that —the love for a wife need never encroach on that for a mother'.[57] On their return to Ireland Adela, brought up in the wilds of the prairie, characterised by her entranced Paris school friends 'La Sauvage D'Amerique', felt intimidated and alienated by the formality and stiffness of the people around her, the one exception being her 67-year-old grandmother, who she describes as the only other 'child' with whom she was able to play. One can only speculate as to how this relationship between his mother and daughter would have gratified Edward, given the exceptional and isolated conditions to which he had previously subjected his daughter.

When we put together the strength and sensitivity of his marriage with Sarah, his relationships with his daughter and his mother, his correspondence with other women, and his commitment to their interests (as in dress reform) there evolves a picture of a man for whom women were extremely important and whose interests remained a very significant part of his outlook. In this context it is interesting to look at the concerns that preoccupied him when Adela was about to marry her first cousin once removed, Goddard H. Orpen, a lawyer by profession. For months preceding the wedding in August 1880 Edward had endeavoured to arrange a marriage settlement for her, first with Goddard's father John H. Orpen, also a lawyer, and then with Goddard himself. His wish was to secure Adela's rights to any property she had at the time of her marriage in the event either of the failure of the marriage or of Goddard's death. He found himself frustrated by the obscure legal problems which these two lawyers raised and which seemed to miss the point of what he was trying to achieve. In the end Edward gave up and relied instead on an appeal to Goddard just days before the wedding, writing, 'I believe you and I are of the opinion that by natural right a woman ought to own her property after marriage as the man does his' and appealing to him 'to give [Adela] before marriage your written consent that she retains after marriage all that the [Married Women's Property] act enables her to do';[58] given the loopholes in that 1870 act, this envisaged a much weaker outcome than he had wanted.

In 1900 Edward transferred the ownership of Monksgrange and the estate to Adela, retiring with his second wife, Ellen, to Rosslare, where he died in 1911. Adela and Goddard Orpen created new lives for themselves, she abandoning a promising career as a novelist and essayist to become a proactive and innovative landed and farming proprietor and he leaving his profession as a London barrister for a life of scholarship that made him one of the most eminent historians of medieval Ireland. They lived on to experience in the last years of their lives a remarkable echo of Adela's childhood experiences. In 1924, in the midst of the Irish Civil War, she reflected on the extraordinary irony:

> Then and now. Three score years and half the habitable globe lie between those two worlds . . . Then I was a fat, red cheeked little girl of seven now I am a white haired old woman and yet how much there is of similarity in my life of today with the life of that faraway time. I was in Kansas and am in Ireland. There was a war in Kansas, men were in battle against each other, brother against brother, son against father. Ye Gods what is it in Ireland today? I know the feeling so well. The cold terror clutching at my heart then and now. Always thinking of what next was to happen, how frightened at the sound of a shot. How fearful of the sight of a stranger—then and now.[59]

It was indeed extraordinary that in her life she had personally participated directly in two civil wars 60 years apart. And in neither case was she merely an observer. In 1923 aged nearly 70 she faced down the republican irregulars who had arrived to search the house and potentially to burn it down, as happened to many others, as part of their campaign of reprisals against the Irish Protestant elite and their property. Probably without knowing at the time that she had a secret ally in a leading rebel Myles Fenlon the house was again saved in a very similar way to that of 1798. Adela died in 1927, her husband Goddard in 1932.

The lives of Edward Moore Richards and his daughter Adela are illustrative of the increasing diversity of experiences and the rapidly changing social and political environment for the Irish landed elite from the middle of the nineteenth century to the early years of an independent Irish state. These were years that posed great challenges for their class, ones that threatened their future not only in terms of their traditional economic and social role but also of their very capacity to continue to contribute meaningfully to the society and country in which they lived. In the case of Monksgrange and the Richards and Orpen families the successive crises of the land war, of dispossession of their estates, and finally the destruction of the wider British framework on which they had come to rely involved unwelcome turbulence in their lives and in the custodianship of the house and estate that was their inheritance. With some difficulty they weathered that storm and their children, grandchildren, great-grandchildren, and now great-great-grandchildren have not only survived as the proprietors of Monksgrange but have also worked assiduously in order to contribute creatively and constructively to the new polity in which they lived. The very unconventional episode of Edward Moore Richards and his daughter in a frontier society in the midst of civil war represented an unusual backdrop and a continuing point of reference for this particular family as they faced those challenges and changes.

These experiences of individuals also suggest ways that migration and movement across national boundaries can produce significant change at least within micro-societies such as, in this case, an Irish landed society faced with very significant challenges. There is now an extensive literature specifically based on the letters that Irish migrants wrote home and those they received from family still in Ireland, most notably Kerby A. Miller in the case of migrants to North America, Angela McCarthy for those who went to New Zealand, and Patrick O'Farrell and David Fitzpatrick for Irish migrants to Australia.[60] In addition D.H. Akenson has published extensively on the Irish diaspora, including a book on the Irish in New Zealand,[61] and in an article published in 1990 he makes a comparison from within the then existing literature on letters from the Irish in North America, New Zealand, and Australia, as well as drawing on a selection of letters held in the Public Record Office of Northern Ireland for his own analysis.[62] In that article he points to one distinction in the literature relevant to the case of Edward Moore Richards. On one hand, Akenson writes, Miller concludes that 'Irish emigrant letters were pervaded by the theme of "exile"' and that, despite most having emigrated voluntarily, they saw themselves as having been forced to leave Ireland, while on the other hand O'Farrell finds no such theme of exile but rather 'evidence of "self-reliance," which came to mean among other things, "freedom from the tyranny of the old place"'.[63] This contrast may raise interesting issues about differences in types of migrants (especially social class or counties of origin), variations in the nature of the host society (including contrasting stages of societal development in North America and the antipodean colonies), and distinctions of religion. In her more recent work, however, on the letters of Irish migrants in New Zealand, Angela McCarthy suggests that Miller's conclusions might need to be revisited.[64] This, to some extent at least, he has done in his later work *Ireland and Irish America*, in which he develops a more nuanced view of the sense in which Irish migrants to America saw themselves as exiles even though having emigrated voluntarily and been conscious of the material advantages that would accrue.[65]

Whatever the outcome of this continuing discourse it is clear that Edward Moore Richards falls into the category of those described by O'Farrell insofar as there is no sense of exile in his letters from the United States while there are remarks that fall within the broad category of 'freedom from the tyranny of the old place,' although given his class and status in Ireland the 'tyrannies' from which he had been freed were very different ones from those applicable to the bulk of migrants to whatever location. In any reassessment of the comparative experiences of Irish migrants to different places, account might also be taken of Edward Richards's observations of Irish labourers in the United States and how they were treated there. Apart from class difference this might point to contrasting receptions afforded

Irish people in different destinations. The experiences of Edward and Adela Richards in the United States thus opens up a personal case that might stand at least as a commentary on different experiences of Irish migrants but with the additional dimension of an eventual assessment of how their roles on their return to Ireland might have been influenced by their American experiences. Continuing work on the archive at Monksgrange, it is hoped, will lead to more conclusions being drawn in relation to such questions.

NOTES

1. The one exception was by reference to a very small selection of documents for the article by N. G. Bowe, 'A Cotswold-inspired Venture towards Modernism in Ireland: Edward Richards Orpen (1884–1967) and the Grange Furniture Industry, 1927–1932', *The Decorative Arts Society 1850 to the Present*, 27 (2003), pp. 95–111.
2. Monksgrange Archive (hereafter MGA), Dorothea Sargent's Journal, vol. 2, 4 September 1851.
3. MGA, Dorothea Sargent's Journal, vol. 2, 31 December 1851.
4. MGA, Edward Moore Richards (hereafter EMR) to Dorothea Sargent (hereafter DS), 15 May 1850.
5. Ibid., 11 September 1849.
6. Ibid.
7. Ibid., 30 November 1850.
8. Ibid., 11 December 1851.
9. Ibid., 7 April 1850.
10. Ibid.
11. MGA, EMR to his Aunt Bess, 4 April 1850.
12. MGA, EMR to Richard Sargent, 28 February 1852.
13. Ibid., 3 February 1850
14. MGA, EMR to DS, 19 March 1852.
15. Ibid.
16. *Wexford Independent*, 7 July 1855.
17. Ibid.
18. MGA, EMR to DAS, 16 June 1850.
19. Ibid.
20. Ibid., 29 March 1859.
21. Ibid., 6 October 1850
22. A.E. Orpen, *Memories of the Old Emigrant Days in Kansas, 1862–1865: Also of a Visit to Paris in 1867* (Edinburgh & London: William Blackwood, 1926), p. 131.
23. Edward Moore Richards, 'The Relative Physical Powers of Man and Woman', *Rational Dress Gazette: Organ of the Rational Dress League*, 6 (March 1899).
24. Edward Moore Richards, 'English Fair Play', *Rational Dress Gazette*, 15 (December 1899).
25. EMR to Adela Richards, 19 May 1871.
26. MGA, EMR, notes, 18 July 1901.
27. See, for example, MGA, EMR to Ann Owen, 15 July 1879.
28. MGA, EMR to Adelia Gates, 19 November 1859.
29. MGA, EMR to DAS, 4 March 1859.
30. Ibid., 16 June 1850.
31. Ibid., 11 December 1851
32. Ibid.

33. Ibid., 17 June 1851.
34. Ibid., 20 February 1860.
35. Orpen, *Memories*, p. 25.
36. MGA, EMR to Richard Sargent, 3 February 1850
37. MGA, EMR to DAS, 27 April 1851.
38. MGA, EMR to his Aunt Bess, 4 April 1850.
39. MGA, EMR to DAS, 17 June 1851.
40. W. G. Thomas, *The Iron Way: Railroads, the Civil War, and the Making of Modern America* (New Haven, CT, and London: Yale University Press, 2011), p. 95.
41. MGA, EMR to DAS, 11 July 1852.
42. A. Castel, *A Frontier State at War: Kansas, 1861–1865* (Ithaca, NY: Cornell University Press, 1958; reprinted in 1979 by Greenwood Press).
43. Orpen, *Memories*, pp. 156–57.
44. Ibid., p. 166; E. M. Richards, '"Price's Raid": Personal Reminiscences of the American Civil War, Kansas, October 1864', edited by A. Bishop, *The Irish Sword*, 7:28 (1966), pp. 234–40. Note that the editor in his introduction reverses the ages of Richards's two children who died and incorrectly runs together their deaths as happening at the same time.
45. Orpen, *Memories*, p. [vii].
46. A. E. Orpen, The *Jay-hawkers: A Story of Free Soil and Border Ruffian Days* (London and New York: Appleton, 1900).
47. Orpen, *Memories*. Another novel, *Perfection* City (London: Hutchinson, 1897), is also set in Kansas but bears little resemblance to the experiences of herself or family.
48. MGA, Dorothea Sargent's Journal, vol. 2, 19 June 1849.
49. Edward Moore Richards, 'Rems' (retrospective journal compiled in 1890s, hereafter EMR 'Rems'), vol. 1, p. 16.
50. EMR 'Rems', vol. 2, p. 23
51. Ibid.
52. EMR 'Rems', vol 1, p. 16
53. Ibid., pp. 15–16.
54. EMR 'Rems', vol. 2, p. 18.
55. MGA, EMR Letter Book, 1876–80: EMR to Catholic priests, 4 July 1880 (copies), fols 714–5; EMR to Revd R. S. Blacker (Woodbrook), 29 December 1879 (copy), fol. 598.
56. MGA, Ellen Richards's Diary, introductory section, 1882/3. This journal, formerly the property of Anne Wood-Roe, has now been donated by her to the Monskgrange Archive.
57. MGA, EMR to DS (n.d.).
58. MGA, EMR Letter Book, 1876–80, EMR to Goddard H. Orpen, 12 August 1880 (copy), fol. 740.
59. MGA, Adela Elizabeth Orpen, Haphazard Memories (transcription by Jeremy Hill).
60. K. A. Miller, *Emigrants and Exiles: Ireland and the Irish Exodus to North America* (New York: Oxford University Press, 1985); A. McCarthy, *Irish Migrants in New Zealand, 1840–1937: 'The Desired Haven'* (Woodbridge, Suffolk: The Boydell Press, 2005); P. O'Farrell, *The Irish in Australia* (Sydney: New South Wales University Press, 1987) and (with B. Trainor), *Letters from Irish Australia, 1825–1929* (Sydney and Belfast: New South Wales University Press and Ulster Historical Foundation, 1984); D. Fitzpatrick, *Oceans of Consolation: Personal Accounts of Irish Migration to Australia* (Melbourne: Melbourne University Press, 1995).
61. D. H. Akenson, *Half the World from Home: Perspectives on the Irish in New Zealand, 1860–1950* (Wellington: Victoria University Press, 1990).

62. D. H. Akenson 'Reading the Texts of Rural Immigrants: Letters from the Irish in Australia, New Zealand, and North America', *Canadian Papers in Rural History*, 7 (1990), pp. 387–406
63. Ibid., p. 388.
64. McCarthy, *Irish Migrants*, p. 264.
65. K. A. Miller, *Ireland and Irish America: Culture, Class, and Transatlantic Migration* (Dublin: Field Day, 2008), especially pp. 79–80.

7 Coming from over the Waves
The Emergence of Collaborative Action in Ireland and Wales

Robert Lindsey

Although we are now more than a century distant from the heyday of pan-Celticism and the enthusiasm of early Celtic Congresses, practical or material cooperation between Irish and Welsh groups with cultural-nationalist objectives is a phenomenon only observable within a much more recent timeframe. While studies into the relationship between the Irish and the Welsh were once restricted to the fields of literary studies and linguistics (often within an ancient or medieval timeframe that investigated a shared Celticity),[1] this has now changed in light of manifold points of connection during the twentieth century. Several historical studies and narratives now exist that explore Welsh and Irish relations, generally in the context of migration between the two countries.[2]

The best example of recent Irish/Welsh scholarship is probably the 'Irish and Welsh Writing' issue of the *Irish Studies Review* in 2009. Several articles used comparative approaches and dealt with a variety of timeframes and disciplines, including cultural, organisational, and biographical history, literary studies, and cultural studies. As noted by editors Claire Connolly and Katie Grammich, although 'it is by no means common for . . . a comparative perspective to be brought to bear on the two countries in the period after 1600 . . . the perception that Wales and Ireland still share a "special relationship" is widespread'.[3] This issue aspired towards exploring that special relationship, which is an aim shared by this present study.

This chapter seeks to outline the way in which Irish and Welsh nationalist and cultural organisations were interconnected in the post-war period, in a way that was not possible before the Second World War. It is clear that the Welsh and Irish non-governmental organisations under discussion were not simply bound by a sense of Celtic fraternity to one another. Instead, they very much looked beyond their own shores for all kinds of moral, organisational, and material support to further their native causes. The organisations discussed in this article were united by the sharing of similar aims and/or philosophies, that is, to the fulfilment of a nationhood characterised by comparable cultural or political objectives, facilitated by historical context and a perceived struggle against British and/or Anglophone authorities. Although at the extreme end we do find that violent nationalist groups probably exchanged equipment with one another in the 1960s, successful 'cooperation' appears to have been best characterised by capturing the attention of the British and Irish media, by acts made in the name of multiple organisations strengthened in solidarity.

This chapter characterises the shifting relationship between Irish and Welsh nationalists during the mid-twentieth century and then outlines the cooperative history of several significant Irish and Welsh organisations. The precursor was the Irish Anti-Partition League, whose activities in Ireland and Britain in the 1940s and early 1950s brought Irish and Welsh nationalists together in a manner only ever imagined at gatherings of the primarily academic Celtic Congresses. From here, further attempts at cooperation can be traced in the civil disobedience campaigns of the Irish and Welsh language movements, and in the activities of paramilitary groups such as the Irish Republican Army (IRA) and Welsh associates such as the Free Wales Army and Mudiad Amddiffyn Cymru. For members of these admittedly disparate groups, their inspiration can generally be traced to the Easter Rising and the leaders of the Irish independence movement.[4]

An organisation is in practice an agglomeration of like-minded individuals operating under specific terms of reference to achieve set objectives, and this needs to be kept in mind as we explore the threads of connection between these groups. In the context of Welsh and Irish relations, Niamh Hourigan has researched organisational and interpersonal connections in her work on minority-language media.[5] She adopted a model of networking and diffusion within a protest movement (*diffusion* referring to a 'process whereby past events make future events more likely'),[6] outlined by sociologists Pamela Oliver and Daniel Myers in 2003. Their modelling specified three key elements underlying the process of diffusion, namely, 'spatial/social', 'movement/organisational', and 'relational/social'. These elements respectively referred to the need for people with common interests to meet in a shared physical space, the need for organisations with similar aims to communicate with one another, and the possibility of organisations being connected to non-members (and the groups they identify with) by personal and social ties.[7]

The primary purpose of the media is described by Pamela Oliver and Daniel Myers as a 'mechanism for having influence on a wider public and the authorities'. It should also be highlighted that the media was the main (and sometimes only) 'mechanism' for the initial transference of information and ideas between Irish and Welsh groups—the Irish response to Saunders Lewis's call in 1962 for civil disobedience among Welsh language activists is a case in point. This model is useful, and I refer to a 'web of diffusion' to describe a network of personal associations that influenced the policies and actions of a range of groups: the IRA, the Anti-Partition League, and the Gaelic League in Ireland and Welsh groups such as the Welsh Language Society and the Free Wales Army. This study does not focus on political (and, more recently, parliamentary) nationalist parties such as Sinn Féin and

Plaid Cymru, yet it must be acknowledged that membership of any of the aforementioned groups often overlapped with membership in these political parties and political life in Wales or Ireland.

Sven Beckert has observed that the recent 'transnational turn' of historical inquiry is a 'way of seeing' that 'takes as its starting point the interconnectedness of human history as a whole, and while it acknowledges the extraordinary importance of states, empires, and the like, it pays attention to networks, processes, beliefs, and institutions that transcend these politically defined spaces'.[8] This chapter contributes to a transnational perspective on Irish history in the twentieth century, by recognising that Irish nationalists and language advocates were sometimes participants of, and undoubtedly subject to, events and debates taking place in Wales in the post-war period.

CELTIC NATIONALISM AND THE ANTI-PARTITION LEAGUE

Irish and Welsh nationalists of the post-war era did have a precedent to draw upon, in the attempted collaboration of Welsh and Irish members of Parliament (MPs) during the 1880s and 1890s on issues such as land reform and Home Rule for the constituent nations of the United Kingdom. For example, Welsh Liberals such as T. E. Ellis sought to remedy the poverty and insecurity of Welsh farmers by instigating a movement along the lines of Michael Davitt's Irish Land League. Ellis and Davitt corresponded in early 1886 on the topic of 'Celtic cooperation', and Davitt was invited to speak at a number of meetings in Wales on the topic of agrarian reform. Ellis was also an avid supporter of Home Rule for Wales and was therefore a supporter of his party leader William Gladstone's call for 'Home Rule all round', voting in favour of an Irish Home Rule bill in June 1886. Subsequently, Ellis visited Ireland in September 1887 to support Irish nationalist William O'Brien, who had been summoned to court for making inflammatory speeches. Speaking at large meetings in Dublin and Cork, Ellis was hailed as the 'Parnell of Wales'.[9]

However, it was widely held at the time that Ireland and Wales were very different countries possessing very different ethnic, religious, and economic landscapes. Most Welsh newspapers treated Davitt's 1886 tour with suspicion, and even prominent proponents of Welsh land reform such as Thomas Gee avoided him on the basis that the Irish campaign for land reform had been too violent and radical in its objectives.[10] More generally, it needs to be recognised that the strength of Welsh calls for separation was not like that of Ireland, where the issue was exacerbated by religious and ethnic tensions that were particularly evident in Ulster.[11] Welsh cooperation in Westminster on the subject of Irish Home Rule was therefore inconsistent. When Gladstone presented a bill for Irish Home Rule in 1886, some members of his own party opposed it in sympathy of Protestant Ulster. While the majority of the 34 Welsh MPs supported Gladstone's defeated bill, seven Welsh

Liberals dissented.[12] This vote, which had led to a split in the Liberal Party and the fall of Gladstone's government, stalled any prospect of a Welsh Home Rule bill and highlighted some fundamental differences in the objectives and tactics of Irish and Welsh nationalists.

Despite being two geographically, culturally and politically related societies, possessing in the words of Irish- and Welsh-speaking activist Máirtín Ó Cadhain a 'close yet unclear connection',[13] there exists a long history of ignorance and prejudice regarding Welsh understandings of Ireland and Irish understandings of Wales. From the Welsh perspective, the Irish experience of conflict and civil strife in the early twentieth century served as a powerful antidote to the electoral prospects of Welsh nationalists. In the words of Harri Pritchard Jones, '[t]he attitude of most Welsh people towards Ireland . . . was coloured by the anti-nationalist propaganda of the Labour Party in Wales, which spoke of Ireland as being poor, priest-ridden and inward-looking, and suffering from censorship of even its own authors'.[14] Moreover, the early 1940s saw an ongoing campaign in Britain to denigrate the Irish nation for its failure to spring to the defence of the Commonwealth, a campaign that did not go unnoticed in Labour-dominated Wales. Welsh nationalist Roy Lewis noted in 1949 that Plaid Cymru, the Welsh nationalist party, had been unusual in supporting nationalist Irish causes throughout this time, but that 'when anti-Irish feeling was sedulously fostered by those in authority', it had been an effective way of losing votes for Plaid.[15] A more direct relationship with Irish groups or the Irish government itself was certainly not desirable at this time.

This sentiment started to shift at the end of the Second World War in 1945. The moral and political implications of de-colonisation and the principle of national self-determination began to manifest itself in the context of localised Welsh politics, dominated by the Labour Party but also starting to witness the growth of Plaid Cymru's base of support. The principle of Home Rule or independence for the constituent nations of Britain inevitably drew momentum from Britain's in-principle support of self-determination, enshrined by its ratification of the Allies' Atlantic Charter in 1941, and of the United Nations Charter in 1945.

In this post-war mood of self-determination, 'partition' re-emerged as a political buzzword. While Irish nationalists wished to tear down the partition between South and North, some Welsh wished to *strengthen* the sense of partition between England and Wales. As a matter of re-defining nationhood within Britain and Ireland, Welsh and Irish nationalists increasingly saw this as a shared battle. The Catholic archbishop of Cardiff, Irishman Michael McGrath, firmly outlined the Irish nationalist perspective in 1947, as the partition of Ireland once again became a key political issue:

> Partition as a policy . . . has been rejected as a solution of the problems in the East, Palestine and India. The experiment, most foolishly tried in Ireland, has shown the evils innate in such a system, open injustice,

blood-letting, deprivation of electoral rights by gerrymandering of constituencies, as a result of which both minorities and majorities suffer. To crown the evil—for the partition of Ireland is a most flagrant moral evil—it digs ever more deeply the grave of any permanent friendship between two peoples, those in Great Britain and those in Ireland, who should be living on terms of the closest friendship. The conditions of the post-war world dot the i's and cross the t's of this statement.[16]

Welsh nationalists clearly took heart from their Irish supporters, and Roy Lewis recalled how Éamon de Valera had called on the big power blocks of the world to be broken up on several occasions. Lewis concluded that whether partition or de-partition was the answer to specific national problems, 'if Celtic nations are to survive, they must turn their bonds of sentiment into practical co-operation.'[17]

Of course, from the perspective of most major British political parties, devolution of the Empire and devolution of Britain's constituent nations were two entirely different issues.[18] Therefore, while the international climate and discourse of self-determination gained momentum, Irish and Welsh nationalists still could not expect support from the Great Powers or from the United Nations in the period after its creation in 1945. Brendan Lynn provides the humorous example of Ireland's initial negotiations to join North Atlantic Treaty Organization (NATO) in 1949. American diplomat T.C. Achilles recalled that upon Ireland being invited to join NATO as a key 'stepping-stone' in submarine warfare against the communist threat, the Irish response was that 'they would be delighted to join provided we could get the British to give back the Six Counties'. According to Achilles, 'We replied in effect, "It's been nice knowing you", and that was that.'[19]

Nevertheless, the very existence of the Irish Free State and succeeding republic, generally finding its 'creation story' in the Easter Rising of 1916, provided a powerful precedent for nationalist minority movements throughout Western Europe.[20] The apparent moral of this story, the necessity for politically autonomous spaces within which oppressed cultures may be liberated and sustained, found continuous expression from the time of the signing of the Anglo-Irish Treaty in 1921 onwards. To take three Welsh examples, separated by time and context:

- Editorial from a Welsh-language newspaper, 1927: 'Irishmen . . . have displayed a determination and perseverance and a willingness to sacrifice for their country which should be a lesson to us in Wales. In our opinion it would be a great advantage to Welshmen to visit Ireland as often as possible at present, and see how the Celtic nation governs itself.'[21]
- Editorial from the *Welsh Nationalist*, 1947: 'Look at Ireland . . . they have fought the good fight against the Empire and they have almost won. Wales should follow the great example given by Ireland.'[22]

- President of Plaid Cymru and the Celtic League, Gwynfor Evans, April 1966: The Irish struggle demonstrated that 'subjection to England and France was neither inevitable nor permanent.'[23]

Nevertheless, for the reasons already outlined, the emergence of cooperation only really starts after the end of the Second World War, with the creation of the 'Anti-Partition League' (APL) at a meeting in Dungannon, County Tyrone, on 14 November 1945. Following the support given by de Valera's government in defeating wartime attempts at conscription in Northern Ireland, and his statement that current conditions favoured the renewal of a 'a big drive to end partition', northern nationalists were given hope that progress might finally be made on this issue. However, despite a high level of grass-roots support from a broad spectrum of Catholic and nationalist groups, both north and south of the border, there was nevertheless little sympathy for the cause in Westminster or on the international stage.[24] In this context, the spread of the movement to Scotland, England, and Wales took on a greater significance at the time, demonstrating that support for the cause went beyond the borders of Ireland itself.

As suggested earlier on, the concept of partition had contrasting significance in Wales and Ireland, but only because Welsh and Irish nationalists had the same goal of creating a unified and independent nation. Roy Lewis responded to this apparent contrast at an APL meeting in Cardiff in 1947 by stating that 'Wales is not blessed with a strip of sea between her and England'.[25] Plaid Cymru opened their new headquarters in Cardiff in March the same year, and during the massive demonstration that marked this occasion, a resolution was passed for the British government to 'right the wrong inflicted on Ireland by the establishment of the Border across the north-eastern part of the country'. While one observer thought that this was a strange demand from a Welsh nationalist perspective, Plaid executive member Glyn Williams told him that '[i]f they want borders, let them make natural ones . . . Let them place a border between two distinct racial territories and then Wales will be free forever from the English.' In a further display of solidarity, he added wryly that 'we'll tell them [the English] we are exporting our surplus coal to Ireland'.[26]

Welsh support on the anti-partition front was justified in terms of 'repayment' for past support from the Irish government and from Irish people in Wales. When prominent Welsh nationalist J. E. Jones wrote to the *Irish Press* about partition in March 1949, he claimed that 'the Welsh nationalist movement has already drawn much moral and material support from Eire as well as from Irishmen in Wales; the party attempts to repay some of this debt by supporting the anti-Partition and other Irish movements'.[27] However, it should be pointed out that this prior 'support' in fact had no organised or collaborative features, purely moral, and can only be in reference to the several well-publicised, Welsh-themed, orations given by de Valera, Lord Ashbourne, and other prominent Irishmen at Celtic Congresses over the previous 25 years.

It is not surprising that the APL, being an Irish cause, was launched in Wales as an initiative of Irish migrants. The central figure in the story of the APL in Wales was John Fogarty, a Cardiff businessman and native of Donegal who set up the Cardiff branch of the APL in 1947. Although APL branches appeared to be limited to South Wales, where the largest Irish communities were to be found, there was a genuinely Welsh aspect to the activities and membership of the Welsh APL. When the Ferndale branch was founded in July 1948 in the Rhondda Valley, the initial meeting attracted 56 members from Cardiff (including Fogarty), as well as members from nearby Tonypandy. On viewing the crowd in front him, the local reverend and branch chairman said that it was 'very gratifying to find the Welsh people joining their Irish friends in their efforts to remove the last barrier to Irish Unity and Freedom'.[28]

Despite concerted electioneering in Northern Ireland and effort expended in drumming up support in Wales and the rest of Britain, the APL made no headway in achieving its aims. The main Welsh contribution to the APL campaign, apart from the moral support provided by Welsh branches, was in the presence of several Welsh speakers at APL events between the years 1950 and 1954.[29] However, with regard to the primary aim of uniting all of the nationalist groups in Stormont by utilising public pressure, this battle was as good as lost as early as 1949. The new inter-party government of Ireland that had ousted de Valera and Fianna Fáil in early 1948, led by Taoiseach John A. Costello, had eventually come around to express renewed support for the nationalists in the North, and did so by repealing the External Relations Act of 1936 that had kept Ireland within the Commonwealth. The impact of this was to unite the Unionists in fear of the proposed republic and the possibility of renewed civil unrest, and while candidates under the APL ticket garnered 27.2 per cent of the votes in the Northern Ireland general election on 10 February 1949, the Unionist Party under Sir Basil Brooke actually increased their share of the vote and gained four extra seats.[30] This defeat ended any short-term hopes that Irish nationalists had of effecting constitutional change through Northern Ireland's democratic processes. In other words, the later involvement of Welsh speakers at APL meetings and rallies suggests that this was little more than an attempt to shore up perceptions of a broad based support for anti-partitionism, at a time when Unionist success at Stormont and international silence suggested otherwise.

From the Welsh perspective, the visibility of the nationalist cause in the media was always welcome, at a time when Plaid Cymru generally attracted less than 1 per cent of the Welsh electoral vote. The APL campaign had succeeded in involving Welsh nationalists in Irish matters and in establishing important points of contact. Gwynfor Evans was the most significant figure, having developed a relationship with Éamon de Valera during this time, and his later involvement with Plaid Cymru and the Celtic League (founded in 1961) ensured that Irish matters would continue to matter in Wales. Having been one of many APL members to express the need for a new relationship between Ireland and Wales, Evans was at least able to say at the APL's St. Patrick's Day dinner in Cardiff in 1952 that there was now a closer cooperation between the 'Celtic races'.[31]

'WELSH TACTICS' AND LANGUAGE ACTIVISM

In light of shared views relating to cultural nationalism, it is not surprising that post-war cooperation was to be increasingly found between cultural organisations in Wales and Ireland. Nevertheless, in the task of safeguarding national cultures through activism and lobbying, the Irish and the Welsh possessed contrasting traditions. As the discourse of pacifism is often seen to be a distinct part of the modern Welsh national character, it is perhaps surprising to find that the more confrontational aspects of modern Irish activism (particularly on behalf of the Irish language) drew inspiration from Wales in the post-War period.

The 40 years following the signing of the Anglo-Irish Treaty in 1921 bore witness to three emerging realities that came to influence the Welsh political landscape: the continued decline of Welsh in its heartland of 'West Wales'; the growing realisation that the 'Gaelic Ireland' promised after Irish independence had failed to emerge even under sympathetic government; and the failure of any advancement of the Home Rule and independence campaigns in Northern Ireland and Wales. The Irish experiences were important to Welsh nationalists, and although it was often asserted that there were few points of contact across the Irish Sea, this viewpoint became increasingly inaccurate over time. This awareness grew into contact, and contact brought about cooperation among cultural nationalists in Wales and Ireland. Some activists advocated the need to disengage the threatened Irish and Welsh languages from questions of political status, whereas a small minority maintained the need for political unity at any cost to save the 'national language'. We will look at both of these divergent traditions.

Historically, the precedence of reviving native culture over the need for political autonomy found its greatest advocate in Saunders Lewis, poet, playwright, novelist, activist, and co-founder of the Welsh Nationalist Party (later 'Plaid Cymru') in 1925. However, he was an admirer of the leaders of the Easter Rising, and as a younger man he was not averse to the use of non-lethal violence at the very least.[32] Lewis was a regular delegate to the only pan-Celtic forum of the interwar years, the annual Celtic Congresses, and his earliest comments reported in the Irish press (in September 1929) illustrate his viewpoint quite succinctly: 'A language should not be kept alive at the cost of every other ideal that made for nationhood. Until Wales was baptised with the same idealistic fire and high-mindedness as that which inspired Ireland, her language would not be the instrument of the finest Celtic literature of the twentieth century.'[33]

In other words, without a political framework to sustain Welsh, the language would suffer and languish, and indeed *should* do so if it was distracting nationalists from the task of achieving political freedom for Wales. His words were translated into action a few years later in 1936, when Lewis and two accomplices started a fire at the RAF Penrhos bombing range in the Llŷn Peninsula. The court cases that followed were a watershed in the history of Welsh nationalism, and their actions constituted the first act of Welsh violence against British hegemony in more than 500 years, but any concrete results fell far short of Welsh autonomy. The years that followed saw the proportion of Welsh speakers in Wales fall to 28.9 per cent by 1951 and awoke Lewis to what he saw as the stark reality: there was almost no more time left to save the Welsh language.

It was in this frame of mind, fearful that the upcoming release of the 1961 UK census statistics would confirm his concerns, that Lewis read his 'Tynged yr Iaith' ('Fate of the Language') speech in a BBC Radio broadcast on 13 February 1962. He said that by the end of the century 'Welsh will end as a living language, should the present trend continue',[34] and he advocated two activities that had hardly been seen in Wales before (and had been declining in Ireland for nearly 50 years): grassroots activism, and nonviolent resistance. In the mass appeal of the Gaelic League, and in the civil disobedience campaigns against the British during the 1919–21 War of Independence, we see that neither activity was foreign to the Irish historical experience, but in a similar way to the Welsh, they had never been combined for the purpose of language revival before. From the Welsh perspective, Lewis cited a single precedent and cause célèbre, that of Trefor and Eileen Beasley, who fought with Llanelli Rural District Council for eight years to have their rates notice issued in the Welsh language.[35]

Although no longer obsessed with the need for independence before saving the language, Lewis still saw value in the lessons of Irish history. He felt that the Welsh had not done enough to protect their country and natural resources from exploitation, citing the dam being built at Tryweryn to supply Liverpool with water as a key example. At the time of the lecture, lots had been said against the construction of the dam, but little done. The authorities surely noted, 'We are not Irishmen', and relied on Welsh apathy to push ahead with their project.[36] In suggesting that the Irish have risen up against authority when threatened at various times across history, it is interesting to observe how this Welsh call to arms now returned to Ireland in the form of language activism. In any case, as a direct result of Lewis's lecture, the Welsh Language Society was founded on 4 August 1962, thus beginning a decades-long campaign to assert Welsh-language rights through the use of direct action—protests, sit-ins, hunger strikes, the painting over of English road signs and the refusal to pay various bills issued in English.

As revolutionary as Lewis's call to action was in Wales itself, it also had a far-reaching influence in Ireland. His ideas primarily manifested themselves in the actions of Irish language advocacy groups such as the Gaelic League. By the early 1960s, the Gaelic League had survived 40 years of neglect and antagonism from the Irish government. Although the league is often credited with slowing the decline of the Irish language in its early years, Irish independence and an association with all-Ireland Republicanism limited the Gaelic League's capacity to attract members and to promote the Irish language via consensus. It often relied on the financial support of the Gaelic Athletic Association and other non-state groups, and in general it was seen to be a relic of the past 'Gaelic League times' very much referring to the early years when there was still widespread support for the creation of a predominantly Irish-speaking nation.[37] Máirtín Ó Cadhain was clearly the figure who altered the trajectory of Irish language activism, the man through whom Saunders Lewis's ideas were initially diffused in the Ireland of the mid-1960s. A fluent Welsh speaker who had maintained links with some of Wales' most eminent public figures for more than 20 years, he took it upon himself to translate Lewis's 'Tynged yr Iaith' within weeks of the original Welsh broadcast.[38] Ó Cadhain had been an admirer of the Gaelic League as a younger man, but came to criticise it for its 'submission to conservatism and the establishment'.[39] He felt at the time of Lewis' lecture that the League was not 'serviceable, inspirational or vigorous enough', even if it was still possible to 'change the League without changing its name'.[40] The conservatism apparently imposed upon the League is to be observed in the fact that while Lewis's call was doing the rounds in Irish language circles, the Gaelic League was trumped by Ó Cadhain's group, 'Misneach' ('Courage' in English), in adopting these new Welsh tactics.

The first expressions of direct action on behalf of the Irish language came in 1963, when the newly formed Misneach marched on the home of Taoiseach Seán Lemass to demand the release of three fishermen from Inis Bearacháin, in Connemara, who had refused to pay their rates because of the poor state of public services in their Gaeltacht.[41] Misneach's activities climaxed in 1966, a significant year when the 50th anniversary of the Easter Rising proved to be a catalyst for much nationalist activity and debate about Irish nationhood. In this year both Ireland and Wales saw campaigns where people refused to pay motor tax bills issued in English, the Irish campaign supported in principle by every major Irish-language organisation. Rex Mac Gall, an Irish-language columnist for the *Irish Independent*, directly credited these events to the influence of Saunders Lewis and Máirtín Ó Cadhain.[42] The following years would see Misneach involved in sign-painting campaigns and, more controversially, physical confrontations with an organisation set up to end the compulsory teaching of Irish in schools, the Language Freedom Movement.[43] The example provided by Ó Cadhain and Misneach continued to diffuse these 'Welsh methods' amongst Irish-language advocates, and these were essentially the same approaches used by the Gaeltacht civil rights movement from 1969 onwards.

Utilisation of these controversial 'Welsh methods' ultimately led to closer cooperation with groups such as the Welsh Language Society. The Gaelic League under the leadership of Maolsheachlainn Ó Caollaí gradually adapted itself to this new approach and, moreover, began to advocate for

Welsh and Breton language rights as part of a collaborative effort in the late 1960s.[44] This process was facilitated by the Celtic League and sustained by personal links between key Welsh and Irish activists, Ó Caollaí and Welsh Language Society chairman Dafydd Iwan in particular. These figureheads worked together on a range of shared issues: both men spoke against the closure of the Irish-medium school at Dún Chaoin, County Kerry, in 1970, and they also organised a joint protest against discriminatory language policies in Northern Ireland and Wales outside the British Embassy in Dublin in November 1971.[45]

Nevertheless, the Gaelic League did not wholeheartedly follow Misneach's lead into the use of 'Welsh methods' until the mid-1970s. At the Gaelic League's *ard-fheis* in 1973, Ó Caollaí was re-elected as president on the promise to adopt 'Welsh methods' in order to achieve a declaration of rights, including the need for Irish-language television.[46] In 1975, he brought over members of the Welsh Language Society to speak to Gaelic Leaguers about their methods of protest, and this proved to be a turning point for many members—in Hourigan's words, 'a key moment of diffusion'. The next few years saw the Welsh ideas put into practice—members refused to pay television licence fees, some formed picket lines or chained themselves to state buildings to attract media attention, and one even dared to climb the RTÉ broadcasting mast in 1976.[47] The Gaelic League also maintained good relations with Plaid Cymru and Celtic League president Gwynfor Evans, at a time when he was despairing about the campaign for a Welsh-language television service. He travelled to Dublin in October 1980 to support the Gaelic League's criticism of RTÉ's programming in a public march, having recently demonstrated the ongoing potential of the 'Welsh methods' by threatening to go on hunger strike in May that year. Margaret Thatcher, who had previously refused to support the creation of a Welsh-language television station, made one of the few backflips of her career by acceding to Evan's demands.[48]

Direct collaboration for Celtic-language television subsequently faded away, and it was nearly 20 years before Teilifís na Gaeilge (now TG4) began broadcasting in 1996. Hourigan suggests that ultimately, these tactics achieved little towards the creation of an Irish-language television station, for by the 1980s public opinion in Ireland and the United Kingdom had turned against the concept of direct action.[49] The final section of this chapter also relates to public reactions to direct action, and so this shift in the public mood is discussed further below.

WELSH EXTREMISTS AND THE IRA

In the long term, the more radical forms of direct action, that is, the use of sabotage or violence, worked against cultural nationalists in Wales.[50] Although it has been argued by writers such as Roy Clews and John Humphries that extreme Welsh nationalists had some success in putting pressure on local and national authorities on specific issues,[51] their methods also tended to alienate them from the electorate, particularly in areas of Wales that were predominantly English speaking.[52] Although the Welsh Language Society in particular took a long and inconsistent path towards divorcing itself from violent extremism, the short jumps from civil disobedience to sabotage and from sabotage to violence tended to attract guilt by association. In addition, shifting and overlapping memberships between members of Plaid Cymru, the Welsh Language Society, and Welsh extremist movements complicated matters further. In the eyes of the British establishment, to quote the Lord Chamberlain Quintin Hogg, the Welsh Language Society only differed from 'the baboons of the IRA' as 'a question of degree and not kind.'[53]

Of course, neither Welsh nor Irish nationalism happen to be monolithic concepts, and if one thing characterises popular notions of post-war Irish nationalism, it is in the way it was given violent expression in Northern Ireland during the era of the Troubles. The perceived necessity of securing political autonomy to achieve cultural ends continued to possess a powerful attraction, despite the public distaste that gradually developed towards the use of violence in achieving this end. As discussed in the introduction, the inspiration that some Welsh people drew from the Easter Rising and the Irish War of Independence meant that non-peaceful methods had long been considered in Wales itself. Before the 1960s, this rarely translated into action, although Saunders Lewis' sabotage of the RAF base at Penrhos in 1936 was a notable exception. It had been noted in the Irish press that Plaid Cymru included an extremist element in its membership during the era of the Anti-Partition League,[54] but it was the building of the Tryweryn dam and Lewis's 'Tynged yr Iaith' speech that finally spurred this element into action during the 1960s.

For these individuals and groups the tradition of Welsh pacifism, deeply rooted in the Nonconformist beliefs of the majority, was a 'nonsense'. Keith Griffiths, a founder of the Welsh Patriotic Front in 1966, spoke of a 'Welsh pacifism foisted onto us. This is a lie, because the medieval Welsh society was a militarist class based on the warrior castes'.[55] In the aftermath of Lewis's 'Tynged yr Iaith' speech, this became *the* topic of the day, and in general Welsh nationalists were radicalised in their rhetoric, if not necessarily in action. Even the famed pacifist and president of Plaid Cymru, Gwynfor Evans, expressed support for three men who sabotaged the construction site at Tryweryn, making an appearance during their court case in March 1964 to publicly shake their hands.[56] Plaid's organising secretary, Emrys Roberts, explained at the time that the party had decided against violence, except 'in certain circumstances', in a vague statement that appeared to make the distinction between violence against buildings and against people. Roberts showed some insight by recognising that being associated with violent direct action could alienate Plaid from the electorate.[57]

Between 1962 and 1969, a network of loosely connected Welsh extremist groups waged a campaign against the British establishment, with the creation of a Welsh republic being their general aim. Having failed to capture the imaginations of those they claimed to fight for, and often operating from a position of financial and material inferiority, these groups had an interest in developing relationships with other rebel organisations such as the IRA. For many of these militant Welsh nationalists, the members of the IRA were highly respected comrades-in-arms and Celtic brethren, and indeed the Patriotic Front declared that its members sought 'an independent Welsh republic within a confederation of Free Celtia'.[58]

The Free Wales Army (FWA) made an initial, mysterious appearance during a nationwide graffiti campaign in the wake of 'Tynged yr Iaith' and the building of the Tryweryn dam in the early 1960s. Commentators at the time were probably right in thinking that this was initially little more than a hoax by disaffected youths, but within three years various Welsh nationalist groups had come to ally themselves under this name. This network of nationalists, organised along military lines, came under the overall command of two colourful leaders, Julian Cayo Evans and Dennis Coslett. Even though the leaders of the FWA subsequently admitted that some of their claims of weapons caches and foreign aid were made to intimidate the authorities, there is no reason to doubt that the FWA and the IRA did cooperate to some extent. Julian Cayo Evans had made friends with IRA sympathisers while serving in the British Army and came to know many high-ranking officers.[59] The FWA marched alongside other rebel movements at the 50th anniversary celebrations of the Easter Rising in Dublin in April 1966, where Cayo Evans told James Nicholson of the *Daily Sketch* that they intended on working more closely with the IRA in the future: 'While we are here, we shall see some of our friends in the IRA. They might give us some idea about fighting for freedom.'[60]

A couple of months later, Cayo Evans claimed that FWA men had already spent time training in guerrilla warfare with the IRA, with at least one man spending several months in the country working undercover.[61] In the following year, the struggling London magazine *Town* devoted a seven-page spread to the FWA, where their training methods, apparently derived from prior IRA training in the 'Irish mountains', were described in great detail. John Humphries is quick to point out that this article is filled with false claims about perpetrating particular bombings, and that quite simply, the journalist who had set up the interview knew that 'Cayo Evans . . . would do anything for publicity or money'.[62] Nevertheless, the IRA training claim was made regularly, and when the FWA leaders were rounded up and tried in Swansea in early 1969, the prosecutor repeated his claims of having attended three-week IRA training courses and of Irish financial backing.[63]

Cayo Evans never retracted the claims of IRA training, but interestingly, he downplayed other IRA links that had been reported in the press.

Speaking to Roy Clews in the late 1970s, he attempted to address the charge of receiving a considerable quantity of the IRA's Belfast arsenal sometime in 1968. It had been suggested that in the political upheavals leading to the split within the IRA in 1969, chief of staff Cathal Goulding and other left-wing members had passed on weapons to Dublin and on to the FWA, on the basis that Wales 'was a greater priority than the Northern question'. When civil rights protesters came under attack by Unionists in early 1969 (most significantly, at Burntollet on 4 January), it was said that the IRA no longer had the weaponry needed to make effective reprisals.[64] If this is what transpired, then it both weakened the IRA in Northern Ireland, and failed to strengthen the FWA, which was soon to fall apart. Cayo Evans denied that this transfer ever happened, stating that the American company ARMCO (probably Samuel Cummings's International Armament Corporation, which dominated the small-arms market at this time) had offered to broker a deal between the FWA and the IRA. The IRA would sell their weapons to the FWA through ARMCO as part of an upgrading deal, but the FWA simply did not have the money to make this exchange.[65] The main concern with Cayo Evans's testimony is one of positioning—a dominant theme of Clews's history is the FWA's aim to threaten violence rather than to act, and this claim smacks of revisionism. Moreover, the weapons transfer was recalled on the Irish side too, with former Provisional IRA member Maria McGuire making reference to it in her memoir *To Take Arms* after her defection in 1972.[66]

The FWA's private scheming, while perhaps fanciful, cannot be dismissed as mere propaganda. Cayo Evans, Coslett, Keith Griffiths, and other FWA commandants had drawn up considerable plans to disrupt Prince Charles's investiture as Prince of Wales at Caernarfon on 1 July 1969 and produced these documents for Clews. In devising their plans to 'fight into the town' on the day, Cayo Evans pointed out that he could call on the IRA if its resources fell short in any way. An Irish sympathiser who owned an Auster light plane in Ireland had already offered its services: 'If the IRA could use helicopters to drop milk-churns full of explosives onto police stations, why couldn't the FWA emulate them using the Auster'.[67] Regardless of how we interpret Cayo Evans's testimony (Johnes considers the practicality of these plans to be 'unclear'),[68] there is little doubt that the FWA leadership had some kind of ongoing relationship with IRA members in the late 1960s.

There is also evidence to suggest that columns beyond Cayo Evans's and Coslett's direct control maintained links with the IRA, with one Swansea-based column linking up with the IRA in Dublin and Cork. According to the commandant of the column, Vivian Davies:

> My column did a lot with the IRA; we had a lot of support, arms, explosives, the know-how on guerrilla and terrorist tactics. The arms were mainly old Thompsons, etc. The boxes would come on a Dutch coaster to Swansea docks, and we would get it from them on the docks.

The boxes were lucky dips really, could be anything in them. Half a dozen deliveries came over a period of time . . . Periodically, some of our boys would go over to Southern Ireland to shift stuff around for the IRA . . . I was pretty close with some of the Irish, I went over myself on a couple of occasions.[69]

Humphries considers this claim to be 'outrageous' and without basis, but the Special Branch did suspect that these South Walian FWA were engaging in similar activities.[70] Nevertheless, it should be noted that Davies was also known to grandstand for the press on occasion. For example, when a small arms cache was discovered in Maes Llyn in September 1968, he announced that the FWA volunteer responsible for the dumping would be subject to 'instant death'.[71]

Later in the same month, it was reported that Belfast Special Branch officers were cooperating with Dublin Gardaí in investigating IRA–FWA links, following reports of ammunition being stolen from Ireland and smuggled into Wales. At the Welsh end, police believed that members of the two groups met periodically, often during rugby internationals to avoid detection. There were two caveats regarding this cooperation, in that the 'IRA [was] thought to have no influence on the Free Wales Army members, who [were] mostly young men who [were] more exhibitionists than extremists', and that police surveillance suggested that the IRA members involved were in no position to pass on weapons to the Welsh.[72]

This same news report suggested that as no FWA member had been convicted of any bombings in 1968, this 'leaves the possibility of another extremist group, but it is not known whether it would have a liaison with the IRA'.[73] There was indeed another group, and regardless of any lingering doubts over FWA/IRA links, this group did have its own unique points of contact with the Irish. Mudiad Amddiffyn Cymru (Movement for the Defence of Wales, or simply MAC) had been founded by Owain Williams, John Albert Jones, and Emyr Llywelyn Jones in 1963 but had been taken over and restructured by John Barnard Jenkins, an officer in the British Army. Jenkins echoed some of Saunders Lewis's sentiments in justifying the bombing campaign undertaken by MAC: 'Of course it can be said that violence is unnecessary, and that Plaid Cymru have the answer. To this I would agree; there is no doubt that Wales will inevitably become independent. My proviso is that by the time independence arrives the Wales we know and love/hate even now, will have long gone.'[74]

MAC and Jenkins had at least two men with contacts in Ireland, Owain Williams and Dai Pritchard.[75] Neither was active in the bombing campaign, having been apprehended for bombings a few years earlier, but Pritchard became Jenkins's main point of contact with the Irish. Jenkins insists that '[a]s for the IRA, one or two came over for a chat but there was no alliance, no specific arrangements.'[76] MAC's bombing campaign, run on the basis of avoiding casualties on either side, took a deadly turn on 30 June 1969 when a bomb being carried by George Taylor and Alwyn Jones exploded prematurely, killing them instantly. Irish republicans decided to honour the men publicly a week later, at the reburial of IRA men James McCormick and Peter Barnes in Mullingar (they had been executed in Birmingham in 1940). Accounts vary, but thousands were present at the ceremony, and a minute (or two minutes) silence was observed on behalf of Taylor and Jones. The secrecy of MAC was such that as far as those gathered were concerned, Taylor and Jones were FWA men, not MAC.[77]

Although MAC began to fall apart following police investigations into this fatal bomb blast, and the ringleader Jenkins was arrested in November 1969, the tactics of the organisation were not completely disregarded by the IRA. This was to have far-reaching consequences. MAC had contrasted from the Free Wales Army in two ways—Jenkins had gone out of his way to avoid publicity, and he structured the group based on the concept of 'cells'. Indeed, he had learned from both the IRA and the FWA that the arrest of one member could easily lead to the arrest of a dozen others.[78] He could not afford to let this happen within a tiny organisation such as MAC. As he explained to John Humphries, '[i]n each cell only the cell leader knew me, and then only by sight, not my name, where I lived or anything else. I vetted every recruit personally and trained each cell leader personally. They were then left to recruit their own people. If there was a job, I would call unannounced, give the leader the target and the stuff, leaving him to organise the rest.'[79]

A significant member of Jenkins' organisation was Owain Williams, who had become well known in nationalist circles for planting a bomb near Trawsfynydd Power Station in 1963, for which he had been jailed for 12 months. Jenkins could not use Williams because he was under constant surveillance by the police, and moreover, he fled to Ireland in early 1968 to escape new explosives charges whilst on bail. It was claimed that Williams stayed for some time at the bungalow of IRA leader Seán Mac Stíofáin in Navan, County Meath. At the time, Mac Stíofáin was in the middle of the IRA's left–right split, and was soon to form the Provisional IRA as its first chief of staff. Humphries suggests that Mac Stíofáin adopted Jenkins's cell system on the strength of Williams's testimony.[80] Mac Stíofáin's hospitality clearly had its limitations, however, as a few months after leaving Wales, Williams was living in a tent on a beach in Kinsale, West Cork, and short on cash and food. Having stayed there for six weeks, he was arrested at Birmingham Airport on 26 August 1968 and subsequently tried.[81]

Mac Stíofáin himself lends indirect credence to this contact in his 1974 autobiography *Revolutionary in Ireland*. Mac Stíofáin, born John Stevenson in England in 1928, had associated with members of other Celtic nationalist movements in the 1950s, during his early IRA days in London. Claiming to have met Welsh and Breton nationalists at a rally in Trafalgar Square around 1952, he recalled that he 'liked and felt close to these people of the other Celtic nations', the Welsh in particular. When he was subsequently jailed for six years for taking part in a raid on an armoury in Essex, he credits his friends from the Welsh republican movement with aiding his wife Máire and their young children.[82] Although he had nothing to say about the Free Wales Army, MAC, or Owain Williams in his autobiography, it is clear that Mac Stíofáin had an ongoing interest in fostering relationships with rebel movements from all over the world, and that he was particularly fond of Welsh nationalists.

CONCLUSION

In general, these collaborating movements were ineffective in achieving their direct and shared aims. The Anti-Partition League's campaign in the late 1940s, if anything, rallied Unionists in Northern Ireland and ultimately buried the issue of partition for a generation. Allied to an attempt to define Wales geographically vis-à-vis England, nothing less than an attempt to *create* a partition, nothing was achieved in the short term. During the 1960s, Irish and Welsh paramilitary groups provided material support to one another but possibly undermined one another with the transfer of IRA small arms and munitions to Welsh militants. Cultural organisations such as the Gaelic League and the Welsh Language Society were arguably more successful in highlighting the common plight of their Celtic tongues, but it has to be recognised that 'Welsh methods' became increasingly ineffective as direct action attracted increasingly unfavourable media and public reactions in the 1970s and 1980s.

What these and other points of contact did achieve was to normalise dialogue between Irish and Welsh nationalists in a range of contexts, primarily cultural and political. Significant examples of diffusion are to be observed in the post-war period, mainly facilitated by personal relationships, and in several cases inspiring or accelerating organisational change. In some instances, this transfer of ideas took place more than once, with an idea (such as civil disobedience) returning to its source but altered to deal with a new age and new circumstances. Where pan-Celts had been talking about the need for collaboration and closer relationships throughout the 'Celtic countries' since before the turn of the twentieth century, this was now happening with increasing frequency, finding its most permanent form in the establishment of the Celtic League in 1961 by Gwynfor Evans and J. E. Jones.

NOTES

1. Representative examples include C. O'Rahilly, *Ireland and Wales: Their Historical and Literary Relations* (London: Longmans, 1924) and A. D. Rees and B. R. Rees, *Celtic Heritage: Ancient Tradition in Ireland and Wales* (London: Thames and Hudson, 1961).

2. H. Llewelyn Williams, *At Anchorage in Dublin* (Dún Laoghaire, Co. Dublin: Genealogical Society of Ireland, 2012; first published 1968); P. O'Leary (ed), *Irish Migrants in Modern Wales* (Liverpool: Liverpool University Press, 2004); P. O'Leary, *Immigration and Integration: The Irish in Wales, 1798–1922* (Cardiff: University of Wales Press, 2000).
3. C. Connolly and K. Gramich, 'Introduction', *Irish Studies Review*, 17:1 (2009), p. 1.
4. For example, G. ap Gwilym, *Stori Saunders Lewis/The Story of Saunders Lewis* (Y Bala, Gwynedd, Wales: Cyhoeddiadau Barddas, 2011), pp. 16–17; J. S. Ellis, *Investiture: Royal Ceremony and National Identity in Wales, 1911–1969* (Cardiff: University of Wales Press, 2008), p. 218; R. Clews, *To Dream of Freedom: The Story of MAC and the Free Wales Army* (Talybont, Ceredigion: Y Lolfa Cyf., 2004), p. 83.
5. N. Hourigan, 'The Role of Networks in Minority Language Television Campaigns', in M. Cormack and N. Hourigan (eds), *Minority Language Media: Concepts, Critiques and Case Studies* (Clevedon, UK: Multilingual Matters Ltd., 2007), pp. 69–87.
6. P. Oliver and D. Myers, 'Networks, Diffusion, and Cycles of Collective Action', in M. Diani and D. McAdam (eds), *Social Movement Analysis: The Network Perspective* (Oxford: Oxford University Press, 2003), p. 174.
7. Ibid., pp. 177–78.
8. C. A. Bayly, S. Beckert, M. Connelly, I. Hofmeyr, W. Kozol, and P. Seed, 'AHR Conversation: On Transnational History', *American Historical Review*, 111:5 (1996), pp. 1454, 1459.
9. J. Graham Jones, 'Michael Davitt, David Lloyd George and T. E. Ellis: The Welsh Experience, 1886', *Cylchgrawn Hanes Cymru/Welsh History Review*, 18:3 (1997), pp. 473–75, 480.
10. Ibid., pp. 471–72.
11. K. O. Morgan, *Rebirth of a Nation: Wales, 1880–1980* (New York: Oxford University Press, 1981), p. 44; M. Johnes, *Wales since 1939* (Manchester and New York: Manchester University Press, 2012), p. 203.
12. Morgan, *Rebirth of a Nation*, p. 43; Graham Jones, 'Michael Davitt', p. 469.
13. 'Dlúthbhaint . . . nach léar', in Máirtín Ó Cadhain's introduction to Saunders Lewis, *Bás nó Beatha?*, trans. M. Ó Cadhain (Baile Átha Cliath: Sáirséal agus Dill, 1963), p. 7.
14. H. Pritchard Jones, 'No Church, No State, Just a Culture: A Welsh-Irish Perspective', *Irish Studies in International Affairs*, 12 (2001), p. 237.
15. R. A. Lewis, 'Welsh Nationalism', *Irish Press*, 16 November 1949, p. 4.
16. 'Welsh Archbishop on Ireland's Partition', *Catholic Herald*, 21 March 1947, p. 7.
17. R. A. Lewis, 'Welsh Nationalism', *Irish Press*, 16 November 1949, p. 4.
18. With the exception of parts of the Labour Party, where a 30-strong 'Friends of Ireland' group was formed in 1945. B. Lynn, 'The Irish Anti-Partition League and the Political Realities of Partition, 1945–9', *Irish Historical Studies*, 34:135 (2005), p. 324.
19. B. Lynn, 'The Irish Anti-Partition League and the Political Realities of Partition, 1945–9', *Irish Historical Studies*, 34:135 (2005), p. 328.
20. D. Leach, '"Repaying a Debt of Gratitude": Foreign Minority Nationalists and the Fiftieth Anniversary of the Easter Rising in 1966', *Éire-Ireland*, 43:3/4 (2008), p. 267.
21. 'An Saoghal Gaedhlach: As Others See Us', *Connaught Telegraph*, 3 September 1927, p. 7.
22. 'Our Letter from Dublin', *Nenagh Guardian*, 8 March 1947, p. 5.
23. Leach, 'The Irish Anti-Partition League', p. 268.

24. B. Lynn, 'The Irish Anti-Partition League and the Political Realities of Partition, 1945–9', *Irish Historical Studies*, 34:135 (2005), pp. 321, 328.
25. R. A. Lewis, 'Wales and its Language', *Irish Press*, 29 September 1947, p. 4.
26. 'Our Letter from Dublin', *Nenagh Guardian*, 8 March 1947, p. 5.
27. J. E. Jones, 'St. David's Day', *Irish Press*, 1 March 1949, p. 5.
28. 'New Anti-Partition League Branch', *Irish Press*, 17 July 1948, p. 2.
29. Including J. F. Roberts, I. Davies, T. Williams, Meirion Lewis, and Harri Webb, representing Plaid Cymru and other Welsh nationalist groups. 'Anti-Partitionists from Britain at Dublin Rally', *Sunday Independent*, 9 April 1950, p. 1; 'Anti-Partition Week in Dun Laoghaire', *Irish Times*, 10 April 1950, p. 1; 'To Protest against New Bill in North', *Irish Times*, 25 June 1951, p. 1; 'Protests against Partition', *Irish Independent*, 20 April 1954, p. 9.
30. B. Lynn, 'The Irish Anti-Partition League and the Political Realities of Partition, 1945–9', *Irish Historical Studies*, 34:135 (2005), pp. 330–31.
31. 'Cardiff Protests on Partition', *Irish Independent*, 18 March 1952, p. 7.
32. Ap Gwilym, *Stori Saunders Lewis*, pp. 16–17.
33. 'The Gathering of Gaels', *Irish Times*, 26 September 1929, p. 8.
34. Saunders Lewis, 'Mi ragdybiaf hefyd y bydd terfyn ar y Gymraeg yn iaith fyw, ond parhau'r tueddiad presennol', in *Tynged yr Iaith* (London: British Broadcasting Corporation, 1962), p. 5.
35. Lewis, *Tynged yr Iaith*, pp. 27–28.
36. Saunders Lewis, 'Nid Gwyddelod mohonom', in *Tynged yr Iaith*, p. 24.
37. For example, 'Bilingual Ireland "Will Never Be a Reality"', *Irish Times*, 19 May 1959, p. 6; P. Ó Fearaíl, *The Story of Conradh na Gaeilge* (Baile Atha Claith: Clodhanna Teo., 1975), p. 51.
38. M. Ó Cadhain, 'Cinniúint na Teanga', *Comhar* 21:4 (1962), pp. 6–13, 20–22 (published in booklet form in August 1963). Saunders Lewis, *Bás nó Beatha?*, trans M. Ó Cadhain (Baile Átha Cliath: Sáirséal agus Dill, 1963).
39. D. Walsh, 'Preserving the Idealism, Vision and Spirit of O Cadhain', *Irish Independent*, 18 February 1971, p. 10.
40. A. Ó Cathasaigh, '"Níl Conra na Gaeilge feidhmiúil, níl sí spreagúil ná spreacúil a dóthain", cé go mb'fhéidir "an Conra a athrú gan an t-ainm a athrú"', in *Ag Samhlú Troda: Máirtín Ó Cadhain 1905–1970* (Baile Átha Cliath: Coiscéim, 2002), p. 198.
41. Sr B. Costigan, *De Ghlaschloich an Oileáin: Beatha agus Saothar Mháirtín Uí Chadhain* (Béal an Daingin, Conamara: Cló Iar-Chonnachta, 1987), pp. 96–97.
42. R. MacGall, 'Ag Machnamh Dom', *Irish Independent*, 16 June 1966, p. 3.
43. Ó Cathasaigh, *Ag Samhlú Troda*, pp. 213–15, 231–34.
44. Ó Fearaíl, *The Story of Conradh na Gaeilge*, p. 55.
45. 'Irish, Welsh Language Protest', *Irish Independent*, 2 November 1971, p. 23; 'Welsh Join Dublin Protest', *Irish Press*, 2 November 1971, p. 1.
46. 'Declaration of Rights for Language Will be Promoted', *Irish Times*, 30 April 1973, p. 13.
47. Hourigan, 'The Role of Networks in Minority Language Television Campaigns', p. 75.
48. H. Pritchard Jones, 'No Church, No State, Just a Culture: A Welsh-Irish Perspective', *Irish Studies in International Affairs*, 12 (2001), p. 240.
49. Hourigan, 'The Role of Networks in Minority Language Television Campaigns', p. 76.
50. H. Pritchard Jones, 'No Church, No State, Just a Culture: A Welsh-Irish Perspective', *Irish Studies in International Affairs*, 12 (2001), p. 240.
51. Clews, *To Dream of Freedom*, pp. 130–34; J. Humphries, *Freedom Fighters: Wales' Forgotten 'War', 1963–1993* (Cardiff: University of Wales Press, 2008), pp. 199–200.

52. D. Balsom, P. J. Madgwick, and D. van Mechelen, 'The Red and the Green: Patterns of Partisan Choice in Wales', *British Journal of Political Science*, 13:3 (1983), p. 315.
53. M. Parker, *Neighbours from Hell?: English Attitudes to the Welsh* (Talybont, Ceredigion, Wales: Y Lolfa Cyf., 2007), p. 61; C. H. Williams, 'Non-Violence and the Development of the Welsh Language Society, 1962-c.1974', *Cylchgrawn Hanes Cymru / Welsh History Review*, 8:4 (1977), p. 444.
54. For example, see 'Our Letter from Dublin', *Nenagh Guardian*, 8 March 1947, p. 5.
55. Clews, *To Dream of Freedom*, p. 97.
56. Humphries, *Freedom Fighters*, p. 34; L. Fellows, 'Welsh Nationalism Is Hardening Its Tone', *Irish Times*, 5 March 1964, p. 8.
57. Fellows, 'Welsh Nationalism', p. 8.
58. A. Butt Philip, *The Welsh Question: Nationalism in Welsh Politics 1945–1970* (Cardiff: University of Wales Press, 1975), p. 266.
59. Clews, *To Dream of Freedom*, p. 83.
60. Leach, 'The Irish Anti-Partition League', pp. 279, 281.
61. 'Free Wales Army Chief Claims Links with Irish Organisation', *Irish Independent*, 23 July 1966, p. 18.
62. Humphries, *Freedom Fighters*, p. 52.
63. '3 Millionaires for "Wales Army"', *Irish Press*, 18 April 1969, p. 5.
64. H. Kelly, 'I.R.A. Policy Split Led to Raid', *Irish Times*, 15 December 1969, p. 1; Clews, *To Dream of Freedom*, p. 71.
65. Clews, *To Dream of Freedom*, p. 71.
66. M. McGuire, *To Take Arms: A Year in the Provisional IRA* (London: Quartet, 1973), p. 34.
67. Clews, *To Dream of Freedom*, pp. 226–27.
68. Johnes, *Wales since 1939*, p. 236.
69. Clews, *To Dream of Freedom*, pp. 143–44.
70. With the IRA in Cork in particular. See 'Cork Ammunition Theft Inquiry', *Irish Press*, 21 September 1968, p. 1; Humphries, *Freedom Fighters*, p. 45.
71. Broadcast on ITV's 'News at Ten', 13 September 1968.
72. 'R.U.C.-Gardai Liaison on Arms Thefts', *Irish Times*, 23 September 1968, p. 1.
73. Ibid.
74. Clews, *To Dream of Freedom*, p. 117.
75. Humphries, *Freedom Fighters*, p. 28.
76. Ibid., p. 141.
77. D. Maguire, 'Re-burial in Mullingar', *Irish Press*, 7 July 1969, p. 1; 'Ex-I.R.A. Man Claims he Planted Bomb', *Irish Times*, 7 July 1969, p. 1.
78. Clews, *To Dream of Freedom*, pp. 163–64.
79. Humphries, *Freedom Fighters*, p. 66.
80. Ibid., p. 66.
81. Clews, *To Dream of Freedom*, p. 203; Humphries, *Freedom Fighters*, p. 83.
82. S. Mac Stíofáin, *Revolutionary in Ireland* (Farnborough, Hants.: Saxon House, 1974), p. 53.

8 Ireland and Scotland
From Partition to Peace Process
Graham Walker

IRISH-SCOTTISH STUDIES

Irish-Scottish Studies is now a well-established area of scholarly endeavour in its own right. The crucial moment in this development came in the late 1990s, perhaps most emblematically in the establishment of a Research Institute of Irish and Scottish Studies at the University of Aberdeen directed by Scotland's foremost historian, Sir Tom Devine.[1]

It should not be forgotten that there had been some notable comparative work carried out before this, especially by social and economic historians such as Devine himself, during the previous decades.[2] However, the Institute at Aberdeen proved to be a catalyst to much creativity and to the flowering of impressive scholarship, particularly around cultural cross-currents in the Irish-Scottish relationship. There have been notable contributions in subject areas such as literature, language, and the arts, and there have been further advances in areas of social and economic history such as migration and diasporas.[3]

The Irish-Scottish scholarly 'moment' of the turn of the last century was essentially a political happening. Without the cessation of violence and the onset of the Peace Process in Northern Ireland, and the constitutional shake-up of the United Kingdom, it is doubtful if the space and the opportunity for the rediscovery and reconstruction of Irish-Scottish links would have transpired. What has been termed earlier as the 'flowering' of scholarship in this area owed much to the transformative political context of the end of the century—to the way that political changes led rapidly to a reassessment and reconfiguration of relationships within 'these islands' of Britain and Ireland.

Yet, somewhat ironically, the study of the political aspects of Irish-Scottish relations has not made the progress of the other subject areas mentioned. This may reflect the slower pace of the development of modern Scottish political history relative to socio-economic history, and it may even be related to the mutual wariness between historians and political scientists that Iain McLean has urged both to make efforts to transcend.[4] Moreover, there still seems to be a reluctance to probe too far into the political dimensions of the Irish-Scottish relationship; perhaps, understandably, the recent

Troubles in Northern Ireland still cast a long shadow. However, it may go further than this: it may reflect habits of political analysis that are so long established that they are exceptionally hard to break. In this respect the notion of Northern Ireland as 'sui generis', a 'place apart', a 'constitutional oddity' is particularly prevalent. Indeed there is still an engrained tendency to exclude Northern Ireland from discussions and debates over devolution and the future of the United Kingdom and of the Union more broadly, notwithstanding the fact that the political reality from the turn of the century has been that of a 'United Kingdom' characterised by governmental pluralism and institutional diversity.

So there needs to be some redressing of the balance: more attention needs to be paid to the political character of relations between Ireland and Scotland since the time of partition and the creation of Northern Ireland as a devolved entity within the United Kingdom. This chapter seeks to highlight the relationship of both Scotland and Northern Ireland to the theme of devolution and constitutional change, and to assess the way Irish-Scottish relations more broadly have been reformulated in the new political circumstances of a relatively peaceful and stable Northern Ireland and a Scotland apparently on the march to either independence or increased autonomy within the Union. In addition, the chapter will address the vexed topic of religious sectarianism in view of its spectacular emergence over recent years in Scotland as an issue of vigorous public debate and soul-searching, and the way it links clearly, if problematically, to Ireland and to Scotland's Irish dimensions. Underpinning the chapter is a strong affirmation of the value of comparative study of historically intimate places such as Scotland and Ireland, and of the insights that might be fashioned from explaining why they have both converged and diverged around themes with broader transnational resonance: politics and governance, religious, ethnic and national identities, surges of cultural activity and crises of confidence. Equally, such an approach has to be aware of the seductive lure of the brand of romanticism that has often surrounded both countries, and the deceptive sense of predestined distinction it has sometimes conjured.

POLITICAL CONTEXTS, CONNECTIONS, AND CONTRASTS, 1921–79

The settlement of the Irish question in 1921–22 had important political consequences for Scotland. It might be said that it allowed Scotland to develop politically along wider British lines; to conform to a left–right and class-based political framework. It opened up more political space for Labour to appeal across the Protestant-Catholic religious divide of west-central, industrial Scotland, and at the same time constrained the Conservatives—known then and for some 40 years afterwards as 'The Unionists'—from making much sectarian capital out of the Irish unrest. As it took over from the

Liberals as the progressive party in British politics, Labour assumed increasingly the character of an urban working-class alliance throughout Britain, and effectively a unionist party on the constitution. The relatively socially disadvantaged Irish community (largely of Catholic religious affiliation) in industrial Scotland became solidly Labour on account of the party's concern for working-class welfare, and its ability to satisfy the Catholic Church that it was committed to the Education Act of 1918 which had provided for full state support for separate Catholic schools.[5]

Scottish Labour had been—and remained—a strong supporter of land reform, but it might be said that the land question, which had been the basis in the late nineteenth and early twentieth century for joint Scottish-Irish radicalism, saw its profile as an issue dip within the predominantly urban British political background of the 1920s onwards. In this sense there was a disconnect politically between Scotland and Ireland compared to the heady days of Michael Davitt and John Murdoch.[6] Furthermore, that notable episode of Irish-Scottish rural radicalism encompassed the mainly Catholic nature of the land agitation in Ireland and the mainly Calvinist crofters of Scotland.

As Scotland's politics were increasingly shaped around the two party class-based structure of the Westminster-dominated world, so, therefore, much of its interaction with the new political entity of Northern Ireland—the United Kingdom's first example from 1921 of devolved government — was curtailed. Popular Protestant politics did register in interwar Scotland and did carry echoes of Ulster; however, they were fragmented, and they were kept at bay by a Unionist Party anxious not to be religiously pigeonholed. Moreover, as the sociologist of religion Steve Bruce has argued, there was little opportunity for tribal leaders to engage in the 'pork-barrel' politics that came rapidly to characterise Northern Ireland.[7]

It thus needs to be appreciated that social and cultural divisions and tensions in Scotland did not map straightforwardly on to political divisions as they did in Northern Ireland and that economic and class concerns were able to cut across sectarian appeals in a way that they could not in the province. Northern Ireland was cut adrift from British party politics, and a 'zero-sum' Orange versus Green political culture afforded little room for secular appeals of any kind.

Yet we also have to be aware of the depth of religious sectarianism during the interwar years, particularly in Glasgow and the west of the country although not exclusively: witness the success in local government elections for a brief period in the 1930s by the Edinburgh party 'Protestant Action'. Several historians have brought to light the anti-Irish Catholic campaign carried on by elements of the Church of Scotland and some leading nationalist figures in this period: there was indeed something of a panic whipped up around perceptions of Irish Catholic immigration and its supposed effects on the country's character, values, and morals.[8]

It was also clearly connected to anxieties over the phenomenally high rate of emigration from Scotland during the 1920s. In this connection Angela

McCarthy's comparative analysis of the experience of emigrants from both Scotland and Ireland to the United States, Canada, Australia, and New Zealand, is of crucial importance.[9] As McCarthy points out, emigration from Scotland in this period was proportionately higher than any other European country—almost half a million Scots emigrated beyond Europe in the 1920s. In Scotland there was understandable fear of the effects of such a loss of, in most cases, skilled and young working people. McCarthy's case studies also testify to the significance of sectarian tensions in Scotland at the time: one interviewee recalled that the Irish Troubles had 'split Scotland right down the middle', while another likened the Lanarkshire steel town of Motherwell to Belfast.[10] Clearly, the economic downturn of the early part of the decade and the slump that hit many of Scotland's heavy industries led many to emigrate and might also be said to have exacerbated communal tensions that had been stoked by the spillover of the Irish Troubles to Scotland in the 1920–22 period. This was when Irish Republican Army (IRA) activity in Scotland resulted in clashes with the authorities and indeed the killing of a policeman in a raid on a prisoner van in the east end of Glasgow.[11] The immediate post-war years were ones of profound social and political turbulence in Scotland, and historians have yet to provide a full assessment of the way that such upheavals, including the impact of the Irish Troubles, set the tone for the socially discordant interwar period.

Indeed, given the bleak economic context, the demoralising loss of so many people to emigration, the lingering bitterness of the Irish question, and controversies over education and mixed marriages, it might be contended that Scotland actually did well to contain religious-based antagonisms and to ensure that scapegoating and calls for Irish people to be sent back home were rebuffed. For every sectarian rabble-rouser there were more tolerant voices. Moreover, it needs to be acknowledged that the mainstream political parties held the line in relation to defusing tensions. Maybe, too, it was Scotland's good fortune in respect of this matter at least, that her political development should have taken place within the broader, more capacious context of the British state; local tensions and squabbles rarely achieved any national political profile or purchase. The contrast with the political conditions of Northern Ireland was stark.[12]

It was also a major point of contrast with Ireland—north and south—that Scotland's own 'national question' was politically muted between the wars. Although bills for a Scottish Home Rule parliament were introduced and debated at Westminster during the 1920s, they were talked out and easily defused. This spurred a small group of mainly culturally attuned nationalists, including the poet Hugh MacDiarmid, to form a Nationalist Party of Scotland in 1928. However, this party's independence demands were watered down to the 'Home Rule within the Empire' stance of the Scottish National Party (SNP) which came into being in 1934 after the fringe fundamentalists such as MacDiarmid had been ejected. It would only be during the Second World War and immediately afterwards that the Scottish question would make political waves. In the meantime some like MacDiarmid looked to Ireland for inspiration in a spirit of Celtic solidarity. However, as Bob Purdie has demonstrated, Scottish Nationalists could make little sense of the civil war in Ireland of 1922–23 and its profound legacy for the subsequent politics of the Irish Free State. Scottish Nationalist visitors to Ireland tended to see only what they wanted to see—usually a kind of romantic Celtic idyll—and ignored the rest.[13] Again it is important to stress how Scotland's largely social class-based political development was at variance with Northern Ireland where the constitutional or 'national' question dominated politics to the virtual exclusion of everything else and with the Irish Free State where the politics of the national question lingered in the shadow of the civil war and where there was a largely rural economy with no significant urban proletariat driving class politics.

The Second World War saw Northern Ireland share the experience, notably the harrowing trauma of the Blitz by German bombers, with the rest of the United Kingdom while the south of Ireland remained neutral. This broadened and deepened the gulf between north and south in Ireland, a development compounded by the extension to Northern Ireland of the Attlee Labour government's post-war welfare-state reforms. Indeed, the combination of the United Kingdom's part in the defeat of Nazi Germany and the sense of a 'People's Peace' to match the 'People's War' provided a signal boost to British identity: notions of common sacrifice rewarded with common social security tightened the bonds of Union.

Nevertheless, there were important stirrings of Scottish nationalist sentiment as well as British during and after the war, and other measures of the Attlee government, such as nationalisation, had the effect of making many Scots fearful of too much London centralisation. The Unionists, opportunistically, formed a rather incongruous alliance with nationalists in criticising the Labour government, but there were also plenty of Scottish Labour voters receptive to the idea of greater Scottish political autonomy. It was in this context that the Scottish Convention movement, led by John McCormick, had such success in the late 1940s with its National Covenant in favour of a Scottish parliament acquiring some 2.5 million signatures.[14]

What is seldom appreciated is the extent to which the Scottish Home Rule movement of the post-war era took its cue from the one existing devolved administration in the United Kingdom: that of Stormont in Northern Ireland.[15] If Northern Ireland's political culture had developed in a very different way from Scotland's, the value of the province's devolution experiment could nonetheless be viewed as pertinent to those dissatisfied by a London-centric Union. Pro–Home Rule Scottish newspapers carried flattering accounts of Northern Ireland's devolutionary achievements and claimed that '[w]hat Ulster can make work so can we in Scotland'. McCormick led a Scottish convention delegation to Northern Ireland for a fact-finding visit in 1949. Rather ironically, as Scots Home Rulers shaped their aspirations around the Stormont model, there emerged at precisely this juncture a body of opinion in Ulster that wished to go further and become a self-governing dominion of the Commonwealth, as the Irish Free State had been until a Republic was declared there in 1948. This dominion state tendency came from within the governing Ulster Unionist Party and was only put down with some difficulty: the clinching argument for the status quo in Northern Ireland being that the province would not enjoy the levels of welfare support and social security recently acquired in any dominion state arrangement. Over the course of the late 1940s and early 1950s it indeed was notable how crucial the factor of enhanced social welfare and health provision was—and would be—to the continuing unity of the United Kingdom, and how relatively well both Scotland and Northern Ireland did in terms of public expenditure from the centre.

By the mid-1950s the campaign for a Scottish parliament had come unstuck as the welfare state bedded down. The Conservatives, returned to power in 1951, conceded a Royal Commission on Scottish Affairs, but it advocated only tinkering with the administrative devolution arrangements Scotland possessed. It should of course be noted that some scholars have argued that the accumulation of powers and responsibilities by the Scottish Office during the twentieth century represented a considerable degree of autonomy, notwithstanding the lack of a democratically elected assembly and the 'behind-closed-doors' nature of this kind of governance.[16] In 1955 the 'Unionists', as the Conservatives in Scotland were still called, won more than half the Scottish vote, an achievement unique to this day. In 1958 the Scottish Council of the Labour Party felt able to drop its historic if, after the 1920s, largely theoretical commitment to Home Rule.

However, with hindsight the apparently harmonious character—based on at least a degree of consensus politics around a more interventionist state—which the United Kingdom assumed in the 1950s and early 1960s, was in a way anomalous, for the late 1960s were to see the arrival of serious challenges to that state in the form of the eruption of the Northern Ireland Troubles and the rise of political nationalism in Scotland (and in lesser measure Wales) to an unprecedented level.

There were important connections and interactions between these phenomena. The impact of the Northern Ireland Troubles on Scotland has too seldom been studied, and the impact of Scottish political developments in Northern Ireland even less so. Yet in separating out the Northern Ireland imbroglio as a kind of freakish anachronistic religious squabble that did not relate in any way to 'normal' or mainstream' Britain and British politics, scholars and commentators have missed many crucial links between Northern Ireland and the other parts of the United Kingdom, in particular Scotland, and they have also failed to assess properly questions of British identity and questions of how the United Kingdom has actually worked or held together, however uneasily. If, to take a commonsense example, it is acknowledged that a substantial number of people in Britain, and, of course, Scotland, value an Irish heritage and background (whether from north or south in Ireland and Catholic or Protestant), then it is reasonable to surmise that their sense of British identity may be qualified, complicated, bolstered, undermined, or even negated by that sense of Irishness and perhaps by the way that the Northern Ireland conflict has been handled by the British state. Similarly, the notion of the United Kingdom as a construct with room for a plethora of national, regional, and ethnic identities might be worth pursuing in explaining the reasons for its longevity even as British identity appears from various surveys and indicators to be in decline.

However, even if the focus is restricted to day-to-day political developments rather than broader existential identity questions, there is much to be said about the effects of the Northern Ireland Troubles from the late 1960s through to the end of the century. First, as the Northern Ireland crisis escalated, successive London governments, whether Heath's Conservatives or Wilson's and Callaghan's Labour, all tried to keep the problem from influencing or 'contaminating' other political issues, and all failed to do so. This was especially the case in relation to devolution and constitutional change in Britain, a subject put on the political agenda by the Nationalist upsurge of the late 1960s. The Royal Commission on the Constitution, set up by the Wilson government in 1968 to convey the impression of responsiveness, incorporated Northern Ireland into its remit. Furthermore, its report in 1973 had greater political impact than had been originally anticipated, and this report drew on the Northern Ireland experience of devolution in framing devolutionary recommendations for Scotland and Wales. Moreover, the Heath government, which had come to power in 1970 pledging some kind of assembly for Scotland, found that it was inhibited by the Royal Commission that was still in the midst of its investigations and distracted by the need to address the Northern Ireland emergency. The moment when the Heath government might have been able to take a devolution initiative for Scotland and carry the Conservative Party with it was allowed to pass. This was crucial in allowing an anti-devolutionary momentum to build within the party, something that came into its own when Margaret Thatcher took over as leader and then became prime minister in 1979.

The Labour governments between February 1974 and May 1979 also found that the objectives of bringing political stability to Northern Ireland and bringing forward devolution schemes for Scotland and Wales often cut across each other in spite of these governments' wish to keep them apart.[17] The strong showing of the SNP in both the 1974 elections ensured that Labour took the devolution route although many in the party were hostile. Labour indeed was devolutionist out of pragmatic political necessity rather than by conviction, although there were genuine devolvers and constitutional reformers in the Scottish ranks of the party such as the intellectual figure of John P. Mackintosh and his protégé, Donald Dewar, the man to whom it was eventually to fall to provide for the Scottish Parliament now in existence. Labour's instincts in relation to constitutional matters in the 1970s were cautious, but the very limited and modest proposals they came up with in 1975 were partly a result of the government's fear of such developments rendering their task in Northern Ireland more hazardous. Equally, the failure of the Ulster Constitutional Convention of 1975–76 was to a significant extent the result of the majority Ulster Unionist demand that Northern Ireland receive the same devolutionary scheme to be offered to Scotland and Wales. In the debate over devolution in Scotland prior to the referendum of 1979 that recorded an insufficient vote in favour, the Irish Troubles were invoked to support the arguments of both pro- and anti-devolutionists, largely by inducing fear of similar mayhem spreading in the event either of a Scottish Assembly being established or an assembly being denied.[18] There was little in the way of constructive reflection on what the Northern Ireland experience of devolution might have to teach Scotland: the political violence, in this respect, simply made most people run scared. An important exception was John P. Mackintosh who insisted on the relevance of the Northern Irish dimension to the broader UK constitutional deliberations, and indeed used Northern Ireland as a research laboratory from which he divined, clarified, and posed problems and dilemmas—some still pertinent today—and from which he yet derived cautious optimism.[19]

SCOTLAND'S SECTARIANISM QUESTION: IRISH ANSWERS AND ASSISTANCE?

There was undoubtedly much concern in Scotland about the possible spill-over effects of the Northern Ireland Troubles. As previously stated, this had significant political consequences for the way the Northern Ireland and Scottish questions of the period intersected and for the missed opportunities that may have been there for both places to learn from each other and support or cooperate with one another. This is a point that might be said to have borne down heavily on the issue of sectarianism.

If it is the case—and this writer would assent—that Scotland should have confronted the issue of sectarianism long before it became a hot potato of public debate and a media obsession at the turn of the last century, then it can be suggested that the impact of the Northern Ireland Troubles was a key factor in causing the delay. From the late 1960s the fear of contagion perhaps led many to deny the extent of the problem in Scotland. Perhaps too, as Scotland largely steered clear of Northern Ireland's tragedy, it was too readily accepted that problems of an 'Orange and Green' nature were without substance. Certainly, there was a strong argument that religious divisions were by the 1960s nowhere near as deep and bitter as the 1930s, and that Scotland had embarked on a more secular course. Historians of religion such as Callum Brown have demonstrated how abruptly and how steeply religious observance and church membership, particularly among Protestants, declined from the early 1960s.[20] Maybe by this time religion was rapidly becoming a badge of identity, a nod to one's background and formative influences, rather than faith as such, yet, equally, Scotland retained its engrained tribalism, and it was this that was arguably fed and nurtured by the nearby Ulster conflict. The vicarious sense in which many Scots related to the Troubles is brilliantly conveyed in Liam McIllvaney's novel *All the Colours of the Town*.[21] Moreover, the tribalism was also sustained by the intense uniqueness of the Rangers–Celtic 'Old Firm' football rivalry which prompted the Scottish government in 2012 to pass special legislation designed to curb the singing of certain songs and expressions of sectarianism at football matches. Support for the Glasgow teams contributes substantially to Ulster/Irish-Scottish connections, particularly in relation to working class communities, and it is the history and current politics of the Irish national question rather than the Scottish one that provides the supporters' emblems and their repertoires of songs and chants.

The contention that public discussion of sectarianism in Scotland was fatally hampered by the crisis across the North Channel is arguably validated by the fact that such discussion only gained momentum when the Northern Ireland Peace Process got underway during the 1990s. By this time the context for the discussion was very different to what it was in the 1960s: by the end of the century there was much more emphasis on ethnicity and identity politics, rather than social class, and much more doubt about the future of the Union and the United Kingdom. The sectarian debate, indeed, has become linked, if ambiguously, to the constitutional debate about what a 'new Scotland' or independent Scotland would look like.[22] However, it might be suggested that the delay in discussing sectarianism has distorted that discussion and that dubious concepts and fashionable preoccupations have been brought to it and have actually rendered it more problematic.[23]

Regardless of conceptual difficulties and disagreements, it is beyond question that there has to be due acknowledgement of the Irish dimension to this Scottish debate. In this respect the Scottish government's football legislation fell short. Although focused on football the new law raised broader questions about the expression of certain identities in Scotland: the social reality with which any legislation of this kind has to deal is the prevalence of Irish and Ulster allegiances in certain parts of Scotland. For many people there is a need for an outlet for identities and emotions arising out of Irish connections and a purposeful sense of tribal belonging. Some fear that the SNP government's measures are designed to curb expression of these identities; some opponents of the government have indeed suggested that it has set its face against expressions of identity that do not sit well with its wish to build what it considers to be a new confident sense of Scottishness.[24]

This constitutes a real challenge for the SNP, especially when it is recalled that its main political rival—the Labour Party—can claim to have achieved much in relation to sectarianism. This is not a reference to former first minister Jack McConnell's somewhat cosmetic 'crusade' against sectarianism in the early 2000s. Rather, it is the way that, historically, Labour was able to counter sectarian passions with class politics, by concentrating minds at election time on jobs, housing, health, and wages. This was arguably the main reason Scotland did not go the way of Northern Ireland when the Troubles erupted in the late 1960s. Moreover, it goes some way to explaining Labour's nervousness over constitutional reform, if not excusing its paucity of thinking around constitutional issues. Labour felt its class politics message was all the more convincing for their links to the politics of the working class in the north of England, the Midlands, South Wales, and so on. As the historian Alvin Jackson has recently put it, '[o]ne of the critical unsung achievements of Scottish Labour was that, virtually uniquely, it created a largely secular unionism—a unionism that largely transcended the religious origins of "Britishness", and the religious polarization which had accompanied the birth of Unionism in Ireland, and been exploited by British Unionists.'[25]

Times, of course, have changed and the context of devolution has boosted the politics of identity at the expense of those of class, notwithstanding the SNP's continuing wish to appeal to voters as the true left-of-centre party in the country. The SNP, though, has yet to devise a credible approach to Scotland's sectarian divisions, one which addresses Scotland's long and complex relationship with Ireland.

It might help if both the spirit and part of the letter of the Good Friday Agreement of 1998 that has formed the basis of the (uneasy) peace in Northern Ireland were revisited. The agreement was designed to accommodate different national and ethnic allegiances. Strand Three, which addressed East–West relations, provided for what came to be known as the British-Irish Council (BIC). The BIC was viewed by some as a potential means of breaking down the either/or endgame of Britishness and Irishness and creating space for different identities to breathe. The BIC was emblematic of the kind of thinking which conceived of identities as expansive and labile rather than solid and exclusivist.[26]

The BIC, however, has languished in the background since the signing of the Good Friday Agreement. It has not featured in the news headlines. It was recently, and belatedly, provided with a permanent base and a secretariat in Edinburgh and the question arises as to whether it might now play a positive role in re-conceptualising identity matters at a time of possible constitutional upheaval. In relation to Scotland's old problem of sectarianism, it has been argued that there could be mileage in the BIC being the facilitator of a purposeful and comprehensive joint initiative between three of the BIC's governments, namely, Scotland, Northern Ireland, and the Republic of Ireland.[27]

There would seem to be much in the way of good practice that such an initiative might highlight and further develop. Northern Ireland's experiments in integrated education may hold lessons for Scotland; the debate over the value of integrated schools has certainly developed much further than in Scotland where the defensiveness of the Catholic Church has rendered even the exploration of issues such as shared school campuses fraught with sensitivities and difficulties.[28] The Republic of Ireland's recent robust handling of the Catholic Church's child abuse scandals has reflected the profound way that attitudes have altered to the role of religion in politics and society in a country where deferral to the hierarchy was once second nature. This development may have wider significance in these islands of Britain and Ireland given the increasing intermingling of peoples and identities.[29] The changes that have occurred, arising out of long-running identity controversies, around the Northern Ireland international football team's fans, and the community initiatives pioneered by the Irish Football Association, may well have relevance to Scotland with its 'Old Firm'—dominated supporters' culture.[30]

By promoting or leading such an initiative, the Scottish government could be seen to pay due respect to the considerable Irish influences on Scotland and to open up the possibility of developing Irish links productively rather than recoiling from the history of conflict that has surrounded them. Moreover, through such an initiative the SNP government could involve itself in a proper dialogue with those constituencies for whom Irish and Ulster-shaped identities remain vital.[31]

THE PEACE PROCESS, THE SCOTTISH PARLIAMENT, AND THE INDEPENDENCE REFERENDUM

The inconclusive devolution referendum result of 1979 was quickly followed by the return of the Conservatives to power under Margaret Thatcher. The long period of Tory rule from 1979 until 1997 was notable for the reassembling of the case for a Scottish parliament as a form of popular protest against the Thatcher government which had no mandate from the Scottish electorate. Besides the evidence that the Thatcherite economic project was deeply unpopular, a perception grew steadily that she and her government had no appreciation of Scottish national distinctiveness, no respect for Scottish institutions, and no grasp of the concept of the Union as a two-way street, of the tacit understandings and balancing acts that the Union always rested on.[32] Thatcher alienated Scottish voters to the point that even now the Conservatives are widely regarded as a 'toxic' political brand. Thatcher's successor, John Major, may have attempted to repair some of the damage, but he was just as opposed to giving Scotland a devolved parliament. Moreover, as Northern Ireland moved towards peace during his premiership, Major left himself open to attack over his inconsistency in supporting devolution for Northern Ireland as part of the Peace Process and in urging people in the province to cast aside the 'old history' that was standing in the way of peace while in relation to Scotland Major was denouncing the idea of devolution and calling for the common history between Scotland and England to be preserved and cherished.[33] The 1990s were years when the UK constitutional debate again brought Scotland and Northern Ireland together. At some points it seemed that Scotland was pushing and advancing the devolutionary and constitutional reform agenda; at others it was Northern Ireland and the Peace Process that appeared to be the catalyst for demands for broader change and, in particular, the redress of the perceived democratic deficit in Scotland. When the Labour government led by Tony Blair was finally returned to office in 1997 developments in Northern Ireland were entering the crucial phase that would lead to the signing of the Good Friday Agreement of 1998, an accord that had at its centre the restoration of devolution to Northern Ireland, in the form of a power-sharing, consociational executive and an assembly with primary legislative powers. Blair, whatever his personal feelings on the matter, could not renege on Labour's commitment to Scottish devolution (or indeed an assembly for Wales), and so the scene was set for the political re-configuration of the United Kingdom. It is certainly true that Scotland and Northern Ireland arrived at their devolutionary destinations by different routes but it is nonetheless important to recognise the extent to which the two cases had for decades rubbed off each other, cut across each other, influenced one another, and finally converged around their new devolved structures and capacities, and their centrality to the future of the re-defined Union, with its accompanying questions of identity and allegiance.

The extraordinary historical moment when peace (at least of a kind) came to Northern Ireland, and the United Kingdom was finally shaken up and de-centralised, proved to be an auspicious one for Scottish-Irish relations. To a significant extent old historic and cultural bonds between Scotland and Ireland were rediscovered and certainly in the academic and media worlds new relationships were formed. There seemed to be a new fluidity and expansiveness about relationships within the two islands, although in the Scottish-Irish case there were also hiccups such as the cancellation of a visit by the Irish Taoiseach Bertie Ahern to Scotland in 2001 for fear of possible trouble given that the visit fell on the occasion of an 'Old Firm' football match.[34]

The potential there may have been for productive interchange and cooperation between the two devolved entities of Scotland and Northern Ireland largely failed to be realised on account of the Northern Ireland assembly's stuttering progress in the early years when the problematic outworking of the 1998 agreement led to suspensions of Stormont. With such thorny issues as the decommissioning of paramilitary weapons and the reform of the police taking time to be resolved, Northern Ireland could not focus on the operation of devolution as such, and it is only since 2007 that there has been proper continuity in respect of the functioning of the institutions. More widely, it is fair to say that since the transformation of the United Kingdom governmentally at the end of the twentieth century, there have been many uncertainties and ambivalences around what is in effect a UK project in transition, and at this juncture it is not clear where that project is heading.

However, in the light of such factors, it is unsurprising that the most politically significant development of the early twenty-first century around Scottish-Irish relations should be the SNP's use of the economic success story of the Republic of Ireland—'The Celtic Tiger'—to support its own case for independence. This song of praise had of course to be abruptly dropped from the SNP repertoire when Ireland, like Iceland, crashed into the economic doldrums in 2008–9. Yet for the time it lasted the Irish success story fed into an influential narrative—the legacy of which arguably remains 'sellable'—of small nations emerging from the shadow of bigger neighbours, playing to their own distinctive cultural strengths, and using them to underpin new economic ventures.

However, even at its height the Republic of Ireland of the 'Celtic Tiger' still had a weak welfare system and a largely agrarian economy with a privileged farming class and was markedly different to Scotland with her higher (British) standards of welfare provision, greater urbanisation, a large public sector, and a historically strong Labour movement reflecting the once dominant heavy industry sector. The obvious Irish parallel was, and is, Northern Ireland. Scotland's twentieth-century experience was shared to a great extent by the province whether in terms of economic profiles, the problems and challenges of deindustrialisation, public-sector reliance, relative religious and ethno-cultural pluralism as well as divisions and tensions emanating from this source, 'national questions', and—as outlined earlier—devolution and debates over the future of the Union, the United Kingdom, and Britishness.

The historian Alvin Jackson has referred to the constitutional proposition first advanced by Gladstone, and still of crucial importance today: 'the paradox that the United Kingdom could be best sustained through devolution.'[35] The Scottish referendum of September 2014 put this proposition to the test. The SNP's period as a minority government in Scotland from 2007 until 2011 and its astonishing Holyrood election victory in 2011 paved the way for the vote on the question, 'Should Scotland be an Independent Country?' The SNP, long enamoured of Irish Nationalist leader Charles Stewart Parnell's declaration about no man having the right to 'fix the boundary to the march of a nation', have played on the teleological notion that Scotland's destiny lies in independence, that it is somehow decreed by history, and that the actual 'No' vote that transpired in the referendum represents merely a setback. Those in favour of the Union, by contrast, were faced with the apparently drier task of upholding Gladstone's proposition, and it seems that they still face the challenge of truly convincing Scots that the Union is capable of evolving to meet the needs of the time, and that the 'best of both worlds' promised by the 'No' campaign will materialise in the form of a stronger Scottish Parliament within a 'rebooted'—perhaps in time federalised—United Kingdom.[36]

The referendum mattered greatly to Ireland, both north and south, and to Scottish-Irish relations. The SNP have laid great stress in what its former leader Alex Salmond has called 'The Social Union': the idea that independence would not in any way attenuate the deep and extensive ties between the peoples of the different parts of the two islands. Politically, however, a 'Yes' vote would have affected Northern Ireland directly and profoundly, leaving it facing dislocation in a truncated United Kingdom that would not have carried the same emotional resonance. Culturally and socially, much of the Northern Ireland Unionists' sense of belonging and sense of who they are is bound with Scotland in particular, and the historic links across a narrow sea. An Ulster-Scots identity has become recognised as part of the complex tapestry of the province and central to the 'culture war' that some see as having replaced the guns.[37] Some Unionist politicians indeed entered the Scottish debate to urge Scots not to break the ties of kith and kin, an anguished echo of similar pleas made at the height of the Irish Home Rule crisis a century ago.[38]

The 'Edinburgh Agreement' of 2012 between the Scottish and London governments ruled out a second question on the ballot paper of the referendum that would have allowed voters to state a preference for the further strengthening of the powers of the Scottish devolved parliament, popularly referred to as either 'devo max' or 'devo plus', although the pro-Union parties vowed to ensure that enhanced powers would follow a 'No' vote. Nonetheless, the campaign yielded a sharper sense of polarisation than many would have wished. Among many academic contributions to the referendum debate, the Scottish historian Colin Kidd indeed made the point that nationalism is historically an ingredient of Scottish Unionism and that most Scots have long been susceptible to both nationalist and unionist sentiments.[39] Historically, nationalism and unionism have been two points on a political continuum in Scotland rather than binary opposites as in Ireland. It would be ironic if, at a time when the unionist/nationalist 'endgame' has apparently been declared a draw in Northern Ireland with the relative loosening of old certainties and atavistic loyalties, the unionist/nationalist interplay in Scotland of over three centuries was to be reformulated in a more adversarial and zero-sum fashion following the referendum. But, if the independence debate can be said to have produced any broad agreement, it is that nothing can ever be the same again.

NOTES

1. The opening of the institute indeed coincided with the publication of Devine's award-winning and best-selling history *The Scottish Nation* (London: Allen Lane, 1999).
2. L. M. Cullen and T. C. Smout (eds), *Comparative Aspects of Scottish and Irish Economic and Social History, 1600–1900* (Edinburgh: John Donald, 1977); T. M. Devine and D. Dickson (eds), *Ireland and Scotland, 1600–1850* (Edinburgh: John Donald, 1983); R. Mitchison and P. Roebuck (eds), *Economy and Society in Scotland and Ireland, 1500–1939* (Edinburgh: John Donald, 1988).

3. Examples include L. McIlvanney and R. Ryan (eds), *Ireland and Scotland: Culture and Society, 1700–2000* (Dublin: Four Courts Press, 2005); R. Ryan, *Ireland and Scotland. Literature and Culture, State and Nation, 1966–2000* (Oxford: Oxford University Press, 2002); J.M. Kirk and D.P.O. Baoill (eds), *Language Links: The Languages of Ireland and Scotland* (Belfast: Queen's University, 2001); A. McCarthy, *Personal Narratives of Irish and Scottish Migration, 1921–65: 'For Spirit and Adventure'* (Manchester: Manchester University Press, 2007); and *Scottishness and Irishness in New Zealand since 1840* (Manchester: Manchester University Press, 2010).
4. I. McLean, 'Political Science and History: Friends and Neighbours', *Political Studies*, 58:2 (2010), pp. 354–67.
5. For an excellent general history see I.C.G. Hutchison, *Scottish Politics in the Twentieth Century* (Basingstoke: PalgraveMacMillan, 2000)
6. See E. Cameron, *Impaled Upon a Thistle: Scotland since 1880* (Edinburgh: Edinburgh University Press, 2010), pp. 68–69; also Scotland First Minister Donald Dewar's Keynote Address at conference in Dublin in 2000 in D. Dickson et al. (eds), *Ireland and Scotland: Nation, Region, Identity* (Dublin: The Centre for Irish-Scottish Studies, TCD, 2001), pp. 1–12.
7. S. Bruce, 'Sectarianism in Scotland: A Contemporary Assessment and Explanation', *Scottish Government Yearbook 1988* (Edinburgh: University of Edinburgh, 1988), pp. 150–65. These issues are discussed at length in G. Walker, *Intimate Strangers: Political and Cultural Interaction between Scotland and Ulster* (Edinburgh: John Donald, 1995), chap. 3; and in contributions to C.M.M. Macdonald (ed), *Unionist Scotland, 1800–1997* (Edinburgh: John Donald, 1998).
8. See T. Gallagher, *Divided Scotland* (Glendaruel: Argyll Press, 2013), chap. 4; S.J. Brown, '"Outside the Covenant": The Scottish Presbyterian Churches and Irish Immigration, 1922–38', *Innes Review*, 42:1 (1991), pp. 19–45.
9. McCarthy, *Personal Narratives*.
10. Ibid., pp. 51–52.
11. T. Gallagher, *Glasgow: The Uneasy Peace* (Manchester: Manchester University Press, 1987), p. 92.
12. Walker, *Intimate Strangers*, chap. 3. For interwar failure of anti-Irish policy see R.J. Finlay, 'The Interwar Crisis: the Failure of Extremism', in T.M. Devine and J. Wormald (eds), *The Oxford Handbook of Modern Scottish History* (Oxford: Oxford University Press, 2012), pp. 569–84.
13. B. Purdie, '"Crossing Swords with W.B. Yeats": Twentieth Century Scottish Nationalist Encounters with Ireland', *Journal of Irish and Scottish Studies*, 1:1 (2007), pp. 191–210.
14. See K. Roy, *The Invisible Spirit* (Prestwick: ICS Books, 2013), pp. 93–6; J. McCormick, *The Flag in the Wind* (Edinburgh: Birlinn, 2008).
15. For a full discussion of this example of political interaction see G. Walker, 'Scotland, Northern Ireland and Devolution: Past and Present', *Contemporary British History*, 24:2 (2010), pp. 235–56.
16. The best example is L. Paterson, *The Autonomy of Modern Scotland* (Edinburgh: Edinburgh University Press, 1994).
17. For a fuller exploration see G. Walker, 'Scotland, Northern Ireland and Devolution, 1945–79', *Journal of British Studies*, 49:1 (2010), pp. 117–42.
18. See the reflections of prominent anti-devolution campaigner of the period, Tam Dalyell, MP, in his autobiography, *The Importance of Being Awkward* (Edinburgh: Birlinn, 2012), pp. 131–35.
19. See G. Walker, 'John P. Mackintosh, Devolution and the Union', *Parliamentary Affairs*, 66:3 (2013), pp. 557–78.
20. C.G. Brown, *The Death of Christian Britain* (London: 2001), pp. 175–76.

21. L. McIlvanney, *All the Colours of the Town* (London: Faber, 2009). See also discussion in Gallagher, *Divided Scotland*, chap. 6.
22. See N. Bonney, 'Religion and the Scottish Independence Referendum', *Political Quarterly*, 84:4 (2013), pp. 478–85.
23. One such preoccupation might be called 'the politics of taking offence', and this phenomenon is explored in Stuart Waiton's *Snobs' Law* (Dundee: Take a Liberty, 2012), a polemical rejoinder occasioned by the Scottish government's legislation on songs and chants at football matches. A report titled 'An Examination of the Evidence on Sectarianism in Scotland', published by the Scottish government in 2013, attested to the still widespread perception of sectarianism as a problem, yet found no significant difference in the level of discrimination experienced by Catholics and Protestant in respect of any of the forms of discrimination explored, and no evidence of structural disadvantage against either Catholics or Protestants.
24. For academic perspectives on the new legislation see J. Flint and J. Kelly (eds), *Bigotry, Football and Scotland* (Edinburgh: Edinburgh University Press, 2013); and for a swingeing critique of the SNP's *modus operandi*, penned before the football controversy, see T. Gallagher, *The Illusion of Freedom* (London: Hurst, 2009).
25. A. Jackson, *The Two Unions* (Oxford: Oxford University Press, 2012), p. 270.
26. See, for example, R. Kearney, *Postnationalist Ireland* (London: Routledge, 1997), pp. 92–95.
27. G. Walker, 'Scotland's Sectarianism Problem: Irish Answers?' *Political Quarterly*, 83:2 (2012), pp. 374–83.
28. See discussion of Catholic attitudes in M. Rosie, *The Sectarian Myth in Scotland* (Basingstoke: Palgrave, 2004), pp. 44–48; also the critical observations in Bonney, 'Religion'.
29. See also Roy Foster's insights into the loosening of the Church's political and cultural grip in the late twentieth century in his *Luck and the Irish* (London: Allen Lane, 2007), chap. 2.
30. See the various essays on sport and national identity in A. Bairner, *Sport and the Irish* (Dublin: UCD Press, 2005).
31. In early 2014 the Irish Consul in Edinburgh weighed in to the Scottish sectarianism controversy alleging 'disturbing' examples of 'anti-Irishness'. See *The Herald*, 27 February 2014.
32. For discussion of the decline of the Conservatives in Scotland and in particular the impact of Thatcherism see D. Torrance (ed), *Whatever Happened to Tory Scotland?* (Edinburgh: Edinburgh University Press, 2012). For a masterly treatment of the workings of the Union over time see C. Kidd, *Union and Unionisms* (Cambridge: Cambridge University Press, 2008).
33. For discussion of Major's inconsistency see P. Lynch, 'The Northern Ireland Peace Process and Scottish Constitutional Reform', *Regional and Federal Studies*, 6:1 (1996), pp. 45–62.
34. See G. Walker and A. Bairner, 'Popular Culture in Scotland and Ireland', in McIlvaney and Ryan (eds), *Ireland and Scotland*, pp. 227–47.
35. Jackson, *Two Unions*, p. 193
36. See D. Torrance, *Britain Rebooted: Scotland in a Federal Union* (Edinburgh: Luath Press, 2014).
37. See the penetrating commentary of Edna Longley in her essay in E. Longley and D. Kiberd, *Multi-Culturalism: The View from the Two Irelands* (Cork: Cork University Press, 2001).

38. See A. Aughey, 'Faraway, so close: Scotland from Northern Ireland', in G. Hassan and J. Mitchell (eds), *After Independence* (Edinburgh: Luath Press, 2013), pp. 224–34.
39. C. Kidd, 'Popular Sovereignty not just for Nationalists', *The Scotsman*, 21 January 2012. See also B. Foley, *Scotland and the United Kingdom* (London and Edinburgh: British Academy and the Royal Society of Edinburgh, 2012), pp. 28–30.

9 Emigration in the Age of Electronic Media

Personal Perspectives of Irish Migrants to Australia, 1969–2013

Fidelma Breen

In the 12 months to April 2013 approximately 63,400 migrants permanently left the island of Ireland to seek love, fun, employment, adventure, and advancement in other parts of the globe.[1] Their journeys continue the lengthy tradition of Irish emigration to places other than Europe which increased, and has continued to grow, since the period just after the Napoleonic Wars.[2] This chapter considers the responses given by respondents to two surveys which enquired about the migration experience from Ireland to Australia. Those surveyed emigrated between 1969 and 2013. The survey samples were small and not representative of the Irish population in Australia and, as such, the information contained herein is not used to make inferences about the general Irish population in Australia. It does, however, reveal that the characteristics of Irish migrants since 2008 differ markedly from the post-1980 period and the years before the collapse of the Irish economy. It also pinpoints some avenues for further research. The main points of interest which are to be developed in future work are the drivers of contemporary Irish migration to Australia with a specific focus on the settlement aspirations of migrants and the compatibility of available visas with those aspirations.

Around 5,839 of the Irish migrant group mentioned above chose Australia as their next new home between 2012 and June 2013.[3] The topics of 'migration' and 'diaspora' are briefly discussed, because these are vital to a study of any migrant cohort, before detailing the results of two surveys. The first survey is 'Ireland Online: So Close No Matter How Far' while the second survey is 'Ireland Online: The Experiences of Irish/Northern Irish Migrants to Australia', both of which were carried out among Irish migrants across Australia in 2012 and 2014.[4] These data sets are compared with the findings of recent academic studies undertaken on Irish migrants to Australia in an effort to uncover changing trends in Irish emigration since the collapse of Ireland's economy.[5] The analysis of the Ireland Online data also refers to the Émigré Project being conducted by University College Cork (UCC) because the results of the two Ireland Online surveys generally support its recently published report.[6] After providing the demographic profile of the respondents, analysis of the data provided by the research is undertaken. This includes the role of technology in migration, contemporary emigration motivators, and Ireland's diaspora engagement policy and practice.[7]

We should note that Irish migration to Australia commenced with the British colonisation of the continent as Australia's first European community had a significant Irish component. Not confined to the convict class, the Irish were part of the officialdom which accompanied white settlement. A number of entries in the *Australian Dictionary of Biography* testify to this fact.[8] Irish-born governors, magistrates, and politicians are numerous.[9] Irish families such as the Bagots in South Australia and the Ryans in New South Wales made fortunes on the land as pastoralists and in mines. The Irish in Australia made significant contributions to relief efforts against pending famine in Ireland in the late 1870s and added moral support and financial muscle to the Irish Home Rule movement.[10] In the 1880s the Irish-born comprised around 9.5 per cent of the total colonial population although the Irish component differed from colony to colony.[11] The numbers of Irish-born in Australia have certainly decreased from pre–First World War levels, but Table 9.1 interestingly shows that the figures given for 1933 and for 2011 do not differ significantly. The data are represented as a line graph in Figure 9.1 where the recent upwards trend of the Irish-born component is clearly visible. It is worth noting that the 29 per cent increase in Irish-born people in Australia from 2006 to 2011 is the largest since the mid- to late 1980s when economic depression in Ireland heralded another great wave of emigration. The collapse of Ireland's boom, known as the Celtic Tiger, has

Table 9.1 Numbers of Irish-born in the Australian Population, 1921–2011

Year	% of Australian population that is Irish-born	Total Australian population	Combined Numbers of people from Northern Ireland and Republic of Ireland
1921	2.18	5,435,700	118,328
1933	1.39	6,629,800	92,235
1947	0.73	7,579,400	55,425
1954	0.68	8,986,500	61,008
1966	0.64	11,550,500	74,132
1976	0.69	13,548,400	93,454
1986	0.61	15,602,200	94,519
1991	0.50	16,850,533	83,760
1996	0.46	17,892,423	82,573
2001	0.42	18,972,350	80,286
2006	0.40	20,061,646	80,366
2011	0.46	21,507,719	99,183

Source: Calculated using data from Australian Census, Australian Bureau of Statistics

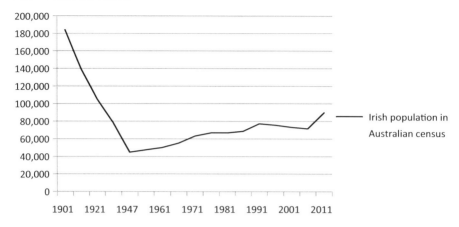

Figure 9.1 The Irish population of Australia, 1901–2011
Source: Australian Bureau of Statistics and Department of Immigration and Border Protection.

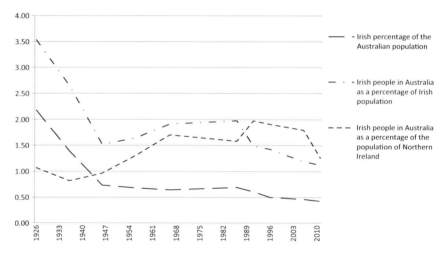

Figure 9.2 The Irish-born as a percentage of the Australian population, 1921–2010
Source: Calculated using data from Australian Census, Australian Bureau of Statistics.

played a part in the country's increased emigration since 2008 but, interestingly, the survey respondents were, by and large, employed at the point of emigration. While the actual numbers vary little what has changed is the proportionate value of the Irish in the total Australian population as shown in Figure 9.2.

MIGRATION

Migration from Ireland has often been characterised as 'exile' or 'victim-driven'.[12] Historians, geographers, and other social scientists have analysed the 'push' and 'pull' factors of centuries of migration and, as much as they change over time, these remain hauntingly similar.[13] Global moves are driven by wishes for an improved lifestyle, better career advancement and employment opportunities, and educational and leisure pursuits not catered for in Ireland. Aside from these, many migrants cite wanderlust or a quest for adventure as the reason for leaving.[14] Whatever the cause of departure, what is striking is the reoccurrence of the theme among survey responses that contemporary emigration may be neither permanent nor a final action. Improvements in the cost, accessibility, and speed of travel, and communication and technology in general, may have contributed to the notion of a smaller world space and ease of connectedness but whatever the social, economic, or political ramifications of migration, the human aspect—feelings of fear, trepidation, loneliness, excitement, freedom, adventure, despair, and homesickness—has not changed.

The Republic of Ireland (ROI) is, once again, experiencing a large exodus of residents due to the financial crises of the past few years and Australia is proving a popular destination. *The Population and Labour Force Projections, 2016–2046*, produced by the Irish Central Statistics Office (CSO), determined that emigration 'ranged from 25,000 to 30,000 between 1997 and 2005 before rising slowly between April 2006 and April 2008. This was followed by a sharp rise in 2009 following the economic downturn in 2008. Emigration has remained high in the years since meaning Ireland has returned to a situation of net outward migration'.[15] The CSO reported that while almost 42 per cent of the 87,100 who had left Ireland in the year to April 2013 represented foreign nationals, the number of Irish women emigrating rose from 20,600 in 2012 to 23,800 in the year to April 2013, while the number of male migrants increased from 26,000 to 27,100 in the same period. More than 17 per cent (15,400) of Irish migrants were destined for Australia.[16] A 2013 report from Australia's Department of Immigration and Border Protection (DIBP) revealed that 4,784 ROI nationals were granted permanent residency in the year to June 2013.

In total 5,209 Irish nationals were granted a permanent visa to Australia through the Migration Programme in 2012–13. The majority (83 per cent) of permanent Irish arrivals were issued 'Skilled' migration visas. Of the 128,973 'Skilled' visas issued in 2012–13, 4,325 (3.4 per cent) were taken up by Irish people. Family visas accounted for the remainder of the total permanent Irish intake. Of the 60,185 family visas in the 2012–13 program, almost 900 (1.5 per cent) were granted to Irish people, the majority of whom (96 per cent) were partners of Australian residents.[17] Most of the visas in these categories were granted onshore (see Figure 9.3). The Business (Long Stay, subclass 457; hereafter 457) visa is popular among the Irish seeking temporary entry to Australia in the first instance. Of the 126,350

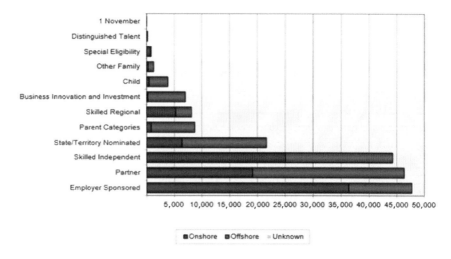

Figure 9.3 Skill and family visa categories, 2012–13: Onshore versus offshore
Source: DIBP 2012–13 Migration Program Report, p. 5.

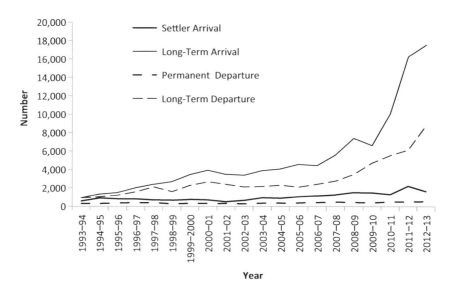

Figure 9.4 Permanent and long-term arrivals and departures of Irish-born persons, 1993–94 to 2012–13
Source: Department of Immigration and Border Protection, unpublished data.

subclass 457 visas issued, 10,290 (8.1 per cent) were granted to Irish nationals. More than 19,000 Irish people were granted the temporary Working Holiday Maker visa (subclass 417; hereafter WHM) in 2012–13 from a total pool of 178,980 representing 10.6 per cent of the total.[18]

As Figure 9.4 shows, the long-term arrivals far outstrip the long-term departures indicating a significant increase in the long-term stay category of migration. Compared to 2009–10, subclass 457 visas issued to Irish nationals have increased by more than 200 per cent.

The top source citizenship country for Temporary Skilled (subclass 457) visa holders in Australia on 31 December 2013 was the United Kingdom (38,860 visa holders), followed by India (30,890), Ireland (12,150), the Philippines (10,270), and the United States of America (8,540).[19]

When comparing the number of Temporary Skilled (subclass 457) visa holders in Australia on 31 December 2013 with earlier years, Figure 9.5 shows that over the past five years, the number of Temporary Skilled (subclass 457) visa holders from the United Kingdom increased by 26.2 per cent from 31 December 2008. India increased by 115.7 per cent, Ireland increased by 242.4 per cent, the Philippines decreased by 14.9 per cent, and the United States of America increased by 44.6 per cent.[20]

In combination with the physical expansion of diasporic communities caused by increased immigration (in the five years from 2006 to 2011 Australia's Irish community increased by 29 per cent), the explosion of online national groups, particularly on Facebook™, in recent years appears to have decreased feelings of distance for some migrants.[21] Evidence for this is provided in the discussion of migrants' feelings regarding distance and the effects of social media below. Paradoxically, then, ethnic communities can seem larger and more widespread as the disparate groups become aware of their counterparts in other regions. These groups, whether government,

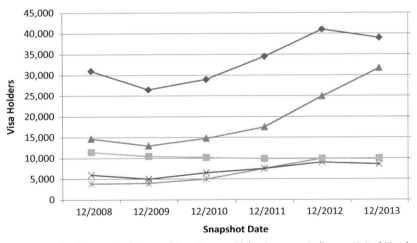

Figure 9.5 Temporary skilled (subclass 457) visa holders in Australia: Top five citizenship countries

Source: Department of Immigration and Border Protection, Temporary entrants and New Zealand citizens in Australia as at 31 December 2013, p. 13.

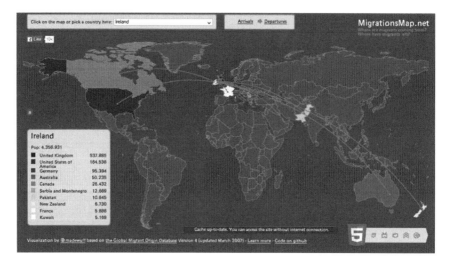

Figure 9.6 World map showing destinations of Irish emigrants (2007)
Source: migrationsmap.net.

media, community, locality, or interest-based, provide the nation with the ability to reach out to members of its diaspora in ways previously unimagined. As of June 2014, Facebook had more than 80 groups dedicated to the Irish in Australia compared with 30 for British/UK expats and just four for the Italian community in Australia.[22] Ireland's attempts to engage with and mobilise its diaspora are discussed briefly below. The reach of the Irish diaspora is evident from the MigrationNet map in Figure 9.6.

DIASPORA

There has been considerable debate among scholars in Irish Studies about the application of the word *diaspora* to the many Irish communities outside Ireland.[23] A diasporic identity is one that allows acceptance of a new physical home to sit alongside the comfort of the emotional or imagined home—that is, it identifies a 'homing desire' without an actual want to return to the country of origin. It is a complex identity which can encompass not just the migrant, but the generations originating from that migrant and involve the accommodation of dual citizenships and many-faceted emotional allegiances. Critics imply that the term sweeps away, or depoliticises, the political and economic causes of mass emigration.[24] Others suggest that its links with the Jewish people hang on it connotations of tragedy and enforced abandonment of home.[25] Patrick Fitzgerald and Brian Lambkin quote Liam Kennedy's MOPE (Most Oppressed People Ever) Syndrome as a description of a trend towards a general culture of victimhood.[26] Kevin Kenny, in 'Diaspora and Comparison', concludes that the Famine is the scarring historical event which ties Ireland to the last of Cohen's five categories of diasporic identity, that of victim.[27] In his critique of Cohen's typology, Donald Harman Akenson states that the categorisation of victim is 'demonstrably false in the case of nineteenth and twentieth century Irish out-migration, considered as a whole' and goes on to make the case that the Irish were as much imperialists as imperialised.[28] Mary Hickman raises the salient point that in Irish Studies the focus on emigration highlights the cause and effects for disparate groups of migrants over time, whereas consideration of an Irish diaspora includes subsequent generations of the migrant.[29] Dianne Hall and Elizabeth Malcolm conclude that 'diaspora' is a legitimate category of analysis if 'clearly defined, and employed with care'.[30]

In May 2013, Joe Hackett, director of the Irish Abroad Unit at the Irish Department of Foreign Affairs, noted that Ireland has an 'inclusive approach to its diaspora. If you are Irish, if you feel Irish, if you feel connected to Ireland then, as far as we are concerned, you are Irish.'[31] The International Organization for Migration (IOM) accepts Kingsley Aikins's and Martin Russell's definition of diasporas as 'obvious collectives of people through which networks can be created and individuals mobilized for mutual benefit' and 'influential bridges to knowledge, expertise, resources and markets for countries of origin'.[32] How a country defines its diaspora will determine its policy and practice of engaging with it. Ireland has many successful diaspora engagement initiatives. Among its five most noteworthy are the Irish International Diaspora Centre Trust, the Ireland Funds, Ireland Reaching Out, Connect Ireland, and, perhaps most famously, The Gathering, which is described in more detail below.[33]

In *Women and the Irish Diaspora*, Breda Gray quotes Khachig Tölöyan's argument that for a consciousness of diaspora to emerge, a discourse of diaspora must be produced by a small group of intellectuals and political leaders.[34] In modern Ireland this was certainly the case. As a phrase, 'the Irish diaspora' gained significance and popularity during Mary Robinson's term as president in the 1990s and has since passed into general usage. Mary Hickman refers to the success of the extent to which 'official imaginings of the nation have dominated public discourses'.[35] *Diaspora* has become synonymous with the Irish nation, as well as other ethnic dispersions, such as the Armenians, Ukrainians, Chinese, Sikhs, Jews, and Hindus.[36] Within the context of this study it is taken to mean the communities of Irish people living outside Ireland, both Irish-born and their descendants. As a concept it is evident in officially promoted events such as 'The Gathering 2013', a Failté Ireland initiative conceived at the Global Irish Economic Forum held in Dublin in September 2009.[37] The Gathering was a year-long programme which provided a national branding umbrella for locally organised activities aimed at bringing members of the diaspora back to Ireland to assist in rejuvenating the economy as well as encouraging those of Irish heritage around the world to connect with the country through genealogy, history, sport, and community events. The strategy appears to be working. A €1 billion boost to the Irish economy was the result of the increase in return travel to Ireland by expatriates and migrants who comprised a quarter of the total visitor number to Ireland in 2012/13. VFR (visiting friends and relatives) tourism was up 9 per cent year on the year between 2012 and 2013. This equates to about 250,000 extra visitors. For Australia and New Zealand, the growth was even more pronounced, up 18 per cent in the year for VFR visitors.[38] Diane Butler, manager of Tourism Ireland Australia and New Zealand, stated that the department aims to 'build on the legacy of the Gathering, continuing to reach out to the Diaspora across Australia and New Zealand.'[39]

The economic and social rejuvenation of rural Irish communities, in particular, is seen as an additional valuable aspect of the country's attention to attracting members of its diaspora to Ireland.[40] Community cooperatives have been formed based on cottage industry manufacturing of cultural artefacts of Irish heritage for an international market as well as increased tourism.[41] Individuals are being urged to speak up for their local areas in business innovation forums through Connect Ireland, which was set up as part of the government's job strategy in 2012. A recent article in *The Irish Times* reported on the 'Building Your Area For The Future Generation' initiative of the Upper Shannon-Erne Future Economy project set up by Bord na Móna and Leitrim County Council to regenerate the economy in the upper Shannon-Erne corridor. The report cites opportunities in artisan agribusiness and tourism which could be capitalised on to bring migrant Irish back home to Ireland. High-speed broadband and better connections have made this area more accessible and parts of the region are only an hour and a half from Dublin Airport. Local people are being urged to be the 'eyes and ears of Ireland' in attempting to attract investment to the region to reinvent their communities for future generations.[42]

While Ireland's diaspora policy and examples of practice have garnered worldwide interest the Irish diaspora has attracted significant academic debate and attention. Studies such as Kerby Miller's *Emigrants and Exiles* and David Fitzpatrick's *Oceans of Consolation*, both of which relied on migrants' letters as source material, contributed to the conversation among scholars as to the most productive method of studying the phenomenon of a national community uncontained by borders and resettling in new and dissimilar (in both geographical location and stage of development) worlds. Akenson's observation that 'the dominant habit of using the passive voice when talking about diasporas' robs the migrant of their agency and relegates them to a piece of 'flotsam on some poorly defined and simplistically explained historical tide' strikes a chord.[43] If one is to categorise contemporary Irish migration to Australia based on responses to the question, 'Did you leave Ireland/Northern Ireland because you had to or because you wanted to?' (a question which was preceded by choices from a list of possible deciding factors), asked in Survey 2, then it would seem the 'exile' motif does not apply. Although almost 30 per cent of respondents stated that the main reason they left Ireland/Northern Ireland was because of the economic/political climate, 73 per cent stated that they left the country because they wanted to, with 27 per cent feeling the move was more 'push' than 'pull'.[44] The varied deciding factors given by respondents to both surveys support the view that the push–pull dichotomy is reductionist and misleading, showing as they do that a mixture of factors that could be characterised as either 'forcing' or 'enticing' were involved in the decision to emigrate.

SURVEY DISTRIBUTION

This chapter is based on two sets of data. One was gathered from a questionnaire which was distributed by post, e-mail, and the Internet (Survey 1) while the second came from a questionnaire that was sent to web-based connections only (Survey 2).[45] Why two surveys one might ask? Survey 1 ('Ireland Online: So Close No Matter How Far') was a brief survey of 33 questions focused on the use of social media and the communication methods of two distinct cohorts: those who arrived in Australia between 1969 and 1985 (Cohort 1) when e-mail, Facebook, and Skype™ were non-existent and a later group who emigrated after 1999 (Cohort 2). Survey 2 ('Ireland Online: The Experiences of Irish/Northern Irish Migrants to Australia'), contained 70 questions and was a more comprehensive questionnaire aimed at filling some of the gaps left by Survey 1 as well as providing pilot data for a PhD proposal.

In addition Survey 1 was aimed solely at Facebook groups self-identifying as Irish and thereby risked missing a portion of people from Northern Ireland who might not self-identify as Irish. This oversight was rectified with Survey 2 which was posted to Irish online forums as well as others such Poms in Oz, Adelaide Brits, and Expats in Adelaide. There were no limitations placed on respondents to the second survey other than considering themselves as having originated from the island of Ireland (self-identifying as Irish, Northern Irish, or British) and having migrated to Australia. All respondents were migrants, although some were dependant children at the time of migration.

Survey 1 targeted two specific groups delimited by the date ranges given above. There was a reason for choosing these two periods: the first group left Ireland and moved across the world at a time when it was generally viewed as a one-way trip.[46] Subsequent communication between the migrant and home was limited to letter writing as few households had a telephone, and even when a connection was available the cost was prohibitive. Respondents from Cohort 1 of Survey 1 report that a phone call from Australia to Ireland had to be saved up for.[47] In contrast, those who moved to Australia in the last decade or so did so in an entirely different technological world. Not only is travel quicker (as in travelling by air as opposed to travelling by sea as some 'Ten Pound Poms' did in the late 1960s) and on the whole more accessible because of cheaper fares, but in the last few years, communication advances, particularly with regard to mobile phone usage, have also meant that very few people in the developed world are unreachable at a moment's notice.[48]

The earliest arrivals (Cohort 1) of Survey 1 represented the tail end of the Ten Pound Poms and those who availed of the assisted passage scheme. Many of these travelled by ship in tourist-class accommodation on Peninsular and Orient (P&O) or other British-owned liners with the less fortunate being allocated to converted carrier escorts owned by the Italian Sitmar Line for a journey from England to Australia that took approximately four weeks.[49] This group benefitted from the later twentieth-century improvements in technology and travel. While still a 'long-haul' flight, travellers from Europe can now reach Australia in less than 24 hours.

Technology was used to reach these migrants in order to find out about their migration experience. Both surveys were formatted on SurveyMonkey, a web-based survey developer. Because SurveyMonkey does not provide a visitation counter it was not possible to determine how many individuals may have viewed the surveys, or links to them, but declined to participate. In total 218 people commenced Survey 1 which was e-mailed using a unique link (this meant it could not be forwarded to another person). It was physically mailed, and posted to various Facebook pages between 27 August and 3 September 2012. Nine responses came from 119 e-mail invitations, seven came from 125 postal surveys, and 202 resulted from the Facebook postings (to six pages). The *Irish Echo* also did an online story on 13 September 2012, but the included link to the survey was corrupted.[50] Of the surveys commenced, 66 per cent (144) were deemed valid and complete.[51] Of these, 22 were in the 1969–85 group compared with 122 in the 1999–2012 group.

Survey 1 was designed with the primary objective of discovering how Irish migrants use technology to connect with home and with each other. It included questions about birthplace, age, gender, education, origin, family composition, marital status, settlement process, use of technology, involvement in Irish sport, dance and music groups, homesickness, regularity of letter writing, and return trips to Ireland. Survey 2 was more comprehensive. As well as these questions it asked for scale ratings of quality of life in Ireland and Australia, employment opportunity and job satisfaction, questions about visa category, integration into Australian society, use of Irish newspaper/radio/food suppliers, remittances to Ireland, use of online forums before and after outward migration to Australia, and the influence of economic factors in the decision to migrate. The response to the request for participation in the survey was impressive. In two days, 208 people submitted their answers and comments to the 70 questions asked of them.[52] Approximately 82 per cent (171) of these were deemed complete and the responses given to both surveys are reflected in this article.

SAMPLE CHARACTERISTICS

Survey 1: Ireland Online: So Close No Matter How Far[53]

Quality of life, particularly for families, was a constant theme of responses concerning the benefits of migration to Australia. Migrants from Northern Ireland represented 57 per cent of Cohort 1 of Survey 1 while 43 per cent were male. Of this group, 13.2 per cent were single, 55 per cent married (58 per cent accompanied by children), and the remainder (31.8 per cent) were child dependants (aged under 18) in a family group. Just over 40 per cent of Cohort 1 left school at age 15 or younger, while 13.6 per cent completed secondary school, gaining A Levels or the Leaving Certificate qualification.[54] More than half (57 per cent) of the child dependants attended university with 75 per cent of these gaining higher degrees.[55] Fewer than 20 per cent of the respondents said they emigrated in search of adventure, 28.5 per cent used the category "Other" and quoted the Troubles as the reason for leaving, while economic opportunity and the search for a more affluent lifestyle was a factor for 42.9 per cent of those questioned. Relationships with Australian citizens accounted for the remaining 9 per cent.

Cohort 2 of Survey 1 differed considerably in both composition and origin. Slightly fewer than 10 per cent of the respondents emigrated from Northern Ireland compared with 90.1 per cent from the Republic of Ireland. Males represented fewer than a quarter (22 per cent) of respondents while 78 per cent were female. Those who emigrated in a de facto relationship accounted for 33 per cent of the Cohort 2 sample, equalling those who travelled with a spouse while 34 per cent came as single persons. Just less than 15 per cent of the married couples were accompanied by children as were 3 per cent of the de facto couples. Slightly more than 66 per cent of the total of Survey 1 respondents were married or in a de facto relationship compared with 76 per cent of Survey 2 respondents. In total, 41 came as single persons, and 103 emigrated in a family group. Three of these left an older child in Ireland when they emigrated. Eighty people (47 per cent) in the second group attended university, with 28 achieving a higher degree. Twenty-seven had a trade or vocational qualification, and only three had left school by age 15. Such is the educational opportunity afforded the last two generations in Ireland.

Survey 2: Ireland Online: The Experiences of Irish/Northern Irish Migrants to Australia

Survey 2 had markedly different demographic results. Almost two-thirds of the respondents were female (62 per cent). While 76 per cent of the total were, at the time of the survey, married or partnered with just fewer than 2 per cent in a same-sex marriage, 30 per cent of this group had arrived in Australia as single people and had formed new relationships post-arrival.[56]

210 *Fidelma Breen*

Overall, spouses were largely Irish (77 per cent) but, of the post-arrival relationships, almost 49 per cent were endogamous, with 46 per cent being formed with Australian citizens and slightly more than 5 per cent with citizens of other countries. Irish women were more likely than Irish men to seek an Irish partner in Australia as female respondents accounted for almost 58 per cent of the post-arrival endogamous relationships. Only 19 per cent of the total respondents from Survey 2 were married to Australian citizens with fewer than 4 per cent of partners being from somewhere other than Ireland or Australia. Around 40 per cent of the migrants who responded to Survey 2 had children. A small number (6.5 per cent) had children living outside Australia.

Of the single, non-parent migrants who responded, 70 per cent lived solely with Irish/Northern Irish people, 13 per cent with a mixture of Irish/Northern Irish people and others, 10 per cent with non-Irish/Northern Irish people, and 7 per cent lived alone. Most tended to socialise with their compatriots more than any other group. Of the total respondents, 64 per cent socialised with Irish/Northern Irish people either 'often' or 'very often' with 11 per cent answering in the categories of 'rarely' or 'never', leaving a quarter in the 'sometimes' category. Similar percentages resulted for the question regarding socialising with Australians with lower rates (47 per cent) of integration with other migrants in a social setting. These high rates of ethnocultural socialisation differ markedly from Patricia O'Connor's study despite the fact that most of the informants also come from the later arriving (post-1980) migrant group.[57] Only 38 per cent of O'Connor's subjects described their friendship group as being predominantly Irish-born, citing workplace relationships and social networking through mutual acquaintances as the main source of new friendships, while 15 per cent of Jean Chetkovich's respondents described their friendship networks as 'mostly Irish'.[58] This lower rate of ethnic insularity may be accounted for by Chetkovich's respondents being longer settled, having arrived between 1945 and 1995. A possible explanation for the responses given by contemporary Irish migrants may lie in the networking opportunities afforded by social media which allows casual but frequent contact between parties. It seems fewer Irish migrants arrive in Australia completely alone and many new arrivals come out to someone they know, even if only distantly.[59] The vast majority of these respondents use social media so this social cohesion is not surprising and points to a level of virtual insularity. The visa class also has an effect here because permanent roots and friendships are not the preserve of temporary-visa holders who are strongly represented in these surveys.

In 2012–13 the Skill Stream was the predominant route for Irish nationals seeking to come to Australia permanently, with 8 in 10 permanent visas granted to Irish nationals—a rise of 5.3 per cent in the number of Skill Stream visas granted. Most of this increase was in the Employer Sponsored component, reflecting the shift towards demand-driven entry. In 2012–13, 2,752 of these visas were granted to Irish nationals, an increase of 15 per cent from 2011–12 and an increase of 158 per cent since 2009–10.[60] Since more than half of Survey 1 and more than 42 per cent of Survey 2 respondents are WHMs and, therefore, not permanent, their general social insularity is perhaps not surprising. Several of the WHM informants reported the convenience of moving in with friends and living with 'their own'.[61] An inherent difficulty in this survey was reaching those who have integrated with Australian society to the point where they make no overt effort to uphold Irish connections. It is possible to speculate that their inclusion may dilute these findings regarding intercommunity socialisation if one were to make the assumption that their friendship networks may be more diversified.

Just over 61 per cent of the total respondents had Irish relatives or friends in Australia prior to arrival. Survey 1 respondents were asked an open-ended question regarding their initial experience of Australia regarding arrival, accommodation, and employment. Almost 45 per cent of new arrivals were met at the airport or stayed with Irish relatives or friends on arrival. Another 14 per cent were greeted by employers/colleagues or chauffeured to prearranged accommodation meaning that 59 per cent of the total had initial settlement assistance.[62] This is slightly lower than the two-thirds (65 per cent) of O'Connor's informants which was similar to both Chetkovich's findings and characteristic of the broad community findings of the Longitudinal Study of Immigrants to Australia.[63]

No Irish community in Australia is large enough to permit its members to be completely insular but many maintain a strong interest in Irish affairs and past times. Almost 55 per cent of Survey 2 informants participated in organised Irish/Northern Irish community activity (but not in conjunction with an Irish club or association), and 58 per cent read online Irish newspapers 'often' or 'very often'. There was no discernible effect on these activities by time of arrival although anecdotal evidence from some respondents suggests that stage of life may be a contributory factor in active involvement with organised ethno-cultural activity.[64] One informant reported that 'since arriving in Australia and becoming a parent I realised how isolated I was (prior to children it wasn't such a big factor), now I actively seek out Irish organisations and clubs to try and forge relationships/contacts with other Irish people.'[65] Her comment reflected the opinions of some others in similar family settings and the popularity of online social networking groups formed around carer/parent responsibilities and family activity points to the surrogacy role some Irish groups fulfil for migrants.[66] The participation in host community activities such as church, sport, music, and charity events in comparison with migrant activity in these areas in Ireland is discussed in the following sections.

VISAS

The *Department of Immigration and Citizenship Working Holiday Visa Report December 2013* stated that Ireland was the third top source country for Australian WHM visas behind Taiwan and the United Kingdom for the program period until 30 June 2013.[67] The report showed that the figure for initial or first-year WHM visas dropped by 39.4 per cent while applications for second-year visas increased by 15.2 per cent.[68] Many WHM visa holders aim to convert this visa to one which will allow a longer stay with the ultimate aim of achieving Australian citizenship as will be discussed later.[69] As of 30 December 2013, 6,660 people from the Republic were in Australia on WHM visas. Almost 24,000 UK residents held this visa meaning around another 700 people from Northern Ireland were likely on a working holiday in the country at that date.[70] As Figure 9.7 and Figure 9.8 show,

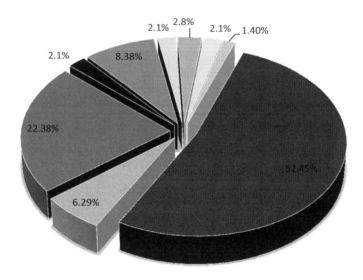

- Working Holiday visa (subclass 417)
- Skilled Independent visa (subclass 189)
- Temporary Work (Skilled) visa (subclass 457)
- Business Innovation and Investment (Permanent) visa (subclass 888)
- Employer Nomination Scheme (subclass 186)
- Regional Sponsored Migration Scheme visa (subclass 187)
- Skilled Nominated visa (subclass 190)
- Skilled—Recognised Graduate visa (subclass 476)
- Skilled Regional (Provisional) visa (subclass 489)

Figure 9.7 Survey 1 visa categories

of the survey respondents who held a visa, the great majority were part of the WHM scheme. The next largest visa cohort was the Temporary Work (Skilled) visa (subclass 457) group representing 22 per cent to 28 per cent of the total in each survey group.

Of those in the sample on a limited fixed duration visa, fewer than 2 per cent intended to return to Ireland on its expiry while another 2 per cent intended to migrate to another country when their visa expires. More than a quarter of this group intended to seek a visa extension or category change to allow them to remain on a different visa if possible. A small number, 2.5 per cent, intended to remain in the country regardless of their visa situation.[71] These figures support the view that even those on a temporary or limited visa regard their movement as a migration.

The fact that most respondents were in the most recent arrival category may explain the high numbers of migrants in the Temporary Work (Skilled)

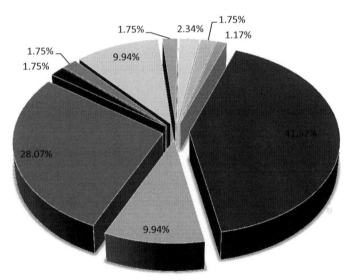

- Working Holiday visa (subclass 417)
- Skilled Independent visa (subclass 189)
- Temporary Work (Skilled) visa (subclass 457)
- Business Innovation and Investment (Permanent) visa (subclass 888)
- Temporary Work (Long Stay Activity) visa (subclass 401)
- Employer Nomination Scheme (subclass 186)
- Regional Sponsored Migration Scheme visa (subclass 187)
- Skilled Nominated visa (subclass 190)
- Skilled—Recognised Graduate visa (subclass 476)
- Skilled Regional (Provisional) visa (subclass 489)

Figure 9.8 Survey 2 visa categories

and WHM visa categories. The argument against an intention to stay in Australia permanently or the removal of such persons from the 'emigrant' classification may be weakened by the fact that many temporary visa applicants subsequently apply for permanent status and this trend is growing. Category jumpers (conversion from temporary to permanent residency) are plentiful. According to DIBP's *Subclass 457 Annual Report 2013–14*, '[i]n the 2013–14 programme year to 31 December 2013, the number of subclass 457 visa holders who were granted a permanent residence/provisional visa was 24,440, 44.2 per cent higher compared with the same period in the previous programme year, which was 16,950'; 3,400 of these were granted to Irish people.[72] Almost two-thirds of Survey 2 respondents indicated that their visa category had changed since arrival.

The change in the nature of Irish migration to Australia, particularly since 2008, is evident. O'Connor noted that migration by skilled transients tended to be career/occupationally motivated while those on WHMs were motivated primarily by recreational stimuli and the rite of passage of the 'gap year'.[73] Australian officials recognise that there has been 'a recent shift in motivation for these visa holders, from a tourism and/or life experience to an employment opportunity.' The WHM programme is often seen 'as a pathway to long-term employment and eventual permanent residence'.[74] Reflecting a shift from O'Connor's figures for 2004–5, in 2012–13, only 547 Irish-born permanent residents indicated at departure that they were leaving Australia permanently representing a drop from 37.5 per cent to 16 per cent of total new permanent residents.[75] The report of UCC's *Émigré Project*, which analysed the responses of almost 3,000 individuals in Ireland and abroad, states that fewer than 10 per cent of its informants intended returning to Ireland and that '68% would like to extend their visas if possible'.[76]

THE AGE OF INFORMATION

Today's migrants are generally much better informed than those of previous years. Information gleaned from friends and family abroad can provide the impetus for some moves. As Stephen Castles puts it:

> It is well known that most migrants follow 'beaten paths' and go where their compatriots have already established a bridgehead, making it easier to find work and lodgings, and deal with bureaucratic obstacles. Older migration scholars spoke of 'chain migration,' while in recent years much emphasis has been put on 'migration networks' and the way these develop as links between communities at home and in destination areas.[77]

Around 57 per cent of Survey 1 respondents and 66 per cent of respondents to Survey 2 had relatives or friends in the location they moved to in Australia, indicating that chain migration, or a migration network, is still a

Emigration in the Age of Electronic Media   215

strong feature of Irish movement to the Antipodes, although fewer people gain entry through family sponsorship.[78] Websites and Internet groups also provide much of the information people seek about their new destination. Migrant forums give a wide range of personal opinion, recounting both good and bad experiences, and provide substantial food for thought for prospective immigrants.[79] Question 41 in Survey 2 asked migrants about the information they sought from online forums. The results are in Figure 9.9.

Because most responses to both surveys were submitted through the web it is not surprising that the majority cited this aspect of technology as one of the most positive of modern-day communication with 66 per cent of the total respondents using video calling services such as Skype. Mobile phone usage was also popular with 62.5 per cent text messaging 'often' or 'very often'.[80] A more recent phenomenon and one that was not included in the questionnaires is the 'group message' on Viber which allows a multi-person conversation to be held.[81]

Online networks usually result in personal connections in host communities: 32 per cent of respondents met with members of their Facebook/online group on a regular basis, with 85 per cent regularly using Irish/British online forums and Facebook groups.[82] For recent arrivals, and those still in Ireland, the most common reason for using the online connection was seeking advice about employment, followed by accommodation costs, inferring that these are the two major concerns of new arrivals. Before relocating, 62 per cent of respondents had used the Australian government immigration website, yet only 15 per cent used online groups for advice.[83] Joining the Facebook

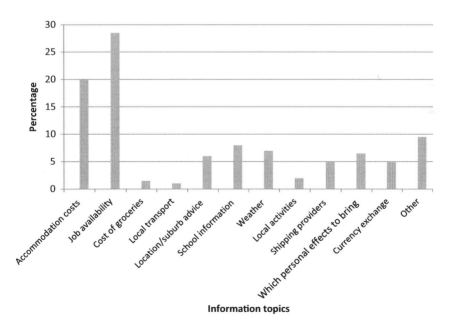

Figure 9.9   Advice sought by migrants in online forums

group relevant to their state or city seemed to happen for the majority of respondents once the move had been made. Earlier pre-1985 migrants relied on information provided in the government literature and by contacts who were, or had been, in Australia.

HOMESICKNESS

Emigration is as much an emotional journey as a physical one, and many migrants experience homesickness at some point. Of Survey 1 informants, 15 per cent reported regularly feeling so homesick that they wanted to leave Australia, while 40 per cent said they felt homesick but contact with the Irish in Australia or at home made them feel better. A quarter of informants felt pangs of homesickness but took no action preferring to let it pass while 20 per cent reported never experiencing longing for Ireland. Of Survey 2 respondents, 73 per cent experienced homesickness 'sometimes', 'often', or 'very often'.

While homesickness was considered a real condition of concern by 77 per cent of respondents to both surveys it was experienced to varying degrees among them. There was no division in opinion between those who arrived recently or long-term residents. Neither did origin, family size, or composition of the migrant's domestic situation in Australia differentiate those who reported suffering from homesickness. The most discernible difference in attitudes towards treatment of homesickness as a condition which required some support or intervention was gender-based. Twice as many men than women felt it was not a 'real/valid' complaint.[84] Among the top life event stressors in society today are death of a spouse/family member, divorce, moving house, and separation.[85] Migration 'involves not only leaving social networks behind (which may or may not be well established) but also includes experiencing at first a sense of loss, dislocation, alienation and isolation'.[86] Considering that migrants experience both changing home and divorce from their support network during migration, it is surprising that specific migration health and counselling services are not more readily available. Illness rates are high among migrants and among persons who move between cultures or move frequently within their own country.[87] While we do not have specific data on either the physical or mental health of Irish migrants in Australia, responses to open-ended questions in the surveys elicited stories of despair, family disintegration when one spouse decided to return, guilt at being away when a family member became ill, separation anxiety, depression, and general sadness, inferring that this may be a matter of concern and an avenue of further research.

Although homesickness appears to be a largely unavoidable part of the migration process, most migrants manage to suppress it, recognising that it presents in waves and that the reason for migration is usually still substantially valid. In response to a thread regarding homesickness, one group member stated that '[d]uring the first two years we would have gone home several times from homesickness. In the next five years we each got homesick at different times and luckily we both were not homesick at the same time so we settled down'.[88] Another wrote, 'At the end of the day you make the decision for you and your children and their future . . . we have a lifestyle that I don't think we would have had in Ireland and our children have opportunities for better lives'.[89]

HOMESICKNESS, COMMUNICATION, AND SOCIAL MEDIA

Anecdotal evidence of feelings of homesickness, isolation, connectedness, settling in, and forming new social networks was gathered from the open-ended questions in the questionnaires. The role of social media was a focus of both surveys, but Survey 1, which was developed specifically to look at communication between diasporic communities and those remaining in Ireland, delved deeper into communication methods than Survey 2.

Facebook was cited in the survey as the most utilised social media platform of recent migrants. The study revealed that it has both benefits and drawbacks from the migrants' perspective. While most (93 per cent) are of the opinion that this portal allows them to keep up with life events of family, friends, and the hometown community, 7 per cent blame it for increasing feelings of loneliness claiming that the almost real-time updates makes them realise what they are missing out on. Conversely, about a quarter made the observation that seeing the lack of activity in peoples' lives at home made them appreciate their new lifestyle, home, and surroundings all the more since some aspects of life at home, particularly their peers' social lives, appear to have stagnated.

Usage of Facebook as a means of keeping in contact with friends and family in Ireland was 70 per cent in the 'often' or 'very often' categories among all respondents. Weekly or fortnightly phone calls from a landline remained the preferred communication method for the Cohort 1 of Survey 1 and, surprisingly, it is those in Cohort 2 who still write letters. The regularity of communication with people in Ireland appears to decline over time as 47 per cent of the earlier group communicated with Ireland once or twice a week compared with 60 per cent of the second group. Of those who arrived since 1999, 94 per cent were in contact with relations in Ireland at least once a fortnight compared with 67 per cent of the earlier arrivals. Skype is perhaps the newest variation in contact methods with 65 per cent of respondents citing this as a service used 'often' or 'very often'. In addition to verbal communication, the Cohort 2 members were physically present in Ireland much more often than Cohort 1. Should these trends continue, it is likely that the 'regret of distance' will figure less for migrants, especially those with children who are thus removed from grandparents and extended family.[90]

The closeness made possible by new methods of instant communication and the affordability of air travel makes familiarity over distance a reality. What this closer communication means for the future Irish diaspora remains to be seen. Taken in conjunction with the Irish diaspora policy it is entirely possible that the generations that were formerly lost to Ireland through either the inability or reluctance of Irish migrants to make return journeys or even maintain regular contact are a thing of the past.

Feelings of connectedness to those still in Ireland appeared strong for most migrants, with 66.6 per cent feeling strong connections with their local community, 80 per cent feeling they still fitted in former friendship groups and, not surprisingly perhaps, 90 per cent reporting slotting easily back into the family circle.[91] Social communication technology assisted here: quick 'chats' via Short Message Service allow regular 'everyday' information flow; Skype calls afford visibility which in turn allows viewing of faces, new hairstyles, 'meeting' newly born members of the family, and witnessing the growth of children. Such seemingly small concerns perhaps, yet it is logical that regular physical viewing of the separated person prevents unfamiliarity; the shock of seeing an aging parent after prolonged absence, for example. About 10 per cent responded that they felt the deep connection among immediate family members was responsible for their connectedness, implying that they would be up to date with events in Ireland with or without electronic media. Only 16 per cent of migrants reported feeling as if they did not belong in their local Irish community anymore, 6 per cent felt alienated from former friends, and fewer than 1 per cent felt they had lost connection with the family circle. Some stated that life experience, including but not solely due to emigration, had changed them and so relationships changed, implying that this would have occurred whether they had left their hometown or not.

Personal experiences displayed on social media and shared in the comments sections of the surveys show a wide variance. There are those who post that they cannot wait to get home because life is too short to be away from the most important people in their lives—parents, siblings, nieces, nephews—and that no amount of sunshine or money can make up for the loss they feel. Such feelings are counterbalanced by posts sharing stories of couples and families becoming closer as they were left to fend without the support of extended family and the local community networks of home. Both ends of the spectrum are important, as are the middle-range experiences of those who feel the pangs of homesickness but 'stick things out'. Further study of the personal experiences of migrants is warranted in this area in order to gain some insight into the health of migrants and ascertain if processes can be streamlined and information improved.

So where is 'home' for the transnational migrant and the diasporic Irish in Australia? The answer to this question did not appear to be dependent on the length of time in Australia. Almost identical percentages of the groups answered to the categories of 'Ireland', 'Australia' or 'Both': 38 per cent of the first group and 37 per cent of the second answered 'Ireland';

14 per cent of each cited Australia as home; and 48 per cent and 49 per cent, respectively, claimed that both were 'home'. Chetkovich reported that 72 per cent of respondents claimed a dual home while 23 per cent named Ireland and 5 per cent named Australia. Of O'Connor's respondents, 38 per cent equally ranked Ireland and Australia as home, and one-fifth of the group considered both locations to be home. From the survey responses given, post-national theories of citizenship are not evident while aspects of transnationalism such as dual, even multi-citizenship, and biculturalism are upheld. Relationships with one's birthplace and chosen homeland can be characterised by fluidity and attachment to place and self-identification can alter over time. The responses of older migrants who are now the grandparents of Australian-born children are a good example of this. Victor Roudometof speaks of 'a perpetual sense of homelessness' for those torn between two places and two identities.[92] Rather than a sense of homelessness, the respondents here felt they had two homes. Family ties in both places appear to be the reason for respondents being unable to define one 'home'. For newer migrants it was extended family in Ireland that kept Ireland in contention for the title, while for the first cohort the presence of grandchildren in Australia left Ireland vying for it: 'Ireland will always be home' was a frequent response.

MIGRATION MOTIVATORS

Although the majority of respondents to both surveys stated that they emigrated because they chose to, there is a strong element of 'push' among the reasons for migration. Economic reasons were cited as the motive for migration for many of the respondents to Survey 1 (46 per cent of the total). For migrants from the north of Ireland there was the added impetus of civil unrest. Of the pre-1980 migrants in Survey 1, 35 per cent left because of the Troubles as did 23 per cent of pre-1980 migrants in Survey 2. The Northern Ireland Troubles are credited with causing the high levels of out-migration which occurred in the early 1970s.[93] This loss resulted in the first decrease in Northern Ireland's population since the early 1930s.[94] As demonstrated by Figure 9.3, arrival in Australia by respondents from Northern Ireland to Survey 1 spiked in 1973. This is likely the result of the impact of increased violence in Northern Ireland during 1972 when 472 people died, 321 of whom were civilians. That year is recognised as the worst year of the Troubles.[95] Those leaving the Republic maintained a fairly steady rate from early in the first decade of this century until around 2008 when the numbers increased sharply and, bar 2010, remain high. The increase from 2008 was the result of the collapse of the ROI economy.

From the data set of Survey 1 only three respondents (14 per cent) of Cohort 1 reported leaving from a county different from their birth place and only one from a different country suggesting that, for this cohort of the sample, rates of internal migration within Ireland were low at this time. This compares with 49 of Cohort 2 (40 per cent) of Survey 1, three of whom were born outside Ireland. From the 2011 Census, the Irish CSO has determined that 'Irish people showed a tendency to live in their birth county. More than three-quarters of the country's 3.76 million Irish born residents were usually resident in their county of birth.'[96] Cohort 2 then appears to be atypical of the general population of the Republic.

Almost one quarter of the respondents to Survey 2 had lived outside Ireland for a period of more than 12 months before moving to Australia. A possible interpretation of this is that Australia may be part of a newer trend of step migration towards a final location. The likelihood of a return to Ireland being the final step seems remote given responses to the last set of questions in Survey 2 as described in the following.

The data from Survey 2 showed that the economic climate in Ireland/Northern Ireland was a 'very influential' or 'extremely influential' factor in the decision to leave for 73 per cent of respondents. Of those who left since 2008, the commencement of Ireland's period of economic downturn, 61 per cent stated that they migrated to find better employment or gain job experience. While 43 per cent indicated that they would like to return to Ireland/Northern Ireland within the next five years either 'very much' or 'quite a lot', only 30 per cent thought it was 'likely' or 'very likely' that they would do so. These figures differ only slightly from those produced in the *Émigré Report*, which said that 'although 39.5% out of all recent emigrants would like to return to Ireland in the next three years, only 22% see it as likely'.[97] Improvement in the economy (aspects of which include reduction in property prices and increased job availability) in Ireland would

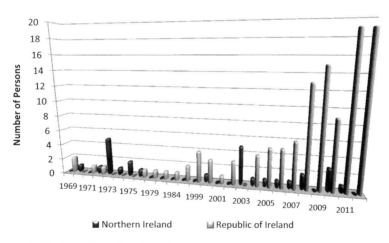

Figure 9.10 Timeline of arrivals for Survey 1 respondents

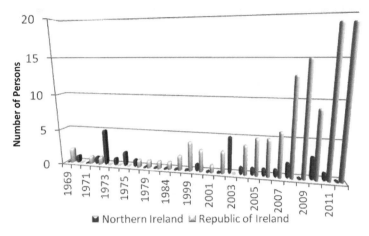

Figure 9.11 Timeline of arrivals for Survey 2 respondents

be enticing for around 52 per cent, while 31 per cent felt this would have no effect whatsoever on a consideration of a move home. A higher percentage (82 per cent) of the *Émigré Report*'s respondents said the likelihood of their return would improve if Ireland's recession showed signs of lifting. Perhaps the greatest differential between the respondents of Surveys 1 and 2, who were all based in Australia, and those who responded to the UCC study is the fact of location. The Émigré respondents were based in several countries.[98] The lifestyle, the weather, recreation, and job opportunities available in Australia appear to offer more enticement than any inducement in Ireland. All travelled to Australia to further their careers, despite holding secure employment at the time of departure. In Ireland/Northern Ireland all held full-time positions, 80 per cent of which were permanent.[99] Given that the economic climate had considerable leverage in the decision to emigrate it might be surprising to read that this was the case. The anecdotal evidence sheds further light on this and reveals layers of intricacy that the data cannot. This group was similarly economically engaged in Australia, with only one reporting being unemployed at the time of submission. Comments about life in Australia reveal that job prospects and career advancement are noticeably better for most.

Lack of permanent resident status, income, stage of life, and relationship status can all affect opportunities for home ownership. Approximately 79 per cent of Survey 2 respondents lived in rental properties while 90 per cent of the homeowners among the group arrived prior to 2009. The great majority were married or partnered (76 per cent) with children (50 per cent). Slightly more than 70 per cent had obtained educational qualifications at diploma level or above, with 85 per cent of these holding a bachelor degree or better. This is congruent with the *Émigré Report* findings which state that '[t]oday's emigrants are much more likely to have a high standard of education than the population in general. While 47 per cent of Irish people aged between 25–34 hold a tertiary qualification of three years or more, 62 per cent of recent Irish emigrants hold the equivalent qualification, suggesting that graduates are over-represented amongst those leaving.'[100] This supports Graeme Hugo's observation of 'brain circulation' in Australia.[101] A lower percentage of O'Connor's informants achieved tertiary or postgraduate qualifications: 'One-third held university or post-graduate qualifications. A further third had attained other tertiary qualifications.'[102] In contrast, 65 per cent of the migrants from Survey 1 had attended university with a higher proportion of this group, mostly from the cohort who arrived before 1986, having left school at the upper secondary level. Obviously visa entry requirements also have an effect on the proportion of migrants who would claim to be non-skilled, but this restriction was not in place during the time of the migration scheme of the 1960s and 1970s when many adult migrants had left school around the age of 14 or 15 because of economic necessity.[103] Quality of life (designated by general satisfaction with work/life balance, leisure time, disposable income, and that vague element, happiness) in Ireland/Northern Ireland was rated by participants on a scale of 1 to 10, where 1 was the lowest: 47 per cent rated quality of life at a score of 5 or below, while 53 per cent rated it between 6 and 10 (6 per cent scored life quality at 10). The same question was asked of life in Australia, and the difference was marked: only 5 per cent rated quality of life below 5 with almost 19 per cent rating it at 10.[104]

In August 2013, Irish Heritage Minister, Jimmy Deenihan, claimed in an interview with ABC News, 'There's [sic] huge connections here [in Australia] in the political world, in the education world, in the medical world and in industry. Irish people feel very comfortable coming to Australia because they know there's a very positive welcome for them here'. While this may be the case for the skilled visa group, commentary from some WHM visa holders described a prejudice against younger Irish workers.[105] Only 34 per cent of respondents had gained work connections from an Irish person in Australia, the majority of whom were known to them before arrival with one-third representing new connections.[106]

One open-ended question regarding the aspects of migration which had been the least pleasant attracted comments that indicated that some new migrants felt they were the victims of discrimination based on their nationality. Some felt their difficulty in having Irish-gained qualifications recognised by Australian employers to be an insidious form of racism.[107] They felt that because they were white and English-speaking such complaints were not taken seriously.

CONSEQUENCES OF EMIGRATION

Return Visits

Survey 1 asked for information about return visits and opinions on how migrants felt they fitted in with family, friends, and the wider community in general when they returned. The phenomenon of the 'American wake' still exists today, although in modified form.[108] It is relatively common for the migrants' family and friends to get together to wish them well in their new life abroad, but there is little of the finality of earlier times. Indeed, Cohort 2 had a much higher rate of return than Cohort 1. Not only did they make a return visit sooner (17.5 per cent within the first year) after the initial departure than their predecessors, but they also returned more frequently and fully intended on keeping up this trend as long as finances permit it. More than 21 per cent returned for a holiday less than two years after emigrating. Where finances are limited migrants have compromised by co-financing holidays by relatives. This arrangement changes as parents age and are no longer able to travel. On average the offspring of Cohort 1 made 2.07 trips each (over a 43-year period), while the children of Cohort 2 have visited Ireland 2.24 times each and that only within a 13-year period. Some children in the second group go to Ireland annually and two, aged 16 months and 20 months, respectively, had already been twice.

High rates of early and frequent return trips are evident among Survey 2 respondents also. Of this group, 2 per cent travel to Ireland several times a year, 25 per cent once a year, 38 per cent once every two or three years, and 10 per cent once each five years, while 25 per cent have not returned. Of those who have not returned yet, 60 per cent reasoned that it was too soon to go back. Other reasons for not having returned included the cost factor, lack of annual leave time available for a decent trip to Ireland, and a wish to see other places during one's free time.[109] Visits by family members to Australia were also a reason to delay a return trip. One development which will be interesting to take account of in the future is to see how the familiarity with Ireland and its cultural aspects through more frequent return travel among child migrants affects the engagement of the diaspora with Gaelic sports and other 'Irish' leisure activities in Australia.

BENEFITS OF EMIGRATION

One of the biggest drawcards for Irish migrants to Australia is its weather and the lifestyle associated with sunshine. While seemingly superficial, 10 per cent of respondents noted that increased outdoor time was a healthier option for growing children and allowed for more 'whole family' activity.[110] Opportunity for career advancement was also highlighted. An article which appeared in November 2013 in the *Irish Times* 'Generation Emigration' series reported that '[e]ven college leavers going on working-holiday visas want a job in their field so they can gain experience ... They don't just want a backpacking job anymore.'[111] As mentioned previously, Australian immigration officials have recognised the shift from casual work intentions and recreational use of the WHM visa towards work experience which can assist with securing a second visa which offers permanent residency. Respondents to the survey confirmed that career prospects were much better in Australia, and many revealed that gaining job experience was a deciding factor when considering migration. When asked to rate career prospects in Ireland/Northern Ireland the majority of Survey 2 informants (61 per cent) rated these 5 or less on a scale of 1 to 10, where 1 was the lowest score. Many commented that although they worked in Ireland they did not see much opportunity for advancement, and newer graduates said they could not get a start in their chosen field at home.

CONCLUSION

Despite their limitations these pilot surveys revealed a number of interesting differences between the two groups of migrants. The earlier group and their offspring do not return to Ireland as often as the newest group of arrivals can and do. Contact between them and family and friends in Ireland is not as frequent as between newer arrivals and home. This is attributed to their longer absences because many gave anecdotal evidence of not feeling as much a part of the home community because of missing out on participation in significant events in the lives of family and friends in Ireland. More frequent return visits by the newer migrants are likely to lessen this distancing effect. The skill level and corresponding income potential of more recent migrants assists frequent return travel. The contribution of the Irish diaspora to the republic's recovering economy is noteworthy as is its addition of threads to the country's social fabric by means of increased familial and community contact.

The widespread and regular use of social media is a conspicuous feature of contemporary emigration. This study suggests it is valuable in the settlement process. The rise in visibility and popularity of online migrant resource and social networking groups may spell the eventual decline of traditional Irish clubs in Australia's capital cities. There are four elements to this conclusion: first, the aging membership and management of clubs appears to lessen their attractiveness and relevancy to contemporary migrants; second, they generally no longer perform the welcoming and networking functions of previous years; third, they require a subscription whereas online groups are free; and, last, they are constrained by the fact that they have a physical location. Participation in online groups and networking through them is not regulated by settlement locality. The accessibility of social media to local, regional, and even prospective migrants cannot be overlooked.

This study's sample has demonstrated differences in attitudes towards the permanency of the move to Australia, in habits of socialisation with their own ethnocultural community and in their intention to return to Ireland compared with earlier studies. That its findings are more in line with the 2013 *Émigré Report* indicates that the characteristics of the trend of migration from Ireland since 2008 differ markedly from the post-1980 period and the more recent years before the collapse of the Irish economy. While world systems and other external forces play their part in migration flows, the agency of the individual migrant is important in determining how much emotion plays a role in this human traffic. This study has demonstrated that economic considerations certainly play a part in the decision to leave Ireland but lifestyle choices, family considerations, freedom, and adventure balance these and suggest that the rising importance of technology in the fields of information provision and in social media will continue to impact successful settlement.

ACKNOWLEDGEMENTS

This chapter is dedicated to the late Professor Graeme Hugo AO (1946–2015), a prolific scholar and a generous supervisor in terms of both his knowledge and his time. I am also grateful for the comments he made on this chapter and his support of the doctoral research project it led to. I am grateful to the anonymous reviewer of this chapter for the extensive and helpful feedback provided.

NOTES

1. Through April 2013, 50,900 Irish nationals left the Republic of Ireland in the year; 'Population and Migration Estimates', Central Statistics Office, Cork, Ireland, http://www.cso.ie/en/media/csoie/releasespublications/documents/population/2012/popmig_2012.pdf (accessed 20 September 2013). Between mid-2011 and mid-2012, 12,500 people left Northern Ireland to live outside the United Kingdom, with indicators of out-migration showing signs of modest increase. See the Northern Ireland Statistics and Research Agency Report, *Long-term International Migration Estimates for Northern Ireland* (August 2013), p. 4, available at Northern Ireland Statistics and Research Agency website: http://www.nisra.gov.uk/archive/demography/population/migration/Mig_Report11_12.pdf (accessed 20 September 2013). Republic of Ireland will hereafter be denoted by the abbreviation ROI. References to Northern Ireland will be denoted by NI. 'Irish nationals' refers to those from the Republic of Ireland. The categories provided here for the motivators of migration are derived from the responses provided by Irish migrants to the survey questions described later in this chapter.
2. Large numbers of soldiers, merchants, and clergy emigrated to Catholic Europe during the seventeenth and eighteenth centuries and there was mass Protestant emigration from Ulster to North America during most of the eighteenth

century. Malcolm Campbell states that the Irish had been emigrating for centuries (p. 4), but only beginning in 1815 did their emigration help create the 'new worlds' of his title. M. Campbell. *Ireland's New Worlds: Immigrants, Politics, and Society in the United States and Australia, 1815–1922* (Madison: University of Wisconsin Press, 2007), p. 5.
3. Department of Immigration and Citizenship (DIAC), *2012–13 Migration Program Report* (Belconnen, ACT: DIAC 2013), p. 5, http://www.immi.gov.au/media/statistics/pdf/report-on-migration-program-2012–13.pdf (accessed 20 February 2014). The *Migration Program Report* stated that the United Kingdom and the Republic of Ireland were the third and eighth top source countries, respectively, for the Australian resident visa program. Visas were granted to 5,209 Irish people and to more than 21,000 UK residents. The figures for the United Kingdom include people from Northern Ireland. Of the 21,711 UK residents who arrived in the program period to June 2013 approximately 630 can be calculated to have been from Northern Ireland. The UK Office of National Statistics states that the population of Northern Ireland constitutes about 2.9 per cent of the total UK population. Because migrants from the constituent parts of the United Kingdom are not treated separately it is difficult to obtain accurate numbers for them. See Office of National Statistics, 'Main Comparisons: Population and Migration', http://www.ons.gov.uk/ons/guide-method/compendiums/compendium-of-uk-statistics/population-and-migration/index.html (accessed 24 April 2014).
4. The surveys were responded to by Irish migrants in each of Australia's states and territories except Tasmania. The state/territory's percentage of the Irish population according to the 2011 Census of Australia is given in parentheses: 6.5 per cent from the Northern Territory (0.94 per cent); 22.2 per cent from New South Wales (32.98 per cent); 15.6 per cent from Victoria (21.95 per cent); 32.4 per cent from Western Australia (21.5 per cent); 16.7 per cent from South Australia (5.23 per cent); and 6.6 per cent from Queensland (16.4 per cent).
5. J. Chetkovich, 'The New Irish in Australia: A Western Australian Perspective' (unpublished PhD thesis, University of Western Australia, 2003); P. O'Connor, 'The Multiple Experiences of Migrancy, Irishness and Home among Contemporary Irish Immigrants in Melbourne, Australia' (unpublished PhD thesis, University of New South Wales, 2005).
6. I. Glynn, T. Kelly, and P. MacÉinrí, *Irish Emigration in an Age of Austerity* (Cork: University College Cork, 2013).
7. The Irish Embassy is running a series of discussion forums with Irish people in Australia throughout June and July 2014 as part of the Irish Department of Foreign Affairs and Trade's Diaspora Policy Review. See https://www.dfa.ie/media/dfa/alldfawebsitemedia/ourrolesandpolicies/Review-of-Irelands-Diaspora-Strategy-Consultation-2014.pdf (accessed 16 June 2014).
8. See the entries for Denis Considen (?–1815), Thomas Jamieson (1753–1811), D'Arcy Wentworth (1762–1827), John Harris (1754–1838), Jacob Mountgarrett (1773–1828), Nicholas Divine (1739–1830), and John Cuthbertson (?-1823) for a few examples of those who held posts such as surgeon, commandant, and superintendent of convicts. Australian Dictionary of Biography, National Centre of Biography, Australian National University, http://adb.anu.edu.au (accessed 10 June 2012).
9. Sir Arthur Kennedy of Cultra, County Down, was governor of Western Australia from 1855 to 1862; Sir Dominick Daly of Ardfry, County Galway, was appointed governor of South Australia in October 1861; Sir Hercules Robinson, of Rosmead, County Westmeath, was appointed governor of New South Wales in June 1872; and Sir Hamilton John Goold-Adams of Jamesbrook, County Cork, became governor of Queensland in 1914. Former Young

Irelander Charles Gavan Duffy was the eighth man to serve as Victorian premier (1871–1872).
10. F. Breen, '"Yet We Are Told Australians Do Not Sympathise with Ireland": A Study of South Australian Support for Irish Home Rule, 1883–1912' (unpublished M.Phil thesis, University of Adelaide, 2013), p. 176; P.J. Naughtin, 'The Green Flag at the Antipodes: Irish Nationalism in Colonial Victoria during the Parnell Era, 1880–91' (unpublished PhD thesis, University of Melbourne, 2011).
11. South Australia, Census of 1881, Historical Census and Colonial Data Archive.
12. Robin Cohen includes the Irish in his 'victim' category of diaspora. R. Cohen, *Global Diasporas: An Introduction* (New York: Routledge, 2008). Irish ballads are renowned for the 'exile' and 'victim' themes: one popular example is 'The Fields of Athenry' which tells of a young man transported to Botany Bay for stealing 'Trevelyan's corn'. Trevelyan was the assistant secretary to the Treasury in London during the Great Famine. This position put him in charge of the administration of government relief to the starving Irish.
13. D.B. Grigg, 'E.G. Ravenstein and the Laws of Migration', *Journal of Historical Geography*, 3:1 (1977), p. 41; Jeannette Schoorl et al., 'Push and Pull Factors of International Migration: A Comparative Report' (Luxembourg, European Communities, Office for Official Publications, 2000), xxi, p. 161. See more at http://www.popline.org/node/180911#sthash.lqw0Pv9a.dpuf. Also see B. Lindsay Lowell, 'Immigration "Pull" Factors in OECD Countries over the Long Term', in *The Future of International Migration to OECD Countries* [electronic Resource], (Paris: Organisation for Economic Co-operation and Development, 2009), pp. 52–137, http://www.keepeek.com/Digital-Asset-Management/oecd/social-issues-migration-health/the-future-of-international-migration-to-oecd-countries_9789264064126-en#page1.
14. F. Breen, 'Survey 1. Ireland Online: So Close No Matter How Far' (Adelaide, SA: University of Adelaide, 2012) and 'Survey 2. Ireland Online: The Experiences of Irish/Northern Irish Migrants to Australia' (Adelaide: University of Adelaide, 2014).
15. Government of Ireland, *Population and Labour Force Projections 2016–2046*, Central Statistics Office (Dublin: Stationary Office, 2013), p. 16.
16. Central Statistics Office, *Population and Migration Estimates*, CSO statistical release, 29 August 2013, http://www.cso.ie/en/releasesandpublications/er/pme/populationandmigrationestimatesapril2013/#.U1-fi_mSySo (accessed 18 February 2014).
17. Economic Analysis Unit, *Country Profile—Ireland* (Belconnen, ACT: Department of Immigration and Border Protection, 2013), p. 3. Available at http://www.immi.gov.au/media/statistics/country-profiles/_files/ireland.pdf (accessed 19 February 2014).
18. Ibid, p. 1. Irish people were issued 11,817 initial WHM visas and 7,300 second-year WHM visas. The WHM visa allows people from a designated list of countries to work in Australia for a period of 12 months. Certain restrictions are placed on WHM visa holders such as placement limits with any one employer and a requirement that some employment is undertaken in a regional area. A second-year visa is an option. Applicants for permanent residency visas usually apply based on having a sought-after skill or trade qualification, are sponsored by an Australian employer, and must meet points-based criteria. They must be self-supporting for the first two years and cannot access social welfare benefits such as Centrelink income support payments for example.
19. DIBP, Temporary entrants and New Zealand citizens in Australia as at 31 December 2013 (BR0169), p. 13, http://www.immi.gov.au/media/statistics/pdf/temp-entrants-newzealand-dec13.pdf (accessed 10 June 2014).

20. Ibid.
21. *Country Profile—Ireland* states that 'At the end of June 2011, 76,590 Irish-born people were living in Australia, 29 per cent more than at 30 June 2006'. Note that the figure of 99,183 given in Table 9.1 is the combined total of ROI and NI born persons. There are numerous online groups initiated and administrated by expatriates for various nationalities. Among the most popular in Australia is Irish People Living in Australia (IPLAUS) in addition to regional variations such as Irish Families in Perth and Adelaide Irish Connect.
22. These are the results of a search on Facebook, carried out on 14 June 2014, using the key words 'Irish', 'British', 'Brits', 'Poms', and 'Ital'. The results exclude pubs and restaurants but include other business-type organisations such as Chamber of Commerce entities.
23. C.E. Orser, Jr. 'Transnational Diaspora and Rights of Heritage', in H. Silverman and D.F. Ruggles (eds), *Cultural Heritage and Human Rights* (New York: Springer 2007), p. 93.
24. D. Hall and E. Malcolm, 'Diaspora, Gender and the Irish', *Australasian Journal of Irish Studies* 8, (2008/9), p. 8; refer to D. Lloyd, *Ireland After History* (Cork: Cork University Press, 1999), pp. 101–2, and B. Walter, *Outsiders Inside: Whiteness, Place and Irish Women* (London and New York: Routledge, 2001), p. 13, as particular critics of the term.
25. Ibid.
26. P. Fitzgerald and B. Lambkin, *Migration in Irish History, 1607–2007* (Basingstoke: Palgrave Macmillan, 2008), p. 53; L. Kennedy, *Colonialism, Religion and Nationalism in Ireland* (Belfast: Institute of Irish Studies, 1996), p. 217.
27. K. Kenny, 'Diaspora and Comparison: The Global Irish as a Case Study', *Journal of American History*, 90:1 (2003), pp. 142–44.
28. D.H. Akenson. 'Diaspora, the Irish, and Irish Nationalism', in A.S. Leoussi, A. Gal, and A.D. Smith (eds), *IJS Studies in Judaica, Volume 9: The Call of the Homeland: Diaspora Nationalisms, Past and Present*, (Boston, MA: Brill Academic Publishers, 2010), pp. 186–87.
29. Mary J. Hickman, '"Locating" the Irish Diaspora', *Irish Journal of Sociology*, 11.2 (2002), p. 18.
30. See Hall and Malcolm, 'Diaspora, Gender and the Irish', p. 7; Kenny, 'Diaspora and Comparison', contains an enlarged discussion on the etymology and expansion of the concept of diaspora, pp. 140–42.
31. K. Aikins and M. Russell, 'Diaspora Capital: Why Diaspora Matters for Policy and Practice', *Migration Policy Practice* (International Organization for Migration and Eurasylum Ltd, 2013), http://www.iom.int/cms/en/sites/iom/home/what-we-do/migration-policy-and-research/migration-policy-1/migration-policy-practice/issues/augustseptember-2013/diaspora-capital-why-diaspora-ma.html (accessed 24 April 2014).
32. Ibid.
33. Ibid.
34. B. Gray, *Women and the Irish Diaspora* (London and New York: Routledge, 2004), p. 6.
35. Hickman, '"Locating" the Irish Diaspora', p. 14.
36. See the contents list in Leoussi, Gal, and Smith (eds), *IJS Studies in Judaica*, p. ii.
37. Fáilte Ireland is the National Tourism Development Authority. *Fáilte* means 'welcome' in Irish. See more at http://www.failteireland.ie/Utility/What-We-Do.aspx#sthash.K2aFXrlt.dpuf, https://www.globalirishforum.ie/2009Forum.aspx (accessed 20 February 2014).
38. 'Emigrants Worth €1bn a Year to Irish tourism', *Irish Echo*, 15 May 2014, http://www.irishecho.com.au/2014/05/15/visiting-emigrants-bring-back-e1-billion-a-year/31753#.U3Qd3VspuDA.facebook (accessed 15 May 2014).

39. Ibid.
40. M. A. Brennan and A. E. Luloff, 'A Cooperative Approach to Rural Development in Ireland: Cultural Artifacts and the Irish Diaspora as an Example', *Journal of International Agricultural and Extension Education*, 12:1 (2005), p. 20.
41. Diane Butler, manager of Tourism Ireland Australia and New Zealand, stated, 'We will also build on the legacy of the Gathering, continuing to reach out to the Diaspora across Australia and New Zealand.'
42. 'Rural Communities Urged to Use Contacts to Bring Emigrants Home', *The Irish Times*, 10 May 2014, http://www.irishtimes.com/news/social-affairs/rural-communities-urged-to-use-contacts-to-bring-emigrants-home-1.1789622 (accessed 10 May 2014).
43. Akenson, 'Diaspora, the Irish, and Irish Nationalism', p. 181.
44. See 'Survey 2', Question 3.
45. Survey 2 was distributed through various social media outlets using a link to the electronic survey hosted by SurveyMonkey.
46. Those who availed of the Assisted Passage scheme (until 1981) were provided with a one-way ticket and were aware of the two-year stay requirement this imposed on them. The provided fare had to be repaid in full if a two-year residency was not completed. K. H. Fouweather, 'Ten Pounds for Adults, Kids Travel Free: An Essay on the Effects of Migration upon the Children of the British Migrants to Western Australia in the 1960s and 1970s; and, the Red Pipe: A Novella Set in Port Hedland' (Unpublished PhD thesis, Edith Cowan University, 2013), p. 20. Considering the trip to be 'one-way' was also largely due to the cost of travel, which is discussed in note 49 of this chapter.
47. There were only 18 telephones per 100 households in Ireland in 1971 and performance of the system was poor. R. Flynn, 'The Development of Universal Telephone Service in Ireland, 1880–1993' (Unpublished PhD thesis, Dublin City University, 1998) p. 314. In the United Kingdom, the penetration rate of domestic telephones did not reach 50 per cent of households until the mid-1970s. See L. Hamill, *The Introduction of New Technology into the Household* (Guildford: Digital World Research Centre, University of Surrey, 2000), http://www.hamill.co.uk/pdfs/tiontith.pdf, p. 5 (accessed 14 October 2012).
48. 'Ten Pound Poms' refers to those migrants who availed of Australia's post-war assisted passage immigration scheme (a joint agreement between the British and Australian governments from 1946 until Britain withdrew in 1972) which was open to residents of the Commonwealth (therefore closed to those from the ROI which left the Commonwealth in 1949) but particularly favoured by migrants from the United Kingdom. *Immigration and Population History of Selected Countries of Birth*, Department of Immigration and Citizenship, http://www.immi.gov.au/media/publications/statistics/federation/body2.pdf (accessed 08 May 2014). Fares for adults cost £10, and children travelled free. In 1973 the cost increased to £75 but without assistance would have cost in the region of £600 for a family of two adults and three children. See A. J. Hammerton and A. Thomson, *Ten Pound Poms: Australia's Invisible Migrants* (Manchester and New York: Manchester University Press, 2005), p. 33; *Ten Pound Poms*, Immigration Museum Victoria, http://museumvictoria.com.au/immigrationmuseum/discoverycentre/your-questions/ten-pound-poms (accessed 8 May 2014). Prior to a fare reduction in April 1972, a one-way airfare from London to Sydney cost £276, which is equivalent to A$2,753.35 at the time of writing. Source: Qantas Airways Ltd. History, http://www.fundinguniverse.com/company-histories/qantas-airways-ltd-history (accessed 8 May 2014). Calculation made using the Inflation Calculator of the Reserve Bank of Australia, http://www.rba.gov.au/calculator/annualDecimal.html

(accessed 8 May 2014). A one-way fare today can cost as little as A$850; Skyscanner, http://www.skyscanner.com.au/transport/flights/lond/syd/141120/airfares-from-london-to-sydney-kingsford-smith-in-november-2014.html?rtn=0 (accessed 8 May 2014). In 2012 Australia had 133 mobile phone devices per 100 persons (in the population) with the total number of mobiles being 30.2 million, *ACMA Communications Report 2011–12* (Melbourne: Australian Communications and Media Authority, 12 November 2012), p. 19.

49. Sea travel tapered off through the early 1970s but it was not until 1977 that air travel took over completely. See E. Richards, *Destination Australia: Migration to Australia since 1901* (Sydney, NSW: University of New South Wales Press, 2008), p. 22; Fouweather, 'Ten Pounds for Adults, Kids Travel Free', p. 47.
50. 'Has Skype ended the expat letter?', *Irish Echo*, Sydney, 13 September 2012, http://www.irishecho.com.au/2012/09/13/has-skype-ended-the-expat-letter/20516.
51. The remaining third either did not meet the date criterion imposed on 'Survey 1' or clicked on the survey link and started but decided not to complete all of the questions.
52. The survey link was posted on 3 February 2014, and data used included responses submitted until 5 February 2014.
53. This survey was undertaken to provide data for a paper given at the nineteenth Australasian Irish Studies Conference, University of Otago, Dunedin, New Zealand, 7–10 November 2012; F. Breen, 'Ireland Online: So Close No Matter How Far'.
54. Advanced or A Levels are usually undertaken at the end of the seventh year of secondary education (Upper Sixth form). The Republic of Ireland equivalent is the Leaving Certificate.
55. These child dependants were frequent return migrants: 75 per cent attended university in Ireland; 50 per cent then returned to Australia and gained a higher degree. See 'Survey 1', Question 8.
56. John Canavan reports that same-sex couples represented 2 per cent of cohabitees in Ireland in 2006. J. Canavan, 'Family and Family Change in Ireland: An Overview', *Journal of Family Issues*, 33:1 (2012), p. 15.
57. Chetkovich's study considered Irish migrants from 1945 to 1995; see Chetkovich, 'The New Irish', p. 3.
58. O'Connor, 'Multiple Experiences of Migrancy', pp. 200, 95.
59. 'Most people I know here have come out to someone they know with a spare bed or couch'—Respondent 'Miss McS' (F, 26, Clare, Ireland), in F. Breen and D. Lonergan, 'Tús maith, leath na h-oibre: Half the Work Is in Having a Good Start. Letters from Pennington', paper given at the 'Hostel Stories: Reflecting on the Past, Looking Forward' symposium at the University of Adelaide, 2014.
60. Department of Immigration and Border Protection, *Subclass 457 Quarterly Report 2013–14* (Belconnen, ACT: Department of Immigration and Border Protection 2013), p. 10; Economic Analysis Unit, *Country Profile—Ireland* (Belconnen, ACT: Department of Immigration and Border Protection, 2013), p. 3.
61. 'Survey 1', Question 20.
62. *Ibid.*, Question 20.
63. O'Connor, 'Multiple Experiences of Migrancy', pp. 195, 24. The Longitudinal Study of Immigrants to Australia was directed at a sample of principal applicants who immigrated to Australia between 1 September 1993 and 31 August 1995. Interviews were conducted in three waves: the first, within six months of arrival; then approximately one year later; and finally, three and a half years after arrival. In total 3,618 persons participated in all three waves.

64. Of respondents, 65 per cent in 'Survey 1' rated the local Irish club as somewhere they visited 'Rarely' or 'Never', while more than 6 per cent did not know where their local Irish association was. The remaining 29 per cent who visit the Irish club 'Often' or 'Sometimes' is in line with O'Connor's data because 28 per cent of her sample were members of Irish clubs or associations. O'Connor, 'Multiple Experiences of Migrancy', p. 201.
65. Case 30, Dublin, Female, arrived in 2005. De facto relationship with Australian male with two children aged 0–4 yrs. See 'Survey 1', Question 21.
66. Irish Mums in Adelaide (76 members); Adelaide Irish Connect (514 members); Irish Mums in Melbourne (180 members); Irish Families in Perth (5,900 members)
67. Department of Immigration and Border Protection, *Working Holiday Maker Visa Programme Report, 31 December 2013* (Belconnen, ACT: Commonwealth of Australia, 2013), p. 7.
68. Ibid, pp. 7, 18.
69. Survey responses of those on WHM visas regarding future intentions. See 'Survey 2', Question 61.
70. Using the proportion of population figure for Northern Ireland in the United Kingdom of 2.9 per cent as stated in note 7 in this chapter.
71. Survey 2, Question 61.
72. DIBP, *Subclass 457 Quarterly Report 2013–14* (2013), pp. 2, 6.
73. O'Connor, 'Multiple Experiences of Migrancy', p. 24.
74. DIAC, *Working Holiday Maker Visa Programme Report, 31 December 2013*, p. 1.
75. O'Connor, 'Multiple Experiences of Migrancy', p. 102. There were 436 permanent arrival figures from Southern Ireland and 164 permanent departures.
76. Glynn et al., *Irish Emigration in an Age of Austerity*, pp. ii, 9.
77. S. Castles, 'Migration and Community Formation under Conditions of Globalization', *International Migration Review*, 36 (2002), p. 1150.
78. Castles states that '[i]n the "classical immigration countries" it was—at least until recently—seen as axiomatic that immigrants of all types, once allowed to settle, should be entitled to bring in close dependents. This principle is now being eroded in Australia and elsewhere'; ibid, p. 153. Slightly more than 61 per cent of respondents had Irish friends or relatives somewhere in Australia when they arrived. Of Irish people known and located at the point of arrival, 45 per cent provided settlement assistance.
79. Newsfeed on many Facebook pages such as Poms in Oz takes the form of prospective and new migrants asking for advice on a range of issues. 'Survey 2', Question 41, asked informants about the categories on which they sought advice. Figure 9 gives the results.
80. 'Survey 1', Question 18; 'Survey 2', Question 35.
81. Members of Adelaide Irish Connect were asked about this at a meeting on 13 April 2014 and 75 per cent of those asked used the Viber app to keep in touch with family and close friendship groups. The fact that the app and communications through it are free was cited as beneficial. More information can be obtained at the Viber website: http://www.viber.com/.
82. 'Survey 2', Question 41.
83. Department of Immigration and Border Protection website: http://www.immi.gov.au (accessed 16 February 2014).
84. 'Survey 1', Question 29; 'Survey 2', Question 63.
85. S. Mestrovic and B. Glassner, 'A Durkheimian Hypothesis on Stress', *Social Science & Medicine*, 17:18 (1983), p. 1315.
86. D. Bhugra, 'Migration, Distress and Cultural Identity', *British Medical Bulletin*, 69:1 (2004), p. 129.

87. Mestrovic and Glassner, 'A Durkheimian Hypothesis on Stress', p. 1316.
88. This quote is from a Facebook post on Irish Families in Perth group page, 23 February 2014. As the group is 'closed' for privacy reasons, the hyperlink to the page cannot be provided.
89. Ibid.
90. Guilt at taking children away from the wider family circle came up several times in the open-ended questions regarding the best and worst aspects of migration. Parents appeared to be regularly weighing up the benefits and opportunities of life in Australia against the loss of familial support and their children's familiarity with extended family members.
91. 'Survey 1', Questions 27 and 28.
92. V. Roudometof, 'From Greek-Orthodox Diaspora to Transnational Hellenism: Greek Nationalism and the Identities of the Diaspora', in Leoussi and Smith (eds), *IJS Studies in Judaica*, p. 158.
93. Northern Ireland Statistics and Research Agency, *The Annual Report of the Registrar General 2012* (Department of Finance and Personnel, Belfast: Office of National Statistics, 2013), p. 9.
94. Office of National Statistics, 'A Demographic Portrait of Northern Ireland', *Population Trends*, 135 (2009), p. 91. Northern Ireland Statistics and Research Agency: http://www.nisra.gov.uk/archive/demography/publications/Pop_Trends_NI_Article.pdf (accessed 15 February 2014).
95. 'Violence—Significant Violent Incidents during the Conflict', CAIN (Conflict Archive on the Internet), University of Ulster, http://cain.ulst.ac.uk/issues/violence/majinc.htm (accessed 15 September 2013).
96. Government of Ireland, *Census 2011 Profile 1—Town and Country*, Information Section, Central Statistics Office (Dublin: Stationery Office, 2012), p. 13.
97. *Émigré Report*, UCC, p.ii.
98. The majority of Irish migrants go to the United Kingdom and Australia with smaller numbers travelling to New Zealand, Canada, and the United States.
99. This compares with 47 per cent of respondents to the *Émigré Report*, p. ii.
100. *Émigré Report*, p. ii.
101. G. Hugo, 'Migration Policies in Australia and their Impact on Development in Countries of Origin', in United Nations Population Fund (ed), *International Migration and the Millennium Development Goals* (UNFPA: New York, 2005), p. 202.
102. O'Connor, 'Multiple Experiences of Migrancy', p. 167.
103. Many of those born in the post-war era accepted that their income was needed to support the nuclear family. This was especially true of the older children of the household. Although educational reform had taken place in Ireland, it was not until the 1967 Education Act that secondary education became a reality for many Irish teenagers. A. E. Raftery and M. Hout, 'Maximally Maintained Inequality: Expansion, Reform, and Opportunity in Irish Education, 1921–75', *Sociology of Education*, 66:1 (1993), pp. 41–62.
104. The combined percentage for ratings 9 and 10 was 40 per cent.
105. 'Survey 2', Question 66.
106. 'More Irish coming to Australia than ever before, according to Immigration figures' *ABC News*, 24 August 2013,http://www.abc.net.au/news/2013-08-24/irish-migration-to-australia-increasing/4910116.
107. Respondents used the terms *racist, bigot,* and *cruel* when describing their experiences as Irish migrants in Australia. Some thought the relationships formed with Australians proved to be superficial after a time. Migrant expectations, perhaps based on an idealistic notion of Irish friendships and sense of community, appear to be disappointed in this regard on occasion. See 'Survey 2', Question 66. O'Connor provides quotes from two respondents

which illustrate this same notion of lack of depth in relationships between the Irish and Australians. See O'Connor, 'Multiple Experiences of Migrancy', pp. 268–69.
108. The traditional American Wake was revived in Co. Clare late in 2011. 'A Party for the Departing', *The Irish Times*, 17 December 2011, http://www.irishtimes.com/life-and-style/people/a-party-for-the-departing-1.12914 (accessed 14 May 2014).
109. Given the cost of return flights a trip of three weeks or more is generally considered a 'decent' amount of time for a visit.
110. 'Survey 2', Question 67.
111. 'Most Emigrants Who Settle in Australia Will Not Return', Generation Emigration, *The Irish Times*, 9 November 2013, http://www.irishtimes.com/life-and-style/most-emigrants-who-settle-in-australia-will-not-return-1.1588651 (accessed 15 November 2013).

Contributors

Fidelma Breen is a native of County Armagh, Northern Ireland, and a graduate of Magee College, University of Ulster, the University of Leicester, and the University of Adelaide, Australia. She is currently undertaking a PhD in the Discipline of Geography, Environment and Population at Adelaide. Her current research focuses on contemporary Irish migrants to Australia, settlement processes, mental health, and social media as a platform for support in the migration process. Her interest in migration, particularly the global movement of the Irish, stems from a lived experience of repeat and frequent migration. You can follow her on Twitter @fidelmab.

Philip Bull is Adjunct Professor at La Trobe University, Melbourne, and a Visiting Professor at the National University of Ireland Maynooth. The author of *Land, Politics and Nationalism: A Study of the Irish Land Question* (1996), he has also written numerous articles on nineteenth- and twentieth-century Irish history. He is currently organising and cataloguing the large archive of papers at Monksgrange, County Wexford, and plans to write a history of that house and it occupants from the mid-eighteenth to the mid-twentieth centuries.

Trevor Burnard is Professor of History at the University of Melbourne, Australia, having previously taught at universities in Britain, New Zealand, and Jamaica. He is the author of *Planters, Merchants, and Slaves: Plantation Societies in British America, 1650–1820* (2015) and *Mastery, Tyranny, and Desire: Thomas Thistlewood and his Slaves in the Anglo-Jamaican World* (2004), as well as other books and numerous articles on plantation societies and planter culture in the Chesapeake and the Caribbean.

Patrick Coleman is a doctoral candidate at the University of Otago, New Zealand, where he is working on a history of the Loyal Orange Institution throughout the British world using a comparative and transnational framework. He is also Academic Coordinator at Lincoln University, where he administers and teaches English for Academic Purposes, which provides language and study skills for international students gaining entrance into undergraduate or postgraduate courses. His research interests have focused on the Irish in New Zealand with an emphasis on the Loyal Orange Institution.

Professor **Richard Hill** is an historian at the Stout Research Centre for New Zealand Studies, Victoria University of Wellington, where he is also Director of the Treaty of Waitangi Research Unit. He holds the degree of Doctor of Letters and is a member of the Waitangi Tribunal, the standing commission of enquiry into Maori claims against the New Zealand state. He has published four books on the history of policing in nineteenth- and early-twentieth-century New Zealand, and two books tracing the relationship between Maori and the state during the twentieth century. More broadly, he has published extensively on historical and contemporary issues of social control, state coercion, and indigeneity.

Stephanie James, with a family background that is totally Irish-born at the great-grandparent level, has a major research interest in Irish Australia, in particular questions of identity and the complex issues of loyalty faced by this group. Her MA looked at the contribution of the Irish to South Australia's Clare Valley from 1841 to 1871, the decades during which this region constituted the most Irish region of the young colony. Her recently completed PhD focuses on Irish Australian identity and loyalty during times of Imperial crisis; it covers the decades from the Fenian alarm of the 1860s through the challenges of World War I and the Irish War of Independence to the end of the Irish Civil War in 1923. Although Irish Catholic newspapers in Victoria and South Australia formed the basis of this research, it also uncovered a wealth of detail about the wartime surveillance of Irish Australians and challenges some of the accepted wisdom about this group's acceptance within Australian society.

Joan Kavanagh is an historian from Wicklow, Ireland. She is the former manager of the Wicklow Family History Centre and was involved in the research for the restoration project of Wicklow Gaol as a visitor interpretative centre. Joan is currently researching convicts who were transported from Wicklow Gaol to Van Diemen's Land. Together with Dianne Snowden, Joan is writing a book about the women and children who arrived in Van Diemen's Land on the *Tasmania* (2) in 1845.

Robert Lindsey is a postgraduate researcher studying in the field of cultural history who has a particular interest in inter-ethnic relations, language maintenance and language revival. He completed his Bachelor of Arts Honours year at the University of Melbourne, Australia, where he investigated ethnic conflict and integration in early Anglo-Saxon England. His more recent work has focused on the history of the Celtic languages, with a special interest in Irish Gaelic and Welsh. Robert is currently a third-year PhD student at the University of Melbourne, where his thesis is proceeding under the working title '"Dlúthbhaint . . . nach léar": The Welsh Language Revival and its Impact on Irish Language Reform in the Twentieth Century'.

Angela McCarthy is Professor of Scottish and Irish History at the University of Otago, New Zealand. She has published extensively on Irish and Scottish migration including *Irish Migrants in New Zealand, 1840–1937: 'The Desired Haven'* (2005); *Personal Accounts of Irish and Scottish Migration, 1921–65: 'For Spirit and Adventure'* (2007); and *Scottishness and Irishness in New Zealand since 1840* (2011). Her most recent book includes consideration of Irish migrants in lunatic asylums: *Migration, Ethnicity, and Madness: New Zealand, 1860–1910* (2015).

Dr Dianne Snowden is a professional historian and genealogist. She is founder and convenor of the Friends of Orphan Schools, St John's Park Precinct, and as Honorary Research Associate at the University of Tasmania is working on a longitudinal study of children admitted to the Orphan Schools, especially those who arrived free with convict parents. In 2005 she completed her doctorate at the University of Tasmania, Australia, about Irish women who committed arson in order to be transported. She is currently working with Joan Kavanagh on a publication about the Irish women and children who arrived in Van Diemen's Land on the *Tasmania* (2) in 1845.

Graham Walker is Professor of Political History at Queen's University of Belfast, Northern Ireland. He has written widely on the history and politics of both Scotland and Ireland. Among his published works are *Intimate Strangers: Political and Cultural Interaction between Scotland and Ulster* (1995) and *A History of the Ulster Unionist Party: Protest, Pragmatism, Pessimism* (2004).

Index

abolitionists 7, 16–17, 19, 20, 24
Achilles, T.C. 165
Adelaide 88–91, 93, 95–8, 101, 207
Aden 71
Africans 20–1
Ahern, Bertie 192
Aikins, Kingsley 205
Akenson, D.H. 3, 4, 81, 157, 205–6
American Civil War 151, 156
American Revolution 15–19, 22–6, 29, 30
Americans 18, 117, 122–3, 140, 143–4
Anderson, Benedict 82
Anderson, J.W. 122
Anglicans 18, 21
Anglo-Indians 19
Anglo-Irish Treaty 165, 168
Anson 44
Anti-Partition League 10, 162, 166–8, 172, 177
Apia 71
Argentina 8, 81, 88
Armagh 95
ARMCO 174
army 46
associational culture 9, 211, 224; *see also* Orange Order
Association of Loyal Orangewomen of Ireland 110, 113, 123, 129
Ashbourne, Lord 166
Ashburton 126
Ashe, Mrs 39, 54
Auckland 87
Australasia 1, 6, 81, 86–7, 92, 94, 96, 103, 128, 129
Australasian Convention 94
Australia 3, 4, 6, 8, 9, 10, 34, 42, 48, 51, 81, 86, 87, 92, 97, 101, 111, 112, 123–5, 144, 184, 198–234

Australian 52, 53, 97, 99, 101, 209–10, 222
Aveling, Marian 35

ballads 137
Baltinglass 38
Baptists 148
Barbados 22
Barnes, Peter 176
Bass Strait 50
Battle of the Boyne 125–6
Battle of the Saints 17, 22
BBC radio 169
Beasley, Eileen 169
Beasley, Trefor 169
Beckert, Sven 163
Beddoe, Deirdre 35
Bedford, Dr Edward 45
Belfast 113, 184
Belfast Special Branch 175
Birkenhead 116, 117
Birmingham 176
Blair, Tony 192
Bodenstown 96
Boling, B. 6
Bombay 46
Boston 120
Bourke, Richard 18
Branigan, St John 70–1
Brennan, T.C. 92, 94
Brisbane 86, 90, 92, 123
Britain 1–3, 7, 15, 19, 21–30, 181, 183, 187, 191
British 18, 121
British Army 50, 173
British Embassy, Dublin 171
British Empire 7, 15–19, 25, 30
British government 24, 28–9, 113, 166, 187

British identity 185–7
British-Irish Council 190
Britishness 18, 190, 193
British parliament 23, 25–6
Brooke, Sir Basil 167
Brown, Callum 188
Brown's River 45
Bruce, Steve 183
Brubaker, Rogers 1
Bryce, David 116
Buenos Aires 88, 90, 96–7, 100
Buffalo 3
Buist, Beverley 129
Burgess, J. 45
Burke, Edmund 20
Burnie 48, 49, 50, 53; *see also* Emu Bay
Burntollet 174
Butler, Diane 206
Butt, Isaac 143

Caernarfon 174
Calcutta 21
California 3
Campbell, Malcolm 3
Campbell Town 45
Cam River 50
Canada 4, 9, 111, 119–21, 116, 124–7, 144, 184
Canada Act (1791), 28
Cape Town 71
Cardiff 166–8
Carlow 40
Carr, Bess (Eliza) 37–41
Cascades Female Factory 44
Cashel 87
Castles, Stephen 214
Catholic Church; abroad 9, 81–2, 90, 102–3, 183, 191; in Ireland 3, 113, 191
Catholics 21, 23, 25–6, 28, 183; abroad 81–2, 86, 88, 91–2, 124; in Ireland 8, 18, 24, 26–30, 40, 110, 153
Cayo Evans, Julian 173–4
Celtic FC 10, 189
Celtic League 166–7, 171, 177
Celtic Tiger 193, 199
Chetkovich, Jean 210–11, 219
child abuse 191
childbirth 37, 40, 44–6, 48, 140, 147–8
children 37–40, 43–4, 46, 49, 113, 210, 223
Christchurch 122

Christie, Margaret 49
Church of England 46, 148
Church of Ireland 27, 154
Church of Scotland 117, 183
Clark, Manning 34
Cleary, Bishop Henry 127
clergy 86–8, 91–3, 95–8, 102, 148, 150, 153–4; *see also* religion
Clews, Roy 171, 174
climate 19, 22
clothing 7, 37, 44, 70, 94, 142, 144–5, 148–9, 154
Clune, Archbishop 92
Colaba 46
Coldhill, Amelia Helen 49
Coldhill, David 51
comparison; of countries 3, 7, 17–18, 21, 29, 82, 111, 130, 157, 161, 164, 181–2; of ethnicities 2, 161, 183–4; of policing models 8, 64, 74
Connemara 170
Connolly, Clare 161
Connolly, S.J. 25
Conservatives 182, 186–7, 191
conscription 92, 166
convict depot, Grangegorman 42–3
convicts 34–6, 43–5, 49–55
convict stain 8, 34, 36, 49, 51–4
Conway, S. 16
Coolgardie 124
Coolkenna 37, 39
Cork 163
Coslett, Dennis 173
Costello, John A. 167
court martial 46
court trial 37–41
crime 41, 43–7, 51
Croke, Archbishop 87, 97
Cronelea 34, 37, 40
Crosbie, Barry 5
Culhane, Francis 37, 39
Cullum, Crofton David 119
Cullum, Mary 119–20, 127
Cummings, Samuel 174

Danbury Park 50
Daniels, Kay 34–5
David Clarke 44
Davies, Vivian 174–5
Davis, Eliza 8, 34, 36–55
Davis, Richard 35, 86, 124
Davis, Thomas 153

Davitt, Michael 94–6, 163, 183
Day, Peter 115–6
death 37, 39, 43–4, 46, 49, 53–4, 140, 147, 149, 152, 155
Declaratory Act (1720) 23, 25
Deegan, Mary 37, 38
Deenihan, Jimmy 222
Delaney, Enda 3, 4–5, 82, 86
Denny, W.J. 98
de Valera, Éamon 165–7
Devereux, Robert 54
Devine, T.M. 2, 181
devolution 165, 182, 185–92, 194
Dewar, Donald 187
diaspora 1, 4, 81–2, 86–7, 95, 103, 204–6, 218
Dillon, Canon 93
Dillon, John 94
disease 140
Dixson, Miriam 35
Doherty, John 37, 39, 40
Dominica 17
Doncaster 46, 48
Donegal 167
Donovan, Revd Samuel 38–41
Doyle, David 3, 6
Drennan, Margaret 127
drink 47, 142, 148, 150
drowning, 39, 40, 45
Drury Lane 20
Dublin 18, 71, 95–7, 103, 110, 112–13, 123, 142, 163, 171, 173–4, 205–6
Dublin Castle 40
Dublin Foundling Hospital 34, 40–41, 51
DuBois, Ellen Carol 112
Duffy, Sir Charles Gavan 98
Duhig, Archbishop 92, 93
Duke of Manchester 17
Dún Chaoin 171
Dunedin 87, 89, 90, 92, 97, 99
Dungannon 166
Dungannon Convention 25
Dwyer, Michael 96

Earl of Halifax 26
Easter Rising 97, 162, 165, 168, 170, 172–3
East India Company 21
Eastwood, Amos 46–51, 54
Eastwood, Jr., Amos 48
Eastwood, Mary 49

Eastwood, Sarah 51, 53
Edinburgh 190
Edinburgh Agreement 194
education 184, 190, 209, 221–2
Education Act (1918) 183
Ellis, Patricia 130
Ellis, T.E. 163
emotions 52, 95, 189, 194, 201, 203–4, 216
employment 40–4, 46, 48, 50–1, 53, 139–43, 155–6, 210–11, 214, 220–4
Emsley, Clive 64
Emu Bay 34, 48, 50
England 9, 15, 50–1, 110–12, 114, 117, 126–7, 142–4, 164, 166, 177, 190–1, 208
English 48, 121, 153
Enlightenment 28, 142
environment 48
Europe 1, 2, 3, 30
Europeans 19
Evans, Gwynfor 166–7, 171–2, 177
exile 4, 6, 43, 98, 157, 201, 206

Facebook 207–8, 215, 217
family history 35, 51–5
Famine, Great 44, 50, 204–5
Farmer, W.R. 39
Fayle, Josiah, 42
Female Protestant Association of Loyal Orangewomen 115
Fenians 88–9, 153–4
Fenlon, Myles 137, 156
Ferguson, Patrick 44
Fianna Fáil 167
First World War 88, 91, 97–8, 115
Fitzgerald, Patrick 204
Fitzpatrick, David 4, 6, 8, 124, 157, 206
Flood, Henry 24–5
Fogarty, John 167
Foley, Catherine 37
food 44–5
France 16, 23, 166
Franklin, Benjamin 15
Free Wales Army 10, 162, 173–6
French Revolution 17
Frost, Lucy 49

Gaelic Athletic Association 170
Gaelic League 10, 162, 169–71, 177
Gaeltacht 170

242 *Index*

Gahan, Eliza 37–8
Gee, Thomas 163
Gellatly, Beverley 51, 54
George III 17
Germany 185
Gilley, Sheridan 82
Gilroy, Archbishop 93
Gladstone, William 94, 163–4, 193
Glanmore Castle 41
Glasgow 116, 129, 183–4
Good Friday Agreement 190, 192
Goulding, Cathal 174
Graigue na Managh 137
Grammich, Katie 161
Grand Orange Lodge of Ireland 113, 125
Grand Lodge of the Loyal Institution of Great Britain 117
Grand Protestant Association of Loyal Orangemen 114–15, 126
Grange *see* Monksgrange
Gratton, Henry 24–5
Gray, Breda 205
Great Famine 139, 143
Greer, Henry 42
Greer, Samuel 42
Grenville, George 26
Grey, George 69
Griffiths, Keith 172, 174
Gunson, W.H. 89–91, 94
Gympie 123

Habel, Chad 54
Hackett, Joe 205
Hall, Dianne 205
Hamilton, A. 16
Hamilton, Dr William 41
Harte, Liam 7
Hastings, Warren 21
Haupt, Heinz-Gerehard 5
Hawkins, Richard 67
health 44, 139, 141
Heytesbury, Lord 37, 40–1
Hibernian Australasian Catholic Benefit Society 99
Hickman, Mary 205
Hilder, Richard 50
Hobart 44–8
Hobart Town Female Factory 44
Hogg, Quintin 172
Holyrood 193
Home Rule 9–10, 94, 112, 115–16, 163, 168, 184–6, 194, 199

homesickness 215–19
Hopkins, Margaret 37–40
Hourigan, Niamh 162
House of Lords 26
housing 37, 221
Houston, Cecil J. 118
Hughes, Alfred 51, 53
Hughes, George 51–4
Hughes, Milton (Mick) 53
Hughes, Robert 51
Hugo, Graeme 222
Humphries, John 171, 173, 176
Huston, G.F. 46

Iceland 193
Impression Bay 46
India 3, 5, 16, 19, 21, 28, 30, 46, 164, 203
Indian Mutiny 50
infanticide 8, 34, 41, 43, 45, 54–5
inheritance 140–1
Inis Bearacháin 170
inquest 37, 39
Irish Anti-Partition League 162
Irish Civil War 89, 98, 137, 156, 185
Irish Confederation 154
Irish descent group 4, 7, 8, 36, 49, 51–2, 81, 86, 95, 98, 102, 121, 204–5
Irish Football Association 191
Irish Free State 185–6
Irish government 29, 166, 169
Irish identity 2, 6, 9, 82, 86–7, 93, 99, 103, 190, 207
Irish Land League 163
Irish Land War 154
Irish National Association 98
Irish National Federation 95–7
Irish National League 95
Irish parliament 24–5, 27, 29
Irish Parliamentary Party 93–4, 96
Irish Republican Army 10, 162, 172–6, 184
Irish-Scottish Studies 3, 181
Irish symbols 9, 99–102
Irish Tenant's Defence Association, 97
Irish Volunteers 24, 27
Irish War of Independence 88, 98, 169, 172
Iwan, Dafydd 171

Jackson, Alvin 190, 193
Jamaica 7, 15, 17–19, 21–4, 26, 28, 30

Jamaicans 16, 20–2, 25–30
Jasanoff, M. 7, 18, 25–6
Jefferson, T 16
Jeffries, Sir Charles 64
Jenkins, John Barnard 175–6
Jenkins, William 3
Johnstone, Mary Elizabeth 113
Jones, Alice 50
Jones, Alwyn 176
Jones, Emyr Llywelyn 175
Jones, Harri Pritchard 164
Jones, John Albert 175
Jones, J.E. 166, 177

Kansas 9, 137, 145, 149, 151–2, 156
Karskens, Grace 36
Kaufmann, Eric 113–14, 117
Keenan, John 93
Kelly, Archbishop Michael 93
Kelly, Fr James Joseph 97
Kelly, John 137
Kelly, Fr W.B. 100
Keneally, Thomas 52
Kennedy, Liam 204
Kenny, Kevin 5, 82, 204
Kidd, Colin 194
Kilkenny 43
Killabeg barracks 37, 39
Killan 137
Killian, Archbishop 92
Kingstown 43
Kinsale 176
Koch, Christopher 54
Koerner, Frederick Martin 88–9, 98

Labour Party 113, 164, 182–3, 185–7, 189–90, 192
Ladies Orange Benevolent Association 119–21, 127
Lalor, Peter 98
Lambkin, Brian 204
Lancashire 114, 126
Lancaster 115
Land League 154
landlords 4, 25, 142–3, 145, 152–4
land reform 10
language 10, 88, 162, 165, 167–72
Language Freedom Movement 170
Lardner, Jason 44
Launceston 48
Leavitt, Mary Clement 122
Leitrim County Council 206
Lemass, Seán 170

letters 138, 140, 144, 157
Levin, Irene 36
Lewis, Edward 127
Lewis, Roy 164–6
Lewis, Saunders 162, 168–72
Liberal Party 163–4, 183
Lincoln, Abraham 149, 151
Linnell, Mary 121
Liverpool 115, 126, 169
Llanelli Rural District Council 169
Llŷn Peninsula 169
Logue, Cardinal 95
London 20, 71, 145
London, Ontario 120
London Metropolitan Police 61
loneliness 6
Long, Edward 20
Long, Samuel Ernest 119
Longford, Aust. 48
Loyal Orange Institution of England 115
Loyal Orange Institution of Great Britain 116
Loyal Orange Ladies' Institution of the United States 118, 120
Lynn, Brendan 165

McArdle, Sarah 44
McCallum, Christi 112–13, 129
McCann, Agnes 113
McCann, Alexander 113
McCarthy, Angela 157, 183–4
McConnell, Jack 189
McCormick, James 176
McCormick, John 185
MacDiarmid, Hugh 184–5
McFarland, Elaine 111
Mac Gall, Rex 170
McGarry, Fearghal 5
MacGinley, Rosa 86, 91–2
McGrath, Michael 164
McGuire, Maria 174
McIlvanney, Liam 189
Mackintosh, John P. 187–8
McLean, Iain 181
McNamara, Heather 82, 90
MacPherson, D.A.J. 111, 116
McPherson, Duncan 45
Mac Stíofáin Seán 176–7
Madison, J 16
madness 45–6
Maes Llyn 175
mail 87

244   Index

Major, John 191
Malcolm, Elizabeth 67, 205
Mannix, Archbishop 92, 99
Maori 65–6, 71, 150
marriage 44–6, 48–9, 53, 113, 140, 142, 145–7, 155, 209–10
Marshall, P.J. 22, 25
Meagher, Thomas Francis 144, 153
media 162
medical officers 37, 39, 40, 44–6, 145
Melbourne 88, 90–1, 93–4, 96, 98–9
memorials 137
memory 36, 53–5
Merseyside 115
Metropolitan police 8
migration, Irish; motives 142, 198, 201, 206–7, 209, 214, 219–22, 225; return 140–1, 153, 205–6, 213, 220–1, 223, 225; statistics 1, 2, 81, 127, 198–9, 201, 209–10, 214, 219, 223
Miller, Kerby 3–4, 6, 157, 206
Minnesota 3
Misneach 170–1
Mitchel, John 153
mixed marriages 184
Molloy, Kevin 90
money 142
Monksgrange 9, 137–8, 140, 149, 153–6, 158
Montagu, Lord Charles 17
Moran, Bishop Patrick 87, 92
Moran, Cardinal Patrick Francis 97
Morton, Henry William 37, 39–42
Morton, Joseph 42
Morven 48
Motherwell 184
Mt Bischoff 48
Mudiad Amddiffyn Cymru 162, 175–6
Mulhern, Gail 51–2, 54
Mullinacuffe, 34, 39–40
Mullingar 176
Munster 4
Murdoch, John 183
Myers, Daniel 162
Mylas, John 48

Nationalist Party of Scotland 184
nationalists 3, 5, 9–10, 25, 28, 96, 162–69, 171–3, 176–7, 183, 185, 194
National Woman Suffrage Association 118
native Americans 144–5, 154

Naughtin, Patrick J. 91
Navan 176
New Brunswick 124
Newcastle, England 116
Newman, Bro. R 120
New Norfolk Asylum for the Insane 46, 49
New South Wales 3, 43, 50, 65, 96, 101, 123–4, 199
newspapers 81–2, 110; *Advertiser* 96; *Advocate* (Melbourne) 87–94, 96–9; *Age* (Brisbane) 86, 92, 93; America 89; Australian 89; *Ave Maria* (US) 86; bans 88; *Belfast Weekly News* 111, 116–18; *Boston Pilot* 86–7, 96; *Catholic Advocate* (Brisbane) 92–3, 99–100; *Catholic Press* (Sydney) 90–3, 96, 99, 101; *Catholic Record* (Perth) 87, 90–2, 99; *Catholic Times* (Liverpool) 86; *Catholic Weekly* (Sydney) 91, 93; *Daily Sketch* 173; editors 9, 81–2, 86–94, 96, 98–9, 101; English 89; *Freeman's Journal* (Dublin) 86, 88–9, 96–7; *Freeman's Journal* (Sydney) 86–7, 90–1, 93, 95–6, 99; Irish 89, 211; Irish American 81, 86, 88; Irish Catholic 8, 81–2, 86–8, 90, 93–5; *Irish Echo* 208; *Irish Independent* 170; *Irish Press* 166; *Irish Times* 206, 223; *Irish World* 86; *Leader* 86, 93; mastheads 9, 82, 91, 99–103; *Nation* 90; *Southern Cross* (Adelaide) 87, 88–93, 95, 98, 101; *Southern Cross* (Buenos Aires) 88–90, 93, 96–7, 100; subscriptions 87; *Tablet* (London) 86, 89; *Tablet* (New Zealand) 82, 86–92, 98–100; *United Ireland* 87; *Universe* 86; *Watchman* 120–1; *Weekly Freeman* 90; *Weekly News* 90; *Wexford Independent* 144
New York 118, 139
New Zealand 4, 6, 8–9, 34, 36, 51, 53, 65–6, 70–1, 86, 90, 92, 96, 110–12, 121–30, 184, 206
Nicholson, James 173
Nolan, Andrew 40
North America 1, 6, 18, 24, 53
North Atlantic Treaty Organisation 165

Northern Ireland 7, 10, 110, 112, 113, 166–8, 171–2, 174, 177, 181–94, 207, 209, 212, 219, 221, 224
Nova Scotia 124

O'Brien, Monsignor 92
O'Brien, William 163
Ó Cadhain, Máirtín 164, 170
Ó Caollái, Maolseachlainn 170–1
O'Connell, Daniel 153
O'Connor, Patricia 210–11, 214, 219, 222
O'Day, Alan 81
O'Donnell, Nicholas 97
O'Farrell, Patrick 6, 90, 93, 97, 157
O'Grady, Michael 98
O'Grady, Fr. T.R. 92, 98
Ohio 119
O'Leary, John 154
Oliver, Pamela 162
O'Loghlin, J.V. 87, 89, 91–2, 96–8, 101
O'Malley, Kate 5
O'Meara, Margaret 54
O'Neill, Ciaran 5
Ontario 119
Opotiki 87
Orange Order; decline 113–4; male lodges 121, 123–4; parades 112, 125–6; ritual 127; songs 110, 126
Orange Order female lodges; decline 112–13, 115–19, 121–3, 130; formation 114, 116–24; growth 112–13, 115–18, 121, 123–4, 130; marching 126; ritual 126–30
Orange Women's Association 112–3
O'Reily, Fr. (later Archbishop) John 91, 95–6, 98
Orientalism 19
Orpen, Adela *see* Richards, Adela
Orpen, Goddard H. 155
Orpen, John H. 155
O'Shannassey, Sir John 98
O'Shaughnessy, A. 17
Otago 71
Oxley 34

Pakenham, Henry 40
Pakistan 19
Palestine 164
Palmer, Stanley 64

Parnell, Charles Stewart 154, 193
partition 164–6, 177, 182
Peace of Paris 25
Peace Process 181, 189, 191–2
Peel, Robert 61, 63
Peninsular and Orient 208
Pennington 44
Pennsylvania 118, 119
Penrhos 172
Perrin, John F. 87, 89, 92, 101
Perrott, Monica 35
Perth 90, 92, 98
Philadelphia 118
Philippines 203
Phoenix Park 71
Pitt, William 16, 24, 29
Pittsburgh 118
Plaid Cymru 163–4, 166–8, 171–2, 175
planters 17, 19–20, 22, 149
Pocock, J.G.A 18
police 37, 45, 47, 62–3, 65, 67, 69–73, 75, 175–6, 192
policing 8, 66–7, 68, 71, 73; colonial 64, 66–72, 74, 76–7; English model 61–6, 68, 71, 73–5, 77; Irish model 61–2, 64–77
politics 86, 93, 181–5, 187, 189, 190–1, 193–4
Pope Pius X 113
Port Arthur 46
Porter, Revd Robert 40
Poynings law 23
Primrose League 116
Prince Alfred 89
Prince of Wales 174
Prince of Wales Bay 44
Pritchard, Dai 175
Privy Council 23
Protestant 7–9, 11, 15–18, 21, 23–30, 41, 43, 110, 112–13, 118, 121, 123–4, 130, 183, 188
Protestant Action 183
Purdie, Bob 185
Pym, Joseph 42

Quebec 139
Quebec Act (1774) 28
Queensland 95, 123
Queenstown 87

railway; in Ireland 142–3, 151; in US 139–42, 149
Ramsay, Revd James 20

246 *Index*

Rangers FC 10, 189
rebellion of 1798 9, 17, 23, 87, 96–7, 137
Redmond, John 94
Reid, Kirsty 34
Reiner, Robert 63
Reith, Charles 63, 65
religion 4, 8, 28, 87, 96, 140, 142, 148, 150, 154, 188–9, 191
remittances 87
Rhodesians 19
Rhondda Valley 167
Richards, Adela 9, 137, 140, 145, 149, 151–3, 155–6, 158
Richards, Dora 140, 149
Richards, Dorothea *see* Sargent, Dorothea
Richards, Edward Moore 9, 137–58
Richards, Ellen 145–7, 155
Richards, Goddard Hewetson 137, 140, 153–4
Richards, John Evelyn 140, 151
Richards, John Francis 140, 149, 154
Richards, Sarah 140, 145, 147, 149, 151, 155
Richards, Solomon 137
Richmond 138, 150–1
Rightboys 29
Risdon 44
River Derwent 44
Roberts, Emrys 172
Robinson, Mary 205
Robson, Lloyd 34
Rodney, Admiral George 17, 22
Roebuck, Amelia Eleanor *see* Coldhill, Amelia Eleanor
Roebuck, Joseph 44–6, 49
Rossendale 126
Rosslare 155
Roudometof, Victor 219
Royal Commission on the Constitution 187
Royal Commission on Scottish Affairs 186
Royal Saxon 46
RTÉ 171
Russell, Martin 205
Ryan, Louise 2, 7
Ryan, Tighe 92, 101

Salmond, Alex 194
Sandwich Islanders 150
Sargent, Dorothea 140, 144, 148–9, 153, 155
Sargent, Richard 140
Saint Domingue 17
Saunderson, Lady Helena 113
schools 183, 190
Schrier, Arnold 6
scientific racism 20, 27–8
Scotland 2, 9, 10, 15, 111, 115–17, 120, 127–9, 166, 181–94
Scottish government 189, 191
Scottish National Party 10, 184, 187, 189–91, 193
Scottish Office 186
Scottish parliament 185–7, 191, 193–4
seasickness 44 *see also* voyage
Second World War 185
sectarianism 10, 182–4, 188–90
Seven Years war 26, 29
Shannon River Navigation Schemes 139
Shaw, A.G.L. 34
Sheller, Mimi 19
Shorthill, Thomas 88
Silvestri, Michael 5
Sinclair, Georgina 64
Sinn Féin 94, 162
Sisters of Mercy 88
Skype 11, 207, 215, 217–18
slavery 17, 20, 137–8, 148–51
slaves 18, 21, 26–30, 145, 149–51
Smith, Babette 35, 52
Smyth, William J. 118
Society of Friends 41
songs 110
South Africans 19
South African War 112
South Australia 88, 91, 94–5, 124, 128, 199
South Carolina 17
Southland, N.Z. 53
Southport 126
Spanishtown 22
Spence, Archbishop 98
Spurway, John 35
St John's Hospital, Launceston 45
St Kitts 20
St Luke's Church 45
St Patrick's Day 95, 97
Stead, W.T. 87
Stewart, Hamish Maxwell 52
Stormont 167, 185, 192
Sturma, Michael 35
Sullivan, Ellen 44

Summers, Anne 35
Supreme Grand Lodge of New York 118
Susquehanna River 140
Swansea 173
Sweden 3
Sydney 8, 65, 87, 89–93, 96–7, 101, 120, 124
Sylvester, James Worral 114
Synge, Francis 41

Taiwan 211
Tasmania, 34, 50, 52–3, 124
Tasmania, 43–4, 54
Tasmanians 54
Taylor, George 176
Teilifís na Gaeilge 171
temperance 112, 123, 142
Tennent, Sir James Emerson 5
Thatcher, Margaret 171, 187, 191
Thomas, William G. 151
Thompson, Margaret 118
Thomson, Harriet 116
Timaru, N.Z. 34, 55
Tisdale, Sarah Elizabeth *see* Richards, Sarah
Tölöyan, Khachig 205
Tone, Wolfe 96
Tonypandy 167
Toronto 4, 120
Town 173
transnationalism 4–6, 9, 81–2, 86, 88, 116–17, 120, 124–5, 127–8, 131, 137, 161, 163–4, 166, 170, 182, 219; of policing models 65, 67, 69, 71, 73, 75–7
transportation 8, 34, 39, 42–6, 50–2, 54–5
Trawsfynydd Power Station 176
Treaty of Union 182, 189, 191, 193
Trew, Johanne Devlin 7
Troubles, the 172, 182, 184, 186–90, 190, 209, 219
Tryweryn dam 172–3
Turner, Eric 123
Twamley, James 34, 40
Twelfth of July 125–6
Tyrone, Co. 166
Tyrrell, Ian 5

Ulster 19, 163, 183, 185, 189. 191
Ulster Constitutional Convention 188
Ulsterisation 18–19

Ulster-Scots 194
Ulster Unionist Party 186
unionists 167, 174, 177, 182, 185–6, 190, 194
Unionist Party 167, 183
United Kingdom 113, 181–2, 186–7, 189, 192–3, 194, 203, 211–12
United Nations 165
United States 2–4, 6, 9, 22, 81, 96, 111–12, 116–19, 120, 122, 126, 137, 140, 142, 144–5, 184, 203

Van Diemen's Land 34–5, 43–4, 46, 50, 52–5
Van Diemen's Land Company 48
Vertigan, Tas 124
Viber 215
Victoria, Aust. 70, 89, 124
Vinegar Hill 96
Virginia 9, 137, 139, 140–1, 143, 149, 150–1
voyage 44, 50, 139, 208

wages 141
Wales 9–10, 15, 35, 115, 163–77, 187–8, 190, 192
Walker, Graham 111
Walsh, Archbishop 95
Walshe, J.W. 94
Ward, Russell 36
War Precautions Act 88
Washington, George 16, 20
Waterford 44, 140
Waterloo 15
Watson, Susannah 35
Waverly Cemetery 97
Wellington 110, 121
Welsh Language Society 10, 162, 169–72, 177
Welsh Nationalist Party *see* Plaid Cymru
Welsh Patriotic Front 172–3
Western Australia 50, 99, 101
West Indians 7, 18–20
West Indies 15–16, 21
Westminster 1, 94, 163, 166, 183–4, 194
Wexford 9, 39, 96, 137
Whelan, Patrick 93
Whelehan, Niall 5
Whiteboys 29
Whitton, Harriet 49

Wicklow, Co. 8, 34, 36–7, 40–1, 43, 49, 51
Wicklow gaol 37–8, 40, 42–3, 54
Wilberforce, William 20
Williams, Chris A. 64
Williams, Glyn 166
Williams, Owain 175–7
Wills, Francis C. 51
Wilson, Dorothy 116
Wilson, Harriet *see* Thomson, Harriet
Winter, Joseph 94
Women's Christian Temperance Union 112, 122–3
Women's Unionist Association 113
Wright, Bro. F.H. 120
Wright, J.J. 5
Wright, Melba 51

York 44
Yorkshire 44, 46, 48, 50
Yorktown 17
Young Ireland Confederates 142, 144

Zeehan 124
Zong 20